Praise for *Conflict*

"I wish I had written Leckie's great book. . . . Here is distinguished writing which makes thrilling reading and is still sound history."
—S.L.A. Marshall

"An enthralling full-dress history about the strange, shifting, heartless conflict of 1950–1953. . . . [Leckie] keeps the battle narrative moving along despite inescapable interruptions to see what the world's statesmen and military chiefs were doing. He handles both with something more valuable than brilliance in history: good judgment. . . . Leckie's opinion, in every case, is perfectly clear; he is blunt but fair." *—New Yorker*

"The Korean War is a vital occurrence in the history of our country that sorely needs knowing about. . . . A masterful work."
—Leon Uris

"An excellent, one-volume history which covers, with accuracy and verbal economy, all the necessary points from Korea's background as a constant pawn in large power struggles to its uneasy truce and internal turmoil. Leckie's lucidity sharpens previously obscured events." *—Library Journal*

"This war was a seesaw affair, difficult for any but a military expert to follow intelligently. With perspective and considerable skill Leckie has written a comprehensive study of the war that can be understood by the interested layman." *—Christian Science Monitor*

"Leckie's a credit to our letters." **—William Carlos Williams**

CONFLICT

THE HISTORY OF THE KOREAN WAR

1950–1953

Books by Robert Leckie

HELMET FOR MY PILLOW

LORD, WHAT A FAMILY

THE MARCH TO GLORY

MARINES!

STRONG MEN ARMED: The United States Marines against Japan

THE WARS OF AMERICA: From 1600 to 1992 (in two volumes)

GEORGE WASHINGTON'S WAR: The Saga of the American Revolution

FROM SEA TO SHINING SEA: From the War of 1812 to the Mexican War, the Saga of America's Expansion

NONE DIED IN VAIN: The Saga of the American Civil War

DELIVERED FROM EVIL: The Saga of World World II

OKINAWA: Final Battle of World War II

CONFLICT

THE HISTORY OF THE KOREAN WAR, 1950–53

Robert Leckie

DA CAPO PRESS • NEW YORK

Library of Congress Cataloging in Publication Data

Leckie, Robert.
    Conflict: the history of the Korean War, 1950–1953 / Robert
Leckie.
      p.   cm.
    Originally published: New York: Putnam, 1962.
    ISBN 0-306-80716-5 (alk. paper)
    1. Korean War, 1950–1953. I. Title.
DS918.L36   1996   96-15600
951.904'2–dc20   CIP

First Da Capo Press edition 1996

This Da Capo Press paperback edition of *Conflict* is an unabridged
republication of the edition first published in New York in 1962.
It is here reprinted by arrangement with the author.

Published by Da Capo Press, Inc.
A Subsidiary of Plenum Publishing Corporation
233 Spring Street, New York, N.Y. 10013

Manufactured in the United States of America

To Those Who Fought for Freedom in Korea

Contents

MAPS

Thirty-two pages of photographs will be found following page 224.

"It's the war we can't win, we can't lose, we can't quit."

—AMERICAN SOLDIER ON THE SECOND RETREAT FROM SEOUL

*D*awn of June 25, 1950, had not yet broken over the hills of central Korea. Throughout the night scattered but heavy rains had been falling along the 38th Parallel, the 200-mile armed border separating the rival Democratic People's Republic of Korea (North Korea) from the Republic of Korea (South Korea). It was the beginning of the summer monsoon, and though the rains gave many South Korean soldiers on outpost duty a soaking, they were generally welcomed— for they would guarantee the rice and barley crops which are the chief products of the agricultural south.

Far away in Washington it was a quiet Saturday afternoon. President Harry Truman had left the White House for a vacation at his home in Independence, Missouri. In Tokyo, General Douglas MacArthur was sound asleep. So were the Communist leaders in North Korea sleeping, for everything that men could do to mount and mask a sudden attack had been done.

Along the border, the soldiers of South Korea talked enviously of their lucky comrades who were back in Seoul on weekend passes. They spoke of the latest "peace proposals" offered their country by the Communists in the north, wondering if the sudden cessation of border clashes could mean that the North Koreans were serious. Some of the soldiers thought they heard the murmur of a storm making up north of the mountains. But they were mistaken. They had not heard the sound of thunder, but the rumble of artillery, and at four o'clock in the morning the enemy shells were crashing and flashing among them.

The "conflict" in Korea had begun.

Chronology of the Korean War

(All dates given are those obtaining in the time zone in which the events occurred. Thus, the invasion of Korea and the UN Security Council resolution calling for a cease-fire both appear to happen on the same day, June 25, 1950. Actually, the invasion was on a Saturday June 25 in the East Zone and the resolution on a Sunday June 25 in the West Zone. In such cases, the Chronology carries the events as separate entries, rather than lumping them together under the same date.)

1950

25 June—North Korean People's Army crosses 38th Parallel to invade South Korea.

25 June—UN Security Council calls for cease-fire in Korea and withdrawal of North Korean troops.

27 June—UN Security Council adopts U. S. resolution taking note of North Korean refusal to heed June 25 resolution and calls upon members to assist South Korea; President Truman orders U. S. air and sea units to support South Korea and orders U. S. Seventh Fleet to "neutralize" Formosa Strait.

28 June—North Koreans capture Seoul, capital of South Korea.

30 June—President Truman orders U. S. ground forces committed in Korea.

3 July—Inchon falls to North Koreans.

5 July—Task Force Smith defeated at Osan as American ground forces enter battle for first time in Korea.

7 July—General of the Army Douglas MacArthur appointed Supreme Commander of United Nations Command in Korea.

20 July—North Koreans capture Taejon. Major General Dean cut off and later taken prisoner.

30 July—Beginning of Pusan Perimeter defense.

1 August—Russia ends boycott of UN Security Council as Delegate Jacob Malik assumes Council presidency.

4 August—North Koreans establish bridgehead across Naktong River.

4 August—Soviet delegate Malik calls Korean fighting an "internal civil war" and demands withdrawal of "all foreign troops from Korea."

6 August—Threat developed against Taegu, Eighth Army headquarters in Korea.

10 August—U. S. delegate Warren Austin states that goal of United Nations is unification of Korea.

17 August—Marine Brigade opens battle for No-Name Ridge, eventually gaining the UN's first victory in Korea and leading way to destruction of enemy bridgehead on the Naktong.

1 September—North Koreans open all-out offensive against Pusan Perimeter.

15 September—United Nations forces land at Inchon.

16 September—Eighth Army begins cautious offensive from Pusan Perimeter.

17 September—Kimpo Airfield recaptured by UN.

19 September—Enemy forces at Pusan begin collapsing.

25 September—North Koreans in full retreat and UN pursuit begins.

28 September—Seoul recaptured by UN troops.

30 September—Communist China's Foreign Minister Chou En-lai warns: "The Chinese people will not supinely tolerate seeing their neighbors being savagely invaded by the imperialists."

1 October—ROK (South Korean) troops cross 38th Parallel in pursuit of retreating North Koreans as General MacArthur calls upon enemy to surrender.

2 October—Chou En-lai informs Indian ambassador in Peiping that if U. S. troops enter North Korea, Communist China will intervene in Korean War.

7 October—U. S. troops begin crossing 38th Parallel.

7 October—UN General Assembly authorizes UN forces to pursue the enemy across the 38th Parallel.

10 October—Wonsan on the east coast captured by ROK troops.

10 October—Communist Chinese Foreign Affairs spokesman repeats warning of intervention in Korean War.

16 October—First Chinese Communist troops—the "People's Volunteers"—secretly enter Korea from Manchuria.

19 October—Pyongyang, capital of North Korea, captured by UN forces.

26 October—Chinese Communist troops attack ROK units at Yalu River and points south of the Sino-Korean border.

1 November—First Russian-built MIGs appear along Yalu to attack U. S. airplanes.

2 November—Chinese Communists with North Korean allies strike at United Nations units on western and eastern fronts.

5 November—General MacArthur notifies United Nations that Chinese Communists are operating in Korea.

7 November—All Communist forces in Korea break off action.

24 November—General MacArthur announces "win-the-war" offensive.

26–27 November—Communist forces, now controlled by People's Republic of China, attack on both fronts; deep penetration around Tokchon threatens to turn Eighth Army's right flank, in the east 1st Marine Division flanked and cut off at Chosin Reservoir.

4 December—United Nations forces in full retreat, Pyongyang recaptured by the Communists.

10 December—1st Marine Division breaks out of Chosin Reservoir trap and begins march to join rest of X Corps at Hungnam.

15 December—United Nations forces begin establishing defensive line approximating the 38th Parallel.

25 December—Evacuation of X Corps from Hungnam completed.

27 December—Lieutenant General Walton Walker, commander of Eighth Army, killed in road accident; Lieutenant General Matthew Ridgway named his successor.

29 December—Communist troop buildup reported above UN line at 38th Parallel.

1951

1 January—Communist forces launch all-out offensive against United Nations; Ridgway begins orderly retreat.

4 January—Seoul again captured by Communists.

7 January—UN forces set up new defense line at Pyongtaek–Wonju.

15 January—Enemy offensive halted.

21 January—General Ridgway issues orders for counteroffensive.

7 February—Communists forced to withdraw north of the Han River.

14 March—Seoul recaptured by UN forces for second time.

31 March—Leading elements of United Nations Command reach 38th Parallel.

11 April—President Truman relieves General MacArthur as Supreme Commander of UN forces and replaces him with General Ridgway; Lieutenant General James Van Fleet appointed as commander of U. S. Eighth Army.

23 April—Chinese Communist forces launch another offensive.

30 April—UN forces complete withdrawal to prepared positions north of Seoul.

3 May—Enemy offensive halted.

16 May—Second phase of enemy offensive given impetus.

21 May—United Nations Command launches counteroffensive which succeeds in driving enemy north of the 38th Parallel.

13 June—UN forces capture Chorwon and Kumhwa in the Iron Triangle.

23 June—Soviet delegate Malik proposes truce in the Korean War.

30 June—General Ridgway notifies enemy he is ready to discuss possibility of arranging a cease-fire.

10 July—Truce talks begin at Kaesong; UN delegation led by U. S. Vice-

Admiral Charles Turner Joy, Communist group led by Lieutenant General Nam Il of North Korea.

27 July—Negotiators at Kaesong agree on agenda.

5 August—UN Command breaks off truce talks on grounds of armed enemy troops in the neutral area.

10 August—Cease-fire talks resumed.

23 August—Communists suspend cease-fire talks on grounds of "bombing" of their delegation at Kaesong.

25 October—Armistice conference resumed at new site, Panmunjom.

28 October—Agreement reached on battle line as the line of demarcation.

12 November—Ridgway orders Van Fleet to cease offensive operations and begin active defense of UN front, thus introducing the stalemate which lasts until June, 1952.

26 November—Agreement reached on location of battle line, "Little Armistice" begins next day.

18 December—Prisoner of war lists exchanged by both sides.

27 December—"Little Armistice" ends but war remains stalemated.

1952

2 January—United Nations makes proposal on prisoner exchange embodying the principle of "voluntary repatriation."

3 January—Communists reject UN proposal in such language as to indicate the 18-month deadlock over voluntary repatriation has been reached.

28 April—Admiral Joy presents UN final offer insisting on voluntary repatriation.

7 May—Communist POWs on Koje Island begin riots; General Mark Clark arrives in Tokyo to succeed Ridgway as Supreme Commander of UN forces; Ridgway thereafter departs for France to take command of NATO.

22 May—Major General William Harrison relieves Admiral Joy as chief of UN delegation at Panmunjom.

8 October—United Nations adjourns armistice talks indefinitely until Communists accept its proposal on prisoner exchange or make a suitable counteroffer.

4 November—Dwight Eisenhower elected President of the United States.

17 November—India introduces compromise truce plan at United Nations.

2 December—President-elect Eisenhower begins three-day tour in Korea.

15 December—Peiping radio announces Communist China's formal rejection of Indian compromise plan.

1953

2 February—President Eisenhower in first State of the Union message ends "neutralization" of Formosa Strait.

5 March—Premier Joseph Stalin of Russia dies.

6 March—Georgi Malenkov named to succeed Stalin.

28 March—Communists accept UN proposal to discuss exchange of sick and wounded prisoners of war.

20 April—Exchange of sick and wounded prisoners—"Operation Little Switch"—begun in Korea.

26 April—Truce talks resumed at Panmunjom.

7 May—Communists accept a UN proposal that prisoners unwilling to be repatriated be kept in neutral custody in Korea rather than removed to a neutral nation.

25 May—New proposals for ending prisoner deadlock offered at Panmunjom, but South Korean observer boycotts meetings; beginning of South Korean President Rhee's campaign to block the cease-fire is indicated.

8 June—Agreement reached on prisoner of war issue.

9 June—South Korean National Assembly unanimously rejects truce terms.

14 June—Communists launch heaviest offensive in two years at ROK troops in eastern sector.

18 June—On orders of President Rhee approximately 27,000 North Korean prisoners are freed and returned to civilian life in South Korea.

20 June—Communists accuse UN Command of complicity in freeing of prisoners; suspend truce talks.

23 June—President Rhee reiterates opposition to truce terms.

25 June—Walter Robertson, U. S. Assistant Secretary of State for Far East, arrives in Seoul to persuade Rhee to accept truce.

8 July—Communists agree to General Clark's proposal to proceed with final arrangements for armistice without South Korean participation.

11 July—Robertson and Rhee announce agreement; Rhee will no longer oppose truce terms.

13 July—Communists launch even larger offensive than June 14 assault against ROK troops.

27 July—Cease-fire agreement signed, Korean War ends.

5 August—Exchange of prisoners—"Operation Big Switch"—begins at Panmunjom.

Part I

The Shooting War

Chapter One

KOREA, the place where the world's peace was broken not five years after the end of World War II, is one of those unhappy little lands fated to be battlegrounds.

Since the end of the nineteenth century Korea has been a pawn in the Asian power struggle between the emergent empires of Russia and Japan as they moved against each other or against the slumbering power of China. And this has been so chiefly because Korea's northern border abuts the Chinese province of Manchuria and the Russian province of Siberia, while to the east over water lies the Japanese archipelago. To Russia and Japan, seeking Asian supremacy through domination of China, the Korean peninsula meant access to Manchuria as well as the use of numerous year-round harbors. To China, control or possession of Korea meant a barrier against Russian or Japanese ambition.

And so it was not for herself that Korea was sought, for she is an iron land and a barren one, an alternating hell of heat and cold, a place of poverty and pain, where death comes early from diseases such as malaria or whatever else may spring from the practice of fertilizing rice with human dung. Nor is Korea made for fighting, for it is actually a great rugged mountain range, the southeast-sloping spurs of which, together with long broad rivers rushing between them, form barriers blocking military movement.

In size, the Korean peninsula is from 500 to 600 miles long, and from 90 to 200 miles wide, except for its broad northern terminus. There the Yalu River border with Manchuria runs for about 400 miles west-to-east, and the Tumen River border with

Siberia extends another ten miles east. West of Korea, 125 miles across the warm waters of the Yellow Sea, lies China's strategic Liaotung Peninsula with the famous port of Port Arthur. To the east, a slightly shorter distance across the colder Sea of Japan, is Japan.

At the time of the invasion there were approximately 30,-000,000 people living in Korea, some 9,000,000 in the Communist north and the rest in the south. But the north possessed most of the nation's resources of gold, iron, wood, tungsten, copper, and graphite, as well as most of the hydroelectric power. In the south, where crops of rice and barley could be harvested twice yearly because of the extra rainfall of the summer monsoon, food and textiles were the chief products.

Until the artificial division of the country after World War II, the south traded its rice, barley, silk, and textiles to the north for wood, coal, iron, and electric power. Economically, then, the nation was an entity and could sustain itself, though the industrial north was always the richer. In the south, primitive farming methods and rapacious loan sharks kept the farmers permanently poor. Korean peasants, borrowing not only for crops, but for food, weddings and the poor man's ultimate triumph of a good funeral, paid interest charges up to 150 percent annually. They were never out of debt. In such a nation, stoicism was the virtue and cruelty the vice: death could be accepted without murmur, and dogs could be tied in sacks and beaten slowly to death to make their flesh the tenderer for eating.

And yet, poverty and pain had not always been Korea's portion. Under the Yi dynasty which ruled in Korea from 1392 until the Japanese annexation of the country in 1910, the people lived under conditions generally prosperous for those times, while a high intellectual and cultural society flourished. It was during the Yi dynasty that Korea came to accept China's nominal suzerainty. It was not outright rule, but Korea, bound to China by the common religion of Buddhism or the Confucian moral code (there are only about 600,000 Christians in modern Korea), strongly influenced by Chinese culture and scholarship, regarded China much as a youth looks up to his older brother. The dynasty, which had been firmly established when General Yi Tae-jo routed the last of the Mongol invaders in 1394, was early recognized by the Ming rulers in China, and Chinese characters had been printed on movable type in Korea fifty years before Gutenberg "invented" movable type in Europe.

At the end of the sixteenth century, however, the Ming nominal suzerainty came under two attacks. In 1592, the Japanese war lord Hideyoshi invaded Korea by sea. Seven years of occupation and conflict followed, until the Japanese withdrew, decisively defeated at sea by Koreans sailing the world's first ironclads, "turtle-shell" ships which had been perfected during wars with pirates. Then, in 1627, the Manchus of China, who eventually replaced the Ming dynasty, invaded and occupied Korea, refusing to withdraw until the Yi ruler acknowledged their sovereignty. Thus Korea became a tributary of Manchu China in name, while remaining independent in fact, and thereafter Korea proclaimed that policy of isolation from the world which, gaining her the name of the Hermit Kingdom, remained in effect until the rise of Russia and Japan as Asiatic powers.

It was in 1530 that Ivan the Terrible formally assumed the title of Russian Czar. Shortly thereafter Russia began to expand eastward through Northern Asia. In 1581 the Cossacks conquered the Tatar Khanate of Siberia, and in 1644 Russian explorers reached the Pacific Ocean. Thereafter Czarist Russia turned south, until China ceded her the Maritime Province which brought her borders as far south as Manchuria and Korea and left her with a Siberian coastline facing Japan. This happened in 1860, by which time European powers and the United States had appeared in Asia.

In 1853 the American Commodore Perry opened Japan to world trade, after which both Japan and the Western powers began attempting to do the same to the Hermit Kingdom in Korea. But the Koreans, never docile, resisted violently. They burned ships and killed their crews. They put a number of Catholic missionaries to death. They fought back against the parties of French, Americans or Japanese which landed on their shores in the hope of punishing them or persuading them to open their harbors. The most famous clash occurred in 1871, after the Koreans had burned the American sailing ship *General Sherman* in the Han River and massacred the crew. The United States sent ships and Marines to Korea on a mission that was to be both punitive and persuasive, if such a combination is possible. The result was, inevitably, only punitive. The Marines landed from U. S. Navy ships which sailed up the Han from the west coast port of Chemulpo (Inchon) and systematically stormed and razed a system of river forts, ending with a circular redoubt called The Citadel. Still, the Koreans clung stubbornly to their isolation until, in 1876, Japan forced them to sign a treaty beginning diplomatic relations between the two countries.

For the next decade, the Korean capital of Seoul was shaken by a series of revolts which the Japanese inspired, but did not lead, against a conservative court still resisting world trade. The court replied by asking help from China. Chinese troops drove the Japanese from Seoul, and in 1885 both China and Japan agreed to withdraw their soldiers from Korea. The Japanese, meanwhile, became stronger. Ten years later they landed at Chemulpo, seized the palace in Seoul, captured the king and declared war on China. The ensuing Sino-Japanese War of 1895 introduced Japan as a military power. China's forces were easily beaten, and the Japanese pursued them across the Yalu River, turning west to take possession of the Liaotung Peninsula with its strategic port at Port Arthur. Stunned, China sued for peace. Japan demanded a huge indemnity, cession of the Liaotung "in perpetuity," and recognition of what she was pleased to call "Korean independence." But energetic little Japan had overdone it. Russia was now alarmed and Russia intervened, for she too coveted the Liaotung and Port Arthur.

With France and Germany, Russia formed the Triple Intervention which compelled Japan to return the Liaotung to China. Russia then came to China as a friend and negotiated in 1896 a secret alliance against Japan. In exchange for promises of help, China gave, or rather surrendered, to Russia the right to build the famous Trans-Siberian Railroad to Vladivostok across Manchuria. Later, she gave her new friend a 25-year lease on the Liaotung Peninsula. Both these Russian gains were not lost upon other European powers, who could see that great China was soft and ripe for despoiling. France and Germany, and later England, began extracting from China those leases of land and trading privileges called "spheres of interest." The seeds of the xenophobia which would inflame the Communist China of a half century later were being planted.

In 1896, meanwhile, Russia and Japan came into conflict in Korea. The year before, the Japanese had murdered a hostile

Korean queen and seized King Yi Tae-wang, forcing him to accept a cabinet of Koreans friendly to Japan. But in February of 1896 the king fled to the Russian legation with his loyal ministers and his great seal and began to rule Korea from there. He dismissed his Japanese advisers and replaced them with Russians, whereupon the Japanese sought an accord with the Russians. In 1896, the two powers signed an agreement recognizing Korea's much-proclaimed "independence" and promising to withdraw their troops. The agreement was renewed in 1898, the year the United States entered the Far Eastern arena by defeating Spain and annexing the Philippine Islands.

Both Russia and Japan consistently violated the pacts of 1896 and 1898, but Japan prepared more realistically for the inevitable showdown. She built her forces, especially her navy, and on the night of February 8, 1904, using the same "sneak-punch" technique with which she was later to stun the American giant at Pearl Harbor, a Japanese squadron launched a surprise attack on Russian ships in Port Arthur. Next, a sizable army landed at Chemulpo again and advanced to the frontier to defeat the Russians in the Battle of the Yalu, a victory which has since been regarded as historic, for it made the West aware that a power of the first order had arisen in the Orient. Korea's value as a strategic springboard was made manifest when Japan's armies were able to move through Manchuria and blockade the Liaotung Peninsula by land, while Japanese ships, operating from Korea's west coast, blockaded it by sea. Port Arthur fell on January 2, 1905, after a bloody, six-month siege. Two more blows brought Russia to the point of capitulation. Japan routed a Russian army of 350,000 men—inflicting 150,000 casualties—during the four-week Battle of Mukden in Manchuria, and on May 27, in the pitiless Battle of Tsushima, Admiral Togo annihilated the decrepit Baltic fleet which the Czar had sent creeping around the curve of the world to save Port Arthur.

The Russo-Japanese War was over by midsummer of 1905. In September of that year, at the Treaty of Portsmouth arranged by U. S. President Theodore Roosevelt, Japan emerged with southern Sakhalin ceded to her by Russia, the Liaotung Peninsula in her possession and her "paramount interest" in Korea recognized by the signers.

In effect, Japan now had Korea firmly in her grasp. Though

the pretense of a protectorate was maintained for five years, outright annexation came in 1910 when the last Korean king, Yi Hyeng, was forced to abdicate and his country—"The Land of the Morning Calm"—became a part of the Japanese Empire. To her credit, Japan did much to improve the land she had renamed Chosen. To her discredit, her policies there were harsh and oppressive, and the Koreans rapidly sank to the level of mere laborers. All leaders, professional men and technicians were Japanese, and so the new masters came to be hated by the Koreans. Bands of irregulars were formed and the legendary guerrilla fighter Kim Il Sung led his countrymen in a harrying war against the despised Japanese. Based in the mountains of Manchuria across the Yalu, Kim's forces struck at the Japanese in northern Korea on an average of several times a day. It was in this hard school, where brains, speed and daring were the weapons used against the superior arms of the Japanese, that many of North Korea's leaders of the future were trained. One of them was a pudgy, stone-faced young lieutenant named Kim Sung Chu. He was to become one of the best guerrilla leaders, and after Kim Il Sung died and the Japanese had driven the guerrillas from Manchuria into Soviet Siberia, Kim Sung Chu became an officer in the Russian Red Army, serving with distinction as a captain in the Battle of Stalingrad.

During the early decades of the century, another expatriate Korean, older than Kim Sung Chu and voluntarily in exile, hated the Japanese from afar. This was Lee Sung Man. A descendant of the Yi dynasty, Lee Sung Man later outraged his aristocratic father by changing his name to its famous Western form, Syngman Rhee. Born in 1875, just as the Hermit Kingdom's isolation had been ended by Japan, Syngman Rhee quickly immersed himself in the tumultuous politics of his day. His father was again outraged when he joined the radical young men demanding democratic reforms and founded, at the age of twenty, Korea's first daily newspaper, *Independence*. Young Rhee was also a remarkable student who had won first place in the national examinations held in the royal court at Seoul, but he emerged, not as a scholar excelling in Oriental philosophy and calligraphy, but as a fiery young leader of students agitating for democratic reforms. Having helped stage an anti-Japanese demonstration in Seoul, he was captured, tortured, and thrown into prison for seven years. A general amnesty brought about his release, and he went to America, studying at George Washington University, earning a master's degree at Harvard and a doctorate in international law at Princeton under Woodrow Wilson. In 1905, Rhee visited Theodore Roosevelt at the Portsmouth Conference to protest against affirmation of Japanese "interests" in Korea. In 1911, he returned to his homeland, but was forced to flee. He became active on Korea's behalf in Hawaii, the United States, China and Switzerland, meeting, in Geneva, Francesca Donner, the Austrian woman whom he later married in New York. In 1919, at a secret session in Seoul, Rhee was elected President of the outlawed Korean Provisional Government, and the Japanese promptly put a price on his head. And so Syngman Rhee spent the long years of his exile as a lonely and empassioned man who had come, through ceaseless activity on behalf of a free and independent Korea, to see in himself the embodiment of his country's cause.

During those years, the Japanese continued to solidify their hold in Korea while acquiring more territory from the old enemy, Russia. The opportunity came during World War I, in which Japan stood with the Allies against the Central Powers led by Germany. Russia was also an Allied nation, but Japan, seeing Russia convulsed by Communist revolution, had no compunction about crossing the border and establishing herself in Siberia. Only U. S. diplomatic intervention persuaded a Japanese army to evacuate Vladivostok three years after the Armistice.

In 1931, Japan once again invaded Manchuria, carving out a puppet state called Manchukuo beneath the eyes of a Western world caught in a severe economic depression, and a Russia and China made powerless by internal problems. In 1937, Japan launched her attack on China proper, and then, two years later, came the great blaze of battle known as World War II.

Korea was forgotten, and she did not reappear in world view again until the interests of Soviet Russia and the United States collided in the vacuum caused by the collapse of the Japanese Empire.

Chapter Two

IT WAS in September of 1945 that Japan's unconditional surrender brought World War II to its formal close. In six years and a day the greatest of all conflicts had ended in the most decisive of defeats: the Nazi beast had been utterly destroyed, along with its Fascist vassal in Italy, while imperialist Japan, driven from island after island by American striking power, was at last broken and made suppliant by atomic bombings which culminated the systematic devastation of her homeland from sea and sky.

The cost to mankind in life and treasure had been staggering, and no war had been more wanton. Millions perished, at the front among the bullets or at home under the bombs; the surface of the earth was strewn with ruin and the floors of the seas were littered with ships and sunken cargo.

In 1945 the very memory of this war was sickening, and in America there began a dash to dismantle the greatest military force the world had known. Angry mothers marched on Washington demanding that their sons be returned home. Across the globe American soldiers—a few of them Communist agents*— demonstrated for demobilization. Everywhere Americans were clamoring for an end to the austerity of war and the high cost of maintaining a large military establishment to oversee the peace. In 1946, a Congressional year, few men ran for office on platforms of continued wartime controls. By the end of that year the U. S. Army had been effectively emasculated, the vast and

---

*General Mark Clark, *From the Danube to the Yalu* (New York: Harper and Brothers, 1954), p. 10.

28

varied American fleet—the majesty of which the world may never see again—was going into mothballs, and there were bellicose pacifists attempting to reduce the Marine Corps to the mission of opening embassy doors. Much of this was urged and accomplished in the sincere belief that the atomic bomb had made conventional military forces obsolete. America did not need a large striking force because she, and she alone, possessed the ultimate weapon. And so the nuclear warhead became the American Maginot Line, while behind it the economy quickly shifted from the making of munitions to the manufacture of playthings. America, which had led the Allies in the great victory over the Axis, was sick and tired of war.

But Soviet Russia was not.

To Joseph Stalin, dictator of Russia, the leader of world Communism, a ruler as cruel at home and as covetous abroad as any Czar before him, the great war just ended was but prelude to the giant conflict then beginning: the struggle for world dominion. Never before, either as a Communist bureaucracy energized by the idea of ruling a world combination of socialist states, or as a Czarist "savior with a sword" striving to make Holy Russia the headquarters of New Rome, had the Russian state occupied such an excellent base of operations as it did in 1945–46.

On her Asiatic flank the old enemy, Japan, lay prostrate, and the power of Chiang Kai-shek in China had been seriously weakened. On the European flank, the old enemy, Germany, was defeated and divided, its eastern half already being formed into the Communist buffer state which would be formally promulgated as the German Democratic Republic (East Germany) in 1949. Although Russia had suffered grievous wounds in her battle with Hitlerite Germany (she was at war with Japan for six days only) her manpower reserves were great and her damaged economy was being rapidly restored by the looting of those Axis territories which had been "liberated" by the Red Army. Russia's army, equipped by an economy still functioning on a wartime basis, was huge—and among a people with a long tradition of suffering and a short history of protest, in a nation which had passed from Khan to Czar to Commissar, there were no demonstrations for demobilization.

Backed by this army, emboldened by American languor, Russia's negotiators in Central Europe insisted upon and achieved the kinds of peace treaties which would make the Central European states setups for the take-overs that were to come.

One by one, beginning with Poland, which Russia had helped invade in 1939 when Stalin was Hitler's partner and which the Communists captured in 1947 by subverting national elections, the nations of Central Europe slid behind what Winston Churchill would call the Iron Curtain. Austria and the rest of Europe would have followed, but for America's monopoly of the atom bomb. By 1949 this monopoly was at an end. Russian and captured German scientists, assisted by nuclear secrets fed them by American and British traitors, made Russia an atomic power sooner than had been anticipated.

Meanwhile, Stalin was also attempting to gain by force what he could not acquire by guile. Communist guerrillas began operations in Greece, and Turkey was also endangered. Only the Truman Doctrine—President Truman's use in 1947 of huge sums of money to fight Communism in Greece and Turkey—kept these Middle Eastern nations from vanishing behind the Iron Curtain.

A year later the Communists tried again, establishing a land blockade against Western Berlin, that half of the former German capital which lay more than a hundred miles inside Communist East Germany. An awakening America responded with the Berlin Airlift. U. S. planes, helped by the British, flew 2,300,000 tons of food and coal into the blockaded city between April 1, 1948, and September 30, 1949, when the Communists at last raised the siege.

Twice, now, Stalin had been rebuffed on his western flank, and to these setbacks were added the Marshall Plan, which gave American financial aid to the recovering nations of Europe, and the inception of the Western military alliance which would be known as the North Atlantic Treaty Organization, or NATO. On Soviet Russia's western flank resistance had begun to stiffen.

But to the east, in Asia, the march of world Communism remained undeterred. Its greatest postwar victory was won in China in 1949, when the Chinese Communist leader, Mao Tsetung, defeated Chiang Kai-shek's Nationalist army and drove Chiang and his remnant to the big offshore island of Formosa. That had been by force of arms, but four years earlier the duplicity of Stalin, the man who once said, "Sincere diplomacy is no more possible than dry water or iron wood," had gobbled up other illicit fruits of war—fruits which were to become in turn the seeds of the new conflict.

Early in 1945 at the Yalta Conference, Stalin made two moves which guaranteed the return of Russian imperialism to the Far East. First he persuaded President Roosevelt that "the wrongs" done to Czarist Russia in 1905 by the Portsmouth Treaty should be righted, meaning that Port Arthur and southern Sakhalin should be recovered by the U.S.S.R., along with certain concessions in Manchuria and Mongolia. In return for this, Stalin consented to sign a treaty of friendship with Chiang as an ally of the United States and to provide military aid in the Pacific. Actually, Stalin was to help his fellow Communist Mao drive Chiang from China and his aid against Japan would turn out to be nothing more than a declaration of war two days after the atomic bombing of Hiroshima, followed by a few actions fought in Siberia against a Japanese army stripped of planes for home defense.

The second move of Stalinist "diplomacy" was to allay any American fears about the future of Korea by agreeing, informally, with the Cairo Conference declaration of 1943 that "in due course Korea should be free and independent." Actually, Stalin had already trained the key Korean Communists who would rule the puppet state he planned to establish. There were exactly 36 of these men, either Soviet-born Koreans or Korean exiles, and their leader was that same Kim Sung Chu who had fought as a guerrilla against the Japanese under the celebrated Kim Il Sung. Another of them was Nam Il, Russian-born and highly educated, a veteran, like Kim Sung Chu, of the Red Army.

Then, of course, President Roosevelt died. President Truman succeeded him, going to Potsdam in Germany to confer with Stalin and Prime Minister Attlee of England. The Cairo agreement on a free and independent Korea was reaffirmed in the Potsdam Declaration. It appeared that the only problem connected with Korea was to find a line north of which the Russians would accept the surrender of Japanese troops, south of which the Americans would accept it. This was settled when Rear Admiral Matthias Gardner pointed to the 38th Parallel, or

38th degree of north latitude, which crosses Korea at its middle and said, "Why not put it there?"

There it went.

On August 12, two days before Japan's collapse, with the nearest American troops 600 miles away in Okinawa, with the 38th Parallel still to be approved by President Truman, a force of 100,000 Russian soldiers under General Ivan Chistiakov crossed the Siberian border into northern Korea. Behind them, other Soviet troops were overrunning Manchuria, making way for the looting of Manchuria's industrial plant. In both Manchuria and northern Korea the Russians began rounding up some 600,000 Japanese soldiers for shipment to Siberia as slave laborers.

The Russian Bear was back in the Far East.

He was wearing a commissar's cap this time in place of the old Czarist smock, but he had not changed in truth or in tactic since Rudyard Kipling wrote of him fifty years before:

> When he stands up like a tired man, tottering near and near;
> When he stands up as pleading, in wavering man-brute guise,
> When he veils the hate and cunning of his little swinish eyes;
> When he shows as seeking quarter, with paws like hands in prayer,
> This is the time of peril—the time of the Truce of the Bear.

The Bear would be joined four years later by that Communist state then rising in China. Farther to the east, preparing an indulgent treaty with Japan, was that other Far Eastern power: the United States of America.

Korea was again to have her destiny decided by a quarrel among foreigners, and more—far crueler for her people—by a conflict between the world's two great contending ideologies.

Chapter Three

THE 38th Parallel separating the world's two great powers in Korea had never been regarded—at least by the American planners—as anything more than a convenience that would speed the surrender of Japanese troops. Because it was an imaginary line, the device of map makers who mark off the world in squares, it ran straight across mountains and rivers and was therefore a military nightmare. It had no political meaning, no place in the history of the country. Nor was it ever intended to separate two zones of occupation, for joint occupation of Korea had never been discussed by the United States and the Soviet Union.

Yet, when American troops arrived in southern Korea on September 8, 1945, four weeks after the Russian entry, the Parallel had effectively divided 9,000,000 Koreans of the industrial north from 21,000,000 Koreans of the agricultural south. There were, in fact, two zones, for the Russians had already begun to seal off the border. Electric power was cut off and railway lines severed. Armed guards patrolled the Parallel. The exchange of goods began to diminish, eventually ending altogether, and the Korean economy began to shrivel and die. Lieutenant General John Hodge, U. S. military commander in Korea, protested to General Chistiakov without result. Prices in South Korea, now without coal or chemicals, soon began to rise in an inflationary spiral. Long before the political division was recognized, the partition of Korea was a fact of daily life. Koreans on both sides of the Parallel, so recently jubilant to feel the fetters of fifty years of Japanese bondage struck from their feet, were consumed with anger. On September 23, two weeks after receipt of the Japanese surrender in Seoul among scenes of exultation, General Hodge sent this message to General MacArthur in Tokyo:

Dissatisfaction with the division of the country grows.

It grew more lustily in the American south, where the U. S. XXIV Corps had the look of alien occupation troops, than in the Russian north, where the Communists had already set up an interim civil government. The Reds also contrived to throw all blame for the division on the Americans. And their interim government, of course, was merely the precursor of the satellite state Stalin intended to create.

Its leaders were the same 36 Soviet Koreans whom Communist Russia had trained, both in Marxist ideology and Communist take-over techniques. They were led by the pudgy and poker-faced Kim Sung Chu and his friend, Nam Il, and they came to the capital city of Pyongyang copiously supplied with pictures of Joseph Stalin and Communist flags. Supported by Russian advisers, these men quickly seized control and silenced all opposition. And then Kim Sung Chu adopted the name of his legendary leader of guerrilla-warfare days, Kim Il Sung.

The peasants of northern Korea were overjoyed to hear that the hero of old had come back to lead them, and they rejoiced when Kim Il Sung proclaimed a program of land reform. Great estates were confiscated and divided among the peasantry. Not until much later would it become plain that the peasant could neither rent nor sell his newly acquired land nor use it as security for a loan, and taxes disguised as "production quotas" would eventually rise to a ruinous 60 percent. Merchants of the north were likewise pleased to join the joint stock companies set up by the Russians, until they found out that these "fifty-fifty" firms were like the famous "fifty-fifty stew" composed equally of horse and rabbit: one horse to one rabbit, and here the Russian was the horse.

Yet these moves were hailed in the beginning and they scored great propaganda victories for the Communists below the Parallel, where there was no land reform and no promise of great things to come. To this was added discontent with General Hodge's rule which, because it failed to understand the Koreans and had a strong military cast, was harsh and fumbling.

In late 1945 against this background there began in Moscow a meeting of the foreign ministers of the United States, England and the Soviet Union. The Moscow Agreement was the result; under its terms the rival U. S. and Soviet military commands in Korea would set up a Joint Commission to make recommendations for creation of a single free government in Korea. This Commission the Soviets began to sabotage from its inception. But far more important was the Moscow Agreement's decision that a four-power trusteeship of up to five years would be needed before Korea attained independence.

News of this latter provision fell like a new bomb in "The Land of the Morning Calm." Trusteeship was repugnant to all Koreans, and demonstrations against the Moscow Agreement were made by the country's political groups, with but one notable abstention: the Communists. All the Red groups had been ordered beforehand to stay silent.

Thus, when the Joint Commission convened, the Russian members proposed that it consult only those Korean political groups which had *not* demonstrated against the Moscow Agreement. Which meant: Let us talk only to Communists. The American members refused, and on this rock all attempts by the Joint Commission to prepare for Korean independence foundered. The Commission continued to meet throughout 1946 and 1947, but it was frustrated by obstacles which were chiefly of Soviet origin.

Meanwhile, the military buildup in what could now be called North Korea had begun. Pyongyang became the headquarters tent of an armed camp. Koreans who had fought either for Red Russia or Red China began pouring across the Yalu into their native land. It was obvious that North Korea was to be the satellite from which the south would be either subverted or invaded.

And so, in 1947, alarmed by Russia's growing intransigence in Korea, the United States took the entire matter to the United Nations. The General Assembly resolved to hold elections throughout Korea in the spring of 1948. A nine-member United Nations Commission on Korea was chosen—although the delegate from the Communist Ukraine refused to attend its meetings—and went to Korea to supervise the first election in four thousand years of Korean history.

The Russians refused to allow the United Nations Commission north of the Parallel. Elections were held only in South Korea, and a National Assembly was named. The deputies chose the aged patriot Syngman Rhee as their president and a government was set up with the capital in Seoul (which is the Korean word for capital). This was the Republic of Korea, which would come to be known as South Korea and whose soldiers would be called ROKs for its initials.

In the north, the Communists retaliated by proclaiming the People's Democratic Republic of Korea with a constitution similar to that of Communist Bulgaria. Kim Il Sung was named its first premier. At the end of 1948, with great fanfare, Russian troops began leaving North Korea. They left behind them a well-trained and well-equipped North Korean People's Army vastly superior to Syngman Rhee's forces in the south.

Even though the last of 50,000 American occupation troops were not withdrawn from South Korea until June of 1949—thereby handing the Reds another propaganda horn to blow—the United States did not give Rhee anything like the military establishment the Russians had turned over to Kim Il Sung. The United States was afraid that President Rhee would satisfy his passion for unifying his country by force. He had often threatened to do so, and had once said that if America gave him the airplanes and gasoline he could conquer North Korea in two weeks. Nor did Rhee's highhanded tactics make him popular in America. Of this, President Truman himself has written:

> President Syngman Rhee is a man of strong convictions and has little patience with those who differ with him. From the moment of his return to Korea in 1945, he attracted to himself men of extreme right-wing attitudes and disagreed sharply with the political leaders of more moderate views. . . . I did not care for the methods used by Rhee's police to break up political meetings and control political enemies, and I was deeply concerned over the Rhee government's lack of concern about the serious inflation that swept the country. Yet we had no choice but to support Rhee. Korea had been overrun and downtrodden by the Japanese since 1905 and had had no chance to develop other leaders and leadership.[1]

But American support carefully excluded tanks, big guns, combat aircraft and even large stocks of ammunition. Without air, armor or artillery, the ROK Army being built by the Korean Military Advisory Group under Brigadier General William Roberts was about as modern as a muzzle-loader.

Further comfort for the Communists came when the U. S. Congress took over four months to authorize Truman's request for $150,000,000 in economic aid to South Korea for fiscal 1949. When Truman asked for another $60,000,000 for the same purpose in the 1950–51 budget, he was actually turned down. The latter appropriation was later passed in a combined South Korea-Nationalist China aid bill, but such dilatoriness could not be missed by the Communists of North Korea. Then, on January 12, 1950, Secretary of State Dean Acheson made his famous speech excluding Korea—and Formosa—from the American defense line in the Far East. That perimeter, said Acheson:

. . . runs along the Aleutians to Japan and then goes to the Ryukyus [and] from the Ryukyus to the Philippine Islands. . . . So far as the military security of other areas in the Pacific is concerned, it must be clear that no person can guarantee these areas against military attack. But it must also be clear that such a guarantee is hardly sensible or necessary within the realm of practical relationship.

In May, Senator Tom Connally, Chairman of the Senate Foreign Relations Committee, said that Russia could seize South Korea without U. S. intervention because Korea was not "very greatly important." Though the remarks were five months apart, though Acheson, at least, had been carefully trying to differentiate between places such as Japan, where U. S. troop commitment was firm, and Korea, where America did not have a policy of employing U. S. troops, it would have been surprising if the Communists had not taken them to mean that the United States would not fight in Korea. And when the invader thinks the defender won't fight, there is always war.

More, that approaching summer of 1950 offered Stalin perhaps the last opportunity to unify Korea under Premier Kim. The American-sponsored republic to the south had showed alarming signs of vitality. It was making economic gains and it had withstood all attempts at subversion. Communist guerrilla activity in the south was also slacking off, and the ROK Army had made enough progress, despite its continued lack of tanks and planes, to cause General Roberts to make the public boast that it was "the best doggoned shooting army outside the United States." Finally the Republic of Korea was beginning to shed some of the features which had made it so unpopular with the U. S. Congress the preceding year. Most notable of all was the National Assembly's move to strip the presidency of some of the broad powers which Syngman Rhee had abused in his tactics of fighting Communist fire with police-state fire. In the elections of May, 1950, 110 independents won seats in the National Assembly, to the satisfaction of many of Rhee's critics in the United States. A shift in American opinion could bring real military help to Korea. If North Korea waited much longer, a true and strong democracy might stand on the frontier of Communist Asia, and pro-Western sentiment would gain in Japan, still the foremost industrial power of the Far East.

So the decision to invade was made, probably by Premier Stalin, whose retouched photograph graced the wall behind Premier Kim's massive mahogany desk in Pyongyang. Certainly Kim had not the power to make it, and the Chinese did not even have an ambassador in Pyongyang by June, 1950. All the arms provided the Reds of North Korea—T-34 medium tanks, Yak fighter planes, submachine guns, 122mm howitzers, 76mm self-propelled guns, 76mm divisional guns, 45mm antitank guns, 61mm, 82mm and 120mm mortars—were Russian, either brought across the northern borders by train or shipped from Vladivostok to North Korean ports on the Sea of Japan. Most important of these were the T-34s, tanks which the German General Heinz Guderian credited with stopping his drive on Moscow. The T-34 fired an 85mm gun, plus a pair of 7.62 machine guns. It had a tough hide—as ROK and American gunners would discover—and there were 150 of them supporting the force which General Chai Ung Chai was moving into position for attack.

General Chai's army numbered about 90,000 men—two-thirds of North Korea's total ground strength of 135,000 men—and was formed into seven infantry divisions, one armored brigade, one brigade of border constabulary, one independent infantry regiment, and one motorcycle regiment. The North Korean division which was to be General Chai's chief striking unit was a body of 10,000 men divided into three rifle regiments of three battalions each. With it went an artillery regiment and a self-propelled gun battalion, medical, signal, antitank, engineer, and training battalions, plus reconnaissance and transport companies. The North Korean division, supported by its tanks, attacking behind its artillery, was a well-balanced, fast-moving force. Many of the men in ranks were combat veterans of the expatriate Korean Volunteer Army which had fought with the Chinese Communist forces. Numerous officers had received special military training in the Soviet Union. General Chai's spearheads had also gained experience during frequent armed raids south of the border, some of them full-scale assaults supported by artillery. These, incidentally, had been made while the Pyongyang radio continued its campaign of vilifying the United States and

South Korea as aggressors planning to attack the "peace-loving" population of North Korea. True enough, Syngman Rhee had made enough saber-rattling speeches to provide ammunition for these propaganda blasts. But no military man in North Korea could have honestly believed that the American Ajax being trained in the south could actually defy his own Communist lightning.

The force below the Parallel was no match for the one above it, either in numbers, in arms, or in experience. The South Korean ground force of 143,000 men actually broke down into an ROK Army of 98,000 and a National Police of 45,000. Worse, the ROK Army split down again into 65,000 combat troops and 33,000 headquarters and service people—an astonishingly high number of noncombat troops. Eight infantry divisions of strengths varying from 6,900 to 9,700 men made up this combat force.

Just as their brothers in the north were Russian-trained and Russian-armed, the men south of the border were armed and trained by America. ROK infantry weapons were those used by GIs and Marines in World War II: the M1 rifle, .30-caliber carbine, light and heavy .30-caliber machine guns, 60mm and 81mm mortars, 2.36-inch rocket launchers or "bazookas," and 37mm antitank guns. They had no mines, no big mortars, no recoilless rifles and, of course, no tanks or planes. Their heaviest weapons were 27 armored cars and 89 serviceable 105mm howitzers of a short-barreled model with an effective range of 7,200 yards (as compared to the 12,500-yard effective range of the normal American 105) and a maximum range of 8,200 yards. Fifteen percent of the ROK weapons were useless and 35 percent of the vehicles unserviceable. Ammunition stocks would last only a few days. Most of the ROK divisions had yet to train in divisional maneuvers. A few of them, engaged in cleaning out Communist guerrillas to the south, were still equipped with Japanese weapons. Many battalions and regiments were led by twenty-five- and thirty-year-old colonels, men whose military training had taken place under the Japanese.

By June of 1950, then, the combat forces facing each other across the Parallel compared to each other as follows: 90,000 North Koreans with 150 tanks and a small tactical air force against 65,000 South Koreans with no tanks and no air force, the North Korean artillery also outnumbering the South Korean by about three to one on the divisional level and possessing an advantage in range—14,000 yards to 8,200 yards—as well as size. The "Russian" Koreans also were better organized than the "American" Koreans and already, as General Chai's troops and tanks began moving south toward invasion points above the Parallel, the Communist propaganda machine was raising the smoke screen intended to obtain the other advantage of surprise.

Pyongyang, girded for war, began talking peace. A "peace proposal" was offered to all Koreans whereby a single national election would be held. But "the traitor" Syngman Rhee and most of his top aides, as well as the United Nations Commission on Korea, would be banned from it. Immediately, Communists of the south, who had boycotted the Republic of Korea's second free election in May, began clamoring for acceptance of the "peace offer." It was, of course, rejected—but it had only been offered to divide the South Koreans and to soften them for the blow that was to come. Refusal of it would also provide later excuses for the "defensive" invasion of South Korea which, as captured North Korean documents later proved, had already been ordered.

And so, between the 15th and 24th of June, the North Korean Army moved into a belt north of the Parallel from which civilians had been cleared. Although the movement did not pass undetected, the intelligence reports that General MacArthur's Far Eastern Headquarters forwarded to Washington were accompanied by estimates discounting enemy intentions to attack. One such report, written less than three months earlier on March 25 had said:

> It is believed there will be no civil war in Korea this spring or summer. The most probable course of North Korean action this spring or summer is furtherance of its attempt to overthrow the South Korean government by the creation of chaotic conditions in the Republic through guerrilla activities and psychological warfare.

Though guerrilla activity did slacken after this estimate was made, the Pyongyang "peace proposal" certainly seemed to bear out the rest of it. And in fairness to Washington, it must be added that reports of Communist military activity were fairly common from almost every point of contact with the Iron Curtain countries: in the west from Scandinavia down through Berlin and Trieste to Greece and Turkey, in the east from the Kuriles in the North Pacific to Korea and Indo-China and Malaya. More, by the time of General Chai's movement to the 38th Parallel, it was too late for any effective action. The die had been cast as long ago as 1948, when, according to President Truman:

> The National Security Council reported to me that we could do one of three things: We could abandon Korea; or we could continue our military and political responsibility for the country; or we could extend to a Korean government aid and assistance for the training and equipping of their own security forces and offer extensive economic help to prevent a breakdown of the infant nation. The Council recommended, however that we choose the last course, and I gave my approval.[2]

That was what had been attempted, and it was a policy all but dictated by the mood of the American people, while harassed by a Congress itself the product of that mood. This policy went into force among a people whom oppression had deprived of modern skills and techniques as well as experienced political leaders, and it was executed through autocratic Syngman Rhee.

The American policy in Korea had, of course, followed the seemingly bumbling way of democracy, which dares not choose more stringent means lest it defeat its own end of political freedom. In the beginning this way seems to have almost no chance against the tighter and more highly organized slave way: either a proletariat accepting dictatorship in the delusion of reaching Utopia, as in Communism, or a people having it forced on them for less noble purposes, as in a despotism. From Xerxes down to Kim Il Sung dangling at the end of Premier Stalin's string, the slave way has always seemed to strike with a fury that is irresistible.

That was how it looked that rainy Sunday morning of June 25, 1950, when the South Korean soldiers mistook the rumble of enemy artillery for the sound of thunder.

41

Chapter Four

A LL along the Parallel, moving from west to east like a train
of powder, the guns of the invasion were flashing alight.
Between four o'clock on the morning of June 25 when the first
blow fell in the west, and the start of the eastern assaults a few
hours later, General Chai sent the North Korean I and II Corps
plunging south along five ground invasion routes and one by
sea. Defending against them were four ROK divisions and one
regiment, but only at Chunchon in the east were these troops
able to withstand that impetuous rush.

In the west, many of the American military advisers to the
ROKs, as well as many of their officers and men, were on weekend passes in Seoul and other towns. The ROK units were not
only surprised but also understrength when the first of the Red
shells exploded on the Ongjin Peninsula jutting into the Yellow
Sea. A half-hour barrage was succeeded by the assault of elements of a division and a brigade. Though the Communists
came on without tanks, they quickly began smashing through a
South Korean battalion. Inside an hour ROK Army headquarters in Seoul about 50 miles south of the Parallel was on notice
that full-scale invasion had begun. Ongjin, only an outpost,
isolated by water and never considered defensible, would have
to be evacuated the next day.

But at Kaesong disaster was impending.

Here, a bit east of Ongjin and a few miles south of the
Parallel, the ancient capital of Korea sat astride the Pyongyang-
Seoul highway. Here the North Koreans launched a strong two-
division thrust behind tanks. The South Koreans fought valiantly to oppose them. Some of them ran at the T-34s with

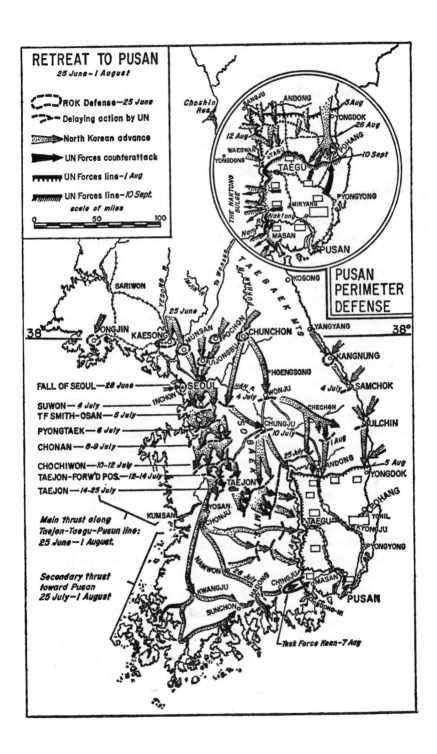

satchel charges or explosive-tipped poles. Others swarmed over the tanks and tried to open the turrets to drop grenades inside. The ROKs sacrificed themselves heroically, but their ardor was unavailing. They were machine-gunned by the tanks or picked off by riflemen, and soon, as is the way of war, there were no more volunteers for suicide duty. The Red onslaught, only momentarily delayed by the efforts of the best ROKs—for the best are often the first to die—rolled on toward Kaesong.

And there were already North Korean troops inside the town.

A regiment of Red troops had ridden into Kaesong by train, as easily as schoolboys on an excursion. The North Koreans had relaid a few miles of pulled-up railroad tracks during the night, and when morning came, had chugged south in a turning movement. And as these Red troops deployed to the rear of the ROKs, their tank-led brothers in front of them applied the pressure. What was to be the North Korean Army's classic maneuver —to hit frontally with one column while another struck at the side or rear—was already succeeding at Kaesong. By half-past nine the city had fallen. Soldiers of the ROK 1st Division continued to fight to its north for three days, particularly in the vicinity of Korangpo-ri, but theirs was a losing battle which was made hopeless when their right flank was exposed by General Chai's main thrust delivered down the Uijongbu Corridor.

This corridor, the historic invasion route to Seoul, was formed by a pair of converging roads running down from the north to meet at Uijongbu, only 20 miles by straight road north of the capital city. And down these roads came the North Korean 4th and 3rd Divisions—the 4th on the west road, the 3rd on the east—behind the bulk of the tanks of the 105th Armored Brigade. There was no stopping these armored columns, for there was nothing with which to stop them. The American 37mm antitank guns were hardly better than pistols against the T-34s, and though a 2.36-inch bazooka might halt one if fired close-up and at a vulnerable spot, there were very few opportunities to get close-up that morning, and still fewer men volunteering to try it. General Chai's armor rolled south almost at will. By noon, the people of Uijongbu could hear artillery fire.

Also by noon the Red air arm had brought Kimpo Airfield a few miles northwest of Seoul under attack, and it was not long before the city itself was strafed by a pair of propeller-driven Yak fighter planes.

An hour earlier the Pyongyang radio had crackled with its usual bombast. The "bandit traitor Syngman Rhee" had attempted to invade North Korea and a "righteous invasion" of Red forces had been launched only as a countermeasure. Rhee, the broadcast said, would soon be arrested and executed. At about half-past one Premier Kim Il Sung announced that his country's forces were attacking because South Korea had rejected his "peace proposal" and had attacked the North Korean Army in the Ongjin Peninsula. Kim did not explain how his "defending" army was already 10 to 20 miles inside the territory of the "aggressor."

Thus by early afternoon in the western half of the battleground, the North Korean I Corps was carrying out its mission with lightning speed. Only on the east at Chunchon, about 60 miles inland from the Sea of Japan, had the invasion fallen behind schedule. Here the ROK 6th Division had issued no weekend passes and the garrison was at full strength. The South Koreans stopped the enemy 2nd Division cold, fighting out of concrete pillboxes built in a high ridge north of the town and hurling the invaders back. Without T-34s to blast a path, the North Koreans failed to carry out II Corps' directive to capture Chunchon the first day. The 7th Division assigned to overwhelm Inje about 30 miles farther east had to be diverted to Chunchon. The 7th arrived the next day with tanks, and that was to prove the end of the ROKs of the 6th Division. They had fought well, but they were ordered to withdraw after three days when their flanks began to collapse.

Across the high, rugged Taebaek Mountains overlooking the Sea of Japan, the II Corps drove south in the last two of General Chai's strokes. One division struck the ROK 8th Division along the coast and forced it to withdraw, while sampans and junks took between 400 to 600 guerrilla fighters downcoast to landing beaches above and below Samchok, about 40 miles southeast of the Parallel. The men deployed among the hills to take up the work of blowing bridges or blocking roads to bar the ROK retreat.

By nightfall of June 25, except for the setback at Chunchon, the North Koreans had achieved all of their objectives and in some places exceeded them. By then, too, the world well knew that it was teetering on the brink of World War III.

The war in Korea was already seven hours old when, at 9:26 the night of Saturday, June 24, this message was received in the U. S. State Department in Washington:

> North Korean forces invaded Republic of Korea territory at several points this morning. . . . It would appear from the nature of the attack and the manner in which it was launched that it constitutes an all-out offensive against ROK.

The report was signed by John Muccio, the U. S. Ambassador to Korea. Hardly another half hour after its receipt, the telephone rang in the library of President Truman's home in Independence, Missouri.

"Mr. President," said Secretary of State Dean Acheson, "I have very serious news. The North Koreans have invaded South Korea."

The President's first reaction was that he had better fly back to Washington, but the Secretary replied that inasmuch as there were no details on the crisis available yet, the President might as well continue his visit with his family. In the meantime, said Acheson, it might be well to request a meeting of the United Nations Security Council. Truman agreed. He asked Acheson to report to him again in the morning, and hung up.[1]

Quickly, Acheson contacted the U. S. Delegation to the United Nations in New York. Ernest Gross, Deputy Representative, was instructed to telephone the UN Secretary-General Trygve Lie and to request the Security Council meeting. Gross called Lie and told him the news. The UN chief was stunned, suddenly bursting out:

"This is war against the United Nations!"

By three o'clock in the morning Gross had made a formal written request for the Security Council meeting and Lie had scheduled it for two o'clock Sunday afternoon.

And 2 P.M. June 25 in New York was three o'clock in the morning below the Parallel in South Korea, where General Chai's regrouped forces were already assembling for the second day's operations.

General Chae Byong Duk was known as the "Fat Boy." He stood five feet six inches tall and weighed 245 pounds, and though he could easily be mistaken for one of those round and pacific Buddhas contained within the numerous red-lacquered temples of Korea, he was, in actuality, the Chief of Staff of the ROK Army. On the morning of June 25, General Chae had decided that the North Korean move was not another "rice raid" and had ordered a counter attack, thus putting into operation part of a previously prepared plan. This called for defending the capital at Seoul by driving the enemy back up the Uijongbu Corridor with reserve divisions moved up from the south.

Accordingly, throughout the Sunday which saw the main North Korean thrust roll down the twin roads converging on Uijongbu, the ROK 2nd Division had been moving north from Taejon, a city some 90 miles below Seoul. General Chae's plan was to have the 2nd counterattack north from Uijongbu along the eastern or right-hand road, while the 7th struck out along the left-hand or western road. Unfortunately, General Chae's plan meant that the 7th, already defending desperately along the right-hand road, had to turn this sector over to the 2nd and march about a half-dozen miles west. The shifting of the 7th presented no great hardship, though it might have been easier to allow the 2nd to march directly to the west road. But the real difficulty was in the delayed arrival of the 2nd from Taejon far to the south. Brigadier General Lee Hyung Koon, the 2nd's Commander, protested that since only a few of his men had reached Uijongbu by nightfall of the first day he could not attack on the morning of the second day, June 26, without committing his forces piecemeal.

General Chae nonetheless ordered General Lee to follow the plan, and Lee became the first of numerous ROK commanders to respond to humiliation by sulking in his tent. And so while the 7th Division counterattacked against the North Korean 4th along the western road and drove it back, General Lee spent the morning of June 26 sitting in his command post surrounded by his staff. The two battalions he had brought into position on the eastern road did not move out.

Then, just as the 7th Division's early success was producing inflated reports of a great victory which had cost the Reds 1,580 soldiers and 58 tanks, catastrophe, in the form of the Red 3rd Division advancing behind a long column of tanks, came down the east road of the Uijongbu Corridor. General Lee's two battalions raked the tanks with artillery and small arms. The T-34s clanked on unscathed. They passed through the ROK battalions deployed on either side of the road and rolled into Uijongbu. Behind them the North Korean riflemen drove the ROKs into the hills. On the left or west, now, the ROK 7th Division was outflanked all along its long axis, and had to pull back. By evening, both North Korean divisions and the armored brigade were safely inside Uijongbu.

The ROK counterattack had failed and the straight road south to Seoul lay open to the invaders.

In New York during the late afternoon of June 25—at about the same time that General Chae Byong Duk's counterattack was sent on its ill-fated way—the United Nations Security Council had assembled. Ten members were present. The eleventh, Soviet Russia, had been boycotting the Council's meetings since January, when it had protested the membership of Nationalist China. Chained by that need for consistency which often handcuffs liars, the Soviet Union remained absent this fatal day—and history may regard this absence as one of the great postwar blunders of international Communism. By staying away, the Soviet Union could not exercise the veto with which any of the five permanent members—France, England, Nationalist China, Russia and America—could nullify the Council's actions.

This historic afternoon of June 25, 1950, the Security Council acted quickly. The United Nations Commission on Korea had already filed its report:

> Commission wishes to draw attention of Secretary-General to serious situation developing which is assuming character of full-scale war and may endanger the maintenance of international peace and security.

The Security Council's response was to call for a cease-fire in North Korea and to direct the North Koreans to withdraw north of the 38th Parallel. A resolution to this end was adopted by a vote of 9–0, with Communist Yugoslavia abstaining, and by early evening copies of it were in the hands of the world press. A few hours later President Truman had begun to confer with Secretary Acheson and his top defense aides at a dramatic meeting in Blair House (the White House was then under repair).

Truman had flown back to the capital after Acheson's second telephone call that morning had confirmed the gravity of the Korean crisis. He departed so quickly that two of his aides were left stranded in Missouri. En route, the President reflected on the shame of the democracies in the decades leading to World War II: how Japan had attacked Manchuria, Hitler had seized Austria and Czechoslovakia, Mussolini had marched on Ethiopia —each confident that no hand would be raised against him.[2] It was plain to Truman that Communist success in Korea would only encourage further aggression elsewhere, until no small nation would have the will to resist stronger Communist neighbors. He made up his mind to help Korea, and sent a message to Acheson to assemble the defense chiefs. The subsequent Blair House conference produced this message to General MacArthur:

> Assist in evacuating United States dependents and noncombatants. MacArthur authorized to take action by Air and Navy to prevent the Inchon-Kimpo-Seoul area from falling into unfriendly hands.

Next, the President secretly issued instructions to alert the U. S. Seventh Fleet to move north from the Philippines to the strait between Chiang Kai-shek's island of Formosa and Mao's Communist China, hoping thereby to forestall attack in either direction and prevent the war from spreading.

America was rushing to the side of embattled South Korea, but in that Inchon-Kimpo-Seoul area which MacArthur was supposed to guarantee, the move was already too late.

The night that General Chae Byong Duk's counterattack collapsed, the city of Seoul was transformed from a calm populace of about a million people into a city quivering with terror. Throughout the night, the muffled thunder of the guns was audible. On the morning of June 27—the third day of invasion— crowds of refugees clogged the streets running south to the broad Han River, just below the city. During the day North Korean airplanes showered Seoul with surrender leaflets, and appeals for surrender were broadcast by the North Korean radio. Confusion, the harbinger of panic, came upon the city—while ROK soldiers to the north of it broke in terror before the real or imagined approach of the dreaded T-34 tanks. Roadblocks were abandoned, bridges primed for demolition were not blown, natural defensive features were left uncovered. At one point along the Uijongbu-Seoul road, a gallant force under a South Korean colonel of engineers struck at the North Korean armor with pole charges and explosives, destroying four tanks. Otherwise, the Communist drive swept ever closer to the city, frightening General Chae so that he fled south of the Han, where Colonel William Wright of the American Advisory Group pursued him and persuaded him to return.

By midnight Ambassador Muccio had departed Seoul for Suwon about 15 miles south, the South Korean government was moving all the way down to Taegu, some members of the National Assembly who had voted to stay were quietly leaving, General Chae had been forced bodily into his jeep by his staff and taken across the Han again, the city's approaches to the Han River bridges were stuffed with leaderless soldiers and miserable civilians clutching a few belongings in parcels or piled in carts —and North Korean foot soldiers and armored vehicles were poking cautiously into Seoul's northern outskirts.

It was then that horrified officers of the American Advisory Group learned that the South Koreans planned to blow the Han River bridges.

There were four bridges over the Han: three for rail traffic, a fourth a three-lane highway crossing. General Chae and Colonel Wright had agreed that they would not be blown until enemy tanks appeared on the street where ROK Army headquarters was located. This was not likely to happen until the next day, June 28, for the fighting on Seoul's northern edge was only sporadic. More, thousands of ROK soldiers, together with most of their transport and heavy equipment, still needed to get across the Han. The bridges themselves were black with humanity. The highway bridge alone held as many as 4,000 people, plodding along on foot or in vehicles that crawled south at a bumper-to-bumper rate. But sometime after midnight, Chae's deputy, General Kim Paik Il, informed Major George Sedberry that he was going to blow the bridges at half-past one in the morning.

Sedberry telephoned Lieutenant Colonel Walter Greenwood, Wright's deputy, getting him out of bed. Greenwood rushed to ROK Army headquarters and began pleading with General Kim to cancel his plans. But the South Korean replied that the Vice Minister of Defense had ordered him to destroy the bridges. At that moment General Lee of the routed ROK 2nd Division came into headquarters. He, too, was horrified. All of his soldiers were north of the river. He, too, pleaded with Kim. Finally, Kim ordered Major General Chang Chang Kuk to drive to the river and stop the engineers, already in position to the south of it, from blowing the bridges. Chang raced for a jeep, jumped in—and plunged into the pitiful, stalled mass of fugitives choking the eight-lane approach to the highway bridge. Agonizing minutes of frustration turned into quarter hours, then half hours, while Chang's jeep inched its way through the throng toward the telephone in a police box on the north side of the river.

At a quarter past two in the morning, Chang had come to within 150 yards of the police box when the night sky flickered orange and there came a terrible rocking roar followed by the sound of rending steel and the giant rustling of collapsing cement. The bridges had been blown. On the south side of the highway bridge alone, where two spans were dropped into the river, between 500 and 800 persons were killed or drowned in the Han. Uncounted other hundreds fell from the rail bridges. And nothing less than military calamity had befallen the Republic of Korea.

Most of the ROK Army was still north of the river when the bridges went down. Some of its soldiers, ironically enough, had rallied to offer the war's most stubborn resistance against the North Koreans driving down on Seoul. But now they had to abandon almost all of their trucks and other vehicles and many of their heavy weapons. They had to get south of the Han by drifting eastward through the mountains, working their way downcoast or crossing the river itself in small boats or rafts. Inevitably, they became disorganized. By the end of June the ROK Army of 98,000 men was down to 22,000. This figure would eventually rise to 54,000 as stragglers began to report in, but 44,000 men had been lost, as well as 30 percent of the army's small arms. Only the 6th and 8th Divisions escaped the debacle with their arms and order intact.

The government of Syngman Rhee was by then operating again from its provisional capital at Taegu, but it had virtually lost its army. Red tanks had routed it and the brutally stupid blowing of the bridges had disorganized it. Up in Seoul, the conquest of the city was completed by the afternoon of June 28. It was then that the Communist fifth column came out of hiding to help the invaders round up trapped South Korean soldiers, police and government officials. Most of the soldiers were spared, either to be impressed as Red troops or sent north as prisoners. Most of the officials were marched off to face the muzzles of the firing squads.

And it was then that the ten little round mouths of Communist freedom began to speak in Seoul.

Chapter Five

DURING the four days of battle in which Seoul fell and the ROK Army was shattered, decisions were reached in New York and Washington which were to change the course of world history.

It was as though each fresh report of Red success and ROK disaster induced a further stiffening of the free world's spine. The first day of attack had produced President Truman's decision to act through the United Nations, as well as his orders to General MacArthur to protect American civilians and send ammunition to South Korea. MacArthur's instructions to guarantee the Inchon-Kimpo-Seoul area were in line with the evacuation of the American women and children, which was carried out without difficulty by the U. S. Navy and Air Force and merchant ships. But there was as yet no disposition to put American forces into the field in actual combat. It was still hoped that the American Advisory Group's optimistic estimate of the ROK fighting capacity would turn out to be true.

On the second day of fighting in Korea, however, when the ROK counterattack collapsed and Uijongbu fell, MacArthur's headquarters in Tokyo sent Washington this ominous message:

> South Korean units unable to resist determined Northern offensive. Contributory factor exclusive enemy possession of tanks and fighter planes. South Korean casualties as an index to fighting have not shown adequate resistance capabilities or the will to fight and our estimate is that a complete collapse is imminent.

President Truman was shocked. As he has since written:

> There was now no doubt! The Republic of Korea needed help at once if it was not to be overrun. More seriously, a Communist success in Korea would put Red troops and planes within easy striking distance of Japan, and Okinawa and Formosa would be open to attack from two sides.[1]

At the end of another dramatic Blair House meeting, President Truman put America into the war on South Korea's side. MacArthur was directed to make immediate use of U. S. air and naval forces against all North Koreans south of the Parallel, and to send the Seventh Fleet, already alerted, into the Formosa Strait to keep Mao and Chiang from extending the area of the war. Truman also approved recommendations for the strengthening of forces in the Philippines and for increased aid to the French then fighting the Communists in Indo-China. These latter decisions, made on the third day of Communist invasion, were announced to the American public on June 27.

Significantly, Truman's orders still did not commit U. S. ground forces, in the hope that air and sea power would save the day, although this optimism was not shared by the Army or MacArthur. And there was another factor: could Korea be a diversion for the true attack against Western Europe? At the very outset of the invasion, Secretary Acheson had dispatched a warning to diplomatic and military leaders in Washington:

> Possible that Korea is only first of series of coordinated actions on part of Soviets. Maintain utmost vigilance and report immediately any positive or negative information. . . .

Truman, determined to repel aggression in Korea, thus had to remain wary—and he could not be blamed for hoping that South Korea's ground forces would be able to hold with U. S. air and sea power at their side. American Presidents do not lightly send American soldiers into battle.

On the fourth day of invasion, Seoul fell. But details of the extent of the catastrophe were not yet available in Washington. In New York that day, the Security Council had put the United Nations into the war against the Communists. In a resolution momentous in the history of the world, the Council declared:

> Having noted from the report of the United Nations Commission for Korea that the authorities in North Korea have neither ceased hostilities nor withdrawn their armed forces to the 38th Parallel and that urgent military measures are required to restore international peace and security, and
>
> Having noted the appeal from the Republic of Korea to the United Nations for immediate and effective steps to secure peace and security,
>
> [The Security Council] recommends that the Members of the United Nations furnish such assistance to the Republic of Korea as may be necessary to repel the armed attack and to restore international peace and security in the area.

For the first time a world organization of states had taken up arms to oppose aggression and keep the peace.

Only Communist Yugoslavia voted against the resolution. India and Egypt abstained from voting. England, France, Nationalist China, Cuba, Ecuador, Norway and the United States voted for it. Soviet Russia was again absent, as she was on July 7 when the Council, by the same alignment of voting and abstaining nations, authorized a unified United Nations command for Korea and asked the United States to appoint a commander for it. Soviet Russia did not return to the Security Council until August, the month during which the rotated presidency fell to her. The Soviets then solemnly pronounced all that had been voted in her absence as "illegal."

But the Communist custom of attempting to outlaw the opposition could not rectify the grave error of Russia's boycott. The United Nations was now at war against the Communist world, committed to protecting the South Korean state which the UN had brought into being, and already asking member nations to contribute arms, money or medical aid to the task. Russia, naturally, ignored this request, as did all Communist nations. But on the fourth day of battle, Admiral C. Turner Joy, Commander of U. S. Naval Forces, Far East, received a message from Admiral Sir Patrick Brind, commander in chief of the British Far Eastern Station at Hong Kong:

> I shall be very glad to know of any operations in which my ships could help. Present dispositions are Task Group 96.8 in South Japan under Rear Admiral Andrewes consisting of *Triumph*, *Belfast, Jamaica,* two destroyers and three frigates. . . .

Australia and New Zealand quickly followed with similar offers. Then Canada. Eventually sixteen nations from East and West rallied beneath the blue-and-white flag of the United Nations. France, her forces already desperately engaged in Indo-China, sent a battalion led by Lieutenant Colonel Ralph Monclar, a veteran of the Foreign Legion who had given up his four-star rank of *Général de Corps d'Armée* to fight in Korea. A brigade came from Turkey, a regiment and ships from Thailand, 5,000 riflemen from the Philippines. Colombia and the Netherlands each dispatched a battalion and a small warship, Belgium and Ethiopia contributed a battalion apiece, a fighter squadron came from South Africa and a company of soldiers from little Luxembourg, while Greece placed an infantry battalion and an air transport squadron in action. And there were hospital units from Sweden, Norway and Italy, a hospital ship from Denmark—even a field ambulance from India.

All these men and arms did not come at once, and it might even be argued that their arrival hindered the United Nations commander in Korea, for there were so many differences in language, food, dress and custom that the already difficult problems of logistics became further complicated. But as much as these men differed, they were bound by the common bond of that historic resolution; and that very variety which would challenge the ingenuity of the American quartermasters would dramatize the great fact that men of differing creeds and races could put aside their differences and fight for freedom together.

The day after the United Nations' adoption of the resolution creating this force, General Douglas MacArthur, the man who would be the first to command it, made a characteristic cannon's-mouth reconnaissance of the Korean battlefront. He flew to Korea and drove north as far as the Han River, beyond which the North Koreans were regrouping for the rush which was intended to overrun the entire peninsula. MacArthur was appalled by what he saw. Flowing all around him, frantically hurrying south, were thousands of Korean refugees and thousands of demoralized South Korean soldiers. MacArthur reported to Washington:

> The South Korean forces are in confusion, have not seriously fought, and lack leadership. Organized and equipped as a light force for maintenance of interior order, they are unprepared for attack by armor and air. Conversely they are incapable of gaining the initiative over such a force as that embodied in the North Korean Army. The South Koreans had made no preparation for defense in depth, for echelons of supply or for a supply system. No plans had been made, or if made were not executed, for the destruction of supplies or materials in the event of a retrograde movement. As a result they have either lost or abandoned their supplies and heavier equipment. . . .
>
> The only assurance for holding the present line and the ability to regain later the lost ground is through the introduction of United States ground combat forces into the Korean battle area. To continue to utilize the forces of our air and navy without an effective ground element cannot be decisive. If authorized it is my intention to immediately move a United States regimental combat team to the reinforcement of the vital area discussed and to provide for a possible build-up to a two-division strength from the troops in Japan for an early counteroffensive.
>
> Unless provision is made for the full utilization of the Army-Navy-Air team in this shattered area, our mission will at best be needlessly costly in life, money and prestige. At worst, it might even be doomed to failure.

There was now no further excuse for withholding American ground forces from Korea. President Truman had already concluded that the Russians were not going to fight there against the United Nations. He had seen a vaguely worded Russian reply to an American query concerning the Soviet's intentions in

Korea, and had quipped, with a prescience of which he was not yet quite aware: "That means the Soviets are going to let the Chinese and the North Koreans do the fighting for them." Moreover, it was now obvious that North Korea planned a swift conquest of the south to be followed by Communist-controlled elections in mid-August. MacArthur's request was imperative, and Truman approved the commitment of a single U. S. regimental combat team, adding later instructions which, in effect, sent every arm of the U. S. military into action and opened up all but a few targets north of the Parallel to attack by American ships and planes.

The historic decision sending American soldiers into battle came at almost the very hour that the North Koreans began their race for Pusan.

The Communist strategy required a quick end to the war to establish the fact of a Communist Korea before the United States and the United Nations could arrive on the peninsula in force. From a military point of view, a landing on hostile shores would be infinitely more difficult for the United States than arrival at ports held open by a still-active ROK Army. Politically, to attack the *fait accompli* of a Communist-unified Korea would be damaging to American prestige: members of the United Nations might not feel enthusiastic about armed attempts to revive a fallen Republic of Korea. The political consideration was paramount; for if ever war was fought on a battlefield with an eye on the conference table, it was this strange, shifting, heartless conflict which moved into its second stage amid the hot moist misery of the summer monsoon.

The Communist plan was simply to seize all the roads south, striking at so many different places that the outnumbered enemy would be unable to meet every thrust. Taegu, where Syngman Rhee had set up his provisional government, was to be seized, along with the little port of Pohang on the east coast—and these blows would deprive the United Nations of air bases in Korea. Roads from Pohang and Taegu ran straight into Pusan, and if one of the lightning thrusts had not yet reached the port, then drives from Taegu or Pohang or both would be mounted to hurl the enemy into the sea.

And so, on the morning of June 30, with the alternating rain and heat of the monsoon at its peak, the Han crossings began. One North Korean drive came down the main Seoul-Taegu-Pusan road on the west, another followed the west-central road to Chongju, a third force came down the corridor of the central mountains to cut the Taegu-Pohang lateral road, and a fourth advanced along an east coast road toward Pohang itself.

It was the westernmost of these that General MacArthur feared most when he made his battlefield reconnaissance, and it was here that the North Koreans had committed their two best divisions, the 3rd and 4th. Here, too, the road seemed to lie undefended, and because of this the Communists were so anxious to cross the Han that they left their tanks behind until a railroad bridge could be repaired and decked for mechanized traffic.

Massed artillery and tank fire on the north bank prepared the way, and then the men of the 3rd Division entered the water, wading or swimming or paddling across in wooden boats strong enough to carry a 2½-ton truck or 30 soldiers. They drove back the ROKs defending the opposite bank and prepared to assault the big industrial suburb of Yongdungpo. The ROKs resisted stubbornly and even attempted to regain the lost positions, after General Chae had ordered a counterattack at the suggestion of Brigadier General John Church, head of MacArthur's advance party in Korea. But the Communist artillery stopped the ROKs. The next day the North Korean 4th Division crossed the Han unmolested at the bridgehead seized by the 3rd. Still the ROK resistance outside Yongdungpo continued. Communist casualties were heavy. Finally on July 3 the T-34s began clattering over a repaired railroad bridge and the end came quickly.

The 3rd and 4th Divisions were in Yongdungpo by nightfall, and the following day they went racing down the peninsula's west coast, capturing abandoned Suwon Airfield and striking ever farther south.

Coming up to meet them was what General MacArthur described as his "arrogant display of strength": 406 American officers and men under the command of a lieutenant colonel, who, ironically, had been at Pearl Harbor the morning of December 7, 1941.

Chapter Six

THE first American force to enter battle in Korea may have been "arrogant" but it certainly lacked strength. As such it exactly reflected the power and spirit of the nation which sent it off to war.

In May of 1945 the U. S. Army had reached its peak of 8,290,000 men (including, of course, the Army Air Corps). Five years later, by the summer of 1950, it had dwindled to 592,000 men or about 7 percent of its former strength. Even at the time of Pearl Harbor, usually regarded as the classic example of American unpreparedness, the Army had 1,600,000 men under arms. Worse, this 1950 Army of 592,000 men was top-heavy with technicians and service people, for the Maginot Line mentality had produced the myth of the push-button war and so downgraded the foot soldier.

In all this army there were only ten combat divisions, plus the equivalent of one more in the European Constabulary, and perhaps the equivalent of another three in nine independent regimental combat teams—an optimistic total, in all, of fourteen divisions of which only the Constabulary was up to strength. The other divisions had infantry regiments functioning with two rather than three battalions and artillery battalions firing but two of three batteries. Other combat arms were similarly depleted.

Of these forces, four divisions were in Japan under General MacArthur. They were the 7th, 24th and 25th Infantry and the 1st Cavalry (dismounted). They were at about 70 percent of wartime strength, varying from a low of 12,200 in the 24th to a high of 15,000 in the 25th, and they were also deficient in such modern arms as 57mm and 75mm recoilless rifles, 4.2-inch mortars and 3.5-inch rocket launchers. The divisional tanks were M-24 lights, no match at all for the Russian T-34 mediums. Together with 5,300 men in antiaircraft artillery, and 25,000 more in other units, these divisions gave MacArthur a total Japanese occupation and defense force of 83,000 men. There were also 6,000 men available in the Fifth Regimental Combat Team in Hawaii and the 29th Infantry Regiment on Okinawa.

American naval strength in the Far East at the time was approximately one-fifth of the total, although roughly a third of the total force was operating in the Pacific. Vice-Admiral Joy's Far East Command consisted of the cruiser *Juneau,* the destroyers *Mansfield, De Haven, Collett* and *Swenson,* three minesweepers and five amphibious vessels. The Seventh Fleet which was to keep Chiang and Mao apart consisted of the carrier *Valley Forge,* the cruiser *Rochester,* eight destroyers, an oiler and three submarines—fourteen ships dignified by fleet status. And only five years before, just one of several American fleets numbered 1,300 ships when it brought a half-million Americans to that very Okinawa where part of this 1950 "fleet" was anchored.

Fortunately the Air Force had withstood economic and pacifist erosion somewhat better, if, in fact, her propaganda war on the Army and Navy had not helped to shrink her sister services. At the end of May in 1950 the Far East Air Force under Lieutenant General George Stratemeyer had available 1,172 aircraft of all types and a force of 33,625 men.

The Marine Corps had shrunk from a wartime peak of 485,-000 men to a little less than 75,000 officers and men on active duty. Two of its six divisions—the First and Second—remained, but these combined would not measure up to one of the big wartime amphibious divisions, while the two Marine air wings had also been vastly reduced. No Marines, except those aboard the Navy's fighting ships, were available to MacArthur. The closest ground force was the First Marine Division in California.

This was the nation's strength in that summer of 1950, and yet no one, from MacArthur down to the fuzziest-chinned teenager beginning his adult life in the heady role of garrison duty in a conquered country, had the slightest doubt that the crisis would be over in a few days, now that the Americans were entering the conflict. MacArthur himself, in the message requesting permission to use ground troops, had spoken of an "early

60

counteroffensive" using just two of his understrength divisions. An Air Force officer, hearing MacArthur's plan, had snorted his derision of the need of as much as a single soldier. "The old man must be off his rocker," he said. "When the Fifth Air Force gets to work there won't be a North Korean left in Korea." And then there was a major of the 24th Division who remarked: "I figure that once the Reds hear Americans are up against them they'll stop and think this thing over a while."

Only one man in authority seemed not to share this ballooning spirit of optimism, and he was the man whose melancholy duty it had been to send those two bare companies of Americans up against a pair of North Korean divisions.

Major General William Dean once described himself as "an in-between, curious sort [of general] who never went to West Point, did not see action in World War I and did not come up from the enlisted ranks." He had commanded the 44th Infantry Division in Europe during World War II, and had come to South Korea in October, 1947, as military governor and deputy to General Hodge. In 1949 he was in Japan as chief of staff of Lieutenant General Walton ("Johnny") Walker's Eighth Army, and in June of 1950 he was in command of the 24th Infantry Division at Kokura, directly across the Tsushima Strait from Korea.

The night of the 24th of that month, as the North Koreans massed above the 38th Parallel, Major General Dean was at a masquerade ball for the 24th's officers, his strong six-foot, 200-pound frame swathed in the long robes of a Korean *yang-ban,* or gentleman, and the black stovepipe hat of that leisurely class perched awkwardly atop his close-cropped sandy hair. The next day General Dean heard of the invasion and concluded that World War III was beginning. Five days later he was under orders to go to Korea to direct a delaying action while other American forces were prepared for battle. He was to do what all commanders loathe doing, to commit his forces piecemeal in an effort to stave off the Communist rush. Which meant, in human terms, that his men must buy time with blood.

To accomplish this mission General Dean called upon Lieutenant Colonel Charles ("Brad") Smith of the 1st Battalion, 21st Infantry.

The day the Japanese bombed Pearl Harbor, Brad Smith was a captain of infantry assigned to Schofield Barracks on Oahu, and he had been called from his bed to lead a company of riflemen to set up a defensive position on Barber's Point. The night of June 30, 1950, Lieutenant Colonel Smith was again in his bed when the telephone rang and Colonel Richard Stephens, commander of the 21st Infantry, told him quickly: "The lid has blown off—get on your clothes and report to the CP."

Smith obeyed, and found that he was to gather half his men immediately and take them, together with a handful of officers loaned from another battalion, to Korea. He was to meet General Dean at Itazuke Airfield and there receive further instructions. At three o'clock in the morning of July 1st what was to be known as Task Force Smith was on its way, riding by truck through a heavy rain to Itazuke 75 miles away. At the airbase General Dean told him:

"When you get to Pusan, head for Taejon. We want to stop the North Koreans as far from Pusan as we can. Block the main road as far north as possible. Contact General Church. If you can't locate him, go to Taejon and beyond if you can. Sorry I can't give you more information. That's all I've got. Good luck to you, and God bless you and your men."[1]

The general's blessing had an ominous sound. To men within hearing distance it seemed like a benediction for the doomed, and they shifted uneasily at the words. Some of them were already grumbling that occupation duty had never been like this before. Others cursed whatever it was that had caused them to be yanked out of warm beds and sent careening through a rainy night with rifles, bazookas and mortars in their hands and two days' issue of C-rations in their packs. They were gloomy, apprehensive, as they formed files to board the six C-54 transports waiting in the rain.

At a quarter of nine that morning the first of these squat gray transports had risen through the rain enshrouding Itazuke Air Base and pointed its nose north toward Pusan.

It was the great good fortune of the United Nations that Pusan, the finest port in South Korea, was also the city farthest removed from the onrushing North Korean armies. Pusan was at the southeastern tip of the peninsula. It had dock facilities capable of handling 45,000 tons daily, although it also had a shortage of skilled dock labor and would therefore never be pressed to capacity. It could receive 24 deepwater ships at its four piers and intervening quays, as well as 14 LSTs on its broad beaches, and it was only 110 miles from the nearest Japanese port at Fukuoka. Pusan was also the southern terminal of a good north-south railroad system which the Japanese had built. Smaller railroads ran westward from Pusan through Masan and Chinju, or northeast to Pohang on the east coast. These railroads came to be the basis of the United Nations' transportation system, for the peninsula's roads were generally inadequate. Nowhere in Korea was there a road meeting the U. S. Army Engineers' "good" standard of 22 feet in width and two lanes. Korea's finest roads averaged only 18 feet in width, and because they had been built for the passage of oxcarts they were unpaved. Even so, many of these roads radiated out of Pusan, and these, complementing the rail system, helped to make the port the nerve center for the United Nations command. Pusan Airport on the outskirts of the city was another asset, and it was to this field that the American air transports brought the men of Task Force Smith.

The last of them had touched down by early afternoon of July 1, to the friendly cheers of hundreds of South Koreans who had gathered to greet them. Then the American soldiers were driven 17 miles by truck to the Pusan railroad station. They passed along flag-bedecked streets lined with thousands of happy, cheering Koreans who shook little flags and banners at them. At the station, Korean bands serenaded them as they climbed aboard a train waiting to take them north to Taejon. Already, some of these young soldiers—who had flown off to battle carrying loaded barracks bags!—were beginning to believe the junior officers who assured them that this was not war but "a police action" and that they would soon be snugly back in Sasebo, Japan.

The next morning Task Force Smith rattled into Taejon and its commander hurried off to confer with General Church.

"We have a little action up here," Church told Smith, pointing to a map. "All we need is some men up there who won't run when they see tanks. We're going to move you up to support the ROKs and give them moral support."[2]

Smith asked permission to go forward to inspect the ground himself. When it was granted, Smith sent his troops off to a bivouac and began driving over miserable roads toward the town of Osan, 90 miles to the north and only 20 miles below Yongdungpo, which one day later would fall to the North Koreans.

On the east coast of Korea, meanwhile, ROK troops were still falling back, while out on the Sea of Japan, the first United Nations action against Communist forces had ended in a victory.

Four sleek, blue-painted aluminum torpedo boats had put out of Wonsan in North Korea on the night of June 27. The Russian-built craft were under orders to pick up a convoy of ten small freighters bringing food and ammunition to Red forces at the east coast port of Chumunjim just below the Parallel. The morning of July 2 the convoy was approaching Chumunjim, when it was sighted by the U. S. and British cruisers *Juneau* and *Jamaica* and the British frigate *Blue Swan*.

The little Communist torpedo boats boldly hurled themselves at the United Nations vessels, trying to get in close enough to launch their torpedoes. But their four heavy machine guns were no match for fifty UN guns ranging from four- to eight-inch.

At the first UN salvo one of the torpedo boats blew up and a second was stopped dead. Almost immediately it was ablaze and sinking. The others heeled and fled, one to beach itself where it was later destroyed at leisure, the other to head for the open sea, zigzagging wildly and eluding the shells of the pursuing *Black Swan*.

Then *Juneau* steamed over to Chumunjim where the ten little freighters had scurried to safety and sank seven of them with her big guns. The other three had taken cover behind a big breakwater and could not be reached.

By the standards of any war other than the peculiar one in Korea, this was not much of a battle. And yet it was the biggest surface naval engagement of the war, ending the brief existence of the North Korean "Navy." From then on both the Sea of Japan in the east and the Yellow Sea in the west were United

Nations lakes, especially after fears of enemy submarines proved groundless. The U. S. Navy and its United Nations allies had only to contend with a highly effective North Korean mine warfare and a relatively ineffective fire from enemy coastal batteries as it carried out its mission of supplying the battle-front, of conducting amphibious assaults, of delivering supporting naval gunfire, of executing its first blockade against a foreign power, and of launching aircraft from the decks of its carriers.

The first car.ier-based operation in Korea occurred the day after the victory at Chumunjim. Standing in the Yellow Sea about 135 miles southwest of Pyongyang, the British carrier *Triumph* and the American *Valley Forge* flew off fighters and dive bombers in a strike against military targets around the North Korean capital.

Below the 38th Parallel that same day, July 3, the Far Eastern Air Force was striking at North Korean columns from skies which had been American since the first of the Japanese-based Mustangs and Shooting Stars entered battle on June 27 to shoot down six Yaks. Unfortunately, the difficulty of distinguishing between friendly and enemy targets still plagued American fliers, as well as their rapidly arriving allies, for also on July 3, a flight of Australian Mustangs shot up the town of Pyongtaek, to which Task Force Smith had come on its trip north, blowing up an ammunition train and with it the railroad station. Many residents of the town were killed in this fatal case of mistaken identity, and the bewilderment of the men of Task Force Smith who witnessed it was increased.

The only good news, in fact, for Smith's troops was that a brother regiment from the 24th Division—the 34th Infantry—had come to Pusan by sea, and that Major General Dean had arrived at Taejon after a wild, mountain-dodging flight through a night fog.

General Dean quickly realized the importance of Pyongtaek. It was a bottleneck which forced the North Koreans above it to keep to the Seoul-Taegu-Pusan road. Below Pyongtaek, the Korean peninsula flared out 45 miles to the west, and here the enemy would be free to maneuver against the United Nations' left flank. Pyongtaek, sitting astride the main road, was also highly defensible. Its left flank lay on an estuary of the Yellow Sea where UN ships were constantly on patrol and was thus secure against attack. On the right a few miles to the east lay the town of Ansong, the right flank of which nestled under a rugged mountain range. And so, General Dean decided to hold at Pyongtaek-Ansong. To this end he ordered the newly arrived 1st and 3rd Battalions of the 34th Infantry to move north into positions there. The 1st Battalion dug in on the south bank of a river just above Pyongtaek, while the 3rd Battalion went east to fortify Ansong.

This movement relieved Colonel Smith's force, now grown from 406 to 540 Americans with the arrival of 134 artillerymen and five 105mm howitzers. Task Force Smith was sent farther north to a point above Osan under orders to intercept the advancing enemy at the position Colonel Smith had scouted a few days before. So his men again boarded trucks and rolled northward through the rain. Above Osan, Colonel Smith began fortifying two hills which bracketed the main road as it came down from Suwon. The only 105mm howitzer serviced with antitank shells—of which there were exactly six—was put into position directly behind the hill to the left or west of the road. This gun was to fire antitank along the road should any T-34s try to run the gantlet between the hills. The other four guns, all firing ordinary high-explosive shells, were placed farther behind this antitank position. They were to support Smith's men occupying the hills to left and right of the road.

Only a platoon of soldiers occupied the left or western height. Most of the men were on the right or eastern hill, with Colonel Smith himself. Smith's intentions, of course, were to halt and delay the enemy—not to defeat him. As long as Smith could delay, the Pyongtaek-Ansong fortifications could be strengthened and new troops and weapons brought into line.

Meanwhile, about 60 miles south in Taejon, General Dean had gone to ROK Army headquarters in the hope of persuading the ROK generals to clear the roads south of Pyongtaek, still streaming with southbound refugees and straggling soldiers. But the ROK generals were busy with internal squabbles, sometimes screaming "Communist!" at each other, offering Dean only excuses for their failure to halt the retreat that had become a rout since the fall of Suwon, frequently asking him to solve their own problems. One of the latter concerned a suggestion by General Lee Bum Suk, the man who had replaced General Chae as chief of staff only to be fired himself a few days later. Lee's idea was to allow the enemy tanks to penetrate the line of defense, then dig ditches behind them to cut them off from their gas supply. Dean thought it not a bad idea, but unfortunately by July 4 the enemy tanks had already blasted into Suwon of their own accord. Massing behind them were foot soldiers of the 4th Division, riflemen who would discourage all ditchdiggers.

Facing this force and its dash to overrun Pyongtaek-Ansong and turn the United Nations left was that 1st Battalion, 21st Infantry, which was still known as Task Force Smith.

It was still raining when July 5th dawned at Osan. American soldiers on the hills crouched glumly in their ponchos while spooning the wet slop of their C-rations from can to mouth. They no longer believed the myth of the "police action," popular though the phrase might become among Administration spokesmen at home. Nor could the Administration euphemism "Korean conflict" convince them that, in President Truman's phrase, "We are not at war." They believed only in their own misery: in the sodden ground beneath their feet and the rainwater filling the foxholes, in the incredibly constant reek of human dung wafted up from the surrounding pale green of the rice paddies, and in the sudden dry clutch of fear in the throat at the sight of eight squat shapes coming out of the rain mists below Suwon and rolling down toward their hills.

At approximately eight o'clock in the morning, Task Force Smith's forward observer called for artillery fire on the North Korean tanks. At sixteen minutes after eight, with the tanks a little more than a mile away from the hills, the first American Army shell of the Korean War howled toward the enemy. Quickly, the artillery observer marked its flash and adjusted range. More shells crashed out. They were landing among the tanks. The observer spoke into his telephone:

"Fire for effect!"

The barrage rose in fury, but the tanks waddled through it as though oblivious to the monstrous fireflies sparking and flashing off their thick hides. The American howitzers were useless as long as they fired nothing but ordinary high-explosive shells.

On either side of the pass, now, Colonel Smith's infantrymen could see a total of 33 squat shapes emerging from the mists. The first eight T-34s had been only the spearhead for the main body which followed in groups of four. Still, the infantrymen on the hills held their fire, for Colonel Smith had instructed the crews of his 75mm recoilless rifles not to shoot until the T-34s were within 700 yards range. Then the lead tanks entered that zone and the 75mm rifles fired.

Direct hits—but still the T-34s rolled down toward the pass.

At last they came abreast of the American infantrymen, and Lieutenant Ollie Connor in a ditch on the right or east side of the road opened up with 2.36-inch bazookas. Connor fired from 15-yard range at the supposedly weak rear of the T-34s. He fired 22 rockets.

The tanks rolled on. Two of them poked through the pass between the hills, and the 105mm howitzer stationed there lashed out with its antitank shells. The tanks lurched and came to a halt. They pulled off the road. One of them caught fire, and two soldiers popped from its turret with hands held high. A third followed and aimed a burp-gun burst at an American machine-gun nest, killing the gunner—the first American to die in the Korean War, though no one ever got his name. Other Americans killed the enemy soldier, but then more tanks shot the pass.

Time after time the American howitzers scored direct hits on the T-34s, but without armor-piercing shells they could only jar them. Each of the guns, firing point-blank from concealed positions 150 to 300 yards west of the road, hurled from four to six rounds at the invaders. But the first wave of T-34s, moving at full throttle with hatches buttoned down, firing so blindly that some of them even pointed their 85s at the east or wrong side of the road, swept past almost without harm.

One of them trapped two bazooka teams led by Colonel Perry and Sergeant Edwin Eversole in the stinking muck of a rice paddy between the howitzers and the road. Eversole's bazooka backlash streamed flame, but his shell bounced off the T-34, now looming above him "as big as a battleship." The sergeant flung himself into a drainage ditch as the tank's gun flashed, and a telephone pole crashed harmlessly across the ditch. Then one of the 105s put a shell into the attacking tank's tread. It stopped, and Eversole lay there while the remaining tanks of the first wave roared down the road. Colonel Perry took an interpreter up to the damaged tank and tried to get its crew to surrender. Failing to get a response, Perry ordered the 105 howitzers to begin battering the tank. Two men jumped out, and the artillerymen killed them.

But then the second wave of tanks arrived, and some of Perry's artillerymen began running away. Officers and noncoms had to load and fire the guns. Gradually, Perry managed to restore order, and soon the howitzers were hammering again at the second wave. Once they hit a T-34 in its treads and halted it for eventual destruction. They damaged a few others, though they did not stop them, and they killed many of the North Korean riflemen who rode the tanks or else blew them into the ditches where they were picked off.

But Task Force Smith had been unable to prevent the enemy armor from moving south to Osan. American firepower was not up to the assignment. More armor-piercing shells might have stopped the tanks, and well-planted antitank mines would certainly have blown up one or two of those recklessly onrushing vehicles and effectively blocked the road. But neither were available, and out of 33 tanks, 26 had run the gantlet in fighting shape and 3 others with slight damage.

By a quarter after ten they had begun to enter Osan unopposed, and worse, they had cut off the rear of Task Force Smith even then under frontal assault from more tanks and two regiments of North Korean infantry.

An hour after the last of the T-34s whined through the pass beneath him, Colonel Smith, on the right-hand hill, saw a long enemy column coming out of Suwon. Three more tanks were in the lead, then trucks loaded with soldiers, then columns of marching men stretching backward several miles. Smith did not know it, but he was looking at the North Korean 4th Division's 16th and 18th Regiments.

The American commander waited. In an hour, when the head of the column was about 1,000 yards away, Smith let go with everything he had. Mortars whuffled overhead, rifles cracked, .50-caliber machine guns chattered—and suddenly there were enemy trucks bursting into flame and tiny figures spinning through the air or jumping into roadside ditches.

The enemy reacted with speed and precision to what might have been a demoralizing blow. The three tanks left the column, rumbled to within 300 yards of the Americans and began to rake the ridgeline with cannon and machine-gun fire. Behind the burning trucks some 1,000 soldiers began to deploy to either side of the road. Still farther behind them out of range of the American mortars and artillery—then firing as well as it could without direction from a forward observer—other truckloads of soldiers pulled over to the sides of the road and waited.

The first infantry thrust against Task Force Smith came from riflemen who occupied a finger ridge running into the main position on the right of the road. From this base two columns moved out from either side in an attempt to encircle the Americans. The attempt was broken up by Task Force Smith's small arms, artillery and mortars. The North Koreans then circled wide to the right or east in an effort to get behind the Americans. On the other side of the road, meanwhile, they seized a western hill overlooking the American positions and sent machine-gun fire plunging into them. Smith called these men to his side of the road.

By one in the afternoon, Task Force Smith had been defeated. Colonel Smith had no support from his artillery, had in fact lost contact with it and presumed it destroyed. A numerous enemy harassed both his flanks. A much larger force sat calmly to his front. An armored column held his rear. He had no hope of help from the air, for the weather would not allow it. He had communication with no one.

At half-past two Smith gave the order to withdraw and Task Force Smith began to fall apart as a military unit.

Colonel Smith had hoped to pull out in the classic leapfrog manner, with the forward unit falling back under the covering fire of the unit behind it, then the rear unit doing likewise, and so on, repeated until the men were safely out of the hills on the road above Osan. But the movement never got started. Accurate enemy machine-gun fire began raking Smith's men, forcing them to retire in a disorderly flight during which most of Task Force Smith's casualties were inflicted.

Smith's soldiers abandoned machine guns, mortars, recoilless rifles. Some threw their rifles away. Others tore off their helmets. Dead were left behind, and worse, 25 to 30 wounded—although an unknown medical sergeant volunteered to stay with them.

Colonel Smith himself, meanwhile, hurried west in search of the artillery. He came upon a wire team trying to string wire up to him, and was directed to the guns. To his astonishment he found them still standing and only Colonel Perry and another man wounded. But there was nothing to do but direct them to join the withdrawal, and the howitzers were also abandoned, after breechblocks and sights had been removed and carried to trucks.

With Smith and Perry aboard, the trucks drove toward Osan, hoping to find a road east to Ansong at the southern end of the town. They assumed that the enemy armor had struck farther south toward Pyongtaek, but in southern Osan, they blundered into a trio of Communist tanks, and the little column wheeled around and sped back north. There they found a dirt road running east and came upon small parties of Smith's shattered force struggling over hills or wading through rice paddies—bareheaded, some of them barefooted with shoes tied together with laces and hung around their necks, a few of them coatless. About one hundred men clambered aboard the trucks, and the column moved on through the enveloping night to arrive in Ansong and continue south to Chonan.

Behind them were the stragglers. For the next two days American soldiers drifted into cities as far south as Taejon. Some trudged west to the Yellow Sea and one went aboard a sampan and sailed down to Pusan. Others walked as far east as the Sea of Japan. Approximately 150 men were killed, wounded or reported missing (probably captured) from Task Force Smith on that first day of American action in Korea. That night a North Korean private wrote in his diary: "We met vehicles and American POWs. We also saw some American dead. We found four of our destroyed tanks. Near Osan there was a great battle."

Chapter Seven

AT OSAN the North Koreans and the Americans met for the first time and the result was a decisive victory for the North Koreans. It might be said that as great battles are measured this was but a skirmish with armor and artillery involved. But great battles are the sum of many little ones, and Osan, because it was the first of a string to be fought along the road south, was vastly important.

It had an exhilarating effect on North Korean morale and caused American spirits to sink. "Everyone thought the enemy would turn around and go back when they found out who they were fighting," an artilleryman of Task Force Smith said later. But after Osan it was the Americans who began to turn and go back, sometimes without waiting to see who it was they were fighting.

The first such voluntary withdrawal occurred the following morning at the Pyongtaek-Ansong line. The 3rd Battalion, 34th Infantry, pulled out of its positions at Ansong on the right flank and moved south toward Chonan. On the left, at the river above Pyongtaek, the 1st Battalion of the same regiment also withdrew after briefly engaging North Korean tanks and infantry in an action which was characterized on the American side by the inability or reluctance of many riflemen to shoot at the approaching enemy. Fire from the American 4.2-inch mortars which began well by knocking out a truck ended poorly when the mortar observer was stunned and no one took his place. American communications varied from poor to nonexistent, either because the distances between command points were too long for radio contact or because southward-flowing South Korean soldiers and civilians cut the telephone wire into strips from which they fashioned pack harnesses.

The Pyongtaek-Ansong withdrawal continued south for 15

miles, and General Dean himself has described his rage and astonishment when he heard of it:

> I learned this at four o'clock in the afternoon of July 6, and I jumped in my jeep and rushed up toward Chonan to find out what was wrong, why they had not held on the river. But by the time I got there the whole regiment was south of Chonan, most of the men having ridden back on the trucks. I should have said, "Turn around and get going now," but rather than add to the confusion and risk night ambushes, I told them, "All right, hold tight here until I give you further orders."[1]

The next day General Dean relieved the 34th's commander and turned the regiment over to Colonel Robert Martin, an aggressive officer who had served with Dean in Europe. But Chonan also fell, on July 8, and Martin was killed while attempting to rally his troops. He had seized a 2.6-inch bazooka and was dueling a tank with it when a shell from the tank's 85mm cannon cut him in half.

So now the 24th Division had suffered three sharp reverses in a row, each of them multiplying the problems of General Dean's delaying action. At Osan it was shown that the North Korean armor could not be stopped by inferior American arms; at Pyongtaek—the worst of all because it opened the western bulge of the peninsula to North Korean maneuver—it was made clear that the general's troops were lacking in ardor; at Chonan the North Koreans were given a choice of attack routes by the fact that the road divided below the town. One arm ran east to Chochiwon, the other continued straight south to Kongju. Both had to be defended, and Dean put the 34th Infantry at Kongju and sent the newly arrived 21st Infantry (which reclaimed the remnants of Task Force Smith, its 1st Battalion) under Colonel Stephens to fight a delaying action between Chonan and Chochiwon.

On July 8, while Chonan was falling, Dean also sent General MacArthur an urgent request for quick delivery of antitank shells and urged immediate airlifting of 3.5-inch bazookas from the United States. He also told MacArthur: "I am convinced that the North Korean Army, the North Korean soldier, and his status of training and quality of equipment have been underestimated."

The next day MacArthur himself considered the situation grave enough to begin using part of his B-29 bomber strength against battle areas and to send a message to the Joint Chiefs of Staff:

> The situation in Korea is critical. . . . His [the enemy's] ar-mored equipment is of the best and the service thereof, as re-ported by qualified veteran observers, as good as any seen at any time in the last war. They further state that the enemy's infantry is of thoroughly first class quality.
>
> This force more and more assumes the aspect of a combination of Soviet leadership and technical guidance with Chinese Com-munist ground elements. While it serves under the flag of North Korea, it can no longer be considered as an indigenous N. K. mil-itary effort.
>
> I strongly urge that in addition to those forces already requisi-tioned, an army of at least four divisions, with all its component services, be dispatched to this area without delay and by every means of transportation available.
>
> The situation has developed into a major operation.

General MacArthur's estimate—especially his concluding line —jolted Washington. Although MacArthur had earlier asked for Marines, and had been given the 1st Provisional Marine Brigade even then embarking for Korea, it had been thought that this force was to spearhead an "early counteroffensive" with just two divisions. But now the Far Eastern Commander was talking of a full army composed of "at least" four full-strength divisions. The Pentagon's reply to this message was to order the 2nd In-fantry Division to begin movement to Korea, along with the sup-plies of the shells and armor requested by General Dean. Mac-Arthur, meanwhile, his earlier optimism cooling, decided that he would have to use his entire Eighth Army under Lieutenant General Walton Walker if Pusan was to be saved.

For above Pusan the North Koreans were pressing steadily southward. The ROK Army, holding off all but the western thrust down the Seoul-Taegu-Pusan road, was battling desper-ately with the support of U. S. warships off the east coast road and some American air strikes in the Chongju and central cor-ridor sectors. But the western drive was still the most perilous, and here the 21st Infantry had begun its delaying action above Chochiwon. On July 10, at a place called Chonui, the enemy was strafed and rocketed by low-flying F-51 Mustangs and F-80 Shooting Star jets. But when the planes disappeared, the North Koreans attacked and broke the American lines. The 21st counterattacked savagely and recaptured the lost ground, where the American soldiers found six of their comrades with their hands tied in back and bullet holes in their heads. This was only the first of numerous North Korean atrocities discovered in the early days of the Korean War, although later the Communists would take great care to prevent the harming of prisoners, whom they hoped to "convert" in their prison camps.

At Chonui on July 10 the American tanks also entered the battle, but these were the lights which had never been considered the equal of the T-34s, and they were of little help. That same day the Fifth Air Force scored one of its greatest successes in Korea. A flight of Shooting Stars swept beneath the overcast at Pyongtaek and found a North Korean column of troops, tanks and trucks halted north of a blown bridge. A report to Fifth Air Force headquarters in Japan brought all available light bombers and jet fighters to Pyongtaek, and the column was scourged in a massive air strike. Although reports of 38 tanks destroyed, along with 7 halftracks, 117 trucks and hundreds of troops, were probably exaggerated, the Pyongtaek strike—together with the air attacks launched at Chonui the same day—produced the greatest destruction of enemy armor in the entire war.

Even so, the 21st Infantry could not hold Chonui against the blows of an enemy desperate to reach Chochiwon. The 21st began withdrawing just before midnight of July 10, setting up new positions a few miles north of Chochiwon.

"Hold in your new position and fight like hell," General Dean ordered Colonel Stephens. "I expect you to hold it all day tomorrow."

The 21st fought well, but it could not hold, and on July 12 Colonel Stephens sent Dean this message:

> Am surrounded. 1st Bn left giving way. Situation bad on right. Having nothing left to establish intermediate delaying position am forced to withdraw to [Kum] river line. I have issued instructions to withdraw.

With that the 21st retreated across the Kum River and Chochi-won was lost, thus becoming the fourth straight victory of the onrushing North Korean 3rd and 4th Divisions. Still, Chochi-won differed vastly from Osan, Pyongtaek and Chonan. These three points along the road had been chewed up in four days in roughly 20-mile bites. Chochiwon, the next 20-mile bite, took three days alone. It had produced rising North Korean tank losses under mounting American air pressure, and had shown the North Koreans an American regiment fighting doggedly. It had also given General Dean time to bring up his third and final regiment, the 19th Infantry under Colonel Guy Meloy, to fortify the Kum River line which he held vital to the defense of Taejon. The 19th went into position at Taepyong-ni, holding the right flank of the 24th Division, while the 34th, still at Kongju about eight miles to the west, protected the left. General Dean hoped to hold at the Kum, because this river, the broadest south of Seoul, flowed like a great curving moat around Taejon some 15 miles southeast of Taepyong-ni. Taejon, small city though it was, was a vital geographical and communications center second in importance only to the Taegu or Pusan areas themselves.

This had been the tactical value of the 21st Infantry's stand at Chochiwon. Strategically, the defeat there had other more far-reaching effects. It impelled General MacArthur to send the 29th Infantry Regiment from Okinawa to Korea, as well as to instruct the Far East Air Force under Lieutenant General George Stratemeyer to use B-26 and B-29 bombers against the North Korean thrust down the central mountains.

Elements of the U. S. 25th Infantry Division had already begun to arrive in Korea as reinforcements for the collapsing central sector, while on the east the American Navy was placing more naval gunfire at the assistance of the embattled ROK divisions. On the east also, it had become increasingly important to hold the little fishing harbor of Pohang, approximately 60 air miles northeast of Pusan. The U. S. 1st Cavalry Division, which MacArthur had been hoarding for his "early counterof-fensive," was going to be rushed to Pohang by sea.

That was the situation on July 12, the day the 21st Regiment retreated across the Kum, the day also that all ground operations in Korea passed under the command of Lieutenant General Walker.

At West Point, Walton Walker was given the nickname of "Johnny," probably for no better reason than the popularity of a brand of liquor of that name. It might have been more properly "Bulldog" Walker, after his short powerful build and his tenacious fighting spirit, a quality and style of battle which exactly fulfilled the requirements of the campaign then developing in southern Korea.

During World War I, Walker led a machine-gun company and won a battlefield promotion. He commanded the 15th Infantry in China during the early 1930's, and became famous during World War II as an armored corps commander in General George Patton's Third Army. In 1948, Walker came to Japan to take charge of the Eighth Army, and on July 6, 1950, he was told by General MacArthur that the Eighth would control the campaign in Korea.

Two days later Walker flew to Korea to join General Dean on a hill below Chonan to watch the retreat of the 34th Infantry Regiment. He saw a platoon of light tanks approaching the front and stopped the youthful lieutenant leading it to ask, "What are you going to do down there?"

"I'm going to slug it out," the lieutenant said in a strained voice, eloquent in his conviction of what would happen when his little M-24s met the big Russian T-34s.

"No," Walker said gently. "Our idea is to stop those people. We don't go up there and charge or slug it out. We take positions where we have the advantage, where we can fire the first shots and still manage a delaying action."[2]

These, in small, were the tactics which Walker would use on a large scale when, on July 13, he began the delaying action with which he hoped to save the United Nations foothold in Korea. From that date on, both the ROK Army and the Eighth Army, as well as the United Nations troops which would subsequently be included in the latter, came under his command. Formal notification of his command of the ROKs did not come until July 17, when MacArthur sent word that Syngman Rhee had made a verbal agreement to this effect. MacArthur was by then, of course, the Supreme Commander of the United Nations Command in Korea, a force which consisted of the U. S. Eighth Army and attached UN units on the one hand, and the ROK Army on the other. MacArthur in turn received his orders from President Truman and the Joint Chiefs of Staff acting as executives of the United Nations Security Council. The field executive of MacArthur's orders was the commanding general of the Eighth Army, in this case Walker, whose directives also controlled the ROKs. And so, on July 17, as General Walker displayed the United Nations flag at his headquarters for the first time, the United Nations Command came into being.

But these were the formalities. The reality on July 13, the day of Walker's arrival, was that a force of 76,000 men—58,000 ROKs and 18,000 Americans—had been thus far powerless to halt the North Korean rush to place all of the peninsula under Communist rule. This force was badly in need of such things as antitank mines, antitank shells, heavy tanks, high-velocity cannon, heavy mortars, trucks, illumination shells, trip flares, spare gun barrels, radios, and, among the ROKs, ample rations of rice and fish. These deficiencies, especially in mines and antitank shells, were at least as corrosive of Eighth Army fighting strength as the well-advertised lack in "guts," if they were not in fact largely responsible for it. Walker's job was to get these weapons into Korea and into the hands of his troops, either by sea or air directly from Japan, or by air from a fleet of about 250 four-engined transports already operating from the United States.

That was the logistics problem. The battle situation on July 13 was as follows:

On the far west, the North Korean 6th Division had fanned out below Pyongtaek and was battling a ROK division and a force of police on a drive south aimed at turning Pusan's left flank. East of this the North Korean 3rd and 4th Divisions continued to strike south along the road from Seoul through the U. S. 24th Division, and still farther east the North Korean 2nd Division was advancing on Chongju against two battered ROK divisions.

In the central mountains three North Korean divisions were pushing back the remnants of two ROK divisions.

On the east coast the North Korean 5th Division was coming down the narrow coastal road against a ROK regiment.

One of Walker's first moves was to begin feeding elements of Major General William Kean's 25th Infantry Division into the central mountains. The 27th (Wolfhound) Infantry Regiment under Lieutenant Colonel John ("Mike") Michaelis had landed on July 10, and Walker ordered it to Andong in a blocking position behind the ROKs. He also charged General Kean with the security of Pohang on the east coast and Yonil Airfield below it.

Pohang was still vital, and thus far the North Korean 5th Division had not been able to capture it. Although the ROKs had not fought well on the east coast road, U. S. naval gunfire had battered the North Koreans and the monsoon rains caused landslides which blocked the road. The 35th Fighter Group at Yonil Airfield also harassed the 5th Division. Nonetheless on July 13 the 5th entered Pyonghae-ri, 22 miles north of Yongdok and 50 miles above Pohang. Obviously, Yongdok would soon be under attack. If it fell it would unmask Pohang.

And yet, with the east coast defenses collapsing, with the ROKs in the central mountains crumbling and the southwestern threat to Pusan at hand, the main road from Seoul guarded by the 24th Division remained Walker's most vital concern. If the enemy 3rd and 4th Divisions got their armor across the Kum River they could race through Taejon toward Taegu itself, with very little between to stop them. And so Walker ordered General Dean's 24th Division to hold the Kum River line.

By the time the North Korean 3rd and 4th Divisions launched their attack on the Americans holding the Kongju-Taepyong line south of the Kum, these divisions were in near-desperate condition. Rising American air power had destroyed much of their armor, the long fighting march south from Yongdungpo had thinned their ranks, and the lengthening supply line was making it increasingly difficult to bring reinforcements or food down to the vicinity of the Kum River. Worse, American air had made it impossible to move by day, and the plan to forage off the countryside was upset when South Korean farmers began hiding their food. The 4th Division opposite the American 34th Infantry at Kongju had done most of the fighting since the Han River was crossed at Yongdungpo and it was down to 5,000 to 6,000 men, about half strength. It had also lost much armor.

The 3rd Division, which would strike at the American 19th Infantry holding Taepyong on the right, was not as badly depleted, but nevertheless its troops were battle-weary. The 3rd's propaganda officers told the men that they would get a long rest after they took Taejon, assuring them that the Americans would surrender if the city fell.

So the North Koreans came on with the ardor born of desperation, and quickly turned the American left at Kongju.

Here the 34th Infantry had blown all the bridges over the Kum to keep the 4th Division's 16th Regiment at bay on the north bank. But with daylight of July 14, the North Korean artillery began pounding the Americans on the south bank, and then troops began to cross by barge. A large force crossed on the 34th's left and began attacking the artillerymen of the 63rd Field Artillery Battalion.

The North Koreans overran this entire position, and captured ten 105mm howitzers, together with all their ammunition and 60 to 80 trucks, as well as 86 American soldiers. The artillery battalion ceased to exist as a fighting force, and once again stragglers struck out for safety by twos and threes. The 1st Battalion, 34th, ordered to counterattack to recapture this equipment as well as to retake Kongju's fallen left, moved forward only to retreat at dusk after being briefly fired upon. The 3rd Battalion on Kongju's right had already collapsed. Kongju was lost, and General Dean's hopes of a long delay there were smashed. Worse, the enemy had a bridgehead on the south bank of the Kum, meaning that the left flank of the 19th Infantry holding on at Taepyong-ni had been turned.

The news of Kongju's fall was received at Taepyong-ni on the afternoon of the 14th, and it soured whatever jubilation Colonel Meloy felt over a fairly good fighting day. Minor enemy crossing attempts supported by fire from tanks dug in on the north bank of the river had been repulsed. Nevertheless, the 19th hung on at Taepyong-ni during the next day, the 15th, falling back only after the North Koreans crossed under cover of the early-morning darkness of the 16th.

At three in the morning, a North Korean plane flew over the Kum and dropped a flare. It was the signal for a fierce North Korean artillery barrage. Then, shortly before four o'clock, the

North Korean soldiers began crossing the river on boats or rafts, wading or swimming. The failure of an American 155mm howitzer to fire flares at this time made it impossible for the 19th's soldiers to spot the enemy and pick them off.

But the assault was not irresistible. At first platoons held all along the line. When C Company's Lieutenant Henry McGill called Lieutenant Thomas Maher to ask how he was making out, Maher replied: "We're doing fine." Thirty seconds later a Red soldier fired a burp-gun burst into Maher's head and killed him. Gradually, the North Koreans began forcing the 19th's right, and then, on the left and below this position, other enemy troops which had simultaneously crossed to the southwest set up a roadblock.

Like the 34th Infantry, the 19th began to withdraw. Colonel Meloy ordered his units to begin falling back on Taejon to the southeast, while down at Eighth Army headquarters in Taegu the news of the Kum River disaster was received with deepest alarm.

Since his arrival in Korea, General Walker had frequently studied terrain maps of the peninsula, while asking his officers: "When and where can I stop the enemy and attack him?" The Kum River defeat answered his question, for it compelled him to review his strength. Taking what he already had in Korea, together with what reserves could be mustered in the next ten days, Walker concluded that his Eighth Army could hold only a line generally following the Naktong River from its mouth west of Pusan and running north to a point west of Andong, then turning east again to Yongdok on the coast. This line would eventually become famous as the Pusan Perimeter, although it was somewhat larger as Walker considered it after the Kum River setback.

To hold this line he needed time for the 1st Calvary Division to sail from Japan to Pohang, about 30 miles below embattled Yongdok, and move west by rail to save Taegu from the approach of the North Korean 3rd and 4th Divisions. Spearheads of the 1st Cavalry would arrive on July 18, and Walker did not immediately worry about keeping Pohang open to receive them. U. S. warships striking the North Korean 5th Division on the east coast road were being augmented by the British cruiser *Belfast,* and Walker had already sent a force to hold the port and Yonil Airfield below it.

Taejon, not Pohang, was Walker's concern. It must hold out until the 1st Cavalry could come west to reinforce the collapsing 24th Division.

And so, on July 18, a few hours after Rear Admiral James Doyle's ships risked the wrath of Typhoon Helene to enter murky Pohang Harbor with men of the 8th Cavalry Regiment, General Walker flew north to speak to General Dean.

General Dean had not planned a last-ditch fight at Taejon, realizing that the North Koreans could now get their armor over the Kum and envelop that city of 130,000 persons. Dean hoped only to delay again at Taejon, while preparing another stand, probably at Yongdong 28 miles to the east. He had already, on July 15, sent his 21st Regiment eight miles east to Okchon with instructions to prepare to blow the railroad tunnels running out of Taejon. Dean planned to use the 34th Infantry—now led by Colonel Charles Beauchamp on loan from the 7th Division in Japan—to fight the delay. The 19th Infantry, Dean thought, had been too badly mauled in the Kum River fighting, and he had sent it east to Yongdong for rest and re-equipment.

But then General Walker flew up to Taejon on July 18 to ask Dean to hold the city an extra day while the 1st Cavalry took its position at Yongdong, and Dean's plan changed.

He postponed evacuation of Taejon to July 20 and ordered the 2nd Battalion, 19th, to return from Yongdong. Then he began blocking the chief approaches to the city. On the east or right flank, the road was already held by the 21st Infantry at Okchon. On the north there was a rail line and a small road, and Dean sent a platoon to block it. On the northwest was the main highway to Pusan, covered by the 1st Battalion, 34th. Directly west or left was a good road from the town of Nonsan, and this was to be temporarily held by a 34th Infantry platoon until the 2nd Battalion, 19th, arrived the next day to take over. To the south along the main road was the Division Reconnaissance Company, and Dean moved it up to the city and turned it over to Beauchamp, thus giving the 34th's commander a scouting force to watch the roads. Unfortunately the effect of this move was to leave Taejon's back door open.

But Dean, of course, was still not planning a diehard stand at Taejon. He was merely extending the delay there by twenty-four hours to enable the 1st Cavalry to arrive in Yongdong on the east, and then he would retire again with his forces intact. Dean was confident he could hold off the advancing North Koreans without great loss, if only because of the arrival of the new 3.5-inch rocket launcher in Taejon. This was the weapon which General Dean had urgently requested on July 3. Its ammunition had gone into production only fifteen days before the Korean War began, but by July 8 supplies of 3.5-inch launchers and shells, together with an instruction team, took off from California and flew to Korea. They were in Taejon on July 12 and that same day Dean's men were instructed how to fire the launcher's 23-inch, 8½-pound rockets. Dean hoped to stop the T-34s with this big bazooka, and he also hoped to encourage his men to do it by staying in Taejon himself. He later explained his other reasons for staying 28 miles forward of his headquarters:

> ... These reasons were compounded of poor communications, which had cost me one valuable position up at Pyongtaek, and the old feeling that I could do the job better—that is, make the hour-to-hour decisions necessary—if I stayed in close contact with what was happening. My staff was quite capable of operating the headquarters at Yongdong, under the direction of Brigadier General Pearson Menoher; and frankly, it was easier to get a message through toward the rear (or so it seemed) than toward the front.[3]

So the general was in Taejon when the two-pronged North Korean onslaught began on July 19, and it was well that he was. When the enemy's 16th and 18th Regiments struck along the western road from Nonsan, Dean rushed to the front with two tanks to help the little platoon roadblock hold out until the 2nd Battalion, 19th, arrived under Lieutenant Colonel Thomas Mc-Grail. This force counterattacked immediately and regained lost ground.

To the northwest along the main highway the North Koreans overran a company which Beauchamp had posted west of the Kap-chon River and hurled one of their heaviest artillery barrages into the lines of the 1st Battalion, 34th. They did not strike with their armor, though—chiefly because they had come to respect American air and had ceased to move boldly along the roads. By nightfall, Beauchamp had come to the optimistic conclusion that he could hold the road another day.

But during the night the North Koreans moved their tanks up, and at three o'clock in the morning of July 20 they struck hard with infantry and armor, coming down both sides of the highway and quickly turning the American right flank. The 1st Battalion, 34th, was driven into the hills in disorder.

On the west, the 2nd Battalion, 19th, was also sent reeling back.

Confusion began to spread among the 24th Division's scattered units, for numerous communications failures had left them leaderless and bewildered. Then, at daybreak, the T-34 tanks rolled into Taejon.

The first of them came down the main highway, but they also began to appear from the west and up from the south through that unguarded back door, and on their decks many of them carried riflemen who jumped to the ground to scoot into deserted buildings and begin the rifle fire that scourged retreating Americans and civilian refugees alike. Hundreds of North Korean infiltrators dressed in civilian clothes joined the sniping. Smoke drifted through the streets from burning buildings and everywhere the smell of cordite mingled with the stench of human dung. Here and there a North Korean tank was burning, for the big new bazookas had proved their worth. General Dean himself had gone tank hunting, moving through town with a bazooka team in a deliberate attempt to inspire his men, to prove, as he has since said, that "an unescorted tank in a city defended by infantry with 3.5-inch bazookas should be a dead duck." The general did get a tank, but unfortunately his gallantry in Taejon that day was not as contagious as he had hoped.

By nightfall the city was completely encircled and much of it was in North Korean hands. An enemy roadblock between the city and Okchon cut the main escape route east, and a mile-long stretch of that dusty, poplar-lined road—littered with burning vehicles and wounded or dying men—became the graveyard of the 34th Infantry.

Only capture or death awaited those Americans who chose to

stay in a city from which the huge sign, WELCOME UNITED NA-
TIONS FORCES, had long since been removed. General Dean
himself prepared to dash for safety and his headquarters at
Yongdong.

> We organized the remaining miscellaneous headquarters vehi-
> cles into a rough column and started out toward the east, the way
> the previous column had gone with the tanks. As we pulled
> through the city we ran into the tail of this column, which had
> been ambushed. Some trucks were on fire, others slewed across a
> narrow street where buildings on both sides were flaming for a
> block or more. Our own infantry, on one side of the street, was
> in a vicious fire fight with enemy units in higher positions on the
> other side.
>
> We drove through, careening between the stalled trucks. It was
> a solid line of fire, an inferno that seared us in spite of our speed.
> A block farther on my jeep and an escort jeep roared straight
> past an intersection, and almost immediately [Lieutenant Ar-
> thur] Clarke, riding with me, said we had missed a turn. But rifle
> fire still poured from buildings on both sides, and turning
> around was out of the question. I looked at a map and decided
> we should go on ahead, south and east, on another road that
> might let us make more speed than the truck-jammed main es-
> cape route. I had been away from my headquarters too long, and
> had to get back very soon. So we bored down the road in the gen-
> eral direction of Kumsan (south), while snipers still chewed at
> us from both sides of the road.
>
> We were all by ourselves.[4]

Thus ended the 24th Division's fifteen-day ordeal that began
when Task Force Smith went up the road to intercept the enemy
at Osan. During the next two days the shattered division regrouped at Yongdong. Then, on July 22, it turned its Yongdong
positions over to the 1st Cavalry Division and went into reserve.

Chapter Eight

THE 24th Infantry Division's performance along the Osan-Taejon road in July of 1950 has been variously described and frequently debated. President Truman has called it "a glorious chapter in the history of the American Army" while in the words of General Douglas MacArthur it was a brilliant holding action conducted with "skill and valor." Elsewhere, in certain newspaper accounts and books on the subject, the retreat to Taejon with its subsequent defeat has been held up as the Exhibit A of the alleged "softness" of the American youths who fought in Korea.

It was, in fact, what MacArthur called it, shorn of the adjectives: a successful holding action, which might have been as much the product of the North Korean failure to exploit the Han crossing as of any brilliance on the part of the Americans. It was very far from being "a glorious chapter" in the annals of American arms, and it did produce sufficient grounds for the charges of softness.

American soldiers, and officers, did retreat against orders to hold, sometimes in disorder; they did abandon artillery and trucks or throw away their rifles and helmets; they did refuse to fight; they did leave their wounded behind; they did sit down to await capture. And it might be well for the people of America, who seem to regard battlefield defeat as being contrary to the will of God, to understand some of the reasons why these things happened—not constantly, it must be understood, but frequently enough to characterize the early fighting and give it its tone. Here is General Dean again, describing Taejon:

> The doom of Taejon was evident to . . . the lost and weary soldiers straggling through the town (the same soldiers who less than a month before had been fat and happy in occupation bil-

lets, complete with Japanese girl friends, plenty of beer, and servants to shine their boots), and to me.[1]

Philip Deane, the British war correspondent who was captured along the Pusan road, quotes one of those riflemen sent out to hold it.

> "Gee, back in Sasebo I had a car, only a Ford, but a honey. You should have seen my little Japanese girl. Gee, she was a honey. Lived with me in my little villa. It was a honey, my little Japanese villa."[2]

Again Philip Deane quotes a conversation with another GI on the road:

> "I don't get this. They told us it was a sort of police action. Some police action! Some cops! Some robbers! What is this police action?"
> "Didn't your officers tell you?"
> "Naw. We don't talk of such things with Bob."
> "Who's Bob?"
> "Bob. You know Bob. Our lieutenant."
> "Well, didn't Bob tell you?"
> "Naw. Not sure he knows himself. You tell me. What's Communism, anyway? Why are we here?"[3]

Another observer who was in Korea, and has since become one of the foremost authorities on the early fighting, was the historian Colonel Roy E. Appleman. Here is his report on the performance of these soldiers who called their officers by their first names:

> There were many heroic actions by American soldiers of the 24th Division in these first weeks in Korea. But there were also many uncomplimentary and unsoldierly ones. Leadership among the officers had to be exceptional to get the men to fight, and several gave their lives in this effort. Others failed to meet the standard expected of American officers. There is no reason to suppose that any of the other occupation divisions in Japan would have done better in Korea than did the U. S. 24th Division in July, 1950. When committed to action they showed the same weaknesses.
>
> A basic fact is that the occupation divisions were not trained,

equipped or ready for battle. The great majority of the enlisted men were young and not really interested in being soldiers. The recruiting posters that had induced most of these men to enter the Army mentioned all conceivable advantages and promised many good things, but never suggested that the principal business of an army is to fight.[4]

Colonel Appleman then quotes the commander of the 24th Division's 21st Infantry, Colonel Richard Stephens:

"The men and officers had no interest in a fight which was not even dignified by being called a war. It was a bitter fight in which many lives were lost, and we could see no profit in it except our pride in our profession and our units as well as the comradeship which dictates that you do not let your fellow soldiers down."[5]

But this "pride in our profession and in our units" applies chiefly to professionals such as Colonel Stephens, in command or in ranks; it does not cover the bulk of the men who fought in Korea, if only because Korea was so different from any other war in American experience. In his book, *The Americans,* the historian Daniel J. Boorstin says:

The belief that American wars would always be fought by "embattled farmers" was rooted in the earliest facts of American life. Military men were to be simply citizens in arms. The military caste, the Man-on-Horseback, the Palace Revolution, the Coup d'Etat, the tug of war between army and civil government —these recurring motifs in continental European political life did not appear on the American scene. Civilian control over the army, clearly asserted in the Federal Constitution, merely declared what was already one of the firmest institutions of colonial life.

The typical American view of the military appeared in Doddridge's description of the backwoodsmen who "formed the cordon along the Ohio river, on the frontiers of Pennsylvania, Virginia and Kentucky, which defended the country against the attacks of the Indians during the revolutionary war. They were the janizaries of the country, that is, they were soldiers when they chose to be so, and when they chose laid down their arms...."[6]

88

In other words, the citizen-soldier or nonprofessional who is the American ideal only kills for a cause. He fulfills Newman's dictum: "Most men will die upon a dogma, few will be martyr to a conclusion." Only the professional soldier will fight for conclusions made in chanceries or foreign offices, and one of the outstanding characteristics of the professional, at least in ranks, is that he rarely "asks the reasons why." To Americans this is repugnant. Americans understand no war but the Crusade (as Dwight Eisenhower frequently calls his conduct of the war in Europe) or that total mobilization which means that "everybody's in it." In World War I when large numbers of American citizen-soldiers first went abroad to fight, it was to win "the war to end wars" or "to make the world safe for democracy" and they went off singing gay songs and joking about what they would do to "Kaiser Bill." Even though the horrible realities of modern war provoked the great pacifist reaction of the Twenties, the next generation of Americans also went aboard ship armed, either convinced that democracy was again the cause, or equating "the day of infamy" at Pearl Harbor with an attack on hearth and home.

Both times the nation was solidly behind its men at arms, so firmly behind them—if we accept the cynical suggestion that patriotism often fails to survive the first artillery barrage—that it was not possible for a reluctant soldier to turn and run. Both times the war effort was total and there was the atmosphere of crusade, even of carnival, with songs and bands and Stage Door Canteens and respectable families eager to entertain young soldiers in their homes, the reverse side of which gay coin was the superpatriotism which seemed to make it the duty of every malicious busybody to inquire of every young man in civilian clothes: "Why aren't you in service?"

But during the Korean War, no clerk or waiter would have dared explain away his inability to fill an order by snapping, "Say, don't you know there's a war on?" For during Korea much of the American public refused to admit there was a war on. They blocked this repugnant thing—this limited war called a "conflict"—from their minds. They called it "Truman's Folly." Senator Taft, the most powerful non-Administration leader in America, openly and frequently spoke of "Mr. Truman's War."

Nor did Mr. Truman improve public morale by his consistent use of the phrases "police action" or "conflict" or by insisting "We are not at war." And yet, as Army historians have described it, the "conflict in Korea" was as miserable and demanding as any war in history.

For these men of the 24th Division, the early days of the fighting were bloody and humiliating. . . . When they tried to retreat by road, they were subjected to a withering cross fire from the hills. Bitter, haggard, tattered and exhausted, they withdrew [through] mud which slowed or stopped vehicular traffic and engulfed the straining leg muscles of the foot soldier. When under fire, the soldier who slipped into the stagnant, sickening waters of a rice paddy might find that only by pulling his feet out of his boots could he escape from the slime and crawl to safety. He could never escape, however, from the eternity of rain . . . it poured, three or four days at a time, drenching every man and coating equipment with mildew, rot or rust. The heat of the Korean summer and the inescapable flies, fleas, and lice constituted other irritants for the exasperated American troops. Nauseated by the earthy smells which thickened the air, caked with dirt, the bruised and sweat-soaked men fought the enemy in filthy, water-filled gullies, in and out of small villages of mud-plastered huts, and over endless mountain ridges . . . as often as not cut off from the rear, jostled by hordes of refugees, sometimes shoeless, frequently bleeding and hungry. . . .

Stately patriarchs in tall black hats, worried bands of women in high-waisted skirts and loose white blouses, bewildered children naked in the oppressive heat, and wiry Korean fathers stooped beneath the staggering weight of overloaded A-frames, clogged the highways to the south. . . . Mingling with the civilians, enemy personnel in native dress moved inconspicuously, waiting for opportunities to stampede the crowds, block bridges, and throw hand grenades into passing groups of U. S. soldiers.[7]

Given such conditions in such an unpopular war, given such soft youths trained to luxury in a nation only recently gone mad in the pursuit of—not happiness, but possessions, pleasure and prestige—the wonder is that they actually stayed to fight at all. But enough of them did to delay the North Korean 3rd and 4th Divisions for seventeen days along a 100-mile route slanting southeastward from Osan to Yongdong. Although they never inflicted very heavy casualties on the enemy infantry, they did, together with supporting air, knock out numerous tanks and guns. And they were, of course, hampered by inferior arms and communications, the latter in particular rendering them singularly vulnerable to the North Korean maneuver of hitting frontally to hold while moving around the flanks to cut off escape routes. Even veterans can be panicked by such tactics.

The 24th Division lost roughly 30 percent of its 12,200 men, as well as enough gear to equip a full-strength division. Among the casualties were 2,400 missing in action, most of whom were presumed dead, although a surprising number later turned up as enemy prisoners. And among these was General Dean.

The night he left Taejon General Dean fell down a slope while going after water for wounded men. He was knocked out. When he awoke, he found his head gashed and his shoulder broken. He wandered for thirty-six days in the mountains, trying to elude capture, shrinking from 190 pounds to 130, until he was finally betrayed by a pair of South Korean civilians who led him into a North Korean trap while pretending to guide him to safety. General Dean spent the rest of the war as a prisoner, as unbreakable in captivity as he had been in battle. And it was characteristic of this gallant and modest commander that he should be astonished when, upon being freed on September 5, 1953, he found himself a national hero and the recipient of the Medal of Honor.

He had not known, of course, that he had accomplished precisely what he had been ordered to accomplish: to hold off the enemy until reinforcements could be brought in. But even as he awoke on the morning of July 21, broken, bruised and bleeding, the 1st Cavalry Division was in line at Yongdong, the 25th Infantry Division had gone into position to the north, and the first phase of the Korean War had ended in failure for the enemy.

Chapter Nine

O N July 20, 1950, it would have seemed difficult for the United Nations forces to catch sight of bright victory moving among the dark ruins of the defeat then developing at Taejon. But MacArthur saw it and proclaimed it.

On that date (Korean time) he sent President Truman a report, parts of which were included in a message the President sent to Congress on July 19 (Washington time). The President asked an end to restrictions on the size of American armed forces along with legislation to establish materials priorities and allocations necessary for the conduct of the war. Truman also requested an additional ten billion dollars for defense while stating that higher taxes and restriction on consumer credit would be necessary. This pill, still a bitter one for Americans to swallow, was sugar-coated with the MacArthur report, which said:

> With the deployment in Korea of major elements of the Eighth Army now accomplished, the first phase of the campaign has ended and with it the chance for victory by the North Korean forces. The enemy's plan and great opportunity depended upon the speed with which he could overrun South Korea once he had breached the Han River line and with overwhelming numbers and superior weapons temporarily shattered South Korean resistance....
>
> The skill and valor thereafter displayed in successive holding actions by the ground forces in accordance with this concept, brilliantly supported in complete coordination by air and naval elements, forced the enemy into continued deployments, costly frontal attacks and confused logistics which so slowed his advance and blunted his drive that we have bought the precious time necessary to build a secure base....
>
> ... the issue of battle is now fully joined and will proceed along lines of action in which we will not be without choice....

Our casualties despite overwhelming odds have been relatively light. Our strength will continually increase while that of the enemy will relatively decrease. His supply line is insecure. He had his great chance and failed to exploit it. We are now in Korea in force and with God's help we are there to stay until the constitutional authority of the Republic is fully restored.

At the time this report was made, the Eighth Army in Korea consisted of the 25th Infantry and 1st Cavalry Divisions moving into line, and the battered 24th moving out of it. The ROK Army was still a week away from completing the reorganization which would give it a force of 85,000 effectives divided among five divisions and a headquarters and training unit. U. S. reinforcements en route to Korea consisted of two battalions of the 29th Infantry, the Fifth Regimental Combat Team, two regiments of the 2nd Infantry Division, and the 1st Provisional Marine Brigade, which, with tanks and supporting air, had been turned at sea and ordered to make for Pusan instead of Japan. Elsewhere, Britain, Australia, Turkey, Canada, and the Philippines had promised troops for Korea, and the U. S. Navy was bringing 48 ships out of mothballs—among them some of the mighty battleships of World War II.

On paper, where strategy usually walks, the situation was exactly as MacArthur described it—and history has upheld his judgment. On earth, where men live and fight to carry out tactics, it seemed not so clear-cut.

As for the North Koreans, they found MacArthur's estimate absurd and they heaped derision on it, broadcasting reiterations of their promise to sweep "the American aggressors and the Syngman Rhee puppet troops" out of Korea by mid-August. The Communists were already preparing to renew the attack with a dozen divisions on the line. Eight were deployed already and four more were being moved south of the Parallel. The North Koreans still expected to take Pusan, and they still struck down four routes, plus that southern thrust which had reached a point south of Pusan on the west and had now turned east to make a flanking dash at the port city.

The North Korean confidence could hardly be scoffed at by General Walker. The initiative was still the enemy's, and it could be argued that Walker's position might actually have

93

been untenable, except for the intervention of American air which made it impossible for the North Koreans to move by daylight, the difficulty of enemy movement through the rugged central mountains, and the presence of U. S. Navy warships hammering the coastal road on the east. Although a steady influx of reinforcements whittled at the enemy's numerical edge, Walker still lacked enough artillery and tanks to deal with the enemy armor. The South Koreans were fighting almost exclusively with small arms. Within the Pusan defense perimeter there were so many blown bridges and roads either mired in mud or clogged with refugees that massed movement of troops rarely reached five miles an hour. At such a rate, Walker had to play the fire chief, and yet, despite the obstacles, he did it well. Trained under the dashing George Patton and indoctrinated to the armored commander's creed of slashing attack, General Walker showed surprising ability to adapt to the shoestring operation he was running. He shuttled troops like a master juggler, gambling again and again while his perimeter steadily shrank.

Along the northwest road to Taegu the Communists gained 25 miles in four days, as their 3rd Division moved out of Taejon after one day's rest and struck at the 1st Cavalry Division in Yongdong. The night of July 25 the North Koreans held Yongdong, and the Americans were falling back east into Hwanggan. Just to the north, the North Korean 2nd Division attacked down the Poul-Hwanggan road, and encountered probably the fiercest American resistance of the war. The 25th Division's Wolfhound (27th) Regiment under Colonel Michaelis fought off the enemy in a five-day delaying action which decimated the already battered 2nd. Still, the Wolfhounds ultimately had to fall back through the 1st Cavalry Division at Hwanggan to go into reserve around Taegu.

In the central corridor the ROKs began to fight furiously as their commanders drove them on in an attempt to save face. They slowed the Communists down about 30 miles north of Taegu, although Eighth Army calculated that the heaviest blows were still to fall on the center.

In the east, Yongdok became a churned, blackened no-man's-land while a fierce seesaw battle raged for possession of the town. It had fallen quickly to the North Koreans on July 17, but the next day the ROKs had counterattacked behind the guns of the *Juneau* and other U. S. ships. On the 19th the North Korean 5th Division retook Yongdok. The following day American fighters from Yonil struck at the Communists, and on July 21, after the British cruiser *Belfast*, along with the American destroyers *Higbee, Mansfield, De Haven* and *Swenson*, had joined *Juneau* in hurling shells into Yongdok, the ROKs retook the town. Came nightfall, when it is difficult for naval gunfire to be accurate, and the ROKs were driven out again. Even so, the North Koreans had little chance to exploit the capture of Yongdok. They were hemmed in by massed artillery and mortar fire, struck at repeatedly from the air, and scourged from the sea. On one day *Juneau* alone killed 400 North Koreans with her shells. On July 24, an entire battalion was pocketed and then annihilated by naval gunfire and air strikes. Three days later the ROK 3rd Division launched the counterattack which recaptured Yongdok on August 2 in the South Korean Army's outstanding action of the war.

Nowhere else did it seem possible to hold, for the Americans as well as the ROKs. Withdrawal followed withdrawal and not even the arrival of the 29th Infantry on July 24 could ease General Walker's disappointment in his troops. On July 29 the Eighth Army commander went to the command post of the faltering 25th Division and issued the controversial order which, as paraphrased from his notes by the historian Appleman, said in effect:

> We are fighting a battle against time. There will be no more retreating, withdrawal or "readjustment of the lines" or any other term you choose. There is no line behind us to which we can retreat. Every unit must counterattack to keep the enemy in a state of confusion and off balance. There will be no Dunkirk, there will be no Bataan, a retreat to Pusan would be one of the greatest butcheries in history. We must fight until the end. Capture by these people is worse than death itself. We will fight as a team. If some of us must die, we will die fighting together. Any man who gives ground may be personally responsible for the death of thousands of his comrades.
>
> I want everybody to understand that we are going to hold this line. We are going to win.[1]

This was the famous "Stand or Die" speech which was widely criticized in the United States, as well as by a few of Walker's commanders. Some of them felt that to stand or die was impossible against an enemy whose outstanding tactic was the flanking movement which cut off the rear. Even so, Walker had ample cause for exasperation. His heart had been chafed for days by the poor showing of his American troops. The allusion to "adjustments of the line" properly sneered at this euphemistic way of describing an unwarranted withdrawal or pullback. "Bugging out" had already become one of the characteristic phrases of the Korean War, and the men of the 24th Infantry, 25th Division, had already cynically adopted "Bug-Out Blues" as its regimental "theme song."* Because of this lack of ardor, the Pusan Perimeter had begun to shrink at such a rate that Walker's remark about a Pusan retreat becoming "one of the greatest butcheries" was no idle threat. History has shown that more men die running from battle than toward it, and the fact that many military men could perceive impending disaster in Korea can be judged from this account from an officer of the 1st Provisional Marine Brigade even then steaming toward Pusan:

> During the long, slow voyage across the Pacific every ship of the Brigade's convoy maintained a prominently displayed situation map of the Korean War. As the radio reports outlining the course of the day's action were received, the front lines were carefully plotted. With each passing day the staggered line of blue and red symbols representing the UN perimeter moved closer and closer to the southern tip of the Korean peninsula. At mid-Pacific the betting in the troop compartments was even money that the defenders would be driven into the sea before the convoy arrived. A few days later only an easy mark would make the same bet without getting odds. By the end of July the maps showed a pitifully small 80 by 50 miles corner of southeastern Korea being held by the UN forces.[2]

Though Walker apparently had grounds for his ultimatum, it was unfortunately true that his glamorous chief, General

*It must be added that the first enlisted man to win the Medal of Honor in Korea was Pfc. William Thompson, a soldier in this regiment.

MacArthur, had only a few days earlier prepared the United Nations for happier tidings. On July 27 MacArthur flew to Taegu from Tokyo to tell the press: "There will be new heartaches and new setbacks" but "I was never more confident of victory—ultimate victory—in my life." The operative word was "ultimate" and the "new heartaches" had been dismissed as a passing woe in prelude to this final triumph, but no one marked this then, as no one suspected that MacArthur's great military mind had already conceived its most daring plan. The UN commander's words were filled with shining hope and for unromantic Bulldog Walker to start dousing the lights again was considered most annoying—just as Walker's issuance of free beer to his fighting men a month later would be taken in some American quarters as the act of a sinful man.

Finally, in Walker's defense, the situation at the end of July could not have been more critical. The northwest drive on Taegu seemed unstoppable, and the ROK government was already prepared for flight to Pusan. Below Taegu lay a wide-open gap of some 50 miles through which the enemy might race to cut off the Pusan road. Worse, an enemy column was already speeding toward it.

As early as the battle for Taejon, UN intelligence had reported North Korean movement in southwest Korea. It was believed that these were troops of the 4th Division which had led the fight down from Yongdungpo, but they were actually of the 6th Division, that unit which had spilled out into the west almost immediately after the fall of Pyongtaek. This unit had nothing to bar its path but a few hundred survivors of the broken ROK 7th Division and a scattering of ROK Marines and policemen. While Taejon was falling, the 6th's troops quickly took Chonju, 30 miles to the southeast. They sped rapidly south and by July 25 were in position for the end run to Pusan, 90 air miles to the east.

"Comrades," General Pang Ho San told his 6th Division troops on that date, "the enemy is demoralized. The task given us is the liberation of Masan and Chinju and the annihilation of the remnants of the enemy. . . . The liberation of Chinju and Masan means the final battle to cut off the windpipe of the enemy."

What "liberation "would mean to the South Koreans can be judged from this entry on July 29 in a North Korean guerrilla's diary: "Apprehended 12 men: National Assembly members, police sergeants and [town of] Myon leaders. Killed four of them at the scene, and the remaining eight were shot after investigation by the People's Court." General Pang's remark about Masan and Chinju forming Pusan's windpipe, however, was exactly correct, and by the time he made it General Walker had also appreciated their value.

Although General Walker knew of the enemy in the southwest by July 20, a few days elapsed before he became fully aware of this peril to his left flank. On July 21 and 22, bad weather covered the enemy's movements and Walker gradually became alarmed. He had no idea of the North Koreans' strength or proximity. The next day the weather cleared, and the Fifth Air Force, by then based at Taegu, sent out scouting patrols. The fliers reported that the enemy was indeed coming strong out of the west and would soon be in position to strike through the gap below Taegu. The critical moment had come and there was nothing for Walker to do but pull the 24th Division out of reserve.

The next day, July 24, Walker summoned Major General John Church, the 24th's new commanding general, to Taegu. Church, promoted since his early days in Korea, had taken over only the day before, after General Dean had been declared missing.

"I'm sorry to have to do this," Walker told him, "but the whole left flank is open and reports indicate the North Koreans are moving in."

Church was ordered to hold an area bounded by Chinju, some 50 air miles west of Pusan, and Kumchon, 65 air miles to its northeast. Thus, only four days after it had been driven out of Taejon, the 24th went back into line again.

That afternoon the 19th Infantry went west to Chinju, and a few hours later Walker sent it reinforcements from the 29th Infantry which had arrived that day. In two of the 29th's battalions, the 1st and 3rd, the depleted ranks had been filled with 400 recruits who had arrived at Okinawa from the United States only four days before. The 29th had expected to spend six weeks training before entering battle. Many of its men had not zeroed-in their rifles. Mortars had not been test-fired. New .50-caliber machine guns were still covered with cosmoline. But the 29th had come into a brush-fire war run by a fire chief whose only hope lay in putting out the biggest fires when and where they erupted. And so the 29th went west to Chinju, was ordered to strike the enemy at Hadong, another 35 miles to the southwest —and was there ambushed.

It was the 3rd Battalion, 29th, under Lieutenant Colonel Harold Mott, which went to Hadong, guided by Major General Chae Byong Duk, the "Fat Boy" who had been ROK Chief of Staff during the Seoul disaster. Chae had pointed out the importance of Hadong, and had gallantly offered to lead the Americans there and act as their interpreter. One of the very first bursts of enemy fire that began the ambush at Hadong on July 27 struck General Chae in the head and killed him. Thereafter the North Koreans raked the Americans until they had killed 315 of them, wounded 52 and captured perhaps 40 more, and sent the 3rd Battalion, 29th, falling back in disorder. Then they moved east again toward Chinju.

But the North Koreans did not reach Chinju until July 31, and though it was apparent to no one at the time, they were beginning to lose the race for Pusan. More reinforcements had come to Walker in the form of the 2nd Division's 9th Infantry Regiment, and the Marine Brigade was two days' sail from Pusan. Walker was also aided by the prior North Korean decision to capture all of the southwest ports before sending the 6th Division racing east for Pusan. The purpose of this decision had been to provide bases for resupply by sea, but in effect it gave Walker time to defend against what had now become, with the reappearance of the North Korean 4th Division, a skillful two-division thrust at his left flank.

In this maneuver, the 6th Division had skirted wide around the Eighth Army's left to come in under it along the southern coast; by July 31, the 6th occupied Chinju. The 4th, meanwhile, had cut inside the 6th on an inner arc, moving down from Taejon to Kumsan, then turning east to capture Kochang-Anui about 35 air miles above Chinju. By July 31, the 4th Division was in position to attack beneath Taegu and seal off its escape routes, while also crossing the Naktong River before Walker had time to fall back behind this natural barrier. And the 6th was poised to smash at Masan, which masked the plum of Pusan.

Walker responded by pulling the 25th Division out of his center and rushing it down to the southwest. The first unit to go south was Colonel Michaelis's 27th Regiment, which came out of reserve to join the 24th Division in blocking the Masan Road. Thereafter, Walker fed the rest of the 25th into the southwest front, taking the gamble which left his center perilously weak for any enemy thrust there, while strengthening his left for what now seemed to him the enemy's most dangerous maneuver.

It was that, but it failed.

The North Korean 6th Division was kept out of Masan, while the 4th was held off beyond the Naktong. Pusan and the United Nations foothold in Korea were saved. The flanking dash from the west had been the enemy's outstanding movement of the entire war, but Bulldog Walker had blunted it. On August 2, the Eighth Army's units began an orderly withdrawal behind the Naktong. They were not, however, falling back to fight to fall back again. The time for such agonizing tactics was at an end. Reinforcements, replacements and supplies had been flowing steadily into the Pusan Perimeter since Walker sent his firehorses galloping west. More than 5,000 officers and men had already been received from Japan to fill the ranks of the U. S. divisions on the line. A battalion of tanks salvaged from the Pacific island battlefields of World War II was, on August 2, only two days out of Pusan. Eighty more Pershings had mounted out of San Francisco on July 26. The Fifth Air Force had risen in strength at Taegu, and Mustangs and Shooting Stars now could patrol the lines for much longer than the twenty-odd minutes available to them when they flew from Japanese bases. And on August 2 the Marine Brigade arrived in Pusan.

The Marines came in 4,725 strong, most of the officers and 65 percent of the NCOs combat veterans, even some of the privates seasoned fighters. They had a few Pershing tanks and many supporting aircraft, and they were, as strength was measured in those days, almost the equivalent of a division. They were also cocky, arrogant even, their invincible assurance that everything would be all right, "Now that we're here," already beginning to irritate soldiers who had been in action a month.

Eighth Army would use the Marine Brigade as a trouble-shooter, Walker told its commander Brigadier General Edward Craig, who had flown to Korea in advance of his troops. Craig passed the information along when he assembled his commanders on the docks.

"The Pusan Perimeter is like a weakened dike," he told them, "and we will be used to plug holes in it as they open. It will be costly fighting against a numerically superior enemy." He paused. "Gentlemen," he said quietly, "Marines have never lost a battle. This Brigade will not be the first to establish such a precedent." Five days later Craig's Marines gave Walker his first victory of the war.

Chapter Ten

DURING those desperate days when Pusan was threatened, open political warfare began in the United Nations and the seeds of one of America's great internal controversies were planted.

First, the Soviet Union ended its boycott of the Security Council in August, the month that the Council presidency fell to Soviet delegate Jacob Malik. The Russians promptly began attacking the presence of the U. S. Seventh Fleet in the waters between Formosa and the Chinese mainland. This fleet seems to have caused the Communists to cancel plans to invade Formosa,* the fall of which, following capture of the other Nationalist island stronghold of Hainan, was intended to crush Chiang Kai-shek forever. The Soviets circulated a petition denouncing the movement of the Seventh Fleet to the Formosa Strait as an act of aggression by the United States against Communist China.

*China Crosses the Yalu, by Allen S. Whiting, Macmillan, 1960, p. 68.

President Truman's reply was to direct Ambassador Austin to refute the charge by pointing out that the Seventh Fleet's mission was to prevent attack from *either* direction and thus narrow the area of the war. With this debate for background, the President and General MacArthur collided in public disagreement over the Administration's policies in Formosa.

On July 29, Chiang had offered 33,000 Nationalist troops for use in Korea. Truman declined the offer, partly because Chiang's troops would need to be equipped and armed just like the South Koreans, partly because their deployment in Korea would weaken Formosa, partly because the use of Nationalist troops in Korea would needlessly offend the Chinese Communists. General MacArthur had already agreed that the offer should be declined for the first reason, and he suggested that he visit Chiang to explain this to him. On July 31 MacArthur flew to Formosa for this purpose, and, immediately, in Congress and among the United Nations allies, his trip was interpreted to portend a shift in U. S. policy from one of neutralizing Formosa to one of military aid to the Nationalists. And this interpretation, of course, tended to support Soviet charges that the United States plotted aggression against Communist China.

President Truman found it necessary to explain to Congress:

> Our desire is that Formosa not become embroiled in hostilities disturbing to the peace of the Pacific and that all questions affecting Formosa be settled by peaceful means as envisaged in the Charter of the United Nations.

Then the President sent his emissary Averill Harriman to Tokyo to talk to MacArthur about Far Eastern policy. Harriman's report said in part:

> In my first talk with MacArthur, I told him the President wanted me to tell him he must not permit Chiang to be the cause of starting a war with the Chinese communists on the mainland, the effect of which might drag us into a world war. He answered that he would, as a soldier, obey any orders that he received from the President. . . .

This seemed to satisfy Truman, and then, on August 10, MacArthur issued a statement firmly denying that his talks with Chiang had any political significance whatever. True,

MacArthur concluded his statement with the remark: "This visit has been maliciously misrepresented to the public by those who invariably in the past have propagandized a policy of defeatism and appeasement in the Pacific," but, taken all in all, the August 10 statement seemed another expression of MacArthur's earnest intention to adhere to Administration policy. President Truman himself assumed that "this would be the last of it."[1]

But then, on August 26, it became clear that the political conflict was just beginning. On that date General MacArthur publicly challenged the Administration policy on Formosa, declaring, in a message to the Veterans of Foreign Wars: "Nothing could be more fallacious than the threadbare argument by those who advocate appeasement and defeatism in the Pacific that if we defend Formosa we alienate continental Asia. Those who speak thus do not understand the Orient. They do not grasp that it is in the pattern of Oriental psychology to respect and follow aggressive, resolute and dynamic leadership—to quickly turn from leadership characterized by timidity or vacillation. . . ."

Though MacArthur's statement was not to be read until August 28, the press had received advance copies of it from his headquarters in Tokyo, and by August 26 one weekly magazine carrying the full text was already in the mails. By the time President Truman heard of it from the White House press room, all the world had heard of it, and Truman, galled by those very bad marks in "Oriental psychology," has described his dismayed reaction:

> I gave serious thought to relieving General MacArthur as our military field commander in the Far East and replacing him with General [Omar] Bradley. I could keep MacArthur in command of the Japanese occupation, taking Korea and Formosa out of his hands. But after weighing it carefully I decided against such a step. It would have been difficult to avoid the appearance of a demotion, and I had no desire to hurt General MacArthur personally. My only concern was to let the world know that his statement was not official policy.[1]

This Truman did by directing MacArthur to withdraw the message. MacArthur obeyed. Much as this face-saving maneuver might reaffirm the Truman policy of neutralizing Formosa, the fact of President Truman's lack of firmness when so publicly defied could not have been lost on such a strong personality as Douglas MacArthur. The time was not a year away when the Commander in Chief would say ruefully, "I should have fired him then."

Chapter Eleven

B Y THE time President Truman and General MacArthur had seemingly settled their differences over U. S. policy in the Far East, the United Nations command in Korea had broken up the first of two furious North Korean onslaughts on the new Naktong River line.

This first stroke followed the same invasion routes as before and was carried out between August 6 and the end of the month. It employed eleven divisions and two regiments, a force which had dwindled from the original number of 90,000 to 70,000 men. Some 58,000 casualties had been inflicted on the North Korean People's Army in its drive south, and even the 70,000 men available for combat by August 4 included thousands of untrained replacements, many of them forcibly conscripted from the South Korean civilian population. Nor did the North Koreans possess that "numerical superiority" of which Brigadier General Edward Craig spoke when he addressed his Marines at the Pusan docks.

Though newspaper articles had popularized the belief of an enemy superiority as high as "4 to 1" in Korea, the fact is that the odds were never greater than 2 to 1, even at the outset. That edge disappeared around July 20 when Walker's force drew even. By August 5, the United Nations army in Korea—still exclusively American and ROK—stood at about 141,000 of which 92,000 were ground combat troops: 47,000 Americans (the 5th Regimental Combat Team as well as another regiment

of the 2nd Division had landed in Pusan by August 5) and 45,-
000 ROKs. Somewhat offsetting this advantage was the fact that
few of General Walker's American units were ever at reported
strength because of the preponderance of "non-battle casualties." Heat exhaustion, for one thing, took a terrible toll. When
the rain stopped, the temperature often rose as high as 110
degrees. Americans climbing Korea's steep hills in such heat
often passed out. Salt tablets became as necessary as ammunition
to keep men fighting. Korea's numerous diseases, notably malaria and hepatitis, also thinned the American ranks, and dysentery was the inevitable punishment for the unwary American
who ate native vegetables. The ROKs, of course, were immune
to much of this, and could live on balls of rice wrapped in
cabbage leaves, hot or cold, clean or crawling with flies. Unfortunately, so could the enemy North Koreans.

Still Walker did possess the numerical edge, and he held the
other important advantage of having the interior lines. From
Pusan it is 63 miles northeast to Pohang, 55 miles northwest to
strategic Taegu, and 29 miles west to Masan. Supplies and troops
still pouring into this safe port could easily be rushed to the
front. Numerous subsidiary depots and dumps had been set up
within a 15-mile radius of the port, and none of these was
endangered by air attack. Walker's supply situation was now
excellent, where it had once been miserable. The U. S. Navy and
Air Force had again shown themselves capable of rapidly re-
trieving a poor logistics position.

On the other hand, the North Korean logistic problem was
increasing. The enemy's long lines of communication were attacked day and night by the planes of the Fifth Air Force, by
Navy and Marine planes flying off the carriers, and by the guns
of the U. S. and British warships parading the east coast. Beginning on August 6, in fact, coincident with the new North
Korean offensive, the planes and the ships became engaged in
what was called "bridge-busting week," thus making it difficult
for the North Koreans to move men or munitions by rail or
road. At night American B-26 bombers flew intruder missions,
supplementing the daily strategic bombing of Major General
Emmett ("Rosy") O'Donnell's B-29 Superfortresses. So the
Communists found themselves resorting to human and animal
transport to keep their fighting men armed and fed. Civilians

were pressed into service as carriers, and horse- or oxen-drawn carts plied the roads, usually disguised as civilian conveyances. Even so, most of the North Korean soldiers were half-starved. Many of those taken prisoner complained of low rations. Unable to forage as planned, the North Koreans had attempted to transport rice from northern warehouses. But the supply columns had been destroyed or scattered by American tactical bombing.

Still, the North Koreans possessed a moral advantage as against the United Nations' material superiority, and Napoleon has said: "The moral is to the material in war as three to one." This moral drive was born of a desperation to fulfill Premier Kim Il Sung's repeated boast that his armies would drive the Americans and the ROKs into the sea in time for the mid-August elections. To make good this boast, the North Korean generals —and Marshal Choe Yong Gun in Pyongyang—were willing to lose men by the thousands. In fact, their very tactics dictated acceptance of such losses, for the standard North Korean assault against a defended United Nations position depended upon manpower exhausting firepower. Three or four waves of troops were used, the first wave, often consisting of forcibly conscripted and untrained South Korean youths, having the mission of overwhelming the enemy by sheer numbers. If they were stopped, and they usually were, then second and third waves of slightly better trained troops renewed the assault. By then, as the North Koreans calculated, the enemy should have run out of ammunition and it was time for a fourth wave of veterans to attack. Often this was so, and the United Nations troops would be forced to evacuate. Another tactic was the "refugee attack" launched by crowds of civilians combed from crowded roads and driven at bayonet point into a United Nations position. Mingling with the civilians or following at their heels were North Korean soldiers.

With such desperation tactics, and not, it must be said, with any skillful and coordinated plan of attack, the North Korean People's Army opened its August offensive, striking on the east, northwest, west and southwest fronts, sometimes simultaneously but more often with an aimless fury which hoped to find and open the soft spot through which troops might rush to Taegu and Pusan. General Walker met this challenge with his old method of shuttling troops back and forth to the danger spots, once the early ominous pressure on the left flank had first been eased.

This latter mission was carried out by Task Force Kean, a group which Major General William Kean formed from the 35th Regiment of his own 25th Division, the 5th Regimental Combat Team and the Marine Brigade. General Kean sent his men southwest of Masan to strike at the 6th Division, which had reorganized and was driving west again for a fresh assault on Masan.

The counterattack began August 7 and quickly collided with an attacking enemy. Task Force Kean was struck by fierce artillery barrages directed by enemy soldiers who had infiltrated as civilians in order to spot American targets. A force of guerrillas surprised the American rear, stampeding units of the reserve 24th Infantry Regiment. Soldiers and Marines wilted in the intense heat, and at one point in the early maneuvering, a unit of the 5th Regimental Combat Team turned down the road assigned to the Marines.

Gradually, however, Task Force Kean rallied. Led by the Marine Brigade they shoved the 6th Division back. The brigade, or actually the Fifth Marine Regiment which formed its nucleus, took the road from Chindong-ni to Chinju on August 9 and drove rapidly into enemy territory. By August 12 it had advanced 26 miles, making devastating use of the supporting Marine Corsairs. Loaded with a 500-pound bomb or tank of napalm jellied gasoline, plus eight rockets and a full load of ammunition for six .50-caliber machine guns, the Corsairs made forays such as these described in the log of the U. S. carrier *Badoeng Strait:*

> 10 Aug: Strike George attacked a large roadblock three miles north of Kaesong at 1500. Steep dive bombing, rocket and strafing runs were made on enemy troops on the hillsides, destroying 75% of the enemy position. After these attacks, Marines of the First Marine Brigade were able to stand up and walk through the roadblock, continuing their advance on Kaesong.

> 11 Aug: Third Battalion standing by to attack Kaesong. Preparatory Marine artillery fire landed in the town. Suddenly, as the Marine artillerymen watched through their binoculars, a column of enemy vehicles, numbering almost a hundred, were

observed, preparing to make a dash for safety. Circling overhead was a . . . flight of four Corsairs [led by Major Arnold Lund]. The ground controllers immediately directed Lund's attention to the column of motorcycles, jeeps, and troop-filled trucks.

The Corsairs made an immediate low-level strafing run in an effort to bring the column to a halt. The Marine airmen spewed rockets and bullets into the column. Vehicles crashed into one another or piled up in the ditch while enemy troops scrambled for cover. Soviet-made jeeps and motorcycles were stopped or abandoned by the rockets and 20-mm. fire. Return fire from enemy's guns on the low-flying aircraft seriously damaged two Corsairs: Lt. Doyle Cole ditched in a nearby bay to be rescued by the helicopter carrying Brig. Gen. Craig: Captain Vivian Moses crashlanded in a rice paddy and was killed. Four additional Corsairs . . . relieved Lund's flight to continue the destruction of the column.

It was with such support from the sky that the Marines gave General Walker his first victory, but on August 13, Task Force Kean marched back to the east. Walker had decided that the 6th Division had been sufficiently battered to keep his lower left secure at least for the time being. His attention was now diverted elsewhere, to the numerous leaks which the attacking enemy had sprung in the Pusan Perimeter, and chiefly to a big one around Pohang.

Here, between August 11 and 20, a North Korean regiment and two divisions nearly wrested the vital eastern corridor to Taegu out of United Nations control. Earlier, the Communists had forced the ROKs out of Yongdok. Then they cut the ROK 3rd Division off by roadblocks erected below Yongdok and above Pohang, while other forces struck out of the west through Kigye. Led by tanks with sirens screaming to terrorize the defense, the Communists struck into Pohang on August 11. Fierce fighting followed, and General Walker was forced to form task force after task force to throw up roadblocks on the vital arteries running from Pohang inland to Taegu, and to protect Yonil Airfield. Early in the east coast fighting the U. S. Air Force had evacuated Yonil, but the planes had returned to help the Americans and ROKs force the North Koreans back. Meanwhile, the

ROK 3rd Division was taken out of the trap. American landing ships ran inshore beneath the bombardment of the U. S. cruiser *Helena* to take the South Koreans off and bring them safely behind the lines at Kuryongpo-ri. Three days later, with Pohang recaptured, General Walker judged the eastern thrust to have been blunted.

Walker's most critical moment, meanwhile, had been reached a week earlier. It occurred when the North Korean 4th Division imposed the threat at the Naktong River Bulge which, if successful, would have isolated Taegu and forced the Pusan Perimeter to shrink to slaughter-pen proportions.

This 4th Division, as has been seen, was, with the 3rd, the best in the North Korean People's Army. With the 3rd it had taken Seoul and bore the honorary title: Seoul Division. It had carried the fight south from the Han bridgehead at Yongdongpo and had performed with distinction at Taejon. Its commander, Major General Lee Kwon Mu, was a friend of Premier Kim Il Sung. General Lee had been a soldier since his youth, had marched with the famous Communist Chinese 8th Route Army and served as a lieutenant in the Russian Army. He had also been the North Korean People's Army's first chief of staff, though he was later mysteriously relieved and sent into obscurity. But Kim had called his friend back to command the 4th, and by August, the forty-year-old Lee had won his nation's highest military honors: Order of Hero of the Korean Democratic People's Republic and Order of the National Flag, First Class.

It was General Lee and his replacement-replenished 4th Division, about 7,000 men, who were to attack from the west below Taegu while the overwhelming bulk of the invading force struck from the north and northwest.

The point of attack was the Naktong Bulge or bend, where the river makes a big curve around an area roughly seven miles long, north-south, and four miles wide, west-east. Within this bulge lies the road to Yongsan and behind that the rail junction of Miryang, about 20 air miles southeast of Taegu. Yongsan-Miryang was obviously vital, and on August 4, General Lee had his 4th Division in place to attack it from the west bank of the Naktong Bulge. His opponent, Major General Church, was also well aware of the importance of this sector, as well as of the impending assault. On August 4 he issued this order to men of his 24th Division holding the Bulge:

> ... There will be no withdrawal nor need there be any if each and every man contributes his share to the preparation [of the defense], and, if attacked, has the will to fight it out here.
>
> Every soldier will under all circumstances retain his weapon, ammunition, and his entrenching tool. Without these he ceases to be a soldier capable of defending himself. Many of our losses have been occasioned by failure to dig a foxhole when the time permitted.

Around midnight on August 5 red and yellow flares burst over the Naktong and about 800 North Korean soldiers, many of them naked with their clothing bundled high on their heads, crossed the river swimming or on rafts. They reached the other side near the top of the Bulge and struck out southeastward through a draw in the direction of the Yongsan road. Another crossing attempt above them was beaten back with heavy casualties by the 34th Infantry.

But the men moving through the draw quickly overran an American mortar position and forced a withdrawal. They had their bridgehead, and they fought to hold it, while more troops were fed into it—and North Korean engineers on the west bank busied themselves constructing "underwater bridges." Actually the underwater bridges were shallow fords made of sandbags, logs and rocks, and built about a foot below the surface of the water. If constructed in muddy water, they were almost impossible to detect from the air. The North Koreans threw many of them across the Naktong, and by August 11 had moved trucks, heavy mortars and twelve artillery pieces over the river and into position to repulse a strong counterattack of the U. S. 9th and 19th Infantry at a place called Obong-ni.

The next day, still pulling regiments out of divisions and forming them into task forces, Walker sent parts of the 23rd and 27th Infantry to clean out smaller enemy holds southeast of Yongsan. But the penetration around Obong-ni in the Bulge held on and began expanding. By August 15 all of General Church's strikes at the Bulge had failed. It was because of this worsening situation, as well as because of the east coast action, that the Eighth Army commander had pulled back Task Force Kean from its advance on the left and put the 1st Marine Brigade in reserve near Miryang. Concerned, Walker went to Church's command post and said: "I'm giving you the Marine Brigade. I want this situation cleaned up, and quick!"

Walker returned to his command post and gave the orders which sent the Marines marching north, his own concern over Yongsan-Miryang and confidence in the brigade echoed in the daily report which a British military observer sent to his superiors in Tokyo next day:

> The situation is critical and Miryang may be lost. The enemy have driven a division-sized salient across the Naktong. More will cross the river tonight. If Miryang is lost Taegu becomes untenable and we will be faced with a withdrawal from Korea. I am heartened that the Marine Brigade will move against the Naktong salient tomorrow. They are faced with impossible odds, and I have no valid reason to substantiate it, but I have a feeling they will halt the enemy.
>
> I realize my expression of hope is unsound, but these Marines have the swagger, confidence and hardness that must have been in Stonewall Jackson's Army of the Shenandoah. They remind me of the Coldstreams at Dunkerque. Upon this thin line of reasoning, I cling to the hope of victory.[1]

The Marines struck at Obong-ni, or No-Name Ridge as they called it, the morning of August 7. Twice they attacked, and twice they were hurled back, but by nightfall they had clawed their way to the summit of two of the ridge's hills.

They resumed the attack next day, until a nest of four Communist machine guns barred their advance. Once more the ground observer called for an air strike. The target was marked with a smoke rocket, and a Corsair flown by Captain John Kelley dove down to plant a 500-pound bomb squarely amid the enemy guns. The explosion was so close it momentarily stunned the watching Marines. But then, the blast still echoing in the surrounding hills, they rose and swept through the destroyed position, their rush gaining momentum until they had taken No-Name Ridge and had put the broken enemy to flight.

"From that moment," General Craig reported, "the issue west of Yongsan was no longer in doubt. A routed enemy fled westward, racing desperately from the continued ground and air assault of the Marines, who, before the day was over, accounted for the destruction of more than 4,000 enemy troops."

The pursuit carried as far as the river, and there, said the log of the carrier *Sicily*, "The enemy was killed in such numbers that the river was definitely discolored with blood."

While the spectacular victory won at No-Name Ridge eased the threat of the isolation of Taegu, it also encouraged General Walker and the Eighth Army to continue the defensive battle raging simultaneously northwest and north of Taegu. Here Walker's forces defended a line following the Naktong's east bank as it wound its way for roughly 50 air miles north of Tuksong-dong through Waegwan to Naktong-ni, and then turned east to run another 30 air miles. All of it, of course, was not defended. Some divisions held as much as 30 miles, and there was contact of the most elementary sort between them. Along this line Walker had disposed the 1st Cavalry Division, the 27th Infantry and the ROK 1st and 6th Divisions. Opposing them were the enemy 1st, 3rd, 10th, 13th and 15th Divisions, with tanks of the 105th Armored Brigade. These units were to deliver the main thrust at Taegu, helped, of course, by the 4th Division throwing a roadblock across the escape route from the ROK provisional capital. Its importance may be judged from a troop exhortation dated August 13 and found on the body of an enemy colonel:

> Kim Il Sung has directed that the war be carried out so that its final victory can be realized by 15 August, fifth anniversary of the liberation of Korea.
>
> Our victory lies before your eyes. Young soldiers! You are fortunate in that you are able to participate in the battle for our final victory. Young soldiers, the capture of Taegu lies in the crossing of the Naktong River. . . .
>
> Pledge of all fighting men: We pledge with our life, no matter what hardships and sacrifice lie before us, to bear it and put forth our full effort to conclude the crossing of the Naktong River. Young men! Let us protect our glorious pride by completely annihilating the enemy!

That biggest Naktong crossing began the night of August 5, simultaneously with the 4th's to the south, and it struck the blows which sent some of the ROK units reeling back as much as 25 miles. All along the northern front the perimeter contracted south toward Taegu. The provisional capital was brought under sporadic shellfire from the west bank of the Naktong, a bare seven miles away, and the city was ordered cleared of a civilian population which had swelled from a normal 300,-000 to an estimated 800,000. The ROK government itself fled to Pusan, the last stopping place on the peninsula. Perhaps as many as 600,000 wretched refugees streamed southward after it, clogging the roads and multiplying the difficulties of the Eighth Army as it fought to hold the city with its vital airfield and communications. Once again General Walker had to call for a troubleshooter.

This time it was Colonel Mike Michaelis and his 27th Infantry Wolfhounds, probably the outstanding Army unit in Korea. Walker sent the Wolfhounds north to hold the Naktong Valley corridor running from Sangju to Taegu. On either side of them were men of the ROK 1st Division, and here the enemy was held off while receiving casualties in the thousands. The Sangju-Taegu road became the avenue for repeated North Korean night attacks, and it was also renamed the Bowling Alley for the whanging of the enemy 85mm shells as the T-34s sent their red-hot armor-piercers hurtling up the road toward the American positions.

Directly west of Taegu, near Waegwan, the 1st Cavalry Division fought furiously to hold off crossing attempts by elements of the North Korean 3rd Division, the effectiveness of the American artillery fire testified to by a Communist soldier who wrote in his diary:

> Gradually advanced toward the river. Enemy shelling is fierce. Arrived at the shores of the river. The terrible enemy has sent up flares. The Naktong River is flowing quietly and evenly. Entered the river. After advancing 200 meters, shooting began with the firing of an enemy flare. The noise is ringing in my ears. Have already crossed the river. Occupied a hill. A new day is already breaking.

The new day was August 9, and thereafter, the fight went back and forth around Waegwan, and also around the critical Tabu-dong area held by the ROKs. Crossings were being made everywhere, and soon the fighting split off into dozens of actions, large and small, the Americans and ROKs sometimes giving ground but always re-forming to counterattack and drive the enemy back to the Naktong's west bank. American airplanes ranged over the battlefield, bombing and strafing the North Koreans' daylight movements and steadily whittling at the T-34s' vital edge in armor. Once, the situation became so critical that the big Superforts were called on to make tactical bombing of enemy troops. An oblong about seven miles long and perhaps three miles wide was marked off west of the river above Waegwan, and nearly 100 B-29s dropped 850 tons of bombs into it in a well-advertised "carpet bombing."

But the bombing had little effect, and the enemy continued to stream to the attack from that area, often driving helpless crowds of refugees before them to block the vision of United Nations troops while they themselves slipped around to the rear to set up roadblocks. The fight for Taegu raged on until August 24, and during it fresh evidence of Communist atrocities was produced. On August 17 the 5th Cavalry Regiment retook Hill 303 around Waegwan and found 26 American soldiers who had been bound and sprayed with burp-gun bullets.

> The boys lay packed tightly, shoulder to shoulder, lying on their sides, curled like babies sleeping in the sun. Their feet, bloodied and bare, from walking on the rocks, stuck out stiffly. ... All had hands tied behind their backs, some with cord, others with regular issue army communication wire. Only a few of the hands were clenched.[2]

It was this atrocity which led General MacArthur to broadcast an announcement on August 20, telling Premier Kim Il Sung: "I shall hold you and your commanders criminally accountable under the rules and precedents of war." Leaflets carrying the MacArthur announcements were dropped while the First Naktong Battle continued to rage. But the enemy's blows gradually grew fainter, and on August 24, with the strongest North Korean drive apparently stopped cold just 13 miles above Taegu, General Walker was able to say: "Taegu is certainly saved."

The words were barely out of Walker's mouth before the

North Koreans were again attacking in prelude to their greatest offensive since they had sped south from Seoul.

Chapter Twelve

THE Great Naktong Offensive launched by the North Korean People's Army lasted from late August to mid-September. It was commanded by General Kim Chaik, who had apparently taken over from General Chai Ung Jun after the drive south from Seoul began to slow down. Kim had thirteen infantry divisions, one armored division and two armored brigades, a force fairly evenly divided between Lieutenant General Kim Ung's I Corps still operating in the west, and Lieutenant General Kim Mu Chong's II Corps still fighting in the east. In all there were about 98,000 men, an increase of 10 percent over the original invasion force. There were also about 50 new T-34 tanks. But one-third of General Kim Chaik's army was formed of raw recruits, and worse, his decision to pursue the tactics of following all the roads to Pusan and fighting whomever he met —good enough when all the advantages were North Korean— was unwisely made in the face of an enemy now his superior in every way. For by the end of August the United Nations force commanded by General Walker had twice as many men as the enemy, its tanks outnumbered the enemy's five to one, its artillery and transport were distinctly superior, and its control of air and sea remained unchallenged.

By September 1, Walker's ground forces stood at 180,000, of which 91,500 were ROKs and the remainder American except for 1,500 newly arrived British soldiers. These men, the first non-Americans to join the United Nations command, comprised a battalion of the Middlesex Regiment which formed the British 27th Infantry Brigade commanded by Brigadier Basil Coad. Thus Walker's ground formations included five ROK divisions, four U. S. Army infantry divisions approaching full strength, the British Brigade and the much larger Marine Brigade. To this were added 34,000 men in the Far Eastern Air Force—including 330 Australians—and 36,000 men of the U. S. Naval Forces, Far East, now grown from its original complement of 14 ships to more than 150 vessels. Some of these were carriers which launched Navy and Marine planes to support Walker's ground troops, or mighty dreadnoughts such as the battleship *Missouri*. The British task force under Admiral Andrews was also still in action.

Logistically, the Navy and Air Force had given Walker great service. An idea of the buildup carried on while the Pusan Perimeter held off the enemy may be gained from the record of the Red Ball Express, the daily rail and water service carrying supplies from Yokohama to Sasebo to Pusan. The Red Ball Express began July 23, and was soon able to bring supplies to Korea in an average of sixty to seventy hours. Its capacity rose from 308 tons on August 5 to 949 tons on August 25.

Among those vital weapons brought to Korea were the medium Sherman and Pershing tanks and one battalion of the big Pattons, which matched or surpassed the Russian-built T-34s. By the end of August the dread of enemy armor had vanished. In all, there were 500 U. S. medium tanks in Korea by the third week of August, together with 30 lights used primarily for scouting.

The problem of caring for South Korea's uprooted civilian population was also nearly solved. After widespread screening —a simple matter of determining whether or not civilian robes covered the uniform and weapons of North Korean soldiers— the refugees had been moved south from the combat zone to about sixty camps which the South Korean government had established in the Taegu-Pusan area. The U. S. 25th Infantry Division alone cleared 120,000 civilians from its sector in mid-August, while the 24th evacuated another 100,000. Slightly smaller movements were conducted by the 1st Cavalry Division and the ROK divisions. Enemy guerrilla operations fell off considerably, especially after the United Nations troops adopted the custom of shooting anyone in civilian clothes who moved at night.

Meanwhile from 30,000 to 40,000 South Korean young men were being fed into the ranks of American units in Korea, under a plan officially labeled the Korean Augmentation to the U. S. Army, but more popularly known and derided as "the buddy system." Ordered on August 15 by General MacArthur, the buddy system was intended to fill the battle-depleted ranks of the four U. S. infantry divisions in Korea, as well as the 7th Division in Japan where Operation Flushout had stripped many units of men needed as replacements in Korea. Some young South Koreans would also find their way into the 3rd Infantry Division, recently ordered to move from the United States to Korea.

The Koreans were recruited by the ROK Army and legally belonged to it. They were paid and administered by the Republic of Korea, although they received American rations and equipment. The idea was to train them on the spot—in battle, if necessary—by pairing them off with American "buddies" who would teach them the tricks of war. Occasionally the method of their recruitment differed not at all from the gunpoint conscription used by the enemy. Many recruits were merely picked up from the streets of Pusan and Taegu. Schoolboys still carried their schoolbooks when they arrived in camp, and one recruit who had left home to obtain medicine for his wife still had the medicine with him when he reached Japan.

Their performance with the American units varied from occasional excellence to a more general grade of fair to poor. Here is one report from an officer in the 25th Division:

> When a fresh batch arrived our First Sergeant ran them through a brief schooling on methods of attack, and they were ready for us. Recon Company's ROK contingent ate with us (our menu plus a huge, steaming plate of rice), but otherwise was a force apart. About sixty ROKs were assigned to each Recon platoon, under the command of an American lieutenant, as support for the Recon platoon leader. In other words, each Recon platoon had two U. S. officers; one for the Americans, the other for the ROKs. I had the latter job for a few weeks. On some occasions I controlled forces consisting of nearly one hundred ROKs,

plus ten or twelve GIs scattered throughout for control. At other times I had a fifty-fifty combination. Sometimes the Americans predominated.

It is difficult for me to evaluate the Koreans who augmented our ranks. All in all, however, I was not impressed by my charges and was happy to see the last of them. Mere recruits, they simply had not had time to become soldiers, and I used them for little more than carrying ammunition and rations. On the occasions I had to use them for fighting I spread my GIs around and prayed that nothing of consequence would happen.

My ROKs were always hungry, and never did understand that the cardboard box of C rations was meant for one day's subsistence. Often, an hour after doling out the one-box-per-man I have heard my interpreter ask me for more "chop-chop." The Koreans had already eaten their entire day's supply! Invariably they fell asleep when on guard, requiring constant checking by the Americans. And to make matters worse, most Koreans I have observed love to greet the morning sun with a song. This habit did not always fit into our security plan.

In one action I had spread my ROKs in a half circle position, with GIs posted here and there along the line for control. Late in the morning one lone sniper fired at us, and immediately my ROKs went to pieces. Hysterical, they lay on the ground with faces pressed into the earth, weapons pointed in the general direction of the enemy, firing madly, wasting ammunition, completely out of hand. There was only one way to straighten out the situation, so my GIs and I went from ROK to ROK, kicking them and dragging them bodily to where they could see. We eventually succeeded in quieting them down, and when the enemy attacked us later in the day my ROKs held pretty well.[1]

Naturally the fear of these unfortunate men so recently dragooned into service would be multiplied by the lack of communications between them and their guardians. It was chiefly on this insurmountable rock that the buddy system foundered, until it was quietly dropped at the end of the year. South Koreans remaining with U. S. units thereafter were used chiefly as laborers who dug fortifications or carried heavy weapons and supplies, though some were employed as scouts.

In early September, however, they were still on the lines

fighting to hold off that massive onslaught which nearly succeeded when their countrymen in the ROK I Corps were sent staggering back toward Taegu.

Although the North Korean offensive was scheduled to begin on August 31, the 12th Division in the north jumped the gun by four days. This unit had supposedly been "routed" in earlier battles. In fact, most of the South Koreans believed that the failure of the First Naktong Battle had put the enemy on the defensive. They believed the war would be over by Thanksgiving, and there had even been a petition from the South Korean government to MacArthur asking that the enemy be cleared from the southern half of the peninsula in time for the fall rice harvest. But the enemy 12th Division struck hard in the early morning of August 27, rolling back the ROK 17th Regiment and forcing the entire I Corps to withdraw. The enemy gained a dozen miles and was poised to cut the lateral Taegu-Pohang road.

General Walker became so concerned that he formed another American task force which he placed, together with the faltering ROK I Corps, under the command of Major General John Coulter. When Coulter took over and ordered the I Corps command to counterattack immediately, he was refused with the remark, "Too many enemy, too many casualties, troops tired." In desperation General Walker issued a special statement to the ROK Army saying: "It is my belief that the overextended enemy is making his last gasp. . . ."

Such it turned out to be, but at the time the North Korean assault sounded more like a roar to the embattled ROKs. Still, they rallied, assisted by the U. S. 27th Wolfhounds whom Walker rushed into position behind them. By August 31 the northern situation had so improved that Walker was able to move the 27th to the south. It was well that he did, for the area around Masan had flamed up in the first of four furious battles, any one of which could have scored the breakthrough that would seal the doom of Taegu, and perhaps even the United Nations forces in Korea.

On this southwestern front around Masan the enemy pushed the 25th Division back within 30 miles of Pusan. Here the fighting was so fierce that the famous Battle Mountain changed hands thirteen times before it finally ended in permanent possession of the United Nations. And even as the southern front became inflamed, the North Koreans on the east coast were once more fighting their way into Pohang, while Yonil Airfield beneath it and the eastern corridor to Pusan were again menaced. This threat was finally repelled by the combined strokes of the U. S. 24th Infantry Division and the ROK II Corps, assisted by the close support of Marine and Navy carrier-based aircraft and naval gunfire.

And then from the west came the fiercest blow of all. Four divisions, nearly 30,000 troops, came swarming over the Naktong to secure a dozen bridgeheads on the east bank. They drove deep into the defenses of the U. S. 2nd Infantry Division, splitting the Americans in two and sweeping past No-Name Ridge until they had penetrated as deep as 12 miles. Once more Taegu's rear was threatened at the Miryang rail junction, and once again Walker called on the Marine Brigade. The Marines made a fighting entry into the line, having to battle to reach the jump-off point assigned them by Walker. Then they counterattacked and regained lost ground. The 2nd Division rallied, and at last the enemy assault fell apart under a series of Marine-Army counterstrokes.

Meanwhile, Taegu was imperiled from still other quarters: from the north where the Communists came down the same mountain passes they had followed in mid-August, and at a thinly defended Naktong sector just southwest of the city. The northern drive finally collapsed of exhaustion after the North Koreans had rolled back the ROK 1st Division and the U. S. 1st Cavalry Division to within seven miles of Taegu. The southwest thrust was parried when Walker put the British 27th Brigade into the line.

These were the four main actions which, with the earlier attack against the ROK I Corps, represented General Kim Chaik's late-summer offensive against the Pusan Perimeter. None, of course, was so clearly separated from the other or so plainly marked out—not even on the big maps in the Taegu headquarters where Bulldog Walker calmly hung on. It was rather in a hundred battles that the Communists were hurled back, with Walker only choosing to commit his reserves in those places where the enemy had broken through or seemed about to do so. Along the Naktong the fighting was especially chaotic: here a ferry crossing was lost, there a bridgehead was erased; some sectors changed hands repeatedly, others sat out the battle like quiet islands in a sea of conflict. Always, the United Nations forces counted on their air, their heavier artillery—markedly in the east where naval gunfire was brought to bear—their superior armor and the great advantage of their interior lines to hold off Communist attacks, which, from a tactical point of view, were nothing more—nor less—than swarmings. To these advantages were added the increasing valor of General Walker's American troops and the general's own decisive movement of his forces within his perimeter.

If the Communist generals had changed tactics the results might have been different. They had already erred in July by overestimating the extent of American intervention and failing to appreciate how badly shattered the ROK Army was. They missed their chance then by not rushing directly and quickly to seize the prize of Pusan. They failed again in August and September by not concentrating their forces. Their piecemeal attacks perfectly fitted the troop-juggling defense forced on General Walker by the intermittent arrival of his reinforcements. If the North Koreans had massed at any one point to score a breakthrough, they might have forced Walker to give up his Naktong line and retreat into a smaller perimeter—might even have forced him to evacuate.

It may well have been that the terrible, ubiquitous American air made it impossible for the North Koreans to mass, or that this same factor made it necessary for them to disperse their supply lines. Whatever the reason, they did spread themselves thin around the Pusan Perimeter, and as they hung there, beating in futile fury on the Taegu gate, one of the great strategic counterstrokes of history slammed the Seoul door shut behind them.

Part II

The Road Back

Chapter One

THE single stroke which was to reverse the Korean War as absolutely as a change in the wind had been conceived by General MacArthur during the first week of disaster. It was then that he came to Korea to reconnoiter the battlefront, standing on a hill overlooking Seoul while the human debris of defeat swirled around him.

At that moment MacArthur decided upon the delaying action which would slow the enemy advance and then keep him in place while an amphibious operation struck him in the rear and destroyed him.

This, of course, was the plan in broad outline. Upon his return to Tokyo, MacArthur ordered his staff to get busy on the details: the time and place of invasion, the forces to be used.

But the North Korean Army kept frustrating these details by refusing to sit still for destruction. Early landings by either the 1st Cavalry Division or the 1st Marine Brigade had to be abandoned while these two units were fed into the battle to stave off MacArthur's own ruin. The need for men in Korea also stripped the 7th Infantry Division of many of its veterans and the attempt to replace them by the buddy system proved a failure. Still, MacArthur held to his vision of the daring surprise blow against the extended North Korean supply line. To defend by attack appealed to his gambler's nature. A long, slow, bloody slugging match back up the peninsula did not. More, MacArthur was an ardent exponent of amphibious warfare who had made masterly use of it during his World War II campaigns. By early July MacArthur had decided that he could hurt the enemy most, both psychologically and physically, by landing at Inchon, the seaport for Seoul. Any landing to the rear, of course, would force the enemy to fight in two places at once. But the one at Inchon had other, greater attractions. Inchon itself was the second-best port in Korea and it was almost in the heart of the city which was the nation's capital, which possessed the nation's best airport at nearby Kimpo, and which sat astride all the supply routes to the North Korean Army in the south. This last was the overpowering consideration, for as MacArthur said later:

> The history of war proves that nine out of ten times an army has been destroyed because its supply lines have been cut off. Everything the Red Army shoots, and all the additional replenishment he needs, comes through Seoul.

MacArthur's plan, in its final form, was for the 1st Marine Division to land at Inchon and capture Seoul, while the 7th Infantry Division followed the Marines and wheeled south to assume a blocking position. These ground forces, to be known as the U. S. X Corps and to operate apart from the Eighth Army, were to be commanded by MacArthur's chief of staff, Major General Edward Almond. The naval commander of the expedition, to be known as Joint Task Force Seven, would be the Seventh Fleet's Vice-Admiral Arthur Struble. And so, on July 10, MacArthur asked the Joint Chiefs of Staff to release the 1st Marine Division to him for this operation.

The request was refused. General Omar Bradley, then chairman of the Joint Chiefs, was a well-known opponent of amphibious warfare in general and Marines in particular. In 1949 he told Congress he doubted if large-scale amphibious warfare would ever again be needed and suggested that most of the big ones of the past had been made by the Army, not the Marines. Five days after the refusal of his request, MacArthur, who had not yet divulged his plans for Inchon, sent this message to the Joint Chiefs:

> I strongly request reconsideration of my need for a Marine division. Its availability is absolutely essential to achieve a decisive stroke. If not made available, a much longer and more expensive effort both in blood and money will result. I must have the Ma-

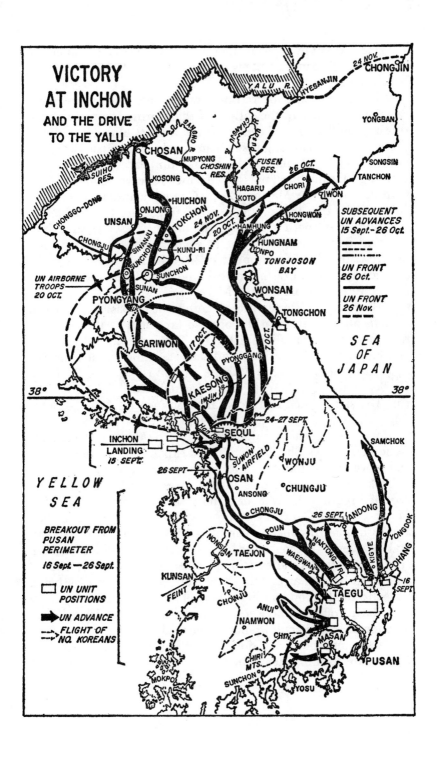

rine division by September 10. I cannot too strongly emphasize the complete urgency of my request.

MacArthur's plea for reconsideration met with a favorable reaction. On July 19 the call-up of the Marine Reserve was authorized by President Truman. It was a cruel blow for many of those men who had fought again and again from Guadalcanal to Okinawa and had come home to take up peaceful pursuits, remaining, meanwhile, in the Marine Reserve. But General Clifton Cates, the Marine Corps Commandant, had told the Joint Chiefs that it was "impossible" to get the 1st Marine Division up to strength without calling up the Reserves, and thus, the next day, orders went out to some 5,000 Americans: "Report to Camp Pendleton for extended active duty." By August 4, another 29,000 had been recalled, and the Marines were transferring veterans from the 2nd Marine Division on the East Coast to the 1st on the West, while cleaning out embassies and naval stations all over the world, going so far afield as the Mediterranean where a battalion of the 6th Marines was redesignated 3rd Battalion, 7th Marines, and sent steaming toward the Sea of Japan and rendezvous with its parent 1st Marine Division. On September 15, the date of the Inchon invasion, the 1st Marine Division, which had stood at 7,789 men on June 30, went into battle as a small army of 26,000 well-armed and well-equipped men, the result, according to Marine Lieutenant General Lemuel Shepherd, of "an expansion, augmentation, and movement without parallel in American military history."

This was the Pentagon's ultimate response to MacArthur's repeated requests for Marines, and it scarcely seems to bear out Major General Courtney Whitney's charge that his chief had always to plan his Inchon gamble with one hand tied by General Bradley's "preconceived notions" on amphibious warfare. It was true that Bradley still mistakenly believed waterborne assault to be outdated, but there were other objections being raised to the Inchon landing—many of them by those very Navy and Marine officers who were the world's most experienced commanders in this difficult branch of the military art.

These numerous professional objections were summarized by Lieutenant Commander Arlie Capps, gunfire support officer for

Rear Admiral James Doyle, who was to be the Inchon amphibious commander.

"We drew up a list of every conceivable natural and geographic handicap," said Capps, "and Inchon had 'em all."

Admiral Doyle's communications officer, Commander Monroe Kelly, said: "Make up a list of amphibious 'don'ts' and you have an exact description of the Inchon operation. A lot of us planners felt that if the Inchon operation worked, we'd have to rewrite the textbook."

Chief among these "don'ts" were the enormous Inchon tides, the second highest in the world with an average 29-foot rise and fall of the sea. Some days the rise and fall measured 36 feet. The tide also moved rapidly, and a boat could be stranded on the mud flats in as little as ten minutes. The mud itself was another problem. Inchon's numerous harbor islands not only heaped the tides high but also broke up wave action. On a windless day the surface of the sea was as smooth as glass, and so, over the centuries, the great unruffled ebb and flow of the tides had built vast mudbanks which ran out from shore as far as 6,000 yards. To clear them, landing ships (LSTs) could only approach the shore on days when the tide rose a minimum of 29 feet, and there were only two or three days a month when this would happen in daylight. Thus, as the naval historian Commander Walter Karig has said, Inchon was "the first time in military history that the date of an invasion was dictated by the moon." MacArthur could only choose September 15, October 11 or November 3 for his D-Day. He chose, of course, September 15.

But, said Admiral Doyle, "Inchon had other objectionable features. For example, we lacked complete information about how much and where dredging had been done in the harbor. Another obstacle was the limited facilities there, even after we won it. Its pier and dock space was small, and the harbor wasn't big enough ever to make it a real logistics base through which we could supply and maintain a big army. The available landing points were spread over a four-mile stretch of the waterfront and consisted for the most part of piers and sea walls. So we had to plan on improving the existing facilities in order that unloading could proceed at an acceptable rate."

"Another major obstacle," said Lieutenant Commander

Capps, "was the very restricted channel and operating space for our bombardment ships. They would be forced to stay in the channel to avoid grounding in the mud, and because of a three-to-five-knot current, would even have to anchor there in order to hold their positions. It was like operating a ship on a dead-end street. There wasn't enough turn-around room or maneuvering space. We felt certain that the Reds were aware of this predicament and that our ships would be sitting ducks out there in the channel."

Major General Oliver Smith, the tall, white-haired scholarly Marine who commanded the 1st Marine Division, did not like Inchon because his troops would be required to land almost in the heart of a city over a seawall which could be easily defended. Worse, the tides dictated that the landing could not be made until 5:30 P.M. Sunset the night of September 15 was expected at 6:43 P.M., meaning that the Marines would have little more than one hour in which to land and fight inland into an Oriental city with a population of about 250,000 and through a port area where warehouses and similar buildings might well be fortified to the teeth, and then to reorganize their positions to hold off the inevitable enemy counterattack. To this difficulty of executing the assault was added the Navy's worries about leaving landing ships stranded on the mud flats. The Marines would need 3,000 tons of supply to guarantee their fight, and by the time these could be unloaded the fast-moving tides would have receded, leaving the LSTs high and dry on the mudbanks, very much those "large stationary targets" of World War II notoriety. As the Navy planners said, the LSTs would be "helplessly vulnerable to enemy fire," and so eight of them were calmly written off, although their officers and ships companies were not, of course, informed that their loss "had to be accepted."

The most serious natural obstacle of all was a tiny pyramid of land with the fanciful name of Moontip Island, or Wolmi-do. Standing just west of Inchon, to which it was connected by a narrow causeway, little Wolmi guarded all the approaches to the inner harbor. It was well fortified. More, Wolmi rose 351 feet above water and was the highest point of land in the Inchon area. Its guns could strike at the Marines attempting to storm the port's seawalls to the north and south. Wolmi would have to be captured to secure the flanks of both landings, but before it could, Wolmi would also have to be subjected to several days of bombardment by air and sea. And this, of course, would forfeit that advantage of surprise so necessary to MacArthur's plan.

Actually, as the Inchon invasion plan progressed, it became known among Tokyo newsmen as "Operation Common Knowledge." Unlike the Pacific invasions of World War II launched from lonely island bases where all plans could be kept secure, Inchon was to be staged out of Japan—a country alive with spies and Communist sympathizers. One week before the landing a North Korean-Japanese spy ringleader named Yoshimatsu Iwamura was captured, according to U. S. Army accusations, with top-secret plans of the invasion in his possession. Nor did high officials remain mum. Syngman Rhee said, "We are about ready to go," and General Walker, asked when the United Nations would take the offensive, replied: "In a very short time." Some secrecy may have been obtained by removing the word "Inchon" from all plans, but there was no doubt that the enemy could judge from the massing of the invasion fleet in Japan that he was about to feel the lash of the American amphibious whip. He might not know where, that was all, and thus it was decided that although the harbor fortress of Wolmi-do must be knocked out by preinvasion bombardment, the enemy had to be kept guessing by two diversionary air attacks—one to the south at Kunsan and another to the north at Chinnampo—while the mighty battleship *Missouri* would batter Samchok directly opposite Inchon on the east coast.

Two final tactical objections to Inchon concerned the possibility of enemy mines in the harbor and the invasion force's apparently complete ignorance of enemy dispositions on shores. As Marine intelligence stated it: "Sadly lacking as was information on the objective area, more so was that on the enemy in the area." Early reports spoke of only 1,500 to 2,000 North Korean troops around Inchon. To check them, the Navy sent Lieutenant Eugene Clark on a perilous scouting mission through the harbor islands. Clark was put ashore the night of September 1 on the island of Yonghung-do, thereafter spending a hair-raising two weeks fending off enemy attacks at the head of his private "army" of Korean civilians. Despite his exploits, Clark was unable to provide exact figures on enemy strength. He did, however, succeed in measuring the Inchon seawall and in locating the position of 20 of Wolmi-do's coastal guns. His most important contribution was to light the lighthouse on Palmi-do the night of September 14 and thus guide the American warships up Flying Fish Channel into the harbor.

Strategically, the one big objection to Inchon was: how would the Communist Chinese react? By the latter part of August it was already known that the Chinese Reds were moving troops north. By mid-September the Communist Chinese 66th and 26th Armies had been shifted from Shanghai to a position supporting two other armies around Tsingtao due east of Inchon across the Yellow Sea, while the 50th and 20th Armies had joined the Fourth Field Army (42nd, 40th and 38th Armies) in Manchuria at a point north of the Yalu River. As the Chinese Communists well knew, a successful landing at Inchon-Seoul would probably mean ruin for the Communist North Korean divisions at the Pusan Perimeter. Would the Chinese Communists sit by and allow this to happen, or would they strike the American invasion fleet when it was most vulnerable—jammed up inside a narrow harbor?

These, then, were the outstanding objections among the myriad raised against the Inchon operation. MacArthur did not ignore them; he studied them and weighed Inchon's drawbacks against Inchon's attractions, deciding that the impossible port was still the only place where he could achieve his purpose of destroying the enemy. He held to this almost visionary goal with a near-mystical assurance. When the Joint Chiefs of Staff themselves came to Tokyo to dissuade him, he was invincible.

The meeting took place on August 23, when General J. Lawton Collins, the Army Chief of Staff, and Admiral Forrest Sherman, Chief of Naval Operations, joined the final Inchon conference at the Dai Ichi Palace. Also present were MacArthur; Major General Almond, his chief of staff who was to command the X Corps; MacArthur's air commander, General Stratemeyer; Lieutenant General Shepherd, commander of Marines in the Pacific; Admirals Joy, Doyle and Struble. The conference began with routine military matters, Doyle's staff presenting a detailed eighty-minute briefing. MacArthur, who was to transform the meeting into one of high drama, sat puffing his corncob pipe, occasionally interrupting one of the speakers to ask a question. Then Admiral Doyle arose and said:

"General, I have not been asked nor have I volunteered my opinion about this landing. If I were asked, however, the best I can say is that Inchon is not impossible."

MacArthur nodded, and General Collins began to present his objections. Inchon, he said, was too far to the rear of the battle to have the effect MacArthur envisioned. To make the landing would require the restoration of the Marine Brigade to the 1st Marine Division, and thus seriously weaken General Walker's hard-pressed Pusan Perimeter. It would be safer, said General Collins, to land at Kunsan about 100 air miles south of Inchon, a port with fewer natural obstacles.

Admiral Sherman seconded the arguments of his colleague on the Joint Chiefs, and for the same reason. There was a momentary silence. MacArthur, the master showman, was allowing tension to rise in the room, waiting for the sound of a shifting chair before he began to speak. He did so in a casual, conversational tone, occasionally jabbing his pipe in the air to underline a point, stopping twice to refill it, leaning forward with his elbows on his desk, his voice rising to a resonance once or twice, then turning husky or dropping to a dramatic whisper.

The very arguments made against his plan, said MacArthur, would ensure its success. "For the enemy commander will reason that no one would be so brash as to make such an attempt." He began drawing a lesson from history. General Wolfe had succeeded at Quebec, he said, because his men had scaled cliffs which the French General Montcalm had considered impossible to climb, and the same would be true of Inchon's tides and seawall.

Once more, MacArthur emphasized the boldness of his plan, how its success would capture the Oriental imagination and score a great victory for the United Nations. The troops who landed at Inchon would become the anvil on which Walker's troops would hammer an enemy forced into retreat by a severed supply line. The port of Kunsan, MacArthur continued, would

133

not achieve this. Kunsan was safer, but it was not far enough in the enemy's rear. It would merely make the North Koreans back up a few miles, and it would not cut their supply lines.

"The amphibious landing is the most powerful tool we have," he said. "To employ it properly, we must strike hard and deep into enemy territory." Inchon, he assured the meeting, would not fail—"and it will save a hundred thousand lives." Turning conversational again, MacArthur reminisced about his landings with the Navy in World War II.

"The Navy has never let me down in the past and I am positive it will not let me down this time. I realize that Inchon is a five-thousand-to-one gamble, but I'll accept it. I am used to taking those odds." He paused dramatically and his voice sank to a harsh whisper: "We shall land at Inchon, and I shall crush them!"

Only Admiral Sherman left the conference room unconvinced. The next day he spent another hour and a half with MacArthur, and emerged persuaded, saying: "I wish I had that man's confidence." Sherman and Collins returned to Washington, and on August 29 MacArthur received the following wire from the Joint Chiefs of Staff:

> We concur after reviewing the information brought back by General Collins and Admiral Sherman, in making preparations and executing a turning movement by amphibious forces on the west coast of Korea at Inchon. . . .

It seemed that the eloquent and passionate Douglas MacArthur had "sold it" again.* But there was one last objection, or vacillation as it may have been. In early September, with the 7th Infantry Division and 1st Marine Division all but embarked, but with the Great Naktong Offensive of the North Koreans seemingly about to hurl the United Nations into the sea, the Joint Chiefs of Staff asked MacArthur for his estimate "as to the feasibility and chance of success of projected operation on

*At a conference in Pearl Harbor during July, 1944, General MacArthur, having persuaded President Roosevelt that the Philippines, not Formosa, offered the best invasion route to Japan, is reported to have told an aide: "We've sold it!" (*History of United States Naval Operations in World War II*, Vol. XII, *Leyte*, Samuel Eliot Morison (Boston, 1958), fn. p. 10.)

planned schedule. . . ." This, says General Whitney, was the one message which "chilled him to the marrow of his bones." But MacArthur replied with a cable which, while reiterating his old arguments, assured the Joint Chiefs of "no slightest possibility" of the loss of the Pusan beachhead, while artfully pointing out that in any case it was too late to call the invasion off. Back came the message: "Approved."

The debate for the gamble had ended in a MacArthur victory, and now it was time to throw the dice.

Chapter Two

ON SEPTEMBER 13, with the invasion force of the North Korean People's Army still flailing wildly at the Pusan Perimeter, the United Nations struck the final blows at Wolmi-do which would pull the cork in the Inchon bottle.

How early the North Koreans became aware of the impending "deep envelopment" maneuver is not known. Surely, by September 13 they knew something was in the offing. Kunsan had been under fierce aerial attack since September 9, and three days later a ROK raiding party landed there supported by the strikes of carrier-based aircraft. In the north, a British task force hammered at Chinnampo. On the east coast a sizable U. S. bombardment force was prowling the Sea of Japan, with the mighty *Missouri* but one day's sail from joining the scheduled September 14th bombardment of Samchok.

Wolmi had also been hammered. Since September 10, carrier-based Marine Corsairs had been dumping thousands of tons of napalm fire bombs on the island fort, burning most of its buildings to the ground. Invasion could come in Inchon, too, absurd as that might have seemed to many North Korean officers. By the morning of September 13 there was probably no longer any doubt that Inchon was the point of attack, for on that date a Communist dispatch to Pyongyang was intercepted and decoded. It said:

> Ten enemy vessels are approaching Inchon. Many aircraft are bombing Wolmi-do. There is every indication the enemy will perform a landing. All units under my command are directed to be ready for combat; all units will be stationed in their given positions so that they may throw back enemy forces when they attempt their landing operation.

Though the message was signed "Commanding General," it was never discovered where or what he commanded. Otherwise, the report was accurate: there *were* ten ships approaching Inchon that morning, the gunfire group of Joint Task Seven. They were the U. S. cruisers *Toledo* and *Rochester*, the British cruisers *Kenya* and *Jamaica*, and the American destroyers *Gurke, Henderson, Collett, Swenson, DeHaven* and *Mansfield*— all commanded by red-mustachioed Rear Admiral John Higgins.

Higgins and his staff had worked out a daring plan to deal Wolmi her deathblows. They not only accepted the risk of the destroyers becoming "sitting ducks" when anchored in daylight against the current of narrow Flying Fish Channel, but turned it to their advantage. Being better targets, the destroyers would draw the fire of guns so far uncharted by Clark or American airmen. Because of this, the oldest destroyers in the Far East—but also those manned by the best gunners—had been chosen. The cruisers would give them covering fire from points seven to ten miles southwest of Wolmi, for Flying Fish Channel was too tricky for such big ships to be risked. If one of them was sunk in it, Joint Task Force Seven might never get into Inchon Harbor. Also, Higgins decided to send his destroyers in at low tide —both to spot minefields and to allow for the lowest possible depression of their guns.

It was a fortunate decision. Sailing warily up Flying Fish Channel, the leading *Mansfield*'s lookouts spotted a string of mines half-submerged in low muddy water. A round from

Gurke's 40-millimeters sent one of them exploding skyward in a geyser of smoke and water, and *Henderson* dropped off to destroy three more before the inrushing tide covered the rest. The column steamed north, past sampans and junks, approaching blackened, silent Wolmi at 1250 in the afternoon, dropping anchor and training their guns broadside, while white-robed Koreans crowded the shores of the harbor islands to watch the battle.

Bombardment was to begin at 1300, but at five minutes before that time Lieutenant Arthur White on *DeHaven* decided he couldn't wait. As his ship came upchannel, White had seen enemy soldiers running into a gun pit—and he had the position bore-sighted. At five minutes before one, White pushed the firing key. *DeHaven*'s five-inchers belched orange flame and smoke, the Wolmi battery went up in a burst of debris—and the battle was on.

It continued for an hour, with the American destroyers opening up with great deliberation, hurling their shells into preassigned areas. The North Korean guns remained silent for ten minutes. Then they returned the fire, on *Collett* at first, hitting her five times and forcing her to shift berths. After that *Gurke* and *Swenson* were hit, and young Lieutenant David Swenson, for whose uncle *Swenson* had been named, was killed by a fragment from a near miss. But each time a Wolmi gun opened up, it marked its own destruction—especially from the eight-inchers of *Toledo* and *Rochester* or the six-inch shells of *Kenya* and *Jamaica,* all of which had joined the cannonading. Then, with Wolmi all but obscured by smoke and dust, the American ships raised anchor and sailed south, having silenced many enemy guns at a cost of three ships damaged—one of them to the point of needing immediate repair—and one man killed and eight wounded.

The next day Admiral Higgins's gunfire group was back, battering Wolmi for a solid seventy-five minutes with hardly a shot fired in reply. When the ships departed, Wolmi was a helpless mass of drifting smoke and quivering flame, and then the American aircraft resumed bombing. By dusk, Wolmi was done—and that night the American armada came creeping up Flying Fish Channel.

There had been a typhoon scare. For three days the planners of General MacArthur's Far Eastern Command had been tensely plotting the movement of the 125-mile-an-hour winds known as Typhoon Kezia. It seemed certain that the storm and Joint Task Force Seven would arrive coincidentally in the Korean Strait. But then, on September 13, Typhoon Kezia veered north from the east coast of Japan, removing this unanticipated obstacle to the invasion.

Even so, the Sea of Japan was turbulent and angry with the winds of a violent backlash when, at about midnight of September 12, General MacArthur secretly boarded his flagship, *Mount McKinley,* and shoved off from Sasebo for Inchon. Throughout that night and the following day Joint Task Force Seven was buffeted by howling winds and mounting seas as it slipped through the Korea Strait following in the wake of the Marines who were to assault Wolmi-do. These were the men of the 3rd Battalion, Fifth Marines, under Lieutenant Colonel Robert Taplett. They and their equipment were stowed aboard the landing ship dock *Fort Marion* and the destroyer-transports *Bass, Diachenko* and *Wantuck.* They had sailed from Pusan on September 12 and were escorted north by British and New Zealand ships. They were well ahead of the bulk of Joint Task Force Seven carrying the rest of the Fifth Marines and all of the First Marine Regiment—the units which would storm the seawalls at Inchon—when September 14 dawned clear and relatively calm. There was only a brisk wind blowing across Korea from the east as these two echelons steamed north through the Yellow Sea.

At half-past twelve that night, the 3rd Battalion, Fifth Marines, and their ships had reached Inchon Harbor. Two hours later they sailed inside its mouth, following the long column of the gunfire ships, spaced about 700 yards apart as they worked their way north through Flying Fish Channel. Then they were rounding brightly lighted Palmi-do, unaware that the intrepid Lieutenant Clark was sitting on top of the lighthouse wrapped in a blanket, shivering, but delighted to see his country's ships approach. One of the Marine officers saw only the anomaly of a homing beacon in an enemy harbor, and he grinned and cracked: "All the comforts of home." At five-forty the gunfire ships resumed their cannonading and soon Wolmi was again

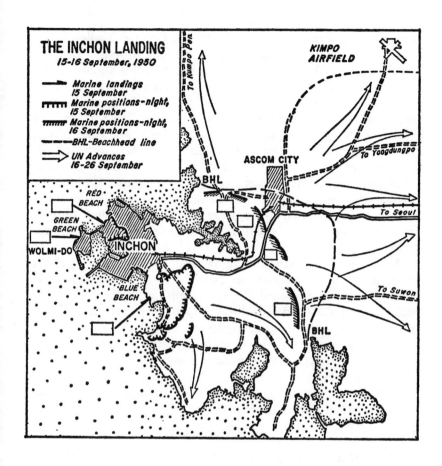

THE INCHON LANDING
15-16 September, 1950

Marine landings
15 September

Marine positions–night,
15 September

Marine positions–night,
16 September

BHL–Beachhead line

UN Advances
16-26 September

To Kimpo Pen.

KIMPO
AIRFIELD

ASCOM CITY

To Yongdungpo

BHL

RED
BEACH

GREEN
BEACH

WOLMI-DO

INCHON

To Seoul

BLUE
BEACH

To Suwon

BHL

aflame, a perfect target for the rocket ships which ran close inshore near daybreak to hurl 6,400 rockets into the island. Then
carrier-based Corsairs dropped from the skies to strafe the
beaches, and at 0627 the first wave of Marine landing boats had
ceased to orbit in the lee of the big ships, had fanned out in
assault formation—and was roaring into Wolmi.

The Marines went into Wolmi while white-robed Korean
civilians were scampering out from Inchon onto the mud flats,
there to seek refuge from the anticipated blasting of the seaport, as well as to watch the Marines hit the beaches. It was 0631,
just a minute past schedule, when the first of the landing boats
grounded up on Wolmi's northern shore and the ramps banged

down to disgorge the first of Lieutenant Colonel Taplett's Marines. They swept rapidly inland, moving through drifting smoke and the heavy smell of powder, meeting almost no resistance at first. Those of Wolmi's 500 defenders who survived the bombardment were still too dazed to fight back. In four more minutes another wave of green-clad "yellow-legs," as the North Koreans called the Marines after the leggings they wore, had stormed ashore. Ten more minutes and the bargelike utility landing ships had brought in nine tanks—three of them equipped with flamethrowers, three others mounting bulldozer blades, the remaining trio the normal medium killers. When one of them rumbled up to a cave and hurled a shell into its mouth, some thirty North Koreans stumbled out with upraised hands.

Resistance was generally light, and the Marines received their biggest surprise when six North Korean soldiers marched a naked comrade toward them, explaining that he was their officer whom they had forced to strip and surrender. But not all of the enemy were so agreeable. Some fought to the death and had to be rooted from their holes in a fight that lasted all morning. Others jumped into the harbor and tried to swim to Inchon. Forty-seven minutes after the Marines had landed, the American flag was flying from Wolmi's highest hill and Lieutenant Colonel Taplett radioed the fleet:

WOLMI-DO SECURED

MacArthur's great gamble had won. Wolmi had fallen at a cost of 20 Marines wounded, with about 120 North Koreans killed and another 180 captured. Many more North Koreans were buried in their holes and an unknown number had sneaked into Inchon along the causeway during the night. But the harbor fort had been stormed, and even though the major part of the operation—the twin assaults on Inchon—was yet to take place, Wolmi's fall all but guaranteed its success. Throughout the day, the guns of two artillery battalions were trundled into place on Wolmi to support the landings to either side of the island, while more tanks were brought ashore for movement over the causeway into the city.

So it was that Douglas MacArthur was filled with exultation when he saw the American flag fluttering over the hill at Wolmi, flung to the breeze from a stick lashed to a shattered tree. Seeing it, he realized that he was on the verge of one of the great strategic counterstrokes of all time, and he rose from his deck chair on the *Mount McKinley* to go below to write the message to Admiral Struble which said:

> The Navy and the Marines have never shown more brightly than this morning.

That afternoon, at 1645, the heaviest bombardment of the operation struck at Inchon in preparation for the evening landings. Cruisers, destroyers, rocket ships and airplanes massed their bombs and missiles. The bigger ships fired at known gun positions, or attempted to knock holes in the thick gray seawall girdling the harbor at heights up to 15 feet, hoping thereby to provide entry for the Marines. Many of the carrier-based airplanes went ranging far afield to destroy reinforcements and supplies which the North Koreans were belatedly rushing to the beleaguered port city. By that time, the North Koreans knew beyond doubt that the impossible landing was being attempted, and that Wolmi had been but the vital preliminary. They were in position, ready to resist, when, at 1730, the bombardment lifted and the Marines attacked two beaches simultaneously.

To the left or north of Wolmi was Red Beach, actually 1,000 feet of seawall designated as a "beach" or landing place. The Marines chosen to assault it carried hooked scaling ladders with them in amtracks. These men formed the two battalions of the Fifth Marines led by Lieutenant Colonel Murray, the man who had commanded at Masan and No-Name Ridge. When they reached the seawall, its top was still four feet above the prows of their boats. Some of the ladders caught and Marines went scrambling up them to vanish in the smoke. The hooks of others were too small, and the men either threw their buddies up-and-over bodily or went leapfrogging into battle. But the first wave landed without being fired at. It was the second and third waves, as well as the LSTs then waddling shoreward, which began to receive fire. One of the LSTs plowed into the seawall at a speed of six knots, the impact shattering the wall sufficiently so that, when the LST's bow doors swung open, bulldozers could clank off and begin covering slit trenches from which enemy rifle fire came. Unloading continued while the Fifth Marines stormed the hilltop cemetery which the Communists had fortified, thus ending Cemetery Hill's threat to the landing of the remaining waves.

On the right or south of Wolmi was Blue Beach, again actually a portion of the seawall, and against this went the First Marine Regiment, commanded by the celebrated Colonel Lewis ("Chesty") Puller, the most decorated man in Marine history. Here fifteen waves of amtracks and amtanks, as well as six waves of landing boats, brought the men ashore—and the dynamiting of entry points which followed nearly took the lives of the commanders of X Corps and Joint Task Force Seven.

Early in the afternoon Vice-Admiral Struble had brought his barge alongside *Mount McKinley* to take Major General Almond aboard. He wanted Almond, who had no amphibious experience, to observe the complications of a seaborne assault. As Puller's second and third waves began landing at Blue Beach, Struble's barge approached the seawall and an angry Marine sergeant bellowed: "Boat there! Get the hell out of here!" Struble called to the coxswain, who quickly took the admiral and the general out of range of the sergeant's charge, which shortly exploded and tore a hole in the wall. So the Blue Beach invasion continued, a 24-inch searchlight providing visibility in the gloom of gathering dusk and drifting smoke. Soon it was dark, but the Marines continued to press inland.

The anticipated nocturnal counterattack in force did not materialize, although the men on Blue Beach still had difficulty cleaning out enemy-infested warehouses, and the next day the Marines on both fronts fanned out in advancing arcs. General Smith came ashore that afternoon to take command, and ROK Marines began mopping up in bypassed Inchon streets. On September 17 the Marines annihilated a force of 200 North Koreans with five tanks in a battle six miles southeast of Inchon, and also captured Kimpo Airfield. That same day, elements of the 7th Infantry Division began an unimpeded landing, while everywhere supplies and heavier weapons poured into the captured port. What Fleet Admiral William ("Bull") Halsey hailed as "the most masterly and audacious strategic stroke in all history" had by then passed into history. The Americans were safely ashore in force and it remained now for them to cut the enemy's supply line by capturing Seoul, and to move south of the city to block off his escape routes from Pusan.

United Nations jubilation over the daring blow struck at Inchon might have been complete, but for the earlier fiasco of a South Korean landing on the east coast, plus the momentary doubts caused by the enemy's failure to relax his pressure on Pusan. This last concern, however, would be dissipated by the North Korean collapse beginning in the third week of September—but the affair at Changsa-dong was a failure from the start.

It was conceived by the ROK Army, which hoped to relieve enemy pressure on Pohang by landing at Changsa-dong ten miles to the north. To this end LST 667 manned by South Koreans took 800 men of the Miryang Guerrilla Battalion to Changsa. The guerrillas were equipped with captured Russian rifles for which they had 50 rounds each. They had no food. And they were to land at places which had not been reconnoitered, moving from the landing points to cut off the Communist supply lines by blowing bridges and blocking roads while the ROK 3rd Division attacked north from Pohang.

On September 14, the day *Missouri* arrived off the east coast to join *Helena*, three destroyers and a minesweeper in battering the port of Samchok, LST 667 stood off Changsa. It was broad daylight, rather than dawn as had been planned, and when the skipper decided to land over rocky surf one mile south of an enemy camp, his stern anchor parted and his ship was driven over the rocks. A hole was torn in her belly and then the wind took her, spun her around and broached her. The guerrillas waded ashore and were immediately attacked by North Koreans.

The outcome of Changsa-dong was that the U. S. Navy had to interrupt hammering the east coast Communists and rush to the rescue. Naval gunfire drew a protective ring around the hapless Miryang guerrillas until 725 of them—including 110 wounded—were pulled out of the trap and brought through wind and high surf to LST 665. Thirty-nine of them had been killed, while thirty-two others flatly refused to come off the beach and risk the balsa-raft passage which had already resulted in ten drownings. That happened on September 18, just as the

Missouri's guns preceded the South Korean 3rd Division's charge into Pohang at the start of the northern drive which earned the men of the 3rd the nickname of "The Rambling ROKs."

> On the night of September 17 [reported Lieutenant Colonel Rollins Emmerich, senior American officer with the 3rd] I decided to ask the Navy to shell the north bank of the Hyong San River, strongly held by many North Koreans. Until we got across that stream, and onto the coastal road, the division couldn't move. Accordingly, I radioed out to the fleet for some destructive and harassing fire. My radio operator, Corporal Leslie Dorn, addressed the message for gunfire support to the cruiser *Helena* but someone interrupted on the circuit and called me:
>
> "Hello *Cliffdweller*, this is *Battle Ax*. We will take that mission." It was the Big Mo!
>
> The next day I accompanied the naval shore fire party to the south bank of the river, where our forces were waiting to cross over. We all found ourselves a deep hole, and then called for the *Missouri* to commence fire. I'll never forget that first round—it really shook the countryside, and it landed 2,000 yards away.
>
> Soon the *Missouri* was dropping her large shells right on the shore, only 300 yards from our spotting position. It was really demoralizing to those Red troops. We practically waded across that river standing up....[1]

So the Rambling ROKs took off, driving the enemy 5th Division ahead of them in disorder, beginning the long spectacular dash which would carry past the 38th Parallel. Below and west of them, the North Korean People's Army was beginning to fall apart.

On September 16 the Eighth Army began its offensive from the Pusan Perimeter. Except for successes scored by the 2nd Division in the Naktong Bulge, there were few gains. The enemy seemed to be holding firm. The next day came the good news of the ROK advance into Pohang to add to the 2nd Division's continued success, but otherwise the enemy still held fast.

That afternoon, an uneasy MacArthur began toying with the idea of a second landing at Kunsan. An alternative plan to this effect had already been drawn up. Under it, one ROK and two

U. S. divisions would be put ashore at Kunsan on October 15. The mere fact that MacArthur considered the operation indicated that the United Nations Commander had begun to doubt the ability of the Eighth Army to break out of Pusan, and this, of course, meant that his faith in his deep envelopment had been shaken. And so, on September 16, with the Marines plunging toward Seoul and congratulations pouring in from all over the world, General MacArthur called Rear Admiral Doyle to his cabin on the *Mount McKinley* and directed him to begin planning the Kunsan landing. In a few more hours, however, there was good news from Pusan. Major General Leven Allen, Walker's chief of staff, telephoned Major General Doyle Hickey, MacArthur's acting chief in Tokyo, and said: "Things down here are ripe for something to break. We haven't had a single counterattack all day."

Now MacArthur began to debate whether he should pull those three divisions out of Walker's force or let them remain at Pusan in hopes of eventual enemy collapse. Signs of that cave-in began to multiply the next day, the 19th, with the capture of Waegwan by the 5th Regimental Combat Team and ROK penetrations in the central mountains. That night, the North Korean 6th and 7th Divisions—those Communist units farthest south from home base—began withdrawing north. And the following day, General Allen gave General Hickey this cautious report: "We have not had any definite break yet. They are softening but still no definite indication of any break which we could turn into a pursuit."

It was still touch-and-go, with MacArthur undecided between continuing the pressure in the south and settling for the Kunsan landing the following month, thereby giving the enemy time to divert a few divisions north to defend Seoul while making a general orderly withdrawal across the peninsula. But then on September 21 it became plain to Generals Walker and Allen that the enemy collapse was at hand, for the chief of staff of the enemy 13th Division had surrendered and given them great news.

Early that morning Senior Colonel Lee Hak Ku had come upon two sleeping soldiers of the 8th Cavalry Regiment on the roadside four miles south of Tabu-dong. He shook them gently, woke them, and told them he wanted to give up. Interrogation of Colonel Lee brought out the fact that the North Korean II Corps had ordered its divisions to assume the defensive September 17. More, the 13th Division knew nothing of the Inchon landing, thus suggesting that the enemy was afraid to let the men encircling Pusan know of the Americans to their rear—and that, of course, meant that the morale of the enemy soldiers was low.

On September 22 a discussion between MacArthur and Walker produced the decision to scrap the Kunsan plan in favor of continuing the Pusan breakout. There was no doubt now that the enemy had collapsed, and that same day General Walker issued this order:

> Enemy resistance has deteriorated along the Eighth Army front permitting the assumption of a general offensive from present positions. In view of this situation it is mandatory that all efforts be directed toward the destruction of the enemy by effecting deep penetrations, fully exploiting enemy weaknesses, and through the conduct of enveloping or encircling maneuver [to] get astride enemy lines of withdrawal to cut his attempted retreat and destroy him.

It was an order for pursuit. The very fact that General Walker had also told his commanders to advance without regard for their flank security was an indication of how complete he considered the enemy collapse to be. And he was right.

By mid-September the morale of the North Korean People's Army had reached its nadir. Both the August and September offensives had failed to make good the boasts of Premier Kim Il Sung, and on September 8 the army lost its most able leader when an exploding land mine killed Lieutenant General Kang Kon. General Kang had been General Kim Chaik's chief of staff and he was the North Korean commander whom MacArthur and Walker most respected.*

Only 30 percent of the North Korean soldiers who had crossed the 38th Parallel on June 25 remained in action by

---

*Whether or not his death had any great or immediate effect on the North Korean cause is virtually impossible to say, though some American commanders believe that it did. At any rate, the force which Kang had done so much to hold together began to come apart about a week after his death.

September 15, and the forcibly drafted South Koreans were showing little interest in fighting for their northern brethren. Many of the North Korean veterans had begun to kill men who refused to advance or who tried to desert, but even these indoctrinated Communists themselves could not refrain from grumbling about the scarcity of food or the wretched state of clothing, arms and equipment. By mid-September the 70,000 combat troops opposing General Walker's combat force of 140,000 men were served by perhaps 50 percent of the tanks and heavy weapons they needed. MacArthur's estimate of what happened to an army at the end of a long supply line was proven correct, and his faith in what happened to it when it was put to rout was borne out with grim exactitude during the last ten days of September.

By the end of the month the North Korean Army was shattered and fleeing north with little semblance of order. Some of the enemy's thirteen divisions simply disappeared. Their men were spread all over the South Korean countryside in disorganized and demoralized small parties. All of the escape routes were in United Nations hands, the sea was hostile to them and the sky roared with the motors of planes that spat death at them or showered them with fire bombs. The roads, rice paddies and ditches of South Korea became littered with abandoned enemy tanks, guns and vehicles. Wholesale surrenders became commonplace and the haul of prisoners would eventually be counted in the tens of thousands. Some of the fleeing enemy soldiers took refuge in the wild Chiri Mountains, there forming guerrilla bands which would harass the United Nations rear in the coming months, but most of them drifted north toward their homeland—leaving behind them a South Korea wasted by war and dotted with the mass graves of thousands of murdered innocents.

Hardly a city which the pursuing United Nations soldiers entered failed to produce evidence of Communist "liberation" techniques. Only hours seemed to separate the pistol shots of the North Koreans, hurrying to liquidate their rivals before they fled, and the arrival of the vanguards of the pursuit. At Sachon the North Koreans burned the jail and the 280 South Korean police, government officials and landowners who were inside it. At Anui, at Mokpo, at Kongju, and at Hamyang and

Chonju, United Nations soldiers uncovered trenches stuffed with the bodies of hundreds of executed civilians, many of them women and children. Near Taejon airstrip 500 ROK soldiers lay with their hands bound behind their backs and bullet holes in their brains. Between September 24 and October 4, in and around Taejon, the remains of an estimated 5,000 to 7,000 murdered civilians were uncovered, together with those of seventeen ROK soldiers and at least forty American soldiers. Most of them had been executed between September 23 and September 26, when the Communists speeded the destruction of their prisoners by marching them in groups of 100 and 200 to previously dug graves where they were killed. The job was finished before United Nations troops came up the old retreat road from Yongdong and recaptured Taejon. Only two American soldiers, one ROK and three civilians escaped the slaughter, all by feigning death and allowing themselves to be buried alive. These, then, were the sights seen during just one of the advances north—a march unfortunately marred by one of the tragic mistakes of the war.

The error involved an aerial strike delivered by American Mustangs against the Argyll Battalion of the British 27th Brigade, then attached to the U. S. 24th Infantry Division. On September 22, after the brigade's Middlesex Battalion had stormed Plum Pudding Hill to the right of the road at a point three miles below Songju, the Argyll Battalion led by Major Kenneth Muir was ordered to take another height standing to the left of the road. This was Hill 282, and the Argylls began climbing it just before dawn of September 23. An hour later the British soldiers surprised an enemy force at breakfast and captured the crest of Hill 282. But this position was in turn dominated by enemy-held Hill 388 about a mile to the southwest across a connecting saddle of land. Soon enemy troops began moving over that saddle against Hill 282, supported, meanwhile, by artillery and mortar fire. The Argylls had no supporting fire, for American artillery had been unaccountably withdrawn and no tanks could reach them over the rugged terrain. So Major Muir requested aerial support. At about noon, three Mustangs appeared overhead and began circling while waiting for the British to mark their own position with white panels. This was done, but then the enemy also put out white panels, confusing the Mustang pilots and tricking them into attacking the wrong hill.

Tanks of napalm fell on the Argylls and their position was engulfed in orange flame. The survivors came plunging down the slopes to escape the burning napalm, but Muir, perceiving that the crest of the hill was still held by a small party of wounded men, turned the survivors around and led them back up. As he reached the hilltop, Muir was mortally wounded by a burst of enemy fire. He was carried below, vowing with his last words that the enemy "will never get the Argylls off this ridge." But the situation was hopeless, and Major A. I. Gordon-Ingram, who succeeded Muir in command there, eventually was forced to evacuate. In all, the Argyll battalion suffered 89 casualties, of which some 60 were the result of the mistaken air strike. The next day Songju fell to the U. S. 19th Infantry and scouts from that regiment entered Taejon on September 28.

Along the west-central route of the United Nations advance, meanwhile, the most spectacular dash of the breakout was made by an armored force drawn from the 1st Cavalry Division and led by Lieutenant Colonel James Lynch. In three days, Task Force Lynch sped 105 miles north from Poun to make juncture with soldiers of the 7th Infantry Division just below Suwon. It had taken the attacking North Korean 2nd Division about a month to travel the same distance during the Communist invasion, and this, if anything, was a measure of how completely the fortunes of war had been reversed. Eleven days after the Marines had landed at Inchon, four days after Walker had issued orders for the pursuit, the Eighth Army and X Corps had effected the juncture which symbolized the destruction of the enemy army in South Korea. General MacArthur could contain his jubilation no longer. That same day, as though to tidy everything up with a single communiqué, the United Nations commander announced the dramatic meeting at Suwon and added: "Seoul, the capital of the Republic of Korea, is again in friendly hands."

But the capital had not fallen and the fiercest fight of the war was being fought over its burning, barricaded streets.

In the pitched battle for Seoul, in the slaughter of thousands of civilians who had remained in the city, in the death of hundreds of Marines who fought for it, in the destruction of 65 percent of the city itself, there can already be perceived the glimmerings of that giddy MacArthur optimism, that passion for the bold stroke, or at least the announcement of it, which was to bring the United Nations army so close to disaster in two more months. That state of mind was shared by MacArthur's former chief of staff, Major General Edward Almond, the man who now commanded the X Corps.

On September 25, the day the Marines began assaulting Seoul, General Almond announced its capture. Like his chief, who followed suit the next day, Almond made no mention thereafter of the fighting which continued until September 28. More, Almond either rejected or did not consider the possibility of surrounding Seoul, of cutting the roads to the northwest, north and northeast and forcing the capitulation of its garrison. This would have been a slower process, and would probably have reduced the psychological effect which bold and sudden victory, as MacArthur often said, could produce upon the Oriental mind. Whatever the reason, Almond's decision to attack vigorously produced the holocaust through which the 1st Marine Division had to pass.

It was this division, and especially Colonel Puller's First Marines, which bore the brunt of the Seoul fighting in the barricaded center of the city.

Here most of the intersections were barred by chest-high barricades made of rice and fiber bags filled with dirt. Enemy soldiers fired antitank and machine guns from behind them, while surrounding buildings held the riflemen who protected the men at the barricades from enemy attack. Ahead of the barricades were numerous antitank mines.

The Marines moved against these obstacles methodically. Their advance was preceded by the rocketing and strafing of Navy and Marine fighters; then mortars and small arms would lay down a protective fire while engineers crawled forward to detonate or disarm the land mines; and finally tanks would rumble forward to knock out the machine guns and antitank guns and perhaps butt down the barricade. Sometimes a flame-throwing tank would burn down the position. Riflemen, meanwhile, came after the tanks to give them protection, cleaning out snipers and making certain no suicider with satchel charge or Molotov cocktail got within throwing range of the tanks. What happened during the night battles, especially what happened to Seoul and its people, has been movingly described by the United Press war correspondent, Rutherford Poats:

I followed the First Marines through the smoldering rubble of central Seoul the day after its premature "liberation." The last desperate Communist counterattack had been hurled back during an eerie 2 A.M. battle of tanks firing at point blank range, American artillery crashing less than a city block ahead of Marine lines, the echoed and re-echoed rattle of machine guns—all against the background of flaming buildings and darting shadows.

Now it was almost quiet. The angry chatter of a machine gun up ahead now and then punctuated the long pauses between mortar and artillery strikes. But on this street corner was condensed the full horror of war, stripped of the vital challenge and excitement which make it bearable to the men who must fight wars.

Telephone and power lines festooned the streets or hung from shattered poles which resembled grotesque Christmas trees. Bluish smoke curled from the corner of a clapboard shack—the only building even partially spared destruction along the left side of the street. A young woman poked among a pile of roof tiles and charred timbers for her possessions, or perhaps for her child. A lump of flesh and bones in a mustard-colored Communist uniform sprawled across the curb up ahead, and the white-robed body of an old man lay on a rice-straw mat nearer the street corner. Marine ammunition and mess trucks churned the plaster and adobe rubble into dust as they shuttled back and forth from the front, six blocks north. Southbound ambulance jeeps, almost always fully loaded with four stretcher cases on their racks, told the story of the pre-dawn battle.

A tiny figure wrapped in a Marine's wool shirt stumbled down the street. Her face, arms, and legs were burned and almost eaten away by the fragments of an American white phosphorous artillery shell. She was blind, but somehow alive. She was about the size of my little girl. Three other Korean children, luckier than she, watched as the child reached the curbing, stumbled, and twice failed to climb up on the sidewalk. The kids laughed.[2]

It was in this agony of civilian suffering and soldierly travail that the last Communist attempt to hold Seoul was crushed. On September 26, the ROK 17th Division advanced toward the eastern edge of the city, while the 32nd Infantry of the U. S. 7th Division attacked the southeast section. The Marines, meanwhile, maintained the pressure. The next day, resistance collapsed, and by September 28, Seoul had truly fallen.

On September 29, General MacArthur flew to Kimpo Airfield to make dramatic restoration of the Korean capital to President Syngman Rhee. There were Marines guarding the new pontoon bridge the Army engineers had thrown over the Han, as well as the streets, as MacArthur's sedan flying the five stars of an American general of the Army drove toward Government House, passing through a desolation of rubble and half-eaten buildings and unburied dead. Even Government House was largely gutted by fire, although the legislative chamber had escaped with only a broken skylight. Splinters of glass fell from it while MacArthur stood in the presence of Syngman Rhee, members of the United Nations Commission, Republic of Korea officials and his own top-ranking officers to say, with visible emotion:

"By the grace of a merciful Providence our forces fighting under the standard of that greatest hope and inspiration of mankind, the United Nations, have liberated this ancient capital of Korea. It has been freed from the despotism of Communist rule and its citizens once more have the opportunity for that immutable concept of life which holds invincibly to the primacy of individual liberty and personal dignity. . . ."

MacArthur then asked the assembly to recite the Lord's Prayer with him, after which he turned to Rhee and said: "Mr. President, my officers and I will now resume our military duties and leave you and your government to the discharge of the civil responsibility."

The aged president seized MacArthur's hand. "We admire you," he said, tears filling his eyes. "We love you as the savior of our race." Turning to his audience, he stretched out his hands, opening and closing them, departing from the speech he had prepared for the occasion to speak directly to the American soldiers before him. "How can I ever explain to you my own undying gratitude and that of the Korean people?"

The ceremony ended and MacArthur drove back to Kimpo for the return flight to Tokyo. From all over the world came messages of congratulations. President Truman cabled: "Few operations in military history can match either the delaying action where you traded space for time in which to build up your forces or the brilliant maneuver which has now resulted in the liberation of Seoul." The Joint Chiefs of Staff said: "We remain completely confident that the great task entrusted to you by the United Nations will be carried to a successful conclusion."

In a few more days the last of the enemy units in South Korea were destroyed at Uijongbu. It had taken only ninety days to restore the *status quo ante bellum*. The Communist challenge had been hurled back with stunning speed. Unfortunately, however, the very brilliance of MacArthur's victory blinded both him and the United Nations to the fact that Communist China was not bluffing when, on September 30, Foreign Minister Chou En-lai announced: "The Chinese people absolutely will not tolerate foreign aggression, nor will they supinely tolerate seeing their neighbors savagely invaded by the imperialists."

By that date General MacArthur had already received a directive from the Joint Chiefs authorizing movement north of the 38th Parallel to carry out "destruction of the North Korean Armed Forces." By then many of the ROK troops had already crossed the border and President Syngman Rhee had said: "Where is the 38th Parallel? . . . It is nonexistent. I am going all the way to the Yalu, and the United Nations can't stop me." By then, too, all the Russian maneuvers to prevent the UN from crossing the Parallel had failed or were obviously doomed to failure. Formal approval of the invasion already begun was only a week away.

The world now knows that the United States—which called the tune in the United Nations—not only failed to unify Korea by force but was nearly driven out of Korea as a consequence of the attempt. Just as the free world had intervened to prevent the Communists from conquering the peninsula, the Communist Chinese were now preparing to halt the United Nations advance. Just as the Communists had not believed the free world would fight, now the free world believed the Chinese Communists would not.

Why this was so must now be examined.

Chapter Three

BY MID-AUGUST of 1950 there was still no indication that the People's Republic of China—as Communist China is officially known—intended to intervene in the Korean War.

On August 11 a "comfort mission" from Peiping arrived in the North Korean capital at Pyongyang, and two days later the first Communist Chinese ambassador to Korea presented his credentials there. But the exchange of greetings was neither unusual nor lavish. Pyongyang propaganda celebrating North Korea's fifth anniversary spoke of gratitude for Russian aid: "Our friendship with the Soviet people is one of the guarantees for victory in the war." Peiping, it seemed then, was vastly more concerned with "liberation" of Formosa.

All the talk about Korea from the Communist camp in early August was made by Jacob Malik, who had returned to the United Nations Security Council to take up the presidency rotated to his nation. Malik ruled proceedings from January to July "illegal" because they had been carried out in the "unlawful" presence of Nationalist China. Then he proceeded to discuss Korean matters in the continued presence of the Nationalist Chinese delegate, T. F. Tsiang. The contradiction did not seem to bother him, nor did the barbed allusions to it made by U. S. Ambassador Austin and the United Kingdom's Sir Gladwyn Jebb. Malik had come back to bluster, to deliver propaganda tirades about "the Anglo-American imperialist bloc and its aggressive policy in Korea," as well as to gain support from neutral India while perhaps isolating the United States from a few of her United Nations allies.

On August 4, Malik introduced a resolution which, in its two main points, proposed that the "internal civil war" in Korea be ended by withdrawal of "all foreign troops" from the peninsula and that delegates from Communist China as well as "representatives of the Korean people" be invited to the United Nations to discuss the Korean question. Malik's proposal seemed conciliatory because it did not employ the usual epithets, such as "Syngman Rhee bandit" in alluding to the rival government in Korea. A week later England's Jebb called on the North Koreans "to go back whence they came" while seeming to suggest that the *status quo* could be restored by negotiations. This idea was seconded by Sir Benegal Rau, the Indian delegate, who proposed that a committee of nonpermanent Council members consider the Korean problem after the North Koreans withdrew. Still, there was no word from Communist China. On August 17, U. S. Ambassador Austin made the statement which was to provoke quick words from Peiping. Austin said:

> The Security Council and the General Assembly have built already a firm base for any future action which might be decided upon to fulfill the objectives for which the United Nations is now fighting. The Security Council has set as its first objective the end of the breach of the peace. This objective must be pursued in such a manner that no opportunity is provided for another attempt at invasion. . . . The United Nations must see that the people of Korea attain complete individual and political freedom. . . . Shall only a part of this country be assured this freedom? I think not. . . . The General Assembly has decided that fair and free elections should be held throughout the whole of the Korean peninsula. . . .
>
> The United Nations ought to have free and unhampered access to and full freedom to travel within all parts of Korea. . . . We are waiting, and while we wait the strength of the United Nations increases.

Austin's statement doomed all hope of compromise. It spelled out the American intention to break out of the Pusan Perimeter and pursue the North Korean Army so that "no opportunity is provided for another attempt at invasion." The whole of the Korean peninsula was to be unified by "fair and free elections." Three days after the enunciation of this policy, the first sign of Peiping's shift of interest from Formosa to Korea was received at the United Nations. On August 20 Foreign Minister Chou En-lai sent the UN his first cable in six weeks, which said: "Korea is China's neighbor. The Chinese people cannot but be concerned about solution of the Korean question." Chou also demanded that Peiping be present in the Security Council when Korean matters were discussed. Two days later Malik warned: "Any continuation of the Korean War will lead inevitably to a widening of the conflict with consequences, the responsibility for which will lie with the United States and its Security Council delegation."

What did all these words mean? Probably that the strength of the Pusan Perimeter was now clear to Soviet Russia and that a new phase of action in Korea was being formulated, with China being taken in as Stalin's reluctant partner. Since the war began on June 25, Communist China had sent the UN just two messages on Korea, and both of these seemed infinitely more concerned with the presence of the U. S. Seventh Fleet in the Strait of Formosa. But after Austin's statement Peiping's attitude changed, and the fact that it changed slowly, and would thereafter evolve piecemeal, seems to suggest that it changed under pressure. Unfortunately, some of that piecemeal change might be traced to the bellicose statements then being made by high-ranking Americans.

On August 25, U. S. Secretary of the Navy Matthews publicly advocated "instituting a war to compel cooperation for peace. . . . We would become the first aggressors for peace." The next day, General MacArthur's controversial message to the Veterans of Foreign Wars was made public in full text, including the parts speaking of "misconceptions currently being voiced concerning the relationship of Formosa to our strategic potential in the Pacific." Formosa, MacArthur's message said, was part of an island defense chain from which "we can dominate by air power every Asiatic port from Vladivostok to Singapore and prevent any hostile movement into the Pacific." And then: "At the present time there is on Formosa a concentration of operational air and naval bases which is potentially greater than any similar concentration on the Asiatic mainland between the Yellow Sea and the Straits of Malacca." The remark which had so infuriated President Truman—"it is in the pattern of Oriental psychology to respect and follow aggressive, resolute and dynamic leadership—to quickly turn from leadership characterized by timidity or vacillation"—might also have raised a few gorges in China. Less than a week later, Major General Orvil Anderson, commander of the Air War College, remarked: "We're at war. . . . Give me the order to do it and I can break up Russia's five A-bomb nests in a week."

On the same day President Truman issued an eight-point policy statement which, while stressing America's intention of working through the United Nations, also said: "We do not want the fighting in Korea to spread into a general war; it will not spread unless Communist imperialism draws other armies and governments into the fight of the aggressors against the United Nations. We hope in particular that the people of China will not be misled or forced into fighting against the United Nations and against the American people who have always been and still are their friends." Although Truman went on to disavow any American designs on Formosa or the Far East in general, the tenor of the remark quoted might have seemed to Peiping an arrogant warning to stay out of her own backyard. And though Truman also moved quickly against the saber rattlers in his own house, suspending General Anderson from his command, ordering MacArthur to withdraw his message, and apparently bringing about the resignation of Secretary of Defense Louis Johnson—believed by many to have backed Navy Secretary Matthew's "aggressors for peace" statement—the net effect on China might have been only one of suspicion or confusion. A scholar highly qualified to pass on this situation has written:

> The top-level denial of aggressive intentions may have been interpreted in China as a crude effort to conceal the true aims of American imperialism, inadvertently "revealed" by military figures of high standing. On the other hand, it may have been accepted as evidence of "contradictions in imperialist circles" which might be scarcely less serious for China since MacArthur

remained at his post and the Truman-Acheson administration was politically vulnerable. We do not know exactly how Peking and Moscow evaluated these developments. However, their occurrence at this particular time gave them special significance for Communist analysts.[1]

However these conflicts be evaluated, the fact is that in late September, 1950, following the staggering blow of the Inchon invasion and the Security Council defeat of Malik's August 4 resolution, Sino-Soviet strategy underwent another change. The scene of Russian maneuver was shifted from the Security Council to the General Assembly, where neutral Afro-Asian states might lend sympathetic ears to proposals offered with the prestige of Foreign Minister Andrei Vishinsky behind them, while in China a Hate-America campaign was launched. Mass rallies and the usual derisive or howling newspaper editorials and cartoons were used to whip into a frenzy of hatred a people unaware that the underlying purpose of this anti-American propaganda was to prepare them for war. Two samples:

> This mad dog [the U. S.] seizes Formosa between its hind legs while with its teeth it violently bites the Korean people. Now one of its forelegs has been poked into our Northeast front. Its bloodswollen eyes cast around for something further to attack. All the world is under its threat. The American imperialist mad dog is half beaten up. Before it dies, it will go on biting and tearing.

> This [the U. S.] is the paradise of gangsters, swindlers, rascals, special agents, fascist germs, speculators, debauchers, and all the dregs of mankind. This is the world's manufactory and source of such crimes as reaction, darkness, cruelty, decadence, corruption, debauchery, oppression of man by man, and cannibalism. This is the exhibition ground of all the crimes which can possibly be committed by mankind. This is a living hell, ten times, one hundred times, one thousand times worse than can possibly be depicted by the most sanguinary of writers. Here the criminal phenomena that issue forth defy the imagination of human brains. Conscientious persons can only wonder how the spiritual civilization of mankind can be depraved to such an extent.[2]

158

Then, following General MacArthur's report to the United Nations, in which he charged that Peiping had "furnished substantial if not decisive military assistance to North Korea" by releasing many of its Korean soldiers to Pyongyang before the war, Communist China replied with this open admission of hostility:

The Chinese people scorn this accusation. They have no fear of it. Furthermore, we clearly reaffirm that we will always stand on the side of the Korean people—just as the Korean people have stood on the side of the Chinese people during the past decades —and resolutely oppose the criminal acts of American imperialist aggressors against Korea and their intrigues for enlarging the war.

This unequivocal answer was received on September 22, the same day that Peiping charged that U. S. aircraft had violated her Manchurian border at the Yalu River town of Antung. The next day, the widely read and highly official Communist newspaper, *People's Daily,* made the following detailed explanation of why North Korea should be supported:

We Chinese people are against the American imperialists because they are against us. They have openly become the archenemy of the People's Republic of China by supporting the people's enemy, the Chiang Kai-shek clique, by sending a huge fleet to prevent the liberation of the Chinese territory of Formosa, by repeated air intrusions and strafing and bombing of the Chinese people, by refusing new China a seat in the UN, through intrigues with their satellite nations, by rearing up again a fascist power in Japan, and by rearming Japan for the purpose of expanding aggressive war. Is it not just for us to support our friend and neighbor against our enemy? The American warmongers are mistaken in thinking that their accusations and threats will intimidate the people of China.

On the following day Chou En-lai sent off his most bellicose cable to the United Nations, accusing the United States of trying "to extend the aggressive war against Korea, to carry out armed aggression on Formosa, and to extend further her aggression against China." Chou concluded: "The flames of war being extended by the United States in the east are burning more fiercely. If the representatives of the majority of states attending the United Nations General Assembly should still be pliant to the manipulation of the United States and continue to play deaf and dumb to these aggressive crimes of the United States, they shall not escape a share in the responsibility for lighting up the war-flames in the East."

And then, almost as suddenly as it began, the Hate-America campaign subsided into silence. It was almost as though Communist China were marking time while Russian Foreign Minister Vishinsky maneuvered to prevent the crossing of the Parallel.

Vishinsky's theme was that if UN troops crossed the Parallel, they would become the aggressors. The fact that the 38th Parallel had already been violated by the invading North Koreans meant nothing to him. He asked, in effect, that the North Korean Army which had violated the Parallel now be given sanctuary behind it. It was as though a man who leaves the sidewalk to break into a house should become immune to pursuit and arrest once he regains the sidewalk. Sir Benegal Rau of India, however, found merit in Vishinsky's arguments, saying: "We cannot help thinking that it would impair faith in the UN if we were even to appear to authorize the unification of Korea by the use of force against North Korea, after we had resisted the attempt of North Korea to unify the country by force against South Korea. The result may be to intensify the North Korean opposition and to increase the tension in that part of the world." The fact that North Korean unification was to be followed by Communist-controlled elections, which, as the Balkans had shown, have one unfailing result, as opposed to United Nations unification being followed by UN-controlled elections, seemed lost on the Indian delegate. It was, of course, the vital fact—the one for which the war was being fought. This was the U. S. position, which Austin restated on September 30: "The aggressor's forces should not be permitted to have refuge behind an imaginary line. . . ." But India was again sympathetic, as she had been to Malik's August 4 proposal, as she was once more when, on October 2, Vishinsky introduced this seven-point proposal in the General Assembly's Political and Security Committee:

1. That the belligerents cease hostilities. (The UN had voted this on June 25, but North Korea had refused.)

2. That United Nations troops be withdrawn to permit the Korean people the sovereign right to settle "freely" their internal affairs. (The UN had voted against returning to the *status quo ante bellum*. Furthermore the troops were to be withdrawn *before* a unified government was formed.)

3. That all-Korean elections be held to establish a unified, independent government. (The Soviet had refused to permit such elections in 1948, thus dividing the country.)

4. That the North Korea Assembly and the National Assembly of South Korea elect a commission of delegates from each to organize and conduct free elections. (This put Pyongyang, representing 9,000,000 people, on an equal basis with Seoul, with a constituency of 21,000,000.)

5. That Red China and Russia be members of the UN committee observing the election. (Russia had repeatedly refused to participate in any previous UN commission on Korea, and now her price seemed to be the recognition of Red China.)

6. That a unified and independent Korea be given economic aid through the UN.

7. That after the establishment of the all-Korean government, the Security Council consider admitting Korea to the UN.

But for the last two points, on which everyone could agree, Vishinsky's final offer was entirely unacceptable to the United States and most of the United Nations. Still, Rau suggested that it be placed side-by-side with the U. S. resolution before a special committee which might work out a compromise. Put to a vote, Rau's motion was rejected, 32 to 24, with 3 abstentions —which might indicate that many United Nations members were eager to end the war at any price. On the Soviet resolution itself, the vote was a resounding defeat: 46 to 5 with 8 abstentions. And so, on October 4, the General Assembly's Political and Security Committee passed the eight-nation resolution backed by the United States. By a vote of 47 to 5 with 7 abstentions, the Committee resolved:

> ... That all appropriate steps be taken to ensure conditions of stability throughout Korea;
> That all constituent acts be taken, including the holding of

elections under the auspices of the United Nations, for the establishment of a unified, independent, and democratic government in the sovereign state of Korea;

That all sections and representative bodies of the population of Korea, south and north, be invited to cooperate with the organs of the UN in the restoration of peace, in the holding of elections, and in the establishment of a unified government;

That United Nations forces should not remain in any part of Korea otherwise than so far as was necessary for achieving the objectives specified;

That all necessary measures be taken to accomplish the economic rehabilitation of Korea; and,

That a commission drawn from Australia, Chile, the Netherlands, Pakistan, the Philippines, Turkey, and one other nation be established to achieve the listed objectives.

The Russian maneuver had failed to halt the United Nations' determination to cross the Parallel, and though the formality of General Assembly approval of the act was still three days off, President Syngman Rhee's jubilant and exultant ROK soldiers were racing north in the central and eastern sectors, urged by Rhee to "unify Korea . . . for all time."

Chou En-lai's last warning was also falling on deaf ears. Chou's remark already quoted—that China would not "supinely tolerate" seeing Korea "invaded by the imperialists"—had been made on September 30. But it had been broadcast for foreign ears and kept from the people at home. Evidently, Peiping was awaiting the result of Russian diplomacy. Then, on October 1, with the ROKs rushing north, General MacArthur broadcast an ultimatum to North Korea demanding unconditional surrender, and stating: "The early and total defeat and complete destruction of your armed forces and war-making potential is now inevitable." That night Chou summoned the Indian ambassador K. M. Panikkar to a dramatic midnight conference. He told him that if U. S. troops invaded North Korea, China would enter the war. This news was relayed to President Harry Truman, who has since written:

Similar reports had been received from Moscow, Stockholm, and New Delhi. However, the problem that arose in connection with these reports was that Mr. Panikkar had in the past played the game of the Chinese Communists fairly regularly, so that his statement could not be taken as that of an impartial observer. ... The key vote on the [Korean] resolution was due the following day, and it appeared quite likely that Chou En-lai's "message" was a bald attempt to blackmail the United Nations by threats of intervention in Korea.

The possibility of Chinese intervention in Korea, however, could not be discounted, and I therefore ... approved the following message to General MacArthur:

"In light of the possible intervention of Chinese Communist forces in North Korea the following amplification of our directive [of September 25] is forwarded for your guidance:

"Hereafter in the event of the open or covert employment anywhere in Korea of major Chinese Communist units, without prior announcement, you should continue the action as long as, in your judgment, action by forces now under your control offers a reasonable chance of success. In any case you will obtain authorization from Washington prior to taking any military action against objectives in Chinese territory."[3]

This directive was issued on October 9, one day after the Hate-America campaign was renewed in Communist China. On October 9 (Eastern time), *People's Daily* printed a front-page editorial which drew attention to the heretofore unpublished warning made by Chou En-lai on September 30 and said: "So far as the situation is concerned with respect to China's neighbor, Korea, the Chinese people have made public their position." The following day a Ministry of Foreign Affairs statement said: "The American war of invasion in Korea has been a serious menace to the security of China from its very start."

So now Chou's warnings had also failed to halt the Parallel crossing. With the fragmented North Korean Army backpedaling wildly before the rush of the ROKs on the east and the advance of the Eighth Army on the west, the vanguard of some 320,000 Chinese soldiers began movement toward the Yalu River.

That these troops had begun to move was already known to MacArthur's intelligence, but his headquarters in Tokyo was apparently not alarmed. In the field, however, Chou's threat and mounting reports of Chinese troops movement burst like a bomb on Eighth Army headquarters, as has been sharply detailed by Eighth Army's operations analyst, Brigadier General S. L. A. Marshall:

> ... A dread apprehension gripped the headquarters. Whereas the threat was greatly discounted in the United States, Walker and his staff gave full weight to the words and to the warning which came from the Indian Ambassador in Peking that Communist China was preparing to enter the war.
>
> Also, as October opened, Eighth Army published to its forces the Chinese Communist order of battle along the Yalu River front, an evaluation which subsequent events proved to be amazingly accurate.
>
> But so delicate was this subject that Intelligence promptly came at cross-purposes with itself. At the merest mention of Chinese intervention in the official reports, our South Korean ally had a tremor phasing into paralysis. The psychological impact upon the field agents was tremendous; they acted like men hexed and their interest in their work dropped to zero. If the periodic report took a pessimistic tone, the effect on the Koreans was such that officers had to be sent forth to calm them with assurances that the words were probably exaggerated. . . . The group of American advisers serving with the South Korean divisions reported that troops had become highly nervous, with signs of demoralization increasing. The Defense Minister, Shin Sung Mo, urged that the advance toward the Yalu be halted. With some mental reservations, Intelligence therefore took a more conservative tone.[4]

At MacArthur's headquarters there was still a firm conviction that these Chinese troops would not enter the war. It was "too late," the theory ran, and this was what MacArthur himself told President Truman at Wake Island.

This famous conference, according to the President, was called by him "to get the benefit of [MacArthur's] first-hand information and judgment" on Korea as well as "to let him see the world-wide picture as we saw it in Washington." More accurately, Mr. Truman's Administration was ailing and there were Congressional elections due that November. To be associated with the man whose Inchon victory had made him wildly popular in America might prove to be wonderful political medicine. As evidence of the Commander in Chief's eagerness to meet his difficult and controversial general, MacArthur was given a choice of two meeting places: Honolulu, about equidistant from Washington and Tokyo; or Wake, eight hours' flight from Tokyo, thirty from Washington. MacArthur chose Wake, and Mr. Truman flew out to see him there on October 15, smiling, affable, bringing with him a fifth Distinguished Service Cross for MacArthur and promising to provide a major general's second star for MacArthur's aide, Courtney Whitney.

At Wake, MacArthur told Truman: "I believe that formal resistance will end throughout North Korea by Thanksgiving" and "It is my hope to be able to withdraw the Eighth Army to Japan by Christmas." Asked about the possibility of Communist Chinese intervention, the general gave his now-famous reply: "Very little. Had they interfered in the first or second months it would have been decisive. We are no longer fearful of their intervention. We no longer stand hat in hand. The Chinese have 300,000 men in Manchuria. Of these probably not more than 100–125,000 are distributed along the Yalu River. They have no Air Force. Now that we have bases for our Air Force in Korea, if the Chinese tried to get down to Pyongyang there would be the greatest slaughter."

The next day the first of 180,000 Chinese troops began crossing the Yalu River into North Korea, and the disaster which awaited General MacArthur's "Home-by-Christmas" drive had begun. That it should have happened at all is one of the great ironies of history: in an age which plumes itself on its communications, there had been a complete breakdown in communications between two great powers. Not all of this was due to the absence of diplomatic relations between the United States and Communist China, or to Peiping's reliance on Soviet Russia for information or to Washington's on India. As one astute observer has written:

> One obstacle to successful communication, particularly between Communist and non-Communist regimes, is the difficulty each side has in projecting itself into the frame of reference within which the other operates. Yet this is necessary if one is to understand the opponent's interpretation of one's own signals, as well as the motives behind his.

Peking . . . ascribed motivations and patterns of decision making to "Wall Street warmongers" and "Anglo-American imperialists" and in other ways departed sharply from reality. Peking ignored the pluralistic political process in the West and failed to differentiate between the true locus of power in Washington and the confusion of voices on both sides of the Pacific Ocean. Utterances by "authoritative spokesmen" in Tokyo were given equal weight (if not greater) with statements from Secretary Acheson and President Truman. *Ad hoc* American decisions on Korea and Taiwan were interpreted as the outcome of carefully designed schemes for "aggression" in Asia. Failure to comprehend the frame of reference within which Washington reacted led Peking to miscalculate the effect of communications designed to deter the U. S. and to exaggerate the threat posed by actual U. S. intentions.

This was not a unilateral phenomenon. American communications for Chinese Communist consumption were inadequately adapted to the Chinese Communist Party's frame of reference. To be sure, hindsight facilitates the reconstruction of Peking's perspective to a degree that was impossible during the actual course of events. Yet a similar if less conclusive exercise, carried out in 1950, might have alerted U. S. officials to the pitfalls of dealing with the new regime as if it were more Chinese than Communist. Judgments in Washington reflected a belief in basic conflicts within the Communist world that, if properly exploited, would inhibit Peking's actions in Korea. One such conflict was seen in a supposed clash between "innately Chinese" qualities and "alien Communism." This theory comfortingly left intact the presumed bonds of "friendship" between "the Chinese and American peoples." Another clash was seen in Peking-Moscow relations, where "Chinese national interests" were thought to conflict with "Russian domination." This, it was said, would keep Mao from pulling Stalin's chestnuts out of the fire. Such assumptions consistently attributed to the Chinese Communists a benevolence they were far from feeling. Hence American "assurances" to Peking were never enough to support the aims of U. S. policy.[5]

Thus, a cogent argument for communications breakdown, to which can be added the abuse of communications, either in a free society such as ours where the press may be and often is capricious, or in a controlled society such as Communism where lying serves the state. Finally, the questions: Why did the United States cross the Parallel? Why did Communist China intervene?

In partial answer to the first, the Inchon victory so thoroughly broke the North Korean Army that the United States and the majority of her allies in the United Nations thought the chance had come to solve the Korean problem for good. On October 7, when the General Assembly approved the crossing, the British Foreign Secretary, Ernest Bevin, said in New York that there could be "no South Koreans, no North Koreans: just Koreans." As Trumbull Higgins has said: "The principal American ally had not restrained Washington at the decisive moment." President Syngman Rhee's intransigence was another reason. He had repeatedly announced his intentions of unifying his nation, with or without United Nations help. Very strong Republican sentiment for a more aggressive Far Eastern policy is a third argument, and it has also been suggested that President Truman needed a great victory to win the November elections, just as the Roosevelt Administration in July, 1942, changed its war strategy in favor of the headlines harvested by the landings in North Africa. The latter may seem a bit hard on Truman, who was honestly concerned with drawing a line somewhere against Communist aggression. That he crossed this line at the 38th Parallel seems to have been caused, again, by the heady wine of Inchon and subsequent MacArthur assurances. The Toynbeean theory of the too-great response to one challenge provoking another challenge was about to be given further melancholy proof, with assistance from the communications breakdown.

China's decision to enter the war may be ascribed to numerous reasons. One spectacular and attractive theory argues that Joseph Stalin had become so jealous of Mao Tse-tung's rising power that he deliberately embroiled Red China with the United States in Korea so that he might emerge supreme in the Far East. Russian responsibility in some part may be adduced from a portion of Nikita Khrushchev's famous speech in 1956 attacking Stalin and "the cult of personality," in which he is reported to have said: "His [Stalin's] anti-realistic consideration of the attitude of the Western Nations in the face of developments in Asia has contributed to the risky situation for the entire socialist cause such as developed around the war in Korea." Certainly Mao's newly emergent Red China was in no position to bargain with Stalin in that year of 1950. Mao needed support, both economic and political, from Moscow. Nor is there any doubt that the Chinese armies which entered Korea came to be supplied—particularly in heavy weapons and air—by Soviet Russia. Unfortunately, how much Stalin or the Russia of the time had to do with China's intervention cannot be known. Stalin is dead, and Mao remains silent behind the Bamboo Curtain.

But Red China had reasons of her own, and the chief of these seems to have been a fear of aggression: would the United Nations halt at the Yalu River as Austin and Truman said they would, or would they go farther under the urging of "the Mac-Arthur-Chiang clique"? This may have been why Chou told Panikkar his nation would not intervene if only South Koreans crossed the Parallel. More, a great American victory in Korea would have enormous psychological effect throughout the Far East. Japan, with whom the Americans were then preparing an indulgent peace treaty, would certainly fall in line behind Uncle Sam, and after Japan perhaps those former Western colonies of Southeast Asia then beginning to emerge as sovereign states. Red China did not, however, fear America's arsenal of nuclear weapons, or at least she did not act or speak as though she did. Mao had already remarked in 1946: "The atom bomb is a paper tiger with which the U. S. reactionaries try to terrify the people." According to K. M. Panikkar, General Nieh Jung-chen, acting chief of staff of the People's Liberation Army, said to him: "We know what we are in for, but at all costs American aggression has to be stopped. The Americans can bomb us, they can destroy our industries, but they cannot defeat us on land. . . . They may even drop atom bombs on us. What then? They may kill a few million people," Nieh said, and added: "After all, China lives on the farms. What can atom bombs do there?" Of course, General Nieh was discussing war on the Chinese mainland, but his words, whether spoken in truth or in bluff, were reflective of the attitude of Chinese leadership at the time.

Even more important, the Chinese may not have feared American attack on their homeland. Whether or not they knew with certainty that MacArthur's directives always carefully prohibited air or naval action against either Manchuria or Siberia in support of his operations, the fact remains that they acted as if they knew. And this security from attack could have been more decisive than any of the reasons cited above. It would almost guarantee the success of a peasant army relying on manpower against firepower, for it would mean that the firepower could not be used in full.

Whatever the actual reasons, on October 16 the Fourth Field Army of the Chinese People's Republic commanded by General Lin Piao began crossing the Yalu River in force.

Chapter Four

THE ROK I Corps commanded by Brigadier General Kim Baik Yil was first to cross the 38th Parallel on October 1, and the 3rd Division was the first of General Kim's units to go over the line.

The Rambling ROKs were in a near-festive mood as they began advancing up the east coast road, with the ROK Capitol Division behind them, bound for the important port of Wonsan about 100 air miles north, and after that, or so they hoped, the Yalu River. President Rhee had already told them, "We have to advance as far as the Manchurian border until not a single enemy soldier is left in our country," and their officers were jubilantly boasting, "We will wash our swords in the waters of the Yalu."

The foot soldiers themselves put on a remarkable drive. Most of them had only canvas shoes to wear, some of them walked on bloody bare feet, yet they marched night and day, bypassing enemy groups which often attacked their supply line in the rear, winning numerous skirmishes, averaging fifteen miles a day and capturing large stores of enemy guns and equipment. Sometimes they were able to seize natural defensive strongholds in the high ground to their left without having to fire a shot, or found still-warm rice balls lying in roadside ditches—evidence that it was now the North Korean soldier who was "bugging out" without a fight. Along the way they were met by cheering crowds. Children ran after them to give them bunches of wild flowers. Women waved flags and the old men stood pulling on their long pipes with expressions of grave satisfaction on their faces. But there were no young men to be seen: the North Koreans had drafted them all.

On October 10, the ROK 3rd and Capitol Divisions made simultaneous entry into Wonsan and began to fight for the city. Within a few days the port and its airfield were secured, and by the 12th there were 22 planes of the Far East Combat Cargo Command flying supplies into Wonsan. Thereafter, the victorious ROKs spent their time patrolling the Wonsan area, marking time for their next lunge to the border.

About the same time, the ROK II Corps—7th and 8th Divisions—began striking up the center of the peninsula toward the Iron Triangle, a complex of industrial towns which was to become famous later in the war. Chorwon, about 20 miles above the Parallel, formed the Iron Triangle's eastern base; its apex was Pyonggang in the north; and its western base was at Kumhwa. The Iron Triangle was also an important rail and road communications center, linking east and west coasts, and its capture on October 13, simultaneous with the fall of Wonsan, augured well for the United Nations counterinvasion.

On the left or western flank, the Eighth Army attack did not begin until October 7, the day before the United Nations General Assembly approved the border crossing. It was here that General Walker hoped to trap most of the broken North Korean Army's straggling units, and the general had already characterized the pursuit in hunter's language: "We have flushed the covey and we are now kicking up the singles. As any quail hunter knows, it's when you're kicking up the singles that you get the most birds." Here, too, the atmosphere was one of elation and optimism. Thirty-year-old Major General Paik Sun Yup, commander of the ROK 1st Division which was part of the U. S. I Corps, smiled broadly when his division received brand-new U. S. tanks. "Now we can be like General Patton," he said. To the question of what his tactics would be during the drive on the North Korean capital of Pyongyang, he grinned and said: "No stop."

Earlier Eighth Army apprehensions about the possible intervention of the Communist Chinese seemed to have vanished by the time the 7th Infantry Division had taken Kaesong and the 1st Cavalry Division struck north along the main Seoul-Pyongyang road, with General Paik's 1st ROKs on the right. Far East Command's daily intelligence summaries still dismissed the possibility, and one dated as late as October 14 said: "Recent declarations by Communist Chinese leaders, threatening to enter North Korea if American forces were to cross the 38th Parallel, are probably in a category of diplomatic blackmail." So the Americans, British, Australians and South Koreans of Eighth Army's I Corps struck confidently north toward the North Korean capital, at the very beginning gaining territory almost at will. Then the North Korean defenses stiffened, and the U. S. I Corps advance slowed. By mid-October it had reached only 20 miles into North Korea and Pyongyang still held out. To enemy resistance had been added the delay caused by a deteriorating supply situation which, in its turn, was the result of General MacArthur's decision to use X Corps for another amphibious landing.

If General of the Army Douglas MacArthur had much cause to complain of the restrictions placed on him in Korea by the Joint Chiefs of Staff, then Lieutenant General Walton Walker had something in his own defense to be said of the restraints placed on him by MacArthur. Chief of these was the United Nations Commander's insistence upon continuing two separate commands, Eighth Army and X Corps. Even though Walker had been placed in charge of all United Nations forces, including the ROK Army, he had no control over Major General Edward Almond's X Corps, and Almond, as often happened among officers who were associated with General MacArthur for very long, had taken onto himself some of his autocratic chief's characteristics. Walker discovered this early in the hammer-and-anvil maneuver from Pusan to Seoul when, upon requesting X Corps to block the central mountain escape routes through Wonju and Chunchon with at least a regiment, he was told that X Corps could not extend the anvil that far. Walker's staff officers were agreed that X Corps should be restored to the Eighth Army after the recapture of Seoul so that there would be a single unified command in Korea, but the bulldog of Pusan had apparently not the temerity to approach MacArthur with this proposal.

At the end of September, Walker was informed that X Corps was to remain in General Headquarters reserve, and soon after he was notified that the 7th Infantry and 1st Marine Divisions under General Almond were to be pulled out of Seoul and sent around the peninsula to land at the North Korean east coast port of Wonsan. Then X Corps would attack west toward Pyongyang along the lateral Wonsan-Pyongyang road while Walker's Eighth Army struck at Pyongyang from the south.

Walker's staff did not like the plan, but their chief did not forward their objections to MacArthur. First, it was argued that the outloading of X Corps from Inchon would delay pursuit of the fleeing North Korean Army—a chase already delayed by the decision not to keep X Corps on the North Korean tail. Instead of an amphibious operation, said Walker's staff, X Corps could march overland to Wonsan. Further, the speed of the ROK east coast advance made it evident that Wonsan would fall to them long before X Corps could land there. On MacArthur's side, it could be argued that the terrain of North Korea was unsuitable for an overland march. Much equipment might be lost. Still, neither the 7th Infantry Division's Major General David Barr nor the 1st Marine Division's Major General Oliver Smith was fond of the Wonsan amphibious maneuver. Least of all was the Navy, from Vice-Admiral Joy on down, for Wonsan Harbor was heavily mined.

The fortunes of war had produced the most fortuitous circumstances imaginable for enemy mine warfare. First, one of the U. S. Navy's initial postwar economy cutbacks had been made at the expense of its minesweeping service; second, the waters off the east coast of Korea were admirably adaptable to mining; third, Russia, which provided the mines and the mine experts in North Korea, has historically been among the most proficient users of mine warfare. Probably this last fact is so because Russia was never a maritime power. A seafaring nation such as Britain is more inclined to work on antimine warfare, and in fact one of its admirals once flatly refused to develop mines on the ground that perfection of such a weapon would be about the worst thing that could happen to His Majesty's Navy. But Russia had been using mines to advantage since the Crimean War, in the days when these moored or drifting sea bombs were known as "torpedoes." Much of the mining in North Korea was accomplished simply by casting the explosives into the long Korean rivers flowing into the Sea of Japan or the Yellow Sea. Others were moored or set adrift by experts disguised as Korean fishermen on innocent-appearing junks and sampans. The bulk of the latter went into the waters off Wonsan and Hungnam, where a large shelf of shallow, muddy water made their use effective. Because of this, as well as because of its shortage of minesweepers, the U. S. Navy also objected to the Wonsan operation.

But General MacArthur was adamant. He accepted the Navy's argument against outloading both the X Corps divisions from Inchon and sent the 7th Division south to Pusan by rail for mounting out there. Otherwise, the Wonsan operation was on as planned. Joint Task Force Seven was re-formed under Vice-Admiral Struble and a fleet of 250 ships assembled to carry the 1st Marine Division on its second amphibious "assault" in five weeks. D-Day at Wonsan was to be October 20, with the 7th Division to land a few days later.

On October 2, Vice-Admiral Struble, an old minesweeping veteran, ordered all available sweepers in the Far East to Wonsan. On October 10, a force under Captain Richard Spofford began clearing a path through the Wonsan minefield. Almost immediately, helicopter reconnaissance spotted strings of mines "too numerous to mention." Countermining was attempted as a quick means of detonating the field. Thirty-nine planes from the carriers *Leyte Gulf* and *Philippine Sea* dropped 50 tons of bombs in the minefield, but even the explosion of 1,000-pounders failed to set off the mines. On the 12th, while *Missouri, Helena, Worcester* and *Ceylon* were battering east coast railyards, bridges, shore batteries and tunnels, the sweeping squadron lost two of its best boats when both *Pledge* and *Pirate* ran into mines and blew up. Thirteen men were killed and 87 wounded. Captain Spofford then decided to try to detonate the minefields by dropping depth charges into them. A precision drop by Navy planes brought no results. On the 18th the Japanese Minesweeper 14 was sunk and on the 19th the ROK Minesweeper 516 went up with a terrific explosion in a "cleared" lane. That made it plain that magnetic countermines were being used, that is, magnetic mines equipped with a mechanism set to allow as many as twelve ships to pass overhead before the mine is triggered. And this meant, of course, that the minesweepers must now make thirteen passes over any given area before it could be considered safe.

In all, it took two weeks to sweep Wonsan free of mines, and during the last six days the invasion transports marked time by sailing up and down the Korean east coast, reversing their course every twelve hours and causing the disgruntled Marines aboard them to coin the derisive phrase "Operation Yo-Yo" for the "assault landing" at Wonsan. Nor were the Marines pleased to learn that Wonsan had been captured by the ROKs on October 13, to which injury was added the insult of October 24 when the comedian Bob Hope and the singer Marilyn Maxwell flew into Wonsan to entertain U. S. Army troops attached to the ROKs with many quips and sallies concerning the Marines still offshore on the transports. On October 26 the Marines at last came ashore at Wonsan with red faces and dry feet.

It seemed to them and to almost everyone else in northeastern Korea that the war was all but over. The ROK I Corps, which had come under Major General Almond's control, had already departed Wonsan; the Capitol Division was poised to move north on the coastal road, while the 3rd had begun pushing northwest to Chosin Reservoir from Hungnam. True, the day before the Marines landed, the ROK 3rd Division had been attacked by the Chinese 124th Division at Sudong 37 miles northwest of Hungnam. The ROKs took sixteen prisoners, from whom it was learned that the 124th, along with the 125th and 126th, the other two divisions of the Chinese 42nd Army, had crossed the Yalu during the third week of October and marched southeast to protect the Chosin Reservoir power complex. That the Communist Chinese Forces were across the Yalu in force was now apparent, and yet there were few top-ranking officers who believed that they intended to intervene. Three days after the Sudong battle, the Far East Command's intelligence summary said:

> From a tactical viewpoint, with victorious U. S. Divisions in full deployment, it would appear that the auspicious time for such [Chinese] intervention had long since passed; it is difficult to believe that such a move, if planned, would have been postponed to a time when remnant North Korean forces have been reduced to a low point of effectiveness.

The last sentence was most true of the North Korean People's Army on the east coast. Its divisions had been fragmented; many of its units were leaderless. So-called "guerrilla bands" were actually nothing but parties of foragers—starving, demoralized soldiers hunting for food in an iron, barren chain of mountains on which the cold breath of a cruel winter was even then beginning to fall. It was because of the enemy's disorganized state that General Almond changed his plans. He decided to make wide and sweeping use of his forces in order to seal off as many escape routes as possible and to seize the Hungnam-Hamhung steel and iron complex as well as the ports and power and irrigation systems of northeast Korea. The 1st Marine Division was to continue mopping up the Wonsan-Hungnam area, but then, with the arrival of the 3rd Infantry Division from the States, the Marine division would go up the Hungnam-Chosin road and relieve the ROKs. Then the ROK I Corps would continue up the coastal road to the border. In the meantime, the 7th Infantry Division would not be brought ashore at Wonsan but would be landed at the little port of Iwon 78 road miles north. The 7th would follow a northwest road to the Yalu River town of Hyesanjin, for the prohibition against using non-Korean troops near the border had been lifted by MacArthur on October 24.

It was a broad dispersal of forces, and as General Almond would admit a few days later: "We are scattered all over the landscape." But he was confident of quick victory. On October 30 he told the staff of the 1st Marine Division: "When we have cleared all this out, the ROKs will take over and we will pull our divisions out of Korea." Similar optimism was expressed in the United States, where, on the same day, an editorial in *The New York Times* declared: "Except for unexpected develop-

175

ments along the frontiers of the peninsula, we can now be easy in our minds as to the military outcome."

And so, on October 29, the 17th Regiment of the U. S. 7th Division was put safely ashore at Iwon high on North Korea's east coast. In a few weeks or less this unit and the ROK I Corps would stand triumphant on the border of Manchuria. Then it would all be over.

The war that seemed almost over in North Korea during that late October of 1950 was far from concluded south of the Parallel, where an estimated 40,000 enemy guerrillas continued to strike at United Nations supply lines. Throughout October and November, the combined strength of the U. S. IX and ROK III Corps was required to contain Communist bands as they ambushed motor convoys on both coasts, raided villages at night for food, clothing and hostages, and sabotaged railroad traffic. On October 15 one of these irregular units ventured into the outskirts of Seoul, attacking and seriously damaging a radio relay station a few miles north of the city. A week later another force struck and scattered sixty ROK policemen and soldiers guarding the Hwachon Dam near the 38th Parallel, and opened the dam's control gates, thus causing the Pukhan River to rise so rapidly that a railroad bridge was swept away. Guerrillas and bypassed units of the North Korean Army also operated west of Wonsan, where railroad trains were ambushed and the men of the 1st Marine Division and the newly arrived U. S. 3rd Infantry Division were frequently subjected to night attack. Enemy irregulars made it difficult for the Eighth Army and X Corps to maintain physical contact by attacking the patrols sent into the vast gap between the separated United Nations forces. They also harried the ROKs guarding the Iron Triangle, particularly at the apex city of Pyonggang, and maintained pressure throughout November—a fact that was to prove troublesome to the United Nations Command when reinforcements had to move through that area to support the faltering "final" offensive.

On the western front, meanwhile, the advancing Eighth Army had begun to break through the crust of enemy resistance. By the third week of October the North Korean defenses along the Seoul-Pyongyang road had begun to collapse, while the return of Inchon's port facilities to General Walker's exclusive use had speeded shipment of supplies to his troops. Everywhere the United Nations forces began to average gains of ten miles a day, even though they were advancing through rugged terrain where narrow winding mountain passes made the possibility of ambush an ever-present danger.

The North Koreans were falling back in disorder along all the western fronts. In the mountainous center, the ROK II Corps advanced rapidly, threatening to outrun the main drive on Pyongyang.

At Pyongyang itself, Major General Hobart Gay's 1st Cavalry Division came up the main road, while the ROKs of General Paik's 1st Division struck along the right flank. To the left of the cavalry division, the 24th Infantry Division with the British Commonwealth Brigade attached veered west in a strike on Pyongyang's port of Chinnampo. Seizure of this supply inlet would ease an Eighth Army logistics situation made vexatious by a breakdown in rail service.

On October 19 both the Americans and the ROKs swept into the southern half of North Korea's capital city. Only desultory sniper fire opposed them. The second largest city in Korea was all but deserted. Premier Kim Il Sung had fled, exhorting his troops to fight to the last man to cover his withdrawal to Sinuiju on the Yalu, where he set up a provisional government. Soviet Russian advisers had also departed, but there were large stores of Russian food and enough pictures, posters and busts of Stalin to indicate who it was who pulled the Korean puppet string. Some streets had also been renamed in the Russian dictator's honor. On October 20 one of the last escape routes to the north had been sealed off when the U. S. 187th Airborne Regiment jumped into action at Sukchon and Sunchon, about 30 miles above the city. On October 21, the United Nations troops crossed the beautiful green Taedong River which cuts Pyongyang in two and brought the northern half of the city under control.

And now began the mass surrender of the North Koreans. By the end of the month 135,000 of them were in captivity all over the peninsula and Premier Kim's army had all but melted away. Everywhere the United Nations forces were moving at will, and as had happened down south at Taejon, evidence of Communist atrocities began cropping up. The bodies of 73 murdered American soldiers were found in and around Sunchon on October 21. The men were part of a group of 370 prisoners whom the North Koreans had marched north from Seoul a month before. According to the 23 men who survived the mass killing (two of them later died of wounds), the Communists became increasingly fearful as the United Nations approached. On October 19, those 300 or so Americans still alive were crowded aboard two trains and sent north from Pyongyang. Each day about half a dozen of them died, either of dysentery, starvation or exposure. Their bodies were removed from the coal cars and gondolas into which the American soldiers had been stuffed, and the trains chugged on. On October 20, the date of the parachute attack on Sunchon, the trains ran into tunnels to take cover. Inside one of the tunnels, 100 Americans were taken from a train in three groups to receive their evening meal. They were shot as they sat on the ground waiting for it. Two days later men of General Paik's division found the bodies of 28 murdered Americans along a railroad track at Kujang-dong, about 30 miles northeast of Sunchon. The frantic North Koreans were lightening their load in the most brutal way possible.

Premier Kim himself fled a second time a few days later, moving east from Sinuiju to the woods around Kanggye-Manpojin in north-central Korea. There he began gathering his remnant for what Eighth Army intelligence expected to be his last stand. Kim's flight had been forced by the advance of the U. S. 24th Division and British 27th Commonwealth Brigade. Leading units of this force crossed the Chongchon River on October 24 for a drive on Sinuiju and the strategic Suiho Reservoir.

In the center of the United Nations advance, the ROK 6th Division had pulled out the plum. On October 26 the division's 7th Regiment marched into Chosan on the Yalu River. Its men attacked and scattered North Korean soldiers retreating into Manchuria over a narrow footbridge. The promise to "wash our swords in the waters of the Yalu" had been fulfilled.

Everywhere in Korea, now, United Nations optimism was ballooning. Morale in the Eighth Army had never been higher. Men of the 1st Cavalry Division boasted they would parade on the Plaza in Tokyo on Thanksgiving Day, wearing their bright yellow cavalry scarves. The division even began turning in some of its equipment preparatory to the anticipated withdrawal from Korea. Men in other outfits spoke openly of Christmas shopping in Japan. To top it all, the Far East Air Force's Bomber Command had begun to complain: "We've run out of targets." One crew from the 92nd Bombardment Group came back from a mission reporting its only target had been an enemy motorcyclist whom they had chased up a road, dropping bombs until one of them hit him. As a result of such reports, Lieutenant General Stratemeyer reduced Bomber Command's sorties to 25 a day and then 15 daily, until, on October 27, the day on which the 22nd and 92nd Bombardment Groups began returning to the United States, he suspended aerial operations for the entire Bomber Command. Only three bridge targets remained in North Korea and it seemed then that they would be of more use to the United Nations than the enemy.

Such was the soaring balloon of optimism in late October, 1950, and it took not jabs but sledgehammer blows—many of them—before this thick-skinned bag of happy gas was finally deflated. The first of these came on October 25, two days before those two bombardment groups began departing Stateside. On that day, just as the Chinese Communist 124th Division struck the ROK 3rd at Sudong on the east, a battalion of the ROK 6th Division stumbled into a Chinese roadblock to the rear of the exultant 7th Regiment on the shores of the Yalu. The South Korean battalion was annihilated, and by that night there was not a company of the 6th Division's 2nd Regiment intact. Next day, the alarmed 7th Regiment turned to pull back from the Yalu. Its withdrawal was barred by the usual enemy roadblock. During the day, supported by U. S. air, the ROKs held their own. After dark they collapsed. Only 875 men of the 7th's original 3,552 escaped the trap.

With astonishing and frightening speed the ROK II Corps had begun to cave in, and its collapse would be complete on November 1 when its men took full flight, a solid mass of frightened soldiers streaming south "indifferent to vehicles moving, indifferent to all that was around them." Thus the center was broken and the right flank of the U. S. I Corps exposed.

On the far left, in the drive on Sinuiju, Australians of the 27th Commonwealth Brigade encountered stiffening North Korean resistance on October 30 as they approached Chongju. But Chongju fell next day to the Argylls, who were relieved in turn by soldiers of the U. S. 24th Division. That night there was a fierce tank battle fought under a silvery moon. The North Koreans lost, and with daylight, the Americans struck out for Sinuiju again.

This unit was the 1st Battalion, 21st Infantry, which had once been famous under the name of Task Force Smith. Lieutenant Colonel Brad Smith, who had led the first American ground forces into battle at Osan four months before, was still in command, and it was probably fitting that Smith's outfit should make the deepest Eighth Army penetration of the Korean War. That afternoon, his soldiers and tanks reached Chongo-dong, only 18 air miles below Sinuiju and the Yalu River. And they were astonished to receive an order to halt and prepare to defend against strong counterattack. Soon they backpedaled into Chongju, and thence farther back toward the Chongchon.

Everywhere the Eighth Army line had begun to contract. That very November 1, the first of the MIG-15 jets appeared in the skies over northern Korea. They stabbed briefly and without success at startled United Nations pilots, displaying that unbelievably bad gunnery which would be characteristic of the enemy fliers throughout the war, and then flashed off to the safety of Manchuria. That night elements of the 1st Cavalry Division were savagely attacked by forces which included Chinese cavalrymen mounted on Mongolian ponies. With the U. S. I Corps' right flank wide open following the collapse of the ROK II Corps, it became necessary for the 1st Cavalry and U. S. 2nd Divisions to fight for their lives, battling to destroy numerous roadblocks to their rear or to hold present positions. From every quarter, now, came reports identifying the enemy as Communist Chinese. The meaning of the forest fires which had raged throughout the northern hills in late October was now clear: under cover of smoke, the Chinese had moved their divisions into place for the sudden stroke. There was no doubt that Red China was in the war against the United Nations. On November 5, General MacArthur issued a special report to the United Nations detailing Communist Chinese acts of war, including the arrival of the MIGs, the antiaircraft buildup on the safe side of the Yalu, and the identification of forces which Peiping called the Chinese People's Volunteers. The next day, MacArthur issued a special communiqué:

> The Korean War was brought to a practical end with the closing of the trap on enemy elements north of Pyongyang and seizure of the east coastal area, resulting in raising the number of enemy prisoners-of-war in our hands to well over 135,000, which, with other losses mounting to over 200,000, brought enemy casualties to 335,000, representing a fair estimate of North Korean total military strength. The defeat of the North Koreans and destruction of their armies was thereby decisive.

> In the face of this victory for United Nations arms, the Communists committed one of the most offensive acts of international lawlessness of historic record by moving, without any notice of belligerence, elements of alien Communist forces across the Yalu River into North Korea and massing a great concentration of possible reinforcing divisions with adequate supply behind the privileged sanctuary of the adjacent Manchurian border.

> A possible trap was thereby surreptitiously laid, calculated to encompass the destruction of the United Nations forces engaged in restoring order and the processes of civil government in the North Korean border area. This potential danger was avoided with minimum losses only by the timely detection and skillful maneuvering of the United Nations commander responsible for that sector, who with great perspicacity and skill completely reversed the movement of his forces in order to achieve the greater integration of tactical power necessitated by the new situation and avert any possibility of a great military reversal.

> The present situation therefore is this. While the North Korean forces with which we were initially engaged have been destroyed or rendered impotent for military action, a new and fresh army faces us, backed up by a possibility of large alien reserves and adequate supplies within easy reach of the enemy but beyond the limits of our present sphere of military action. Whether and to what extent these reserves will be moved forward remains to be seen and is a matter of gravest international significance. . . .

The following day a communiqué from Premier Kim Il

Sung's government officially admitted the "participation" of "volunteer units formed by the Chinese people" in the counterattack against the United Nations troops, and four days later Peiping calmly announced:

> This reasonable expression of the Chinese people's will to assist Korea and resist American aggression is not without precedent in the history of the world, and no one can object to it. As is well known, in the eighteenth century, the progressive people of France, inspired and led by Lafayette, assisted the American people in their war of independence by similar voluntary action. Before the Second World War, the democratic people of all countries of the world, including the British and American people, also assisted the Spanish people by similar voluntary action in the Spanish civil war against Franco. Since the expression of the Chinese people's will . . . is so reasonable, so just, so righteous, magnanimous, and so flawless, the People's Government of China sees no reason to prevent their voluntary departure for Korea.

Meanwhile, a strange thing had happened on the battlefront. The Communist Chinese had pulled back. For almost three weeks, from November 7 to November 26, there was only desultory action in North Korea. Patrols sought the enemy and rarely found him. An eerie wasteland filling with the first snows of winter separated the two antagonists. Unknown to the United Nations, the Communist Chinese "First Phase Offensive" was over.

Chapter Five

THE "new and fresh army" of which General MacArthur complained in his November 6 communiqué was also something new in modern history: a force of trained Chinese soldiers with a tradition of victory.

This force, the People's Liberation Army, or Chinese Communist Forces as United Nations intelligence would call it, was the creation of a remarkable group of a dozen men who broke with Chiang Kai-shek in 1927 and began the struggle which eventually won China's millions for Communism.

Through the lives of these twelve Communists runs an unusual thread of association in education and training in early life, and later in planning and executing the military campaigns which brought them ultimate victory. All are about the same age. Chu Teh, the oldest, was born in 1886, while Lin Piao, the youngest, was born in 1908. The others were born between 1893 and 1900. Nine of them met as youths in grammar or military schools. Seven of them studied in France and Germany and were expelled for subversive activities. All have studied in Moscow, except Mao Tse-tung, Kao Kang and Ho Loung. These last two have no formal education, learning their military trade in the hard and crafty school of organized banditry. All but two of the twelve—Kao and Chen Yi—were veterans of the celebrated Long March from Kiangsi Province in South China to Shensi Province in the north. Chu Teh was tactical commander for the march and Mao Tse-tung was his political commissar. Chou En-lai, a product of the finest western schools and the Whampoa Military Academy—the West Point of China—was Chu's deputy. Peng Teh-huai, deputy commander of the Communist Chinese Forces in 1950 under Chu, was in charge of the 3rd Army Corps which formed the vanguard. Liu Shao-chi, who had been associated with Mao since 1921, was Peng's political commissar.

These men, then, and three others, comprised the twelve Communists who fought Chiang in the late Twenties and the early Thirties, only to come, as it seemed then, to the brink of doom in October, 1934. By then the Communists in South China had been defeated at Nanchang, and later at Swatow and Canton. The only alternative was to withdraw from Kiangsi to the sanctuary of Yenan in northern Shensi Province and to continue the fight there side by side with Kao Kang's forces. In the meantime, Chen Yi would remain in Kiangsi to harry Chiang Kai-shek with guerrilla warfare. Accordingly, on the night of October 16, 1934, the Long March or *Chang Cheng* was begun.

Living off the land, moving its supplies on carts or donkeys or on the backs of some 50,000 civilian men and women drafted en route as porters and carriers, this army of between 90,000 and 100,000 struck out for Yenan in Shensi Province, more than 6,000 miles away. It was a brutal and heroic march, with survival going only to the strong. Those who straggled or deserted were rounded up by a rear guard. If they did not agree to continue, they were shot. Those who fell by the wayside were also executed, or left to die. Some of the men marched barefooted, others with straw sandals on their feet—and yet they had to cross 24 rivers and 18 mountain ranges. There were battles en route, and always the danger of ambush from the Nationalist armies. On October 20, 1935, 20,000 survivors met units of the 25th, 26th and 27th Red Armies which had been in Shensi since 1933. The veterans of the Long March had passed through 12 provinces and had captured and occupied 62 cities while fighting 15 major battles. Of the year they had spent in transit, an actual 235 days and 18 nights were spent marching—at an average daily rate of 24 miles.

It was in this crucible that all but two of the men who led the Communist China of 1950 had been tested; and it was these men, with Kao and Chen assisting, who reorganized the Red Chinese armies and began operating from their secure base at Yenan. For sixteen years the People's Liberation Army knew nothing but war. They fought the Nationalists, and then, when Japan invaded China, they made a loose alliance with the Nationalists to fight Japan. For the first time they received modern arms, most of them through the United States, or through the venality of Nationalist Chinese generals who sold U. S. arms out the back door of their private "go-downs." When Japan was defeated, more arms fell to them. Then, turning to fight Chiang again, they captured additional stores of weapons with the final blows that drove the Nationalists from the mainland in 1949.

In the forefront of this endless fighting had been the men who were to order the Korean intervention or command it: Mao Tse-tung, the military and political theorist, and now Premier of Red China; Chou En-lai, the western-educated Communist, his foreign minister; Chu Teh, tactician of the

Long March and now commander of the Chinese Communist Forces, with Peng of the Long March his deputy; Chen Yi, commander of the Third Field Army still massed north of the Yalu, and Lin Piao, commander of the Fourth Field Army which was first to cross into Korea.

These men had also molded the new China and made it no longer fashionable to quote the proverb: "As you do not use good metal for nails, so you do not use good men for soldiers." That may have been true in the old days when war lords bought the services of peasant soldiers for a few pennies and a bowl of rice. Then a soldier was truly an object of scorn, fighting on one side today, on the other tomorrow—trying only to stay alive and pick up enough plunder to finance a civilian future. Chu Teh and the other generals sought to change this attitude the moment Communist reorganization began in Yenan.

Political instructors were assigned to all units and the men subjected to as much as four hours of daily indoctrination in Marxist theory. Nationalist troops who surrendered or deserted were carefully screened before they were allowed to join the People's Liberation Army. Informers were fed into all units to weed out "reactionaries" who might speak aloud of ideas dangerous to Marxism.

Gradually, as Communism triumphed throughout China, military school cadres were formed. Young men and women of seventeen to twenty-three "of pure ideology and good health, with junior high school and higher elementary school education" were enrolled in courses ranging from eight months to two years and graduated as junior officers for the Communist Chinese Forces. By the fall of 1950, however, the effects of this program had yet to be felt in any large degree, and the Chinese Communist Forces were still a peasant army dependent on animal transport and relying on the numbers and hardiness of their soldiers.

These men were able to march and fight on small rations. Each of them carried from three to five days' food in a cloth shoulder roll, containing either rice from home or the Korean staple of millet seed, rice, and dried peas ground into a powder. Whenever possible the soldier cooked these rations, but otherwise mixed them with water and ate them cold.

In winter, the Chinese Communist soldier was issued a heavy mustard-colored quilted cotton uniform which he wore over his summer dress. The winter uniform was white on the inside and was often reversed for fighting in the snow. The Chinese Communist soldier wore no helmet, only a heavy cotton cap with big earflaps. His shoes were usually rubber or canvas sneakers fitted over layers of cotton socks, although many of the first men across the Yalu had been issued fur boots.

The Chinese Communist Forces were very effective at night, especially on patrol, and their most efficient battle tactic was similar to the one used by the North Koreans—if, in fact, the North Koreans had not learned it from the Chinese while fighting in the Korean Volunteer Army. This was called *Hachi Shiki* and was nothing more than a V formation with the mouth open toward the enemy. When the enemy had entered the V, the sides closed around them while another force moved below the mouth to intercept enemy reinforcements. Individually, the Chinese Communist soldiers preferred to get "in close," crawling toward the enemy under cover of darkness, and then, to the blaring of bugles, the shrilling of whistles and clanging of cymbals, jumping erect to hurl grenades and charge. Their commanders considered a three-to-one superiority ideal for attack, but they did not use those fictitious "human sea" assaults of which some American writers were so fond, and which led one anonymous Marine to ask: "Hey, Sarge, how many hordes in a Chinese platoon?" Nor were the bugle calls and whistles intended to terrify troops, as was originally supposed. They were merely signals, a means of controlling troops in the dark, and though they did cause some United Nations units to panic in the beginning, they became more of a help than a hindrance after they had been decoded and their meaning disseminated among all units.

The Chinese Communist Forces division was composed of about 10,000 men, and three of these divisions made an army, which, with its special troops, included about 40,000 men—the equivalent of a United States Army corps. Five or six armies formed an army group, and two of these comprised a field army, such as the Fourth commanded by General Lin. A Communist Chinese field army, then, is a vast force of 300,000 to 600,000 men.

It was the XIII Army Group of Lin's Fourth Field Army which was first over the Yalu, crossing from Antung in Manchuria to Sinuiju, and from Chian to Manpojin. These units, fighting as "volunteers," struck the first blows which forced the Eighth Army and ROK II Corps back to the Chongchon bridgehead. Why they did not continue is not known, though there are many theories, both military and political, which attempt to explain that lull which fell over the battlefield on November 6 and 7 and continued until the full-scale Communist onslaught of November 26.

On the military side, it could have been that General Lin's divisions were "fought out." As has been mentioned, the Chinese carried only five days' supply, both of food and ammunition. When this was gone, Chinese divisions had to stop to await resupply by a primitive communications system depending upon the Korean A-frame on the backs of conscripted men and women or on a variety of pack animals which included camels. While the fought-out divisions were marking time, fresh ones had to be moved into position. Unfortunately for this argument, the hiatus in Korea lasted not one week but three.

A second military theory is based on the writings of Mao Tsetung, particularly the famous sixteen-word tactical credo which characterized the early Communist guerrilla actions against Chiang:

> *Enemy advancing, we retreat;*
> *Enemy entrenched, we harass;*
> *Enemy exhausted, we attack;*
> *Enemy retreating, we pursue.*

Oversimplified though this may be, Mao's later theories, set down in *The Protracted War* which he wrote during the Japanese invasion of 1938, give a more sophisticated clue to the sudden Chinese disengagement in Korea. In this work, Mao says: "We have always advocated the policy of 'luring the enemy to penetrate deep' precisely because this is the most effective military policy for a weak army in a strategic defense against a strong army." So, it is argued, the lull in Korea was a retreat designed to lure MacArthur on to his doom. His already extended supply line would be stretched out to the full. More, during the three weeks which intervened, the North Korean winter would have fallen, and as Marine Major General Smith has said: "Even Genghis Khan wouldn't have tried Korea in the winter."

The third military argument is simply that the Chinese, having forced the United Nations to back off, were now spending the interval in transporting all possible troops and supplies into Korea. During this period the IX Army Group under General Sung Shin-lun was detached from General Chen Yi's Third Field Army and rushed into positions opposing the U. S. X Corps in northeast Korea. In addition, Lin Piao sent two more armies to join the XIII Army Group in northwest Korea, a move which seems to have impressed General MacArthur, not as theory but as fact, for the Yalu River bridges in the Antung-Sinuiju vicinity were then crowded with nocturnal enemy traffic. On November 6, the day of his communiqué, MacArthur decided to give his directives the broadest interpretation and ordered General Stratemeyer to send 90 B-29 bombers against the Yalu River bridges the following morning. MacArthur had already begun to give the widest latitude to the September 29 message he had received from Secretary of Defense George Marshall, who had replaced the departed Louis Johnson, which instructed him "to feel unhampered tactically and strategically" in pursuing the enemy army. The United Nations Commander had thus lifted restrictions on the use of non-Koreans along the border, and he had answered the Joint Chiefs' subsequent criticism of this move by citing Marshall. And so General MacArthur made the momentous decision to bomb the Yalu bridges and thus strike at Manchurian territory.

An information copy of his order was received by the Joint Chiefs of Staff in Washington, and the reaction reached all the way to Independence, Missouri, where President Truman had gone to vote in the November elections. Truman, reminded of the U. S. promise to consult Britain before taking any action against Manchuria, ordered postponement of the bombing pending MacArthur's explanation of why he thought such a serious step necessary. The United Nations Commander sent back this reply to the Joint Chiefs:

> Men and materials in large force are pouring across all bridges over the Yalu from Manchuria. This movement not only jeopard-

izes but threatens the ultimate destruction of the forces under my command. The actual movement across the river can be accomplished under cover of darkness and the distance between the river and our lines is so short that the forces can be deployed against our troops without being seriously subjected to air interdiction. The only way to stop this reinforcement of the enemy is the destruction of these bridges and the subjection of all installations in the north area supporting the enemy advance to the maximum of air destruction. Every hour that it is postponed will be paid for dearly in American and other United Nations blood. The main crossing at Sinuiju was to be hit within the next few hours and the mission is actually being mounted. Under the gravest protest that I can make, I am suspending this strike and carrying out your instructions. What I had ordered is entirely within the scope of the rules of war and the resolutions and directions which I have received from the United Nations, and constitutes no slightest act of belligerency against Chinese territory, in spite of the outrageous international lawlessness emanating therefrom. I cannot overemphasize the disastrous effect, both physical and psychological, that will result from the restrictions which you are imposing. I trust that the matter be immediately brought to the attention of the President as I believe your instructions may well result in a calamity of major proportion for which I cannot accept the responsibility without his personal and direct understanding of the situation. Time is so essential that I request immediate reconsideration of your decision pending which complete compliance will of course be given to your order.

MacArthur's plea, which amazed the Joint Chiefs in that it so completely reversed his more optimistic message of November 3, had the effect of gaining him permission to bomb the Yalu bridges from the Korean side only. No dams or power plants on the Yalu were to be touched, for political theories explaining the Chinese disengagement in Korea were already having their effect on Administration policy. And so, the last bridling restriction had been placed on that military mind which, as General Charles de Gaulle has said, is "bred upon imperatives." The order to bomb only the Korean side of the bridges was a military absurdity, and it seems to have been no more

189

than a bone to stop the angry barking of the old wardog in Tokyo. Studying that order, General Stratemeyer is reported to have said: "It cannot be done—Washington must have known, it cannot be done."* By then, of course, Stratemeyer knew that the enemy had built his antiaircraft defenses on the assumption that his border would not be violated. American bombers could attack the Yalu bridges only along certain courses which the enemy had zeroed-in. As a result, they had to bomb from 18,000 feet, buffeted by high-level winds up to 120 knots. Under such conditions, accuracy was next to impossible. More, the B-29s were also exposed to the "cat-and-mouse" tactics lately adopted by enemy fighter planes. The Communists rose from their base at Antung to about 30,000 feet on their side of the river, slashing down across the border in firing passes on the Americans below, then turning to recross the border and gain that "privileged sanctuary" from which they might repeat the maneuver. Because of this tactic, MacArthur had requested the right of "hot pursuit," whereby American fighters so attacked might be allowed "two or three minutes" in which to follow the enemy aircraft north of the border. This, too, was denied by Truman, after consultation with United Nations allies, and again as a consequence of his determination to limit the war, as well as of hopeful interpretations being placed upon the battle-field lull.

The most cheerful of the latter stated that Red China had made only "limited intervention" in Korea. This theory, supported by Chinese Communist propaganda, was that the "People's Volunteers" had drawn a *cordon sanitaire* to protect Manchuria and Yalu River power plants while securing a territorial base for Premier Kim Il Sung's fugitive government. It was accepted by the U. S. Central Intelligence Agency as well as by such allies as Britain and France. These two nations helped lead a United Nations Security Council maneuver which resulted in a draft resolution offering "to hold the Chinese frontier with Korea inviolate" and protect Peiping's interests in a frontier zone if the Chinese would withdraw. Some nations, and some of President Truman's advisers, thought that Red China would not renew her attack if the United Nations forces stayed where they

*MacArthur: His Rendezvous with History, Maj. Gen. Courtney Whitney, New York: Alfred A. Knopf, 1956, p. 407.

were or withdrew farther south. Communist China, however, had made no official statement of her objectives in Korea. All the talk of buffer zones and volunteers came from anonymous propaganda statements which bound no one. Still, the buffer-zone notion had some influential advocates. President Truman writes:

> Secretary Acheson expressed himself as feeling that the Russians were especially interested in the idea of defense in depth. He suggested, therefore, that a buffer area in Northeast Korea be established under a UN commission, with a constabulary but no UN armed forces. The Chinese, Acheson said, had two interests; the first was to keep us involved, while the lesser interest was in the border and the power plants. He thought that we ought to explore privately the possibility of a twenty-mile demilitarized zone, ten miles on each side of the Yalu. He went on to say that the trouble with any such proposal, of course, would be that the Communists would insist on all foreign troops leaving Korea, and thus abandon Korea to the Communists.[1]

In that last sentence is reflected the bewilderment which gripped the Truman Administration: the Secretary of State offering a course of action foredoomed by that Communist intransigence which was his daily hair shirt. At the conclusion of this National Security Council meeting of November 9 it was agreed that General MacArthur's directives should not be changed. Except for the prohibition against bombing Manchuria, he remained free to act as he thought best. In other words, the problem of Korea was still to be solved by force of arms. Truman did, however, give public assurance to Red China in the statement: "Speaking for the United States Government and people, I can give assurance that we are supporting and are acting within the limits of United Nations policy in Korea, and that we have never at any time entertained any intention to carry hostilities into China. . . ." The British Government also promised Peiping that no invasion of China was intended. But soon the United Nations was to learn that Communist China was in no way disposed to negotiate for a buffer zone. On November 8, the Security Council had voted to invite Peiping to attend a discussion of General MacArthur's special report of November 5. The invitation was harshly refused by Chou En-lai three days later. Soon Peiping propaganda mills were grinding out insulting and belittling descriptions of the United Nations. On November 18 *World Culture* said:

> American imperialists threaten that if China does not stop helping Korea, not only America will be China's enemy but the entire United Nations will be the enemy. The Chinese people do not fear this threat. If the United Nations is used by the U. S. as its tool of aggression, the United Nations is not then the instrument of the peoples of the world for peace. The United Nations loses its strength in becoming an aggressive instrument of the American imperialists and their satellites. Without the participation of the People's Republic of China, the United Nations is nothing more than a name.

Such language reminded United Nations diplomats that Red China had recently begun to help Communist forces in Indo-China, and that she had invaded ancient Tibet in late October, thereby offending an Indian government which had been friendly and helpful to her. Further proof that Communist China had set her face against the United Nations came later in the month, when General Wu Hsiu-chuan arrived at Lake Success. His government had belatedly accepted a UN invitation of September 29 to discuss the Formosa problem, although Chu spent his time at Lake Success "discussing" Korea by vilifying the United States and the United Nations while defending the right of the "People's Volunteers" to fight for North Korea.

Thus the considerations which might have led Communist China to suspend her offensive during the three weeks November 7–26, 1950. Of all interpretations here described, the events seem to support the theory that this was no strange interlude at all, but merely a pause during which the Communist Chinese brought more troops and supplies into line. Nor is it possible to ignore the fact that the attempt to bomb the Yalu bridges on the Korean side only, with all the risks and difficulties which this entailed for the United Nations airmen, must have made it plain that Manchuria was indeed to be, in General MacArthur's words, "a privileged sanctuary." All the talk about buffer zones and anxiety to protect the Yalu River power plants turned out to be persiflage. The facts show that General Mac-

Arthur was indeed "lured deep" into a harsh and barren land in the midst of a dreadful winter. By the time that his "win-the-war" offensive had begun, the Central Intelligence Agency had reversed its earlier estimate of Chinese Communist intentions, saying that they would "at a minimum" increase their commitment in Korea and had sufficient strength to force the United Nations to withdraw. By then, it was too late. As Senator Saltonstall asked Secretary Acheson during the famous Joint Senate Committee on Armed Services and Foreign Relations Hearings in 1951:

"They really fooled us when it comes right down to it, didn't they?"

"Yes, sir," Acheson replied.

Chapter Six

THE offensive with which General MacArthur expected to end the war was to begin November 24, 1950. The plan was to attack with the Eighth Army on a broad front northward in the west and center, while the X Corps in the east struck northwest to cut the enemy supply line at the Manpojin-Kanggye-Huichon axis.

Thus the division of the United Nations command would be continued, with General Walker in charge in the west and General Almond in the east. Between them lay the high mountainous spine of the peninsula, a gap of as much as 50 air miles in places, but one which was to be kept under aerial observation while communication between the two forces was maintained by radio, air and courier.

The fact that MacArthur had decided on this bold and obviously risky stroke suggests how his cautious mood of early November had shifted back to optimism by mid-month. On November 7 he had told the Joint Chiefs that organized Chinese Communist forces were "unquestionably" in the field against him, estimating that his new enemy would be able to force the United Nations to withdraw if he chose to build up sufficient strength. MacArthur's concern then was to determine whether or not he could halt the flow of enemy reinforcements, as well as to sound out enemy intentions by renewing the offensive. On November 9 he wrote the Joint Chiefs:

> I believe that with my air power, now unrestricted as far as Korea is concerned except as to hydroelectric installations, I can deny reinforcements coming across the Yalu in sufficient strength to prevent the destruction of those forces now arrayed against me in North Korea.

Six days later he changed from his November 7 intention of advancing to "take the measure" of the enemy opposing him to the plan which was to gain complete victory. From November 15 until the all-out assault began nine days later, the Communist strength in Korea was steadily estimated at about 100,-000 men opposite Eighth Army in the west and center, and, as far as figures go, just a fuzzy "fleeing remnant" in the east. Major General Charles Willoughby, MacArthur's intelligence officer, broke that 100,000 down into 30,000 or 40,000 North Koreans and between 60,000 and 70,000 Chinese "volunteers." Actually, there were about 300,000 Chinese in Korea, and they were not "volunteers" but the organized divisions and army groups of Lin Piao's Fourth Field Army and Chen Yi's Third.

Many American officers, among them MacArthur's chief of staff, Major General Hickey, and the X Corps chief of staff, Major General Clark Ruffner, questioned Willoughby's figure as too low, but Willoughby repeated his theory that only volunteers were in Korea, probably at the rate of a battalion of volunteers to each so-called Chinese division. The basis for this theory is not known, unless it was that Willoughby was fooled by the Communist Chinese trick of using the words "unit" and "battalion" to disguise full armies and divisions. Thus, the "55th Unit" was actually the 39th Army and the "1st Battalion, 55th Unit" was the 115th Division, 39th Army. Willoughby continued to figure divisions as battalions in the face of mounting reports giving the true identity of some of the forces opposing the United Nations. Many of the Chinese prisoners had not had time to become consistent in the code subterfuge. Identifying units as a battalion in one breath and a division in the next, they provoked the suspicion of their interrogators, who eventually discovered the ruse.

On Willoughby's side, however, it can be argued that United Nations aerial reconnaissance had still failed to detect any signs of massed Communist Chinese movement, obviously, of course, because the Chinese hid by day and moved by night. When the weather was clear, the Chinese, experts in the art of camouflage, took cover in hillside caves, in the numerous railroad tunnels of North Korea, in village huts or in mine shafts. They marched only at night, and here they surely proved themselves among the hardiest foot soldiers in history.

In a well-documented instance, a CCF army of three divisions marched on foot from Antung in Manchuria, on the north side of the Yalu River, 286 miles to its assembly area in North Korea, in the combat zone, in a period ranging from 16 to 19 days. One division of this army, marching at night over circuitous mountain roads, averaged 18 miles a day for 18 days. The day's march began after dark at 1900 and ended at 0300 the next morning. Defense measures against aircraft were to be completed before 0530. Every man, animal, and piece of equipment were to be concealed and camouflaged. During daylight only bivouac scouting parties moved ahead to select the next day's bivouac area. When CCF units were compelled for any reason to march by day, they were under standing orders for every man to stop in his tracks and remain motionless if aircraft appeared overhead. Officers were empowered to shoot down immediately any man who violated this order.[1]

Under such discipline, the Communist Chinese had succeeded in arraying 30 full divisions in the field: 18 divisions or 180,000 men of the XIII Army Group in the west and center opposing Eighth Army and the ROKs, and 12 divisions or 120,-000 men of the IX Army Group facing the U. S. X Corps in the east. With the entry of these forces, Premier Kim's North Korean Army ceased to be autonomous. The fiction of a combined North Korean and Chinese Communist headquarters under Kim around Kanggye was maintained, but the actual orders came from Peng Teh-huai who had set up his headquarters in Mukden.

Henceforth the Chinese would supply manpower and leadership—with the North Koreans taken in as junior partners—while Russia sent supplies. It was a situation somewhat similar to the American position in Korea, at least in that the United States provided approximately ten times more troops than all other United Nations members combined—never, of course, equaling the Republic of Korea manpower contribution—along with the leadership and most of the supplies.

As of September 30, MacArthur's United Nations command stood at 230,000 troops, of which 85,000 men were in air and naval arms. MacArthur's ground forces, then, were about 165,-000, and this number was augmented by the arrival in late November of the U. S. 3rd Infantry Division, another British brigade, a Turkish brigade, and a battalion each from Canada, the Netherlands, the Philippines and Thailand—giving MacArthur a land force of about 205,000 men. The figure might even have been higher, had not the rebounding optimism of MacArthur's headquarters dissuaded other United Nations members from sending troops to a war that was nearly over. Canada, for instance, had trained 10,000 soldiers especially for Korea, but then, expecting the war to be over by Christmas, had sent only one battalion, the Princess Pats.

Cheerful and unflagging optimism had again become fashionable in top-level command. MacArthur himself had told American soldiers that some of them would be "home for Christmas." His statement might have been intended only to reassure the Chinese that the United States intended to withdraw its troops from Korea, as has been said in MacArthur's defense, but it certainly helped swell the bag of happy gas again. The swift advance of X Corps in the east also inflated hopes. By mid-November the ROK Capitol Division had fought into the steel town of Chongjin, only 60 miles from the Siberian border. Farther west, on November 21, elements of Major General Barr's U. S. 7th Division marched into the Yalu River border town of Hyesanjin. MacArthur sent a message to X Corps' General Almond, saying: "Heartiest congratulations, Ned, and tell Dave Barr that the 7th Division hit the jackpot."

Next day Almond sent off his own message to Barr: "The fact that only twenty days ago this division landed amphibiously over the beaches at Iwon and advanced 200 miles over tortuous mountain terrain and fought successfully against a determined foe in subzero weather will be recorded in history as an outstanding military achievement." Once again the self-pluming, preening pride that had preceded the reverse of late October, again the bombast about "history" characteristic of the Seoul "liberation" announcement. The facts about Hyesanjin were simply that the 7th Division had landed unopposed at Iwon, had advanced toward Hyesanjin chiefly by vehicle, had not met any "determined foe" but only an occasional and brief defense of a town, and had suffered more casualties from frostbite than combat. Almond continued to speak of "enemy remnants fleeing north" while his own chief of staff, as has been seen, was dubious of General Willoughby's estimates of enemy strength, and after the commander of his Marine division had repeatedly voiced his fears of an enemy trap being set in the north.

Major General Oliver Smith's 1st Marine Division had already been in battle with the Communist Chinese 124th Division. On November 2, the 7th Marines collided with the Chinese at Sudong along the road to Chosin Reservoir, at virtually the same site of the ROK 3rd Division's late October defeat. The Marines drove the Chinese back and advanced steadily up to the high Koto-ri plateau, about 50 miles northwest of Hungnam. From captured prisoners they learned of large enemy forces being deployed around Chosin Reservoir. Unfortunately, it was not accepted until much later in the war that enemy privates often knew of broad plans to an extent and detail usually reserved for battalion commanders and above in the American Army. And so, the remarkable story of ten divisions of the Chinese IX Army Group setting a trap for X Corps was not completely believed, in spite of corroborating reports from North Korean civilians. Nonetheless, Smith was worried. The movement of the enemy 124th Division above Sudong appeared to him to be a blocking action meant to delay the 1st Marine Division in its march north. Smith feared large-scale enemy intervention in the north, and on November 15 he wrote to the Marine Commandant in Washington:

So far our MSR [main supply route] north of Hamhung has not been molested, but there is evidence that this situation will not continue. . . .

Someone in high authority will have to make up his mind as to what is our goal. My mission is still to advance to the border. The Eighth Army, 80 miles to the southwest,* will not attack until the 20th [sic]. Manifestly, we should not push on without regard to the Eighth Army. We would simply get further out on a limb. If the Eighth Army push does not go, then the decision will have to be made as to what to do next. I believe a winter campaign in the mountains of North Korea is too much to ask of the American soldier or marine, and I doubt the feasibility of supplying troops in this area during the winter or providing for the evacuation of sick and wounded.

Smith's letter of November 15 ended by reiterating his concern over his "wide open left flank" as well as his disquiet at "the prospect of stringing out a Marine division along a single mountain road for 120 air miles from Hamhung to the border." It was on this day that MacArthur decided to launch the November 24 offensive, with the X Corps attacking northwest into Manpojin-Kanggye-Huichon rather than advancing all the way to the border. The 1st Marine Division was to move up to Chosin Reservoir to assume position for that strike. Smith, still uneasy, approached Almond to ask that he be allowed to bring his units together as well as to begin constructing an airfield midway along the road to Chosin. Almond granted the first request but saw no reason for the second. Finally he agreed to allow Smith to build an airstrip on his own. On November 16, Smith and Major General Field Harris, commander of the First Marine Air Wing, drove up to Hagaru-ri about a dozen miles below Chosin Reservoir, looking for possible airfield sites. They found one in a frozen bean field, and on November 19, the airstrip was begun. In the meantime, Smith deliberately ordered the commanders of his 7th and 5th Regiments to drag their feet en route to the jump-off point for the assault from Chosin

*At the time Smith wrote the gap was at its widest, for the Marines had been advancing north to Chosin. Generally, however, the gap was about 50 air miles.

Reservoir, while carefully stockpiling arms along the Hungnam-Hamhung-Chosin road.

That "wide open left flank" of which Smith complained—the gap between Eighth Army in the southwest and X Corps in the northeast—remained open. It could not actually be closed, of course, because of the wildness of the terrain. But it could be penetrated, and the Chinese were already poised for this purpose. Twin offensives were to come along either side of the mountains to turn Eighth Army's right and X Corps' left. Then both commands would be pressed back against the coasts while other Communist divisions plunged directly south to link up with guerrillas and bypassed North Korean units in the United Nations rear. This was the plan, envisioning nothing less than utter destruction of MacArthur's forces, and on November 19 the Moscow radio had already predicted that this would happen.

On November 23, meanwhile, Thanksgiving Day turkey dinners were served to the troops, and the next day, with its American soldiers joking grimly about having been "fattened up for the slaughter," Eighth Army attacked in the west.

General Walker's forces advanced three corps abreast along a 50-mile front north of the Chongchon. From left to right they were the U. S. I and IX and ROK II. The division order was the U. S. 24th, ROK 1st, U. S. 25th and 2nd, the ROK 7th and 8th. In reserve were the U. S. 1st Cavalry Division, the ROK 6th Division, the British 27th and 29th Brigades and the Turkish Brigade. Other newly arrived United Nations units had not yet been fed into battle formations.

The men attacked behind the heaviest artillery barrage of the war, moving out at ten o'clock of a Friday morning with the cold already at zero levels, the roads glazed with ice, the bare brown hills blotched with snow, and a savage north wind biting at their faces. They made quick gains, bearing out the confidence expressed in the MacArthur communiqué which had been read to all hands before the offensive began. It said:

> The United Nations massive compression envelopment in North Korea against the new Red Armies operating there is now approaching its decisive effort. The isolating component of the pincer, our air forces of all types, have for the past three weeks,

in a sustained attack of model coordination and effectiveness, successfully interdicted enemy lines of support from the north so that further reinforcement therefrom has been sharply curtailed and essential supplies markedly limited. The eastern sector of the pincer, with noteworthy and effective naval support, has now reached commanding enveloping position, cutting in two the northern reaches of the enemy's geographical potential. This morning the western sector of the pincer moves forward in general assault in an effort to complete the compression and close the vise. If successful, this should for all practical purposes end the war, restore peace and unity to Korea, enable the prompt withdrawal of United Nations military forces, and permit the complete assumption by the Korean people and nation of full sovereignty and international equality. It is this for which we fight.

By nightfall the Eighth Army's advance could be measured in terms of as much as ten miles in the far west where the U. S. 24th Division was again racing toward Chongju, and nearly as much in the center-right, where the U. S. 2nd Division had reached Kujang-dong ten miles or so above its departure point at Kunu-ri. Only on the far right had there been nonappreciable gains. Here, the ROK II Corps, moving through mountainous central Korea and against gradually stiffening opposition, had advanced very little from its jump-off point at Tokchon. The ROK failure did not sit too well with Major General Laurence Keiser, commander of the 2nd Division, for Tokchon was about 15 miles southeast or below and to the right of his troops in Kujang-dong. More, Keiser had heard from air observers that the enemy was transforming the oxcart trail linking Huichon and Tokchon into a broad road.

"Goddam it!" Keiser swore, "that's where they're going to hit. That will be the main effort—off our flank and against ROK II Corps."

Unfortunately for his division and his troops, Keiser was right. Before dawn of the next day, Saturday the 25th, the Chinese Communists launched probing counterattacks. On the western end of the Eighth Army front they rolled back the ROK 1st Division for two miles before General Paik's men stiffened and held. Then, they began striking all along the line except at the U. S. 24th Division in the west. It may have been

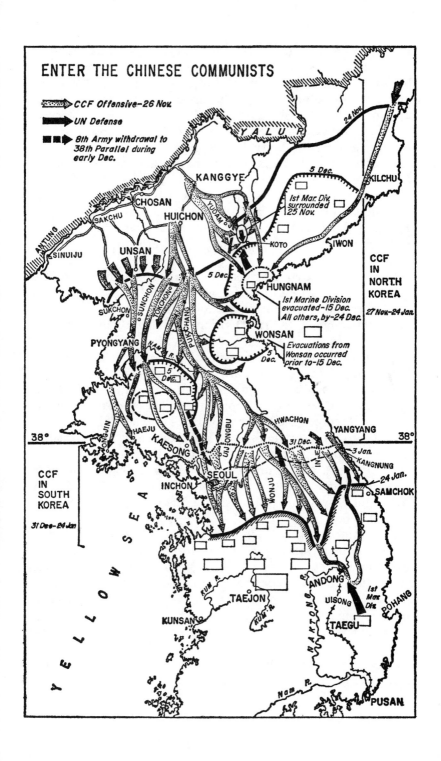

that they were hunting for the South Koreans, as has since been suggested. At any rate, by accident or design, the Communist division did find that ROK II Corps which they had mauled only a month before. That night, under a bright moon, to the blare of bugles, the shrilling of whistles and clanging of cymbals, the Chinese came swarming over the Tokchon hills, infiltrating and setting up their customary roadblocks to the rear while other massed divisions in the north came marching down the new road from Huichon. Meanwhile, bypassed detachments of North Korean regulars moved through the gap separating the United Nations command to slip inside the exposed right rear of the ROK II Corps. And then the massive Chinese counterstroke fell in full fury on the 7th and 8th divisions of that luckless II Corps.

They were broken, fragmented, and then smashed into bits and pieces of leaderless units streaming south.

Another enemy column struck south from Unsan against the U. S. 25th and ROK 1st Divisions, driving them back and threatening to cut off the U. S. 24th Division on its far western end run to Chongju. For the third time since it entered the Korean War, the 24th or Taro Leaf Division was ordered to withdraw, pulling back from Chongju to the south bank of the Chongchon River around Sinanju Airfield, a distance of 30 miles. This represented General Walker's new left flank.

To the right, 40 miles east at Tokchon, there was no flank, only that gaping void brought about by the destruction of the ROK II Corps. And Chinese were pouring through it in great numbers. Their intention was obvious: they would wheel to their right or west and pin the entire Eighth Army back against the Yellow Sea.

The Chinese began to close the trap on the morning of November 26 by advancing troops southwest from Tokchon, thus threatening to cut off the 2nd Division to the northwest of that city. If the threat was effected, the Communists could then race due west to the Yellow Sea undeterred and seal off escape routes at some point below Sinanju Airfield.

General Walker began committing his reserves, and the first to go was the 5,000 man Turkish Brigade. The Turks were actually ordered into battle by Major General John Coulter, commander of the IX Corps to which they had been attached. They were to march north from Kunu-ri to Tokchon, a distance of 20 miles, and halt the onrushing enemy masses, thus saving the 2nd Division's right—a maneuver which, as S. L. A. Marshall has observed, "was like applying an aspirin bottle cork to a bunghole in a beer barrel." The Turks moved out, and then, after reaching the village of Wawon about seven miles east, were brought to the battle which American newsmen, eager for a victory to report (especially, it seems, if it could be about those "Terrible Turks" of whom Americans knew so little), proclaimed around the globe.

> No small fight ever won more impressive headlines around the world. The word was flashed that the Turks, meeting the Chinese for the first time, had dealt them a bloody repulse at bayonet point; it was the first stirring bit of news from the November battle. But what precisely happened in the first few hours at Wawon is still an open question. The brigade also boasted the capture of several hundred enemy prisoners from among these first "Chinese" waves. The word gave a lift to the neighbors. Lt. Sukio Oji, a Nisei interpreter, was sent by 2nd Division to interview the prisoners. Instead of Chinese, he found 200 forlorn ROKs who had blundered into the Turkish column while beating their way back from the fight at Tokchon.[2]

This was not, of course, the fault of the Turks, and they fought gallantly the next day when the vanguard of the Chinese onslaught caught them still astride the road at Wawon. But they, too, were broken by this flood of armed men, and when the remnants of the brigade drifted north to join the 2nd Division, the brigade was no longer battle-worthy. In the meantime, throughout November 27, the Chinese Communists and their North Korean allies were causing the collapse of General MacArthur's win-the-war offensive. Worse, they confronted the reeling Eighth Army with catastrophe.

Once again, Lieutenant General Walker found himself battling to save his army. His divisions were falling back all along the Chongchon River. Further efforts to plug the gap on the right with the 1st Cavalry and the British Brigades proved futile. The Chinese were too numerous and had penetrated too far. Fierce battles were raging everywhere. Southbound roads were jammed with traffic, with soldiers of all races, with fleeing civilians, with tanks. Chinese gunners had more targets than they could shoot at.

It was now obviously impossible to hold at the Chongchon River, either above or below it, and General Walker began the retreat which ultimately preserved the United Nations forces in Korea. All the while, this withdrawal was covered by the northernmost 2nd Division fighting a dogged delaying action back to the Chongchon. That it was successful was also due to the overwhelming air and naval superiority which Walker possessed, especially the air power in those sectors too far inland to be reached by naval gunfire.

But the 2nd Infantry Division's trial by fire, a most literal and terrible running of the gantlet, was yet to come. On December 1, having successfully held off the enemy while retreating south from Kujang-dong, having crossed to the south bank of the Chongchon and regained their original jumping-off point, about 7,000 men of the 2nd Division boarded trucks for rapid movement south to Sunchon. They drove into ambush. Unknown to General Keiser, an entire Communist Chinese division had set up a roadblock along a five-mile stretch of the road from Kunu-ri to Sunchon. Their guns were in position on all the high ground to either side, some of them only 100 yards from the road. At the end of this ambuscade was "The Pass," a narrow quarter-mile defile through high embankments of dirt and loose rock—and it was here that the battered and reeling 2nd Division was struck and scourged as no other United Nations division before or since.

General Keiser had been phenomenally lucky in his jeep run through the greater part of the gantlet. After leaving his command post in the bivouac area at about 1330, he doubled along the stalled parts of the column almost without stopping and got to the final ridge at about 1515. This placed him in "The Pass" approximately twenty minutes after the column had wedged there. He personally witnessed the atrophy of the troops who had closed in just prior to his arrival. The dead lay in the ditches and sprawled across the roadway. Most of the living—even those still unwounded—were in such a state of shock that they responded to nothing, saw nothing, and seemingly heard nothing. The Chinese fire beat like hail among the rocks and next the vehicles where they stood or reclined. But they neither cried out nor sought better cover. Their facial expressions remained set, appearing almost masklike because of the heavy coating of dust and the distortion from the dropping of the jaw. An occasional one whispered, "Water! Water!" as if he had been saying it over and over and could not stop, but there was little else which was intelligible. They were saying nothing and doing nothing except that a few shuffled about aimlessly, seeming to reel in their tracks. The division commander walked among them, moving from group to group, barking questions, trying to startle them back to consciousness. "Who's in command here?" "Who *are* you?" "Can any of you do anything?" He got not a single response. The Americans remained as mute as did the ROKs and the Turks, who probably didn't understand his words.

Keiser decided to walk to the south end of "The Pass." He wanted to see if the Chinese had effectively blocked the exit with fire, and he was still looking for men who might be rallied. It was an incredible reconnaissance for the top man. The Air Force was now working back and forth along the embankments on both sides, and the bullet stream was chipping the rocks less than 75 yards above the floor of the cut. Napalm spilled down onto the road, as it bounced off the cliffs, and set several vehicles afire. Clips from the .50-caliber guns were flying about everywhere. The din was terrific.

One thing made his heart leap up. A sergeant from the 9th Infantry had taken an 81-mm mortar from a ¾-ton truck, set it up in the middle of the roadway, and was now single-handedly firing the piece on line of sight against the Chinese positions atop the south exit. It was the only fire Keiser saw being delivered by an American. But he noted a few other self-possessed individuals, most of whom were trying to help the wounded. One man sat on the hood of a jeep trying to bandage the wound of a second man braced up against the windshield. Keiser saw that the man's foot had been shot away clean at the ankle. He passed another badly wounded man who was lying in a ditch. A second soldier, himself wounded, was trying to drag him to a better cover behind a jeep, but was having a hard tussle. So he was helping with his voice. Keiser heard him say: "Now get your Goddamned leg around the corner of that jeep. Do it, I say! That's the way. Goddamn it, I knew you could make it ..."

The pile-up of American, Turk, and ROK dead in the ditches and along the roadside was mute proof that the enemy gunners were on their mark. Keiser started back toward the top of "The Pass" . . .

As he trudged uphill, he found that his feet were leaden. His journey along this terrible ambush was sapping his physical energy at an excessive rate, even as it drained the last reserve of the private soldier. Never had his shoe pacs weighed so heavy! Directly in his path, crosswise of the road, lay the body of one of his men. He tried to step across it, but failing to lift his foot high enough, struck his toe against the figure's midriff. Thereupon the supposed corpse sat bolt upright and said: "You damned son-of-a-bitch!" Keiser was so astonished that he replied only: "My friend, I'm sorry," and continued on his way.[3]

So went the dreadful ordeal of the 2nd Infantry Division moving through the enemy's five-mile ambush. By the end of the day, roughly 3,000 of the 7,000 men who had run the gantlet were dead or wounded—and the loss of vehicles was enormous. And it might well have been worse, but for the intervention of American air, and the inexplicable, but fortunate, failure of the Communists to exploit the temporary aerial advantage which their fast-flying Russian-built MIGs had won them in northwestern Korea. Eventually the 2nd Infantry Division escaped, assisted by a British column holding open the bottom of "The Pass." It had lost a quarter of its total strength since the abortive United Nations offensive began on November 24, and on December 2 the division went south to regroup behind the blocking position held by the 1st Cavalry Division at Sunchon.

Far to the east, meanwhile, the 1st Marine Division had begun to march through a much longer ambuscade—one prepared by no less than seven enemy divisions—to which was added the further trial of a cruel and incredible cold.

Chapter Seven

THE severity of the Korean climate has been exaggerated in the American press, probably because it has been assumed that the cold white beast of wind and snow that howls over northeastern Korea is typical of winter throughout the peninsula.

This is not so. Except for the lofty plateaus of the northeast, Korea's winters are normally no more rigorous than those of the northeastern United States. Although temperatures do fall to -10° or -15°, they rarely hold at that level for more than a few days. This is not, of course, a mild winter, but it becomes so when compared to the climate on the Koto-ri plateau to which the 1st Marine Division had come in November of 1950.

There the temperatures were consistently at from -20° to -30° or -35° during the night and only infrequently above zero during the day. The winds were sharp and strong and constant snowfalls were sometimes whipped into blizzards. In such cold, weapons froze, food froze, human flesh and blood froze. Medical corpsmen had to put morphine syrettes in their mouths to thaw them out before using them on the wounded. Hungry men who had unwisely consumed the food that froze in their packs were afflicted with terrible gnawing stomach pains known as enteritis, and many other men were felled by frostbite, either from normal exposure to this extreme cold in the course of battle, or because, having ceased to exert themselves, the sweat forming inside their shoepacs froze around their feet and thus encased them in sheaths of ice. In such cold, mechanized vehicles broke down; the motors of tanks and trucks had to be started and run every few hours lest they freeze solid. Weapons would not work because the gases generated by burning powder were too weak to move frozen parts. Shells did not go off and artillery pieces would literally creep back into place once fired, rather than leap back. Entrenching tools were next to useless when struck against that iron earth, and many battles were fought from behind "fortifications" formed by dead and frozen bodies. Simply to bury the dead required feats of engineering ingenuity. Nowhere was food or sanctuary to be found, for the land was barren and deserted but for the few pitiful Koreans who lived on in their mud-hut villages, while the bitter winds of Manchuria came whistling down their desolated mountain peaks, freezing the rivers, choking the gorges with snow and glazing the rocks with ice.

It was in this winter that the men of the 1st Marine Division had been marching north toward the light blue sheet of ice that was Chosin Reservoir—"Frozen Chosin" as it would be forever called—while the Chinese Communist IX Field Army came stealing down from Manchuria to set a trap for them.

This force was commanded by General Sung Shin-lun. Forty years old, Sung was already a veteran of more than two decades of combat. He had been handling troops since his graduation from Whampoa Military Academy at the age of seventeen, and he had commanded a regiment on the Long March at the age of twenty-six. His secret movement of twelve divisions of men from Manchuria to Chosin Reservoir can be regarded as being among the masterly feats of modern arms.

Sung's plan was to annihilate the Marine division and subsequently destroy the entire U. S. X Corps. His attack was, of course, the eastern wing of the twin offensive ordered by Peng Teh-huai up in Mukden. Sung was to move down the east side of the gap dividing the United Nations forces, and then wheel east to the Sea of Japan, thus ensnaring the 105,000 Americans and ROKs of X Corps. These forces consisted of the U. S. 7th Division's 17th Regiment, already beginning to withdraw southeast from Hyesanjin to Iwon on the coast and eventual evacuation; the ROK Capitol Division, which had turned around at Chongjin 60 miles below the Siberian border and was marching south along the coastal road to the safety of Hungnam; the ROK 3rd Division farther down the coastal road also retreating toward Hungnam; the U. S. 3rd Infantry Division newly arrived at Hungnam and charged with protecting the port area; and the U. S. 1st Marine Division and elements of the 7th strung out in the Chosin Reservoir area 53 to 78 miles northwest of Hungnam. To sweep all of these forces into his net, Sung had to annihilate the 1st Marine Division and a task force of 2,500 men from the 7th Division. Then his troops would race down the road to Hungnam unimpeded to prevent the 3rd Infantry Division from making contact with Eighth Army in the west, while slamming shut the X Corps' escape door at Hungnam.

By November 26–27 these United Nations forces chosen for destruction were strung out along the 78 miles of narrow winding road between Hungnam and Chosin Reservoir. Fortunately, Major General Smith had been able to concentrate the bulk of his 25,000-man division at three points: at Koto-ri, 53 miles north of Hungnam, where Colonel Puller commanded 2,500 Marines, some ROKs, 1,500 U. S. soldiers and 250 commandos of the British Royal Marines, about 4,200 men; at Hagaru-ri another 11 miles north, where the airstrip was being built and where Smith had his headquarters, 3,000 more; and at Yudam-ni still 14 miles farther north, where the 5th and 7th Marines were poised for the enveloping attack northwestward to the Yalu, another 8,000 men. Yudam-ni was a little town to the west or left of Chosin Reservoir. On the right or east of the Japanese-built reservoir, one of the world's largest, was the village of Sinhung-ni, and here were the 2,500 men of the 7th Division task force.

Under General Sung's plan to destroy these forces, the 5th and 7th Marines at Yudam-ni would be allowed to move west along the road to the border before being cut off. Then Sung would overwhelm the 7th Division task force to the east of the reservoir. After that he would knock out the Marines at Hagaru-ri and those at Koto-ri, and the road to Hungnam would be open. To inflame his troops against the Marines, he had the composition *The Bloody Path,* by Captain G. Doidzhashvili of the Russian Navy, disseminated among them by pamphlet or lecture. It said in part:

> When, in the summer of 1950 the American imperialist marauders, the newly appeared pretenders to world domination, provoked the bloody holocaust in Korea, the Wall Street housedog General MacArthur demanded that the American so-called "Marines" be immediately placed at his disposal. This professional murderer and inveterate war criminal intended to throw

them into battle as quickly as possible for the purpose of inflicting as it seemed to him then, a final blow on the Korean people.

In putting forward such a demand, MacArthur proceeded
from the fact that US "Marine" units have been trained more
than any other types of American forces for the waging of the un-
precedently brutal and inhuman, predatory war against the free-
dom-loving heroic Korean people.

It was precisely to US Marines that the Ober-bandit Mac-
Arthur addressed the words: "A rich city lies ahead of you, it has
much wine and tasty morsels. Take Seoul and all the girls will be
yours, the property of the inhabitants belongs to the conquerors
and you will be able to send parcels home."

The events in Korea have shown graphically that the Marine
Corps stalwarts did not turn a deaf ear to the appeal of their
rapacious ataman. They have abundantly covered Korean soil
with the blood and tears of hundreds and thousands of Korean
women, old people and children. . . .

Continuing for a few more foaming pages, Captain Doidzhashvili's harangue detailed the crimes of the "monsters" in their
"role of stiflers of small states and peoples," after which the
troops were read General Sung's battle message, which said:
"Soon we will meet the American Marines in battle. We will destroy them. When they are defeated the enemy army will collapse and our country will be free from the threat of aggression.
Kill these Marines as you would snakes in your homes."

By November 24 the trap northwest of Yudam-ni had been
set, but the two Marine regiments, under orders from the wary
General Smith to drag their feet, did not poke their way into it.
That same day the Eighth Army offensive jumped off in the
west, and the following day, November 25, with the Marines
still marking time at Chosin Reservoir, the XIII Army Group
of the Chinese Communist Third Field Army launched its massive counterstroke against the Eighth Army. In the east, General Almond quickly ordered General Smith to attack west on
November 27 to relieve the pressure on Eighth Army's right
flank. The 5th and 7th Marines moved out cautiously. They
were struck. They halted, moved forward again, and were
struck again. They pulled back to Yudam-ni. Throughout the
dusk and early darkness, the 5th under Lieutenant Colonel

Murray and the 7th under Colonel Homer Litzenberg began organizing and fortifying the Yudam-ni ridges.

That night the Chinese attacked with savage force. The 79th and 89th Divisions hurled their assault battalions against the Yudam-ni ridges, where seesaw fighting raged until dawn, while the 59th marched south to cut the road between Yudam-ni and Hagaru. This division also assaulted a company of Marines on a high hill overlooking vital Toktong Pass, but were unable to dislodge them. The pass would prove to be vital in the Marine withdrawal to come.

The same night the Chinese struck hard at the 7th Division task force to the east of the reservoir, splitting it and isolating the two groups.

On the night of November 28, two more Chinese divisions attacked Hagaru and came within an eyelash of capturing it, with its important new airfield, and the following night elements of two more struck at Koto-ri. During these three days the Chinese blocked the road at points along the 35 miles from Yudam-ni south to Chinhung-ni, building log barriers which were covered by small arms, mortars and artillery located on the heights to either side of the road. Still more units were sent south overland for the eventual strike at Hungnam. Meanwhile, pressure was maintained against the main Marine concentrations at Yudam-ni, Hagaru-ri, and Koto-ri. But for that providential airport which was nearly completed, General Oliver Smith's fears had been fulfilled: he was cut off and his division was flanked fore and aft. It was no wonder then that General Walter Bedell Smith, Chief of the Central Intelligence Agency, glanced at the ominous red dots on the map showing the X Corps situation at the end of November, and said:

"Only diplomacy can save MacArthur's right flank."

On November 28, the heady wine of Inchon having now become the hangover of the Chongchon, General Douglas MacArthur changed his plans from the offensive to the defensive, and sent a special communiqué to the United Nations:

Enemy reactions developed in the course of our assault operations of the past four days disclose that a major segment of the Chinese continental forces in army, corps and divisional organization of an aggregate strength of over 200,000 men is now arrayed against the United Nations forces in Korea. . . . Consequently, we face an entirely new war.

General MacArthur also contacted Washington to report: "This command has done everything humanly possible within its capabilities but is now faced with conditions beyond its control and its strength." Then the United Nations commander asked that the Truman Administration reconsider the offer of troops made by Chiang Kai-shek five months before. This sequence of messages, on the one hand seeming to prepare an excuse for failure, on the other portending a renewal of MacArthur's demands for the right to bomb Manchuria, together with reports which erased all doubts that there had been a stunning United Nations defeat, caused Truman to call a special meeting of the National Security Council:

... General Bradley and the Chiefs of Staff had been in session all the day before, examining the situation, and they felt that while it was serious they were doubtful that it was as much a catastrophe as our newspapers were leading us to believe.

General Bradley, however, stressed the danger that might arise if the Communists decided to use their air potential. It was our information that there were at least three hundred bombers on fields in nearby Manchuria. These bombers could hurt us badly, both by attacks on the airlift and by surprise raids on our closely jammed planes on Korean fields. Despite these facts, General Bradley said that the Joint Chiefs of Staff did not believe that General MacArthur should be authorized to bomb airfields in Manchuria.

... [Secretary of Defense] Marshall then talked about the diplomatic aspects of the situation, saying he thought it essential for the United States to go along with the United Nations approach to the Korean question, even if going along with the United Nations meant some difficult problems for us. He said that he felt it essential for us to keep a unanimity of approach in the UN. He was emphatic on one point, on which he said the three service Secretaries were agreed as the most important: that we should not get ourselves involved either individually or with the United Nations in a general war with China.

Bradley said this reflected the Joint Chiefs' thinking too. If we allowed ourselves to be pulled into a general war with China, it would be impossible to continue the build-up of forces in Europe. Secretary [of War] [Frank] Pace added that it was important that everyone in the room understand that we had only the 82nd Airborne Division available at home and that the National Guard units that had been called into federal service would not be ready for combat until the middle of March.

. . . [Secretary of State Dean Acheson] said that we needed to bear in mind that the Soviet Union was behind every one of the Chinese and North Korean moves and that we had to think of all that happened in Korea as world matters. We should never lose sight of the fact that we were facing the Soviet Union all around the world.

Of course, Acheson continued, if we openly accused the Soviet Union of aggression, the United Nations would be demolished. If we came out and pointed a finger at the Soviet Union, it would serve no purpose, because we could do nothing about it. To make the accusation, however, and then to do nothing about it would only weaken our world position. If we proposed action against the Kremlin, on the other hand, we might find ourselves alone, without allies.

. . . As for the conflict in Korea, the Secretary of State was of the opinion that we should find some way to end it. If we went into Manchuria and bombed the airfields there with any degree of success, "Russia would cheerfully get in it." We had banked our entire foreign policy on the idea of keeping Russia contained, and we had succeeded in repulsing her attempts to break out. If we allowed the Russians now to trap us inside their perimeter, however, we would run the risk of being sucked into a bottomless pit. There would be no end to it, and it would bleed us dry. The Russians had tried to lure us into traps time and again. This one differed only in being bigger than the earlier ones.[1]

From this November 28 emergency meeting, then, came the conclusions shaping the policy which thereafter guided the American conduct of the United Nations cause in Korea. The Truman Administration recognized that it was no longer possible to unify Korea by force and that some way to end the war must be found. In no case would Manchuria be bombed or anything done to give Premier Joseph Stalin a chance to involve America, in General Bradley's subsequent and famous phrase, "in the wrong war, at the wrong place, at the wrong time, and with the wrong enemy." Defense of Europe and containment of the Soviet Union remained the objectives of American foreign policy.

Unhappily, only two days later, during a question-and-answer exchange with newsmen at a Presidential news conference, Mr. Truman gave the world the impression that he was considering using the atomic bomb in Korea. Although Truman quickly issued a statement pointing out, "Consideration of the use of any weapon is always implicit in the very possession of that weapon," the reaction among the United Nations allies was still not good, and in England it was bad. One hundred Labor MPs signed a letter to Prime Minister Clement Attlee protesting possible use of nuclear weapons in Korea.

Amid widespread criticism of General MacArthur's failure to win the war, a long and anxious debate was begun in the British Parliament. Conservatives such as Winston Churchill, Anthony Eden and R. A. Butler also expressed uneasiness at the prospect of being involved in World War III by American "rashness." Butler said that "the British people as a whole wished to be assured before their fate was decided that they were helping to decide their own fate." The debate, probably as much a consequence of MacArthur's defeat as of Truman's indiscretion, ended with cheers when Prime Minister Attlee announced that he was flying to Washington to consult Truman. During that consultation, Attlee's fears were allayed on the use of the atomic bomb—though he was unable to convince Truman that Red China was not a Russian satellite but a Communist power in her own right who could be detached from the Kremlin as "a counterpoise" to Russia in the Far East—and a solid allied front was again presented to the world. This was the outstanding public disagreement between the United Nations allies of the war. Thereafter, disputes were less vital and more private and the negotiation of a cease-fire became the goal.

Red China, however, wanted no cease-fire. It was now Peiping's turn to attempt to unify Korea by force. As the events of December, 1950, have shown, Mao Tse-tung and the men around him were in belligerent and imperious mood. They had won at the Chongchon, they seemed to have prepared enemy disaster at Chosin, and now they would destroy the United Nations utterly.

They pressed the pursuit south with great speed. The Chinese soldier, unburdened but for what he carried on his back, was capable of great mobility, and within a week of the Chinese counteroffensive the Eighth Army had been forced back 50 miles in its center. Retreat on the flanks was slower only because General Walker had committed his reserves. And on the right flank the situation was almost constantly critical. Here the 1st Cavalry and 24th Infantry Divisions fought stubbornly, assisted by various remnants of the shattered ROK II Corps, battling not only Chinese but regiments of bypassed North Koreans with whom the Chinese had made junction.

Despite such efforts, the Chinese Communist Forces still rushed south, so eager to deliver the knockout blow that they abandoned the march and camouflage discipline which had brought them into Korea almost undetected. Massed battalions moved along the roads in bold daylight movement, and at night Chinese motor columns ran with their lights on. Such indifference to American air superiority was paid for in heavy casualties. General Stratemeyer estimated that his airmen had killed or wounded 33,000 enemy soldiers in the first two weeks of December. Casualties, however, seemed no deterrent to the Communist high command, and as a result of their willingness to accept them, they were able to effect speedy liberation of Premier Kim Il Sung's capital city of Pyongyang.

General Walker had hoped to hold around Pyongyang, along a line roughly following the road from Pyongyang to Wonsan on the east coast. But the Chinese fought into Songchon in between the two cities and cut the road there. Now the Eighth Army would have to retreat farther south, to a line in the vicinity of the 38th Parallel. Even withdrawal all the way back to Pusan was now a grim possibility, and on December 4, again drawing attention to the benefit which restriction of American air power to the battlefield gave to the enemy, General MacArthur concluded a message to Washington with these words:

It is clearly evident . . . that unless ground reinforcements of the greatest magnitude are promptly supplied, this Command will be either forced into successive withdrawals with diminished powers of resistance after each such move, or will be forced to take up beachhead bastion positions which, while insuring a degree of prolonged resistance, would afford little hope of anything beyond defense.

This small command actually under present conditions is facing the entire Chinese nation in an undeclared war and unless some positive and immediate action is taken, hope for success cannot be justified and steady attrition leading to final destruction can reasonably be contemplated.

Although the command up to the present time has exhibited good morale and marked efficiency, it has been in almost unending combat for five months and is mentally fatigued and physically battered. The combat effectiveness of the Republic of Korea Forces now at our disposal is negligible; for police and constabulary uses they would have some effectiveness. The other foreign army contingents, whatever their combat efficiency may be, are in such small strength as to exercise little influence. Each United States division at my disposal other than the First Marine Division is now approximately 5,000 men under strength and at no time have they achieved their full authorized numerical complement. The Chinese troops are fresh, completely organized, splendidly trained and equipped and apparently in peak condition for actual operations. The general evaluation of the situation here must be viewed on the basis of an entirely new war against an entirely new power of great military strength and under entirely new conditions.

. . . The strategic concept suitable for operations against the North Korean Army which was so successful is not susceptible to continued application against such power. This calls for political decisions and strategic plans in implementation thereof, adequate fully to meet the realities involved. In this, time is of the essence as every hour sees the enemy power increase and ours decline.

President Truman quickly approved a reply by the Joint Chiefs of Staff which said: "We consider that the preservation of your forces is now the primary consideration. Consolidation of forces into beachheads is concurred in." Then, as evidence of how alarming he considered the situation, Truman ordered General J. Lawton Collins, Army Chief of Staff, to fly to Tokyo to talk to MacArthur. The next day, the Eighth Army began pulling out of Pyongyang.

General Walker had already ordered a "scorched earth" withdrawal. For days, demolition crews had been setting explosives and torches to bridges, railways, power plants, airport facilities, warehouses—whatever might serve the approaching enemy. Sadly enough, almost all of these installations had been similarly destroyed by the North Koreans before they retreated, and then repaired by the U. S. Army during its occupation of the city. Millions of dollars' worth of supplies which could not be rapidly moved were destroyed by fire. A great red-tinged pall of smoke hung over the city, while across the Tae-dong River to the north, men of the U. S. 25th Division, the British brigades, and the ROK 1st Division fought a covering action. A unit of British tankers was the last to withdraw, and then American engineers blew the bridges, and the United Nations retreat to the 38th Parallel was on.

Accompanying it was a mass migration of North Korean civilians. In numbers variously estimated at between one and two million persons, they crowded aboard locomotives or packed their belongings on their backs or in oxcarts and left their devastated villages to the approaching Communists. Some of them were evacuated south by ship, for the United Nations navy was already at work assisting the Eighth Army in what was now an ordered and model withdrawal.

On December 3 the U. S. Navy commenced evacuating United Nations personnel and equipment from Wonsan on the east coast. Here, too, the civilians were anxious to get out before the Communist arrival. According to the action report of Captain Albert E. Jarrell, commander of Transport Division Eleven:

> We commenced loading Korean civilians aboard the SS *Lane Victory* at anchor at 0500 on December 7. We had previously made arrangements with the local police to screen the civilians to be evacuated. Specifically, only those persons whom the North Koreans might classify as "enemy"—with all the finality which

that word implies—were to be taken out. Originally, we'd expected about 1,000 civilians, but it became quickly apparent that this number would be greatly exceeded.

That excess produced another neuralgic pain—if we refused asylum to any of those selected, our refusal would be two strikes against them after we left. I therefore gave orders to continue loading to capacity. By midnight, 7,009 people—many of them women and children—were embarked. There were many more than that still left. I estimated that the entire population of Wonsan (75,000) plus an equal number from outlying towns, wanted desperately to leave. About 20,000 were still clambering about the barbed wire and tank barriers long after we were chockablock with passengers.

The Wonsan evacuation was matched by one at Chinnampo, the port for Pyongyang, though here there was greater risk. About 8,700 persons, among them civilians and wounded soldiers, were aboard transports at Pyongyang but unable to move because of numerous mines in the Taedong River estuary down which they had to sail to reach the Yellow Sea. The night of the 5th, under cover of darkness and a heavy snowstorm, one American, two Australian and three Canadian destroyers from the west coast fleet of British Vice-Admiral W. G. Andrewes picked their way up the estuary, shelled Pyongyang and brought the transports back down in safety. Sea evacuations were also made in Inchon and at Iwon, but the biggest of all, the redeployment of X Corps from Hungnam, was still to be effected. The Hungnam operation was begun on December 11, the day after the 1st Marine Division broke out of General Sung Shin-lun's trap at Chosin Reservoir.

In the first few days of December the predicament of the 1st Marine Division seemed hopeless. The Chinese had already flanked the Marines on the west to a depth of 35 miles and had fragmented them by seizing the road linking the four strongholds from Yudam-ni at the reservoir south to Hagaru-ri to Koto-ri to Chinhung-ni. By nightfall of December 1, the right flank was also turned with the destruction of the 7th Division task force to the east of the reservoir.

This unit, composed of elements of the 31st and 32nd Infantry Regiments, was originally led by Colonel Allen MacLean. But Colonel MacLean was reported missing in action during the first Chinese onslaughts and Lieutenant Colonel Don Faith, commander of the 1st Battalion, 32nd, took over. The formation then became known as Task Force Faith. On December 1, Lieutenant Colonel Faith decided to try to fight his way down to Major General Oliver Smith's headquarters in Hagaru, twelve miles to the southwest. Destroying his howitzers and all but essential equipment, loading hundreds of wounded aboard trucks, supported by Marine air, Faith began his movement. Though his column was attacked all the way, yet it seemed on the verge of reaching Hagaru when at dusk, four and a half miles above Hagaru, Faith was killed and his unit fell apart. Men drifted across the hills and the frozen reservoir, trying to reach the Marine lines. Ultimately, 670 of them did so. The truck convoy of wounded was attacked by the Chinese and many were killed, although about 350 of them were rescued by the Marines at Hagaru.

And so, with Task Force Faith gone and both Marine flanks thus exposed, with the only escape route south blocked, General Sung was able to commence piecemeal destruction of the four Marine strongholds. Major General Oliver Smith's response was to counter Sung's tactics: the Marines would hold firm and gather their strength, the Yudam-ni garrison withdrawing south to join the Hagaru garrison, these two then fighting down to Koto-ri, and these three then moving down to Chinhung-ni and so on to the safety of the sea at Hungnam. The movement would require the utmost discipline, and would rely heavily on air power for supply and close support. It also depended on each of the garrison towns standing firm, and for a time Smith's own headquarters at Hagaru—with the vital airfield already in operation by December 1—was under heavy attack. The Marine general's attempt to relieve it produced his only defeat.

A force of about 1,000 men, 150 trucks and 30 tanks under Lieutenant Colonel Douglas Drysdale of the British Royal Marines left Koto-ri for Hagaru on November 29. Midway along the 11-mile march, Task Force Drysdale ran into a roadblock and was ambushed. The Chinese quickly chopped the Marine force into three fragments and succeeded in killing, wounding or capturing 650 of its men while destroying half its vehicles. But 300 men and a dozen valuable tanks fought their way into Hagaru and helped save the garrison the next night in the face of the heaviest of the Chinese onslaughts.

Meanwhile, the other strongholds stood fast, especially the company of Marines holding Fox Hill, the height which commanded Toktong Pass through which the Yudam-ni garrison would have to retreat. This gallant band held out until a battalion made a night march overland from Yudam-ni to relieve it. The march was made on a black night over snow-covered hills with the temperature at 24 degrees below zero and the men who made it already near exhaustion from five days of constant combat. Two of them went mad during it. But Fox Hill was relieved and Toktong Pass was in friendly hands as the 5th and 7th Regiments moved down from Yudam-ni to Hagaru-ri. Thereafter the march became a matter of seizing the heights which the enemy had fortified to either side of the road.

> It was war by battalions. In that early-morning blackness of December 2, the rifle battalions were fighting everywhere, for the enemy was swarming everywhere—to the front, to the rear, on the flanks. Marines climbed mile-high mountains, and fought. They stumbled through jumbles of snow-filled scrubs, up draws, and across saddles, and fought. They withdrew, fighting. It was a fight for their own survival, and for the protection of the wounded and the regimental trains still crawling south as the fighting flared on, their enshrouded trucks and guns glinting fitfully in the flashing and the thundering of the hills.
> . . . Men who had lost the sensation of movement, who had felt the numbness rising slowly from their frozen feet, would suddenly slump, pitch into the snow. They would be seized, shaken, shouted at—kicked, if need be—and made to march on. They might plead to be left alone, but stronger, angry wills forced them forward. No one was left behind. Not even the dead. Their bodies were lashed to gun barrels, strapped to running boards, stretched across the hoods of trucks. They were dragged in sleds. They were brought out.[2]

By the afternoon of December 4, the Yudam-ni column had successfully gained Hagaru, having suffered 1,500 casualties—a third of which were from frostbite. General Smith, meanwhile, had already arranged to fly out his casualties, as well as to fly in reinforcements. The last decision was indicative of his determination to bring his division out fighting. He had already refused Far East Combat Cargo Command's offer to evacuate his men by air, and on December 4, annoyed by news reports that U. S. Marines were retreating for the first time in their history, he gathered the correspondents who had flown into Hagaru and said: "Gentlemen, we are not retreating. We are merely attacking in another direction." The remark became historic, although the popular version has it that the scholarly, mild-mannered Smith, who, unlike most Marine commanders, neither drank nor swore, had said: "Retreat, hell—we're just attacking in another direction." Smith's remark was apt: it *is* impossible to retreat when the enemy has you flanked on both sides and cut off fore and aft—in effect, surrounded. Smith's movement was a breakout, and on December 6, some 10,000 men and 1,000 vehicles at his command, the 1st Marine Division's commander ordered the attack south to be resumed.

In the meantime, he made preparations to remove two big obstacles lying below the town of Koto-ri, still held by Colonel Puller's force. These were a blown-out water-gate bridge three and a half miles below the town, and a height known as The Big Hill commanding Funchilin Pass a few miles farther south. The bridge was actually a crossing over four penstocks, or large steel pipes, which came out of a tunnel to the left of the road facing south. These pipes carried water from Chosin Reservoir to power plants in the valley below. Men on foot could cross the mountains to the left or east of the bridge, but vehicles couldn't. To the right of the bridge was an abyss. So the blown water-gate bridge could effectively block the Marine column's movement south, while Chinese guns on The Big Hill could destroy the column as it wound through Funchilin Pass. Smith's moves were to ask the Far East Air Force to airdrop the steel sections for two Treadway bridges into Koto-ri—asking for two to guard against the possibility of damage or capture by the enemy —and to order the 1st Battalion, 1st Marines, then in Chinhung-ni, to march north to capture The Big Hill. The laying of the bridge and the seizure of the height were to be coordinated. And so, MacArthur's headquarters in Tokyo ordered Brigadier General Armistead Mead, assistant commander of the 3rd Infantry Division, to form a task force to march north to Chinhung to relieve the Marine battalion for this movement. This unit, known as Task Force Dog, was activated December 6. That same day, Smith's main body began attacking down to Koto-ri, with Colonel Homer Litzenberg's 7th Marines in the spearhead, and the 5th Marines under Lieutenant Colonel Murray fighting a covering action.

"We're going to take our dead, wounded, and equipment when we leave," Murray told his officers. "We're coming out, I tell you, as Marines—or not at all."

As Murray's men began pulling down from the Hagaru hills, the last of the American transports flew the last of 4,312 U. S. casualties out of the trap. Then the demolitions experts set to work, giving the unfortunate little hill town its death blows, raising a great cloud of black smoke, and then covering the withdrawal by blowing the last bridge out of town. Out of the smoke, crossing frozen streams and emerging from hillside huts to follow the retreating Marines, came thousands of North Korean refugees.

By ten o'clock the night of December 7 the column from Hagaru had fought its way into Koto-ri, and there were now 14,000 men under General Smith's command, of whom a little less than 12,000 were Marines, 2,300 were U. S. soldiers—800 survivors of Task Force Faith and about 1,500 engineers and artillerymen from X Corps stationed in Koto-ri—150 British Royal Marines and 40 ROKs. Smith decided to take them out the next morning, and ordered Lieutenant Colonel Donald Schmuck at Chinhung-ni to march his battalion north to capture The Big Hill.

Schmuck's battalion moved out at three o'clock in the morning of December 8 in the midst of a howling blizzard. New snow had already fallen to a depth of six inches, the temperature stood at $-14°$, and visibility was nil as the Marines began the four-mile march. One column moved up the road, while another struck off through the hills to take the Chinese by surprise. Within a few hours, the hillbound column would have to ascend from an elevation of 1,200 feet to one of 3,500 feet—and the men climbed by clutching at rocks for handholds or forming human chains to pull one another up the rises. The ground of the narrow hogback over which they moved was hard and frozen beneath the snow, and men frequently slipped and fell to go rolling and clanking down the slopes.

The roadbound column, meanwhile, forced its way through a series of enemy roadblocks. At ten o'clock in the morning, having slipped within 200 yards of the enemy ridges under cover of the storm, the overland column began attacking. They destroyed the Chinese and girded for the following day's assault to take the crest of The Big Hill.

Just below Koto-ri, meanwhile, the Marine column of 1,400 vehicles and 14,000 men seemed blocked. The Chinese fought savagely to prevent the relaying of the blown bridge, pouring down fire from the heights they held. Colonel Litzenberg of the 7th Regiment committed all his rifle units in an effort to dislodge them. When one of his battalion commanders reported no progress, Litzenberg radioed: "Commit your reserve company." He received the reply: "All three companies are up there—fifty men from George, fifty men from How, thirty men from Item. That's it." And that—130 men out of an original force of 1,000 riflemen—was an example of the attrition among the rifle companies as they fought to lead the division column through the trap. In the meantime, one of two huge trucks which were to transport the bridge was lost when its driver parked it on a "turning circle" which turned out to be a frozen pond. The truck sank into the water, and though later pulled out by its brother, was coated with ice and useless. With the long motor column lined up bumper-to-bumper along the two and a half miles below Koto-ri, bridge building had to be suspended until the following day.

On December 9, Schmuck's battalion stormed The Big Hill and killed its defenders to the last man. At the blown bridge site, the remaining truck began lowering the 2,500-pound sections into place over the gap. Some of the sections had been damaged or lost in the airdrop, but Smith's foresight in ordering two bridges had provided enough sections to make one. Below the blown bridge, the Marines who had crossed overland on the mountainous left had overrun the enemy heights, finding many Chinese soldiers frozen stiff in their holes. By late afternoon the bridge was in place and the column stretching back to Koto-ri lurched forward. Heavy equipment began crossing—tractors, snowplows, big trailers carrying construction gear—and then a huge bulldozer hauling an 8-cubic-yard earth pan. The bridge's wooden centerboard cracked and collapsed and the big bulldozer was jammed inside the sections. A skillful driver backed it off the bridge, the damaged board and spacer bars were removed, and the bridge sections moved as far apart as possible—136 inches. This allowed the tanks to cross on the bridge sections, the wheeled vehicles to cross the 45-inch space between sections by rolling over the metal lips on the sections' inboard edges. The tanks had two inches to spare on either side, the wheeled vehicles had a half-inch clearance. In darkness, guided by Marines with flashlights, the column began crossing the bridge. Below them, The Big Hill was in Marine hands and the roadblocks between Chinhung-ni and Koto-ri had been blasted away. The crossing took most of the night, and then:

> It was December 10 and they were coming down The Road to Chinhung-ni. They were moving through Funchilin Pass, debouching into the low ground that let them down the mountainsides. They could be seen by the exulting Marines atop The Big Hill—these lines of marching men, that long dark column of vehicles extending backward for eleven miles.
>
> They were coming down, and there were refugees with them. . . . There were cattle with them too, and occasionally the crying of a baby rose above the crunching of shod feet on snow, the murmuring of many motors. They were coming down, bringing out their wounded, their dead, their prisoners. There was fighting still going on behind them, below Koto, and they would lose some tanks in the confusion of it, but they were coming down with nearly all of their vehicles and their guns. There would be sporadic skirmishes to the flanks, even a battle below Chinhung-ni, but most of them would survive it—and here they were, coming down that bitter road, descending the glittering cruel hills of northern Korea.[3]

And so the 1st Marine Division and its attached soldiers broke out of General Sung's trap, suffering about 7,500 casualties, half of which were frostbite, while inflicting, with supporting air, an estimated 37,500 on the enemy. So far from having been annihilated, they had stopped and shattered the entire IX

On June 25, 1950, the North Korean Army attacked across the 38th Parallel. The only Americans on the peninsula were the members of the Korean Military Advisory Group, seen above marching to Seoul's Kimpo Airbase for evacuation. But within a few days, American infantry units, hastily assembled in Japan, were on Korean soil and heading for a rapidly diminishing front.

As American troops moved north into combat, they passed South Korean civilians fleeing the battle. The refugees were to remain a serious problem for the UN forces, not only because they clogged already meager transportation arteries, but because of the "refugee attacks" mounted by a ruthless enemy. Nonetheless a steadily increasing stream of American soldiers reached Korea in those summer months of 1950.

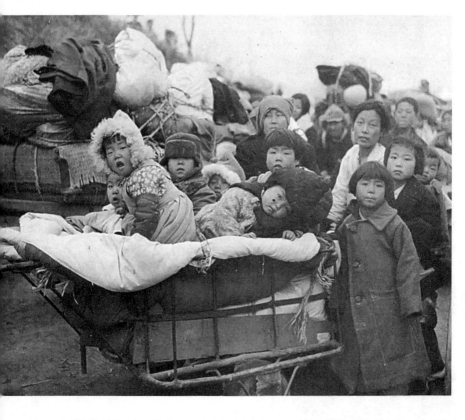

The army was the first to see action, but the GIs were followed closely by members of the First Marine Division. And, as is always the case in combat, the elements made life as miserable for the foot soldier as did the enemy.

The necessary but demoralizing delaying action of the first months of the war took a heavy toll in American lives (see corpsman, *below left,* filling out casualty tags). And on the GIs, few of whom had seen combat and most of whom had just left soft garrison duty in Japan, the horrors of war left indelible scars.

Less than three months after the outbreak of hostilities, UN forces took the offensive. First came the battering of Wolmi-do Island in Inchon Harbor, followed by the brilliant amphibious landings at Wolmi (*above*) and then at Inchon itself (*below*).

American troops advanced quickly from Inchon (*above*) to Seoul (*below*).

On the drive north all available means of transportation were used. And by mid-October soldiers of the First Calvary Division were mopping up in Pyongyang, the capital of North Korea (*below*).

The ground advance was aided immeasurably by the firepower of the U. S. Navy (*above* the USS *Missouri* delivers a 16″ salvo at Chongjin, just 29 miles below the Siberian border) and the devastating bombing of behind-the-lines installations by the Air Force.

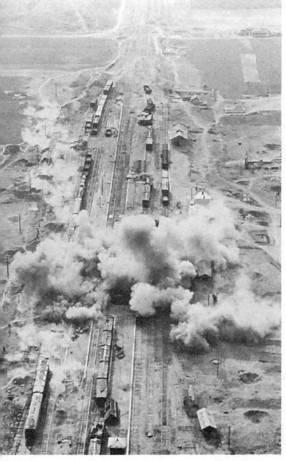

Thus on October 15, 1950, General Douglas MacArthur, Commander in Chief of UN forces, could greet President Truman on his arrival at Wake Island with unmitigated optimism.

And thus, on October 20 at Pyongyang, MacArthur could congratulate Lieutenant General Walton H. Walker, Eighth Army Commanding General, for a job well done.

On the battlefield U. S. troops advanced toward the Yalu virtually unopposed, their commanders seemingly oblivious of the trap which lay waiting for them.

The first inklings of the trap came on October 26 when Chinese Communist troops attacked ROK units at the Yalu and points south, but its full and terrible impact was not felt until late November. Within a week the once invincible UN army was in full retreat before the Chinese, and the First Marine Division was cut off and surrounded at Chosin Reservoir. But the proud Marines broke out fighting and, though crippled by the onrushing winter and the hordes of attacking Chinese, reached Hungnam and evacuation in what has been called one of the greatest such operations in military history.

With the United Nations troops in retreat, winter set in—the mercilessly cruel Korean winter, and it affected them all, be they from the 3rd Division (*above left*), the 187th Regimental Combat Team (*below left*), the Greek detachment (*above right — with mascot*) or the Canadian battalion (*below right*).

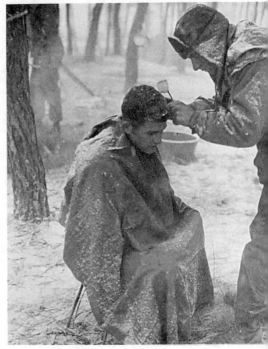

Not until January, 1951, after Seoul had been recaptured by the Communists, did the United Nations hold. Late in December Lieutenant General Walker was killed in a road accident, and his place as Eighth Army commander was taken by Lieutenant General Matthew B. Ridgway, seen *(left center)* on one of his frequent visits to the front. (Major General Courtney Whitney is second from left. Major General William B. Kean is in the right background behind General MacArthur.) It was Ridgway who ordered the UN counteroffensive on January 21, and on March 14, 1951, Seoul was recaptured by UN forces for the second time.

From early 1951 until the end of the Korean War a year and a half later, a virtual stalemate was maintained between the belligerents, and this despite furious offensives and counteroffensives and awful human sacrifice. The United Nations cause was aided materially by aerial strikes and by the aerial superiority of the Sabrejet over the Mig. And on the ground, the unloved, unwashed foot soldier continued his fight against weather, terrain and determined enemy.

For the trooper in the field, the fighting was no less intense for the tactical stalemate. And the elements were a constant foe, as below where men of the 2nd Infantry Division work desperately to save equipment in the swollen Soyang River.

Chances for relaxation were few and far between with only an occasional USO show (*above*) and the far more desirable "R & R" in Japan to break the tensions of war.

To the South Koreans fighting for their homeland and the Americans fighting for nebulous goals far from home, war was war.

The cry of "home for Christmas" was long forgotten and names like Old Baldy, Bloody Ridge, The Punchbowl, Pork Chop Hill, Heartbreak Ridge were added to the American military tradition.

On April 11, 1951, Lieutenant General James Van Fleet *(above left)* took over command of the Eighth Army, while General Ridgway replaced MacArthur as Supreme Commander. Then on May 8, 1952, General Mark W. Clark *(below, foreground,* hat in hand) replaced Ridgway, accompanied here by Ridgway, Vice-Admiral C. Turner Joy, and General Van Fleet.

By day and by night the fighting continued while the truce talks— over a year old — continued at Panmunjom.

In December, 1952, President-elect Dwight D. Eisenhower fulfilled his "I will go to Korea" campaign promise with a tour of frontline installations. But not even Ike's presence could keep the war from entering its third winter.

Prisoners proved a constant burden to the UN forces, and their value for interrogation was far outweighed by the overt insurrections (*below right*) at the Koje-do compounds, culminating in the capture and ransom of Koje's commander and a smashing propaganda victory for the Communists.

The truce talks, begun on July 10, 1951, at Kaesong, continued intermittently at Panmunjom in acrimonious debate for over two years. Among the Communist negotiators were (*below, left to right*): General Hsieh Fang and Teng Hwa (Chinese); and Lt. Gen. Nam Il and Maj. Gens. Lee Sang Cho and Pyong San Chang (North Korean).

And among those who spoke for the United Nations were (*below, left to right*): Major General Lawrence C. Craigie, USAF; Major General Paik Sun Yup, CG, 1st ROK Army Corps; Vice-Admiral C. Turner Joy, Senior Delegate and COM-NAVFE; Major General Henry I. Hodes, Deputy Chief of Staff, U. S. Eighth Army; and Rear Admiral Arleigh A. Burke, USN.

Finally, on July 27, 1953, it was over (although an armistice has never been signed). And when it was over—"the war we can't win, we can't lose, we can't quit"—this conflict, this police action—much of Korea looked like Bloody Ridge.

Army Group of perhaps 120,000 men. Seven of General Sung's divisions were now ineffective. What S. L. A. Marshall has called "the greatest fighting withdrawal of modern times" had saved X Corps, for Admiral Doyle's evacuation fleet of 193 ships was already taking its men and arms aboard. The 3rd Infantry Division was entrenched in a defensive perimeter protecting the evacuation beachhead, beating off nocturnal attacks which became constant by December 15, the day after the 1st Marine Division began boarding ship. All the American or ROK forces which had been high in the Korean north when the Chinese Communist counteroffensive began either had been evacuated from smaller ports or were safely in Hungnam awaiting withdrawal. Protecting them all were the Navy and Marine planes from seven U. S. aircraft carriers, and the guns of thirteen U. S. warships, including mighty *Missouri*. The effectiveness of the naval gunfire can be judged from these entries in the log of the cruiser *Rochester:*

1251: "Hello, *Rochester*. This is *Spot 1*. Fire mission, azimuth 4,500 mills, co-ordinates 768–068. Your target is an enemy-held town. Many troops. Fire one gun, with 8-inch high-capacity shell. I will adjust your hits. Over."

1257: "Hello, *Spot 1*, this is *Rochester*. On the way—Splash;* Over."

1258: "Hello, *Rochester,* this is *Spot 1*. Right 500 yards, add 300 yards. Over."

1259: "Hello, *Spot 1*, this is *Rochester*. On the way—Splash! Over."

(After four more adjustments of range and deflection.)

1307: "Hello, *Rochester,* this is *Spot 1*. We just hit an ammunition dump. Keep 'em coming! Over."

1308: "Hello, *Spot 1,* this is *Rochester*. On the way!—Splash. Over."

1309: "Hello, *Rochester,* this is *Spot 1*. No change! No change! You're on target! You're on target!"

1310: "Hello, *Spot 1*, this is *Rochester*. On the way!—Splash! Over."

1311: "Hello, *Rochester,* this is *Spot 1*. No change! Fire two sal-

*The signal "Splash!" indicates that by then the shells should be exploding.

vos, three guns immediately. Chinks are on the run!
Over."

(Nine minutes later.)

1320: "Hello, *Rochester,* this is *Spot 1.* Cease fire! Cease fire!
End of mission. Enemy is completely annihilated. The
senior spotting officer told me to relay to you that this was
the most spectacular shooting he had ever witnessed.
Many bull's-eyes!"

On land, meanwhile, the carrier planes struck at General
Sung's men in the hills, while howitzers lined up on the city's
streets sent shells howling north and west. Great heaps of supplies and acres of drums of gasoline vanished inside the bowels
of LSTs drawn up on the beaches. Gradually, the perimeter
shrank, until there was only the 3rd Division fighting a skillful
covering action, falling back on a shortened line. Meanwhile,
the refugees had once again begun clamoring for evacuation.

"We could have evacuated the entire area, for they all wanted
to leave," Admiral Doyle said later. "As we left, in fact, refugees
with bundles under their arms were still pouring in for a sealift
south. The Army did a magnificent job ashore with the refugees. Since Hungnam was wrecked and there was little shelter
and it was terribly cold, I ordered all ships with baking capacity
to bake extra bread and cook rice. We distributed rice to all
the ships to help keep the people alive."

Finally, there was only one regiment ashore and the demolitions men and engineers had taken over to accomplish nothing
less than destruction of the port and its facilities. The magnitude of the job may be estimated from the following report of
the 185th Engineer Combat Battalion, charged with railroad
destruction:

> The 2,100-foot railroad bridge consisted of 29 spans, 8 of which
> were wooden-tie cribbings built up to the deck level. When Com-
> pany B was ordered to destroy this bridge and all the rolling
> stock in the Hungnam area, it was decided that the projects
> should be linked. Spans of the railroad bridge would be de-
> stroyed individually and as many cars and engines as possible
> would be pushed into the void before blowing the next span.
> About 15 engines and 275 cars were assembled for demolition.

Korean railroad men helped shuttle the railroad cars from Hungnam to the bridge. When the Koreans learned that the rolling stock was to be destroyed they became reluctant—and had to be prodded to do the job. By contrast, the engineers found the job enjoyable—a release for their pent-up emotions.

At 1545 [December 15] the southernmost span was blown. Ten cars and several engines were pushed into the gap until it was filled. Some of the cars were loaded with gasoline and the engines had steam up. As they were pushed into the defile the wreckage caught fire. This process was repeated at each span. When the men reached the section of wood cribbing, several carloads of POL [Petroleum, Oil, Lubricants] and an engine were spotted on top of it, and the cribbings ignited. The heat was so intense that the locomotive became cherry-red and its whistle started blowing. In a few minutes the whole section had crumbled.

As some of the cars were pushed into the gaps, the ends of the rails would spread and rip. This prevented other cars from being pushed off. Blocked spans were, therefore, blown with the rolling stock on them. By mistake, a boxcar loaded with demolitions was pushed into some flaming wreckage. The resulting blast injured two men. The destruction continued throughout the night.

Throughout the ensuing days Hungnam became a mire of slush and mud churned up by the passage of trucks and tanks headed for the docks, and the air was foul with floating coal dust and the soot from burning warehouses and factories. Finally, the last squads of the 3rd Division had fired their last rounds at the enemy and were hurrying for the ships. They were taken aboard. The engineers set time fuses to their last charges and scurried aboard. A series of mighty explosions rocked the waterfront and it was all over.

Admiral Doyle had every right to boast: "They never laid a glove on us." The U. S. Navy had brought off the greatest evacuation in its history and one of the most masterly ever: 105,000 men of X Corps, 91,000 Korean refugees, 17,500 vehicles and 350,000 tons of material had been taken out of Hungnam. Lieutenant R. B. Mack of the carrier *Princeton*, the last pilot to fly over Hungnam, reported:

> As the LSTs cleared the beaches, several of our destroyers moved in and did their best to ruin the real estate for future

Communist use. I circled Hungnam until 2045. The ships below formed up single file, nose-and-tail like circus elephants, and headed seaward and then south to Pusan.

As I took departure for *Princeton,* I called for the *Mount Mc-Kinley* and we exchanged greetings. "Merry Christmas," we said, for it was Christmas Eve. . . .

President Truman, hearing of the successful evacuation, called it "the best Christmas present I've ever had."

Part III

Stalemate

Chapter One

THE Chinese Communist "second phase offensive" had ended in victory, not as complete as had been hoped, but a triumph, nevertheless, and one that would stand in history. Red China's crossing of the Yalu in 1950 and subsequent defeat of the United Nations was an achievement even greater than Japan's victory over Russia in the Battle of the Yalu in 1904, for the 1950 engagement involved much larger numbers of troops armed with more sophisticated weapons. But in no case was Peiping's success the calamity for which much of the U. S. press, with that zest for flagellation which is one of its peculiar traits, had set up a melancholy wailing.

Time magazine said:

> It was defeat—the worst defeat the United States ever suffered. The Nation received the fearful news from Korea with a strange-seeming calmness—the kind of confused, fearful, half-believing matter-of-factness with which many a man has reacted upon learning that he has cancer or tuberculosis. The news of Pearl Harbor, nine years ago to the month, had pealed out like a fire bell. But the numbing facts of the defeat in Korea seeped into the national consciousness slowly out of a jumble of headlines, bulletins, and communiqués; days passed before its enormity finally became plain.

Newsweek called it "America's worst military licking since Pearl Harbor. Perhaps it might become the worst military disaster in American history. Barring a military or diplomatic miracle, the approximately two-thirds of the U. S. Army that had been thrown into Korea might have to be evacuated in a new Dunkerque to save them from being lost in a new Bataan."

The truth about this "enormity" or "disaster" quoted in these magazines of December 11, 1950, was that by then the Chinese Communist attack had begun to slow down and the Hungnam redeployment had begun. Within two more weeks, Eighth Army and X Corps were out of North Korea with forces preserved, and U. S. air had begun to interdict the faltering enemy. Though the Communists in pursuit were carrying out Mao's admonition, "Enemy retreats, we pursue," they were also contradicting his theory of luring the enemy "to penetrate deep." It was *their* supply lines which were now being extended—in the face of an interdictory power far greater than their own—while those of the United Nations were being shortened. General Walker, with X Corps now part of his overall command, though it was still aboard ship and bound for Pusan to the rear, had begun to set up his defense line a bit south of the 38th Parallel and running for 135 miles coast-to-coast, from the Yellow Sea to the Sea of Japan. That was the situation in mid-December, and it was no calamity, much as such descriptions could and did find wide acceptance in a nation already discouraged, if not disgusted, by the perplexities of limited war.

On the other side of the coin, however, are those disavowals of defeat or "explanations" of General MacArthur's decision to advance to the Yalu, which also have helped confuse the outlines of an already complicated war. MacArthur himself later explained his advance as "a reconnaissance in force" undertaken "to find out what the enemy had and what his intentions were." But the bulletin issued the day his offensive began said: "The United Nations massive compression envelopment in North Korea against the new Red Armies operating there *is now approaching its decisive effort*." This doesn't sound like a "reconnaissance in force." If it was, all the forces were on reconnaissance—and that, of course, is a contradiction in terms. MacArthur's aide, General Whitney, while hailing the withdrawal as "one of the most successful military maneuvers in modern history," goes on to write: "In less than a month MacArthur had reached up, sprung the Red trap, and escaped it." But MacArthur's communiqué the night of November 24 said: "The logistic situation is fully geared to sustain offensive operations." That doesn't sound like a spoiling attack which would reach up and spring the Red trap. MacArthur also told a Senate hearing six months later: "The disposition of those troops, in my opinion, could not have been improved upon had I known the Chinese were going to attack." If the gap of 50 air miles between his divided forces is dismissed—and it cannot be—this statement might be true enough in the west but it was certainly not true in the east. At the time of the Communist attack the five divisions of X Corps were in five different places, and some of these divisions were so fragmented that Major General Almond himself could say: "We're scattered all over the landscape." No, all of the evidence—and it is abundant—points to an attempt to do just what General MacArthur said he was going to do: win the war and withdraw leaving the ROKs in charge before winter set in. MacArthur failed because he miscalculated the strength and intent of the enemy opposing him. This failure was further complicated by his division of forces, the attendant logistics slowdown, and the gap lying between these forces. The miscalculation, of course, was vital; and all things considered, it seems due to the heady draught which General MacArthur drank at Inchon.

He was not, unfortunately, alone in his overconfidence. Inchon apparently caused the Truman Administration to make that single, melancholy deviation from its policy of "containing" the Communist world within the limits it had reached at the end of 1949. This policy had produced in 1950 the 15-nation North Atlantic Treaty Organization which, with General Eisenhower as its chief, was to protect Europe. Intervention in Korea had been consonant with this policy, for Communism was seeking to break out of "containment" by gobbling up the Republic of Korea. Invasion of North Korea, already Communist by the end of 1949, was a direct shift from the wary policy of "containment" to the more belligerent—and to Communism, menacing—policy of "liberation." Nor was America's principal ally, England, immune to the wine of Inchon: Prime Minister Attlee's Labour Government was also enthusiastic about the Parallel crossing. And nowhere is there a shred of evidence suggesting that the bellicose statements of President Syngman Rhee, vowing to unify Korea "with or without the United Nations," were conclusive in the decision to invade. In fine, the chance was taken because it seemed as though the United Nations would get away with it. It would be all right if it turned out all right, and no one changed General MacArthur's instructions to continue the action even "in the event of the open or covert employment anywhere in Korea of major Chinese Communist units, without prior announcement."

After Chosin and the Chongchon, with "sermons and soda water" being dispensed all over the free world, the policy of containment was remembered for the loyal friend it had been and rushed back to the head of the table, never, thereafter, to be dislodged. Because this policy pivoted on the theory that Europe—with its factories and shipyards and millions of technicians and skilled workers—was the true object of Stalin's intentions, it had always found favor with the U. S. allies in the United Nations, most of whom were European nations or, like Canada and the other countries of Latin America, the distant sons and daughters of Europe. But because it was also tantamount to writing off North Korea as once again within the Communist sphere, while also suggesting that Chiang Kai-shek was being "sold down the river," it angered the Asia-First group which was very powerful in America. This group, rallied around the conservative Senator Robert Taft, had always been in favor of a more aggressive American policy in the Far East, an attitude expressed, though oversimplified, by the phrase: "We ought to turn Chiang loose on the Communists." President Truman would one day bitterly attack the Asia-Firsters as Americans who "saw nothing wrong in plunging headlong into an Asian war but would raise no finger for the defense of Europe; who thought a British Prime Minister was never to be trusted but Chiang Kai-shek could do no wrong." Even so, there was considerable sympathy for this group in America, most of it among nationalists. Truman had to consider them, no matter what he might think of them, and the supporters of Chiang Kai-shek were on President Truman's mind when, during the December 4–7 conferences with Prime Minister Attlee, the British leader proposed buying off Red China by admitting her to the United Nations.

"I think," said the Prime Minister, "if China were in the United Nations, there would be a possibility of discussion. That, I know, is distasteful to you. But I think if there is to be a settlement, it is better to have it come through the United Nations.

I'm inclined to think myself that if the present Chinese government were in the United Nations, we would get less loss of face
than if we were dealing with someone outside."

. . . I [said] that we would face terrible divisions among our
people here at home if the Chinese Communists were admitted
to the United Nations, and I could not see what we could gain
that would offset this loss in public morale.[1]

Attlee, according to Truman, sought a quick cease-fire under
such terms because he doubted the wisdom of limited war in
Korea: many people would clamor for total victory, which
would inevitably bring on all-out war. The American reply
was that seeking an immediate cease-fire would seem to be negotiation from weakness, and thus would damage U. S. prestige
in Japan and the Philippines. Secretary of State Acheson spoke
in favor of holding on in Korea and attempting to improve the
military position, and then beginning to negotiate from
strength. And if the Chinese Communists should hurl the
United Nations out of Korea there would be no need for negotiations, but the point of United Nations determination to defend South Korea would have been made.

And so, one of the worst results of the Chinese Communist
victory, the move among the U. S. allies to seek peace in Korea
by "every means," the move, in fact, to buy off Red China, was
resisted. There was more behind this stiff U. S. policy than
sympathy for Chiang Kai-shek in America or fear of what a
"soft" attitude toward Peiping might do to the U. S. position
in the Far East. Truman and Acheson were bitter about Chinese
intervention, as well as the vituperation then being poured on
America by General Wu since his arrival at Lake Success.* Truman has written: "I said their handling of our missionaries
and of our consuls was a blot on humanity. There was nothing
in getting them admitted to the United Nations until they
changed their ways." The final communiqué of the Truman-
Attlee conference declared:

For our part, we are ready, as we have always been to seek an
end to the hostilities by means of negotiation. . . . We are confi-

*United Nations headquarters were maintained at this village on Long Island
from 1945 until 1951, when they were moved to their present site in New York
City.

dent that the great majority of the United Nations take the same view. If the Chinese on their side display any evidence of a similar attitude, we are hopeful that the cause of peace can be upheld.

There was, then, to be no "appeasement," even though some of the conservative opposition to Truman regarded this flat, nonconciliatory statement as a sellout to British interests.

The Communists, however, regarded it with contempt. On December 14, when the United Nations General Assembly voted to seek an armistice in Korea and set up a three-man Cease-Fire Committee to approach Peiping and Pyongyang, Russia voted against the proposal. Then the Peiping radio announced Red China's terms for agreement to talk peace: United Nations withdrawal from the peninsula, American withdrawal from Formosa, an end to all Western rearmament. Meanwhile, Premier Kim Il Sung was again broadcasting pledges to "annihilate" the United Nations. On December 15, General Wu went home with a last blast at the cease-fire offer as an "American plot" to gain time while the U. S. rearmed and regrouped in Korea. Seven days later Premier Chou answered the Cease-Fire Committee's twice-repeated request for a reply to its proposal. He added recognition of Red China as a fourth term to the three proposed in the radio broadcast. He said the 38th Parallel had been "obliterated forever" as a demarcation line. Obviously, the Chinese Communists had no intentions of negotiating unless all that they wanted and more was handed to them on a platter. Otherwise, they would take it.

Chou's harsh and propagandistic reply had the effect of rallying the United Nations behind the U. S. policy of negotiation "from strength." It was recognized that the Chinese Communists would not parley unless forced to do so. Promises of increased aid to the Korean effort were made by the UN allies, and all hopes for an eventual cease-fire were placed in the Eighth Army's ability to deflate Peiping's military pride.

By Christmas of 1950, the Eighth Army had lost its commander. Lieutenant General Walton Walker was killed on December 23 in a highway accident. Walker had been riding along a narrow, icy road toward the British 27th Brigade's command post north of Seoul when a ROK truck pulled out of line and into the path of the jeep. There was a collision and Walker died almost immediately, coming to the same end that had overtaken his mentor, General George Patton, shortly after World War II. Within a few hours of notification of Walker's death, the Joint Chiefs of Staff appointed Lieutenant General Matthew Ridgway to take his place.

Ridgway, hawk-nosed and hard of body and mind, was an inspirational leader with an excellent World War II combat record and a reputation for being a general who understood the shifts and turns of international politics. He had been graduated from West Point in 1917, although he saw no overseas service in World War I. In the next World War, he organized the 82nd Airborne Division—America's first paratroop division—and led it on its first combat jump in Sicily. He also jumped with the division during the Normandy invasion. In 1945 he commanded the XVIII Airborne Corps, and was selected to lead all airborne troops during the scheduled invasion of Japan, taking command of the U. S. Mediterranean Theater when Japan's surrender made the invasion unnecessary. In 1947 Ridgway was on the United Nations Military Staff Committee. The following year he commanded the U. S. Caribbean Theater. By then Ridgway was under consideration as a possible successor to General Collins as Army Chief of Staff. He was brought to Washington as deputy chief of staff for administration, and told, with the outbreak of the Korean War, to stay abreast of the "conflict" in the event that something happened to Walker. When it did, Ridgway was ready to move on short notice. He was in Tokyo by December 26, tactfully removing the label "Washington's man" by assuring General MacArthur that he was proud to serve under "one of the greatest military leaders in history," and just as tactfully—by requesting "permission to attack" if need be—extracting MacArthur's assurance that the Korea field command was his with no strings attached. The restrictions which inhibited Walker would not bind Ridgway.

The Korean command had undergone some marked changes by the time of Ridgway's arrival the next day. For one thing, the arrival of F-86 Sabrejets in Korea had ended the temporary superiority of the MIG-15s. On December 17 a flight of Sabrejets from Kimpo flew up to the Yalu under Lieutenant Colonel

Bruce Hinton. They were attacked by four MIGs, which, thinking they were engaging the old and slower Shooting Stars, approached Hinton's patrol in a leisurely climb. The swift Sabres flashed through the sky, and Colonel Hinton's .50-caliber machine guns sent one of the enemy down in flames, making him the first American to destroy a MIG-15 in air-to-air combat. Thereafter, the Sabres killed off Russia's finest fighter plane at a ratio of 14 to 1, and United Nations aerial supremacy was re-established, never again to be lost.

Eighth Army, meanwhile, had taken on a truly international character. Fifteen nations—the United States, Great Britain, Australia, Canada, New Zealand, India, South Africa, France, Greece, the Netherlands, the Philippines, Thailand, Turkey, Belgium and Sweden—now had troops in Korea. Ridgway followed Walker's practice of training them in U. S. military doctrine at a United Nations Reception Center before attaching them by battalions to the seven U. S. divisions then deployed in Korea. Only the British brigades, which eventually were combined in the 1st Commonwealth Division, operated as autonomous units. Supplying this multinational army became a quartermaster headache which did not cease to throb until the truce was signed.

U. S. rations were generally acceptable to all but the Oriental troops, though the Moslem Turks would not eat pork and the Greeks did not like sweet potatoes, corn or peas. Extra bread was required for European soldiers, as well as rations of olive or vegetable oils for troops from the Mediterranean. Oriental troops wanted only rice. Anything else was supplemental, and the quartermaster officers who thought to cheer them by issuing them steak found that the Orientals simply cut it up and boiled it with the rice. U. S. troops had already been denied issues of "alcoholic beverages" by the puritan storm at home, but the others—particularly the French and British—insisted on their wine or tot of rum. U. S. clothing was also generally acceptable, although broader shoes had to be made for the Greeks and Turks and smaller sizes of all gear found for the Thailanders and Filipinos.

All told, General Ridgway had a force of about 365,000 men to command when he took charge in Korea. Its combat formations were disposed on a line beginning in the flats of the Han

River delta south of the 38th Parallel and running northeast along the Imjin River before bending eastward through high mountains to the Sea of Japan. The U. S. I Corps under Major General Frank Milburn was on the left or west of this line, then Major General Coulter's U. S. IX Corps in the center, with the mountainous right held by the ROK I, II and III Corps. X Corps, which had landed its troops and equipment at Pohang and Pusan, had begun reorganizing in Pusan.

Opposing this force were an estimated 485,000 enemy troops. The battle formations consisted of 21 divisions from General Lin Piao's Fourth Field Army and 12 divisions of Premier Kim's North Korean Army, some of them having been reorganized and rearmed in Communism's "Manchurian sanctuary." General Lin was in command. He had concentrated the bulk of his forces north of Seoul, hoping to deliver the knockout blow by shattering the United Nations in a furious rush for Pusan. His "third phase offensive" was to begin in the last days of the Old Year or the first of the New.

And so, General Ridgway flew into Korea to meet much the same situation that had greeted Walker five months before. His response was vigorous and dramatic. First, he put on the paratrooper's jump harness which, with its ever-present hand grenade, would identify him as long as he remained in command. Next he flew over the battleground to trace on a map the series of ridgelines where he believed the Eighth Army could stand and fight. Then, arriving at Eighth Army's advance headquarters in Seoul he expressed his shock and anger to find only a handful of officers present. The rest were back at Taegu, 200 miles from the front. Meeting President Syngman Rhee for the first time, Ridgway said: "I am glad to be here. And I've come to stay." The following three days Ridgway spent traveling the front, trying to refresh his battered army and renew its fighting spirit.

> I rode in an open jeep, and would permit no jeep with the top up to operate in the combat zone. Riding in a closed vehicle in a battle area puts a man in the wrong frame of mind. It gives him an erroneous sense of warmth, of safety. His mental attitude is that of an ostrich poking his head in the sand. Also, I held to the old-fashioned idea that it helped the spirits of the men to see the

Old Man up there, in the snow and sleet and the mud, sharing the same cold, miserable existence they had to endure. As a consequence, I damn near froze. . . .[2]

During those three days the Eighth Army's new chief was everywhere among his commanders, encouraging those who seemed anxious to turn and fight, insulting those who showed him their plans for further withdrawal, deriding those who complained of mechanical failures, and telling division commanders he wanted them up with their forward battalions, and corps commanders to stay with their engaged regiments.

Ridgway did not only exhort. He asked Rhee for 30,000 Korean laborers and began to construct the battle line where he expected to meet the enemy onslaught.

In the meantime, on December 30, General MacArthur warned the Joint Chiefs that the Communist Chinese could, if they wished, drive the United Nations out of Korea. This warning came at a time when the move to appease Red China in some way had been revived and was gaining strength, but with the United States still determined to resist the aggression. MacArthur was instructed to defend his positions, to inflict as much damage as possible on the enemy while retiring, if necessary, all the way back to the old Pusan beachhead. Though some of the free world allies in the UN were again despairing of stopping Red China's seeming juggernaut, the United States was not. So the Korean laborers were also put to work building fortifications south of Seoul around Suwon, preparing the next place to stand and fight in the event that Eighth Army should once more be forced back.

The enemy attack began on New Year's Eve. All night long mortars and artillery bombarded the United Nations line. At daybreak on New Year's Day advance elements of seven Chinese Communist armies and two North Korean corps struck southward toward Seoul and the rail center of Wonju 50 air miles to the southeast. Again it was the U. S. I and IX Corps which received the brunt of the enemy's blows, although the action was general with only the U. S. 24th Division and the Turkish Brigade in the far west, and the ROK Capitol Division in the far east, escaping its full fury. Thousands of Chinese were killed during this first fierce onslaught, but on they came

—many of them screaming "Kill GI!" as they swept over snowy hills and frozen paddies. By midmorning they had driven deep into the United Nations lines and had broken the ROK 1st and 7th Divisions. What happened to these men has been described by General Ridgway.

> At dawn I headed for the front by jeep, toward the ROK sector, the point of deepest penetration. Only a few miles north of Seoul, I ran head-on into that fleeing army. I'd never had such an experience before, and I pray to God I never witness such a spectacle again. They were coming down the road in trucks, the men standing, packed so close together in those big carriers another small boy could not have found space among them. They had abandoned their heavy artillery, their machine guns—all their crew-served weapons. Only a few had kept their rifles. Their only thought was to get away, to put miles between them and the fearful army that was at their heels.
>
> I jumped from my jeep and stood in the middle of the road, waving them to a halt. I might as well have tried to stop the flow of the Han. . . . The only solution was to let them run—and to set up road blocks far enough back where they could be stopped, channeled into bivouac areas, calmed down, refitted, and turned to face the enemy again. . . .[3]

This was done, and tough old Syngman Rhee flew north in the icy cockpit of a canvas-covered scouting plane to speak to his countrymen and renew their willingness to fight again. Meanwhile, Ridgway committed the U. S. X Corps in the collapsing center and began fighting a covering action to blunt the Chinese Communist drive while his forces withdrew from Seoul.

There was no other alternative. The Communists had obviously committed most of their forces in the assault. To stand in place and fight would invite destruction, for the United Nations was pressed with its back against the broad Han River. Two 50-ton floating bridges over the half-frozen Han offered the only route of withdrawal. Better to pull back quickly to the positions already being prepared farther south, than to turn Seoul into a slaughter pen. Withdrawal also would make capital of the Chinese Communist Forces' inability to sustain a lengthy advance. November had already shown how a supply train geared to human and animal transport could not keep pace with fast-moving, lightly armed Chinese soldiers. Inevitably, the spearheads had been forced to sit down to await resupply. So General Ridgway ordered Eighth Army to break contact. It was done, rapidly and with precision. As one Eighth Army staff officer said: "We *ought* to be good at this—we've had plenty of practice." On January 3, with the enemy crossing the Han ice both to the west and east of Seoul, bumper-to-bumper movement out of the capital began. President Rhee and his government left the city and nearly 500,000 gallons of fuel and 23,000 gallons of napalm stored at Kimpo Airfield were destroyed in a great red roaring holocaust. Barracks, hangars and other installations were burned—and the Fifth Air Force found itself based far from the front at Taegu. Eventually, most of its fighter planes would be withdrawn to Japan. This, too, was an unpleasant consequence of the decision to retreat. Another was the misery once more visited upon the city's inhabitants. General Ridgway has described it:

> Off to the right and left of the [Han] bridges was being enacted one of the great human tragedies of our time. In a zero wind that seared the face like a blow torch, hundreds of thousands of Koreans were running, stumbling, falling, as they fled across the ice. Women with tiny babies in their arms, men bearing their old, sick, crippled fathers and mothers on their backs, others bent under great bundles of household gear flowed down the northern bank and across the ice toward the frozen plain on the southern shore. Some pushed little two-wheeled carts piled high with goods and little children. Others prodded burdened oxen. Now and then an ox would go down, all four legs asprawl, and the river of humanity would break and flow around him for in this terrible flight no man stopped to help his neighbor.
>
> There was no weeping, no crying. Without a sound, except the dry whisper of their slippers on the snow, and the deep pant of their hard-drawn breath, they moved in utter silence. Until long after dark, I stood there watching that endless flow, while across the bridges men and guns, tanks and trucks, moved in an unbroken stream.[4]

To the north, the Chinese had begun entering the city, and to the U. S. 25th Division and the British 29th Brigade fell the assignment of holding them off while the rest of the Eighth

242

Army gained the south bank of the Han. British Brigadier Thomas Brodie told his men: "If you meet [the enemy], you are to knock hell out of him with everything you have got. You are only to give ground on my orders." Ground was given only slowly while air and artillery steadily scourged the Chinese as they fought to press Eighth Army against the river. The attempt failed. The ROKs in the right and center also fell back, and the entire United Nations command took up a position beginning with Pyongtaek on the west, stretching northeast to Wonju in the center, and from there due east to Samchok on the east coast. Intermediate positions were taken at Suwon to cover the withdrawal of great stocks of supplies. In Seoul itself, General Ridgway had departed, leaving a derisive greeting for General Lin Pao. While packing, Ridgway had found a pair of pajamas with a hole in the seat of the trousers. He tacked it up on the office wall. Above it, in big block letters, he printed the message:

TO THE COMMANDING GENERAL
CHINESE COMMUNIST FORCES—
WITH THE COMPLIMENTS OF
THE COMMANDING GENERAL
EIGHTH ARMY

Then Ridgway, too, took his leave. Fires broke out in the city. Buildings which had escaped the destruction of two prior withdrawals were engulfed in flames. Inchon was desolated. Docks and cranes were destroyed. Port troops and thousands of civilians were evacuated by U. S., Dutch, Canadian and Australian warships under cover of carrier-based U. S. Marine aircraft. The last two LSTs were floated off the mud flats just as the Chinese appeared at the shore. And then the enemy continued his pursuit south of the Han.

Gradually, in good order, the Eighth Army's units fell back from Suwon after the supplies had been saved and the airfield destroyed. Osan, too, was abandoned. The position at Pyongtaek was occupied. And then the enemy attack in the west petered out.

Failing to trap the U. S. I and IX Corps in the west, the Chinese Communist Forces and their North Korean allies had shifted their strongest blows to the center and the east. These came against the U. S. 2nd Division and the ROKs, and were assisted by actions against the United Nations rear by the North Korean II Corps, which had infiltrated the eastern mountains during December. The objective was Wonju, the central bastion of Ridgway's new line. Here the 2nd Division, reinforced by the French and Dutch Battalions, fought a gallant action which took ample revenge for the beating suffered in the December running of the gantlet below the Chongchon River. The 2nd's soldiers held off the enemy in battles fought during fierce snowstorms with the temperature at 20 degrees below zero. On January 10, with the collapse of the ROK divisions on the 2nd's right, Wonju was abandoned. The Chinese rushed into the city, and were subjected to saturation bombardment by American B-29s and lighter planes. On January 10 also, Ridgway ordered the 1st Marine Division to move to the front from Masan against the thousands of enemy soldiers who had poured through the gap on the 2nd Division's right and infiltrated to the rear of the ROK III Corps.

By midmonth, the United Nations front became silent. The west saw almost no action at all, and though the center and east were still seriously threatened, the fury of the enemy attack had diminished there as well. The bubble of Chinese pride had been pricked, the "third phase offensive" which was to knock out the United Nations had failed, and the proud and sharp-tongued Lin Piao, having received the first defeat of his career, was already bitterly assailing "the failure of the Chinese Central Government to furnish air and tank support as promised." But neither General Ridgway nor his staff were aware of this yet, nor were any of his soldiers. Not even the moral victory won at Wonju by the 2nd Division could solace the spirits of men making their second retreat from Seoul. And the peculiar character of the "conflict" in Korea was given definition by one of those weary infantrymen who had experienced its ups and downs since July. He said:

"It's the war we can't win, we can't lose, we can't quit."

Chapter Two

WHILE one of the shooting phases of the conflict so aptly described was thus simmering down, a talking phase was beginning to boil. In late December of 1950, the Joint Chiefs of Staff, still fearful of being drawn into a trap which would fall in with Stalin's plans for European conquest, sent MacArthur this message:

It appears from all estimates available that the Chinese Communists possess the capability of forcing United Nations forces out of Korea if they choose to exercise it. The execution of this capability might be prevented by making the effort so costly to the enemy that they would abandon it, or by committing substantial additional United States forces to that theater, thus seriously jeopardizing other commitments including the safety of Japan. It is not practical to obtain significant additional forces for Korea from other members of the United Nations.

. . . We believe that Korea is not the place to fight a major war. Further, we believe that we should not commit our remaining available ground forces to action against Chinese Communist forces in Korea in face of the increased threat of general war. However, a successful resistance to Chinese-North Korean aggression at some position in Korea and a deflation of the military and political prestige of the Chinese Communists would be of great importance to our national interest, if they could be accomplished without incurring serious losses.

Your basic directive . . . requires modification in the light of the present situation. You are now directed to defend in successive positions . . . subject to the primary consideration of the continued threat to Japan, [and] to determine in advance our last reasonable opportunity for an orderly evacuation. It seems to us that if you are forced back to position in the vicinity of the Kum River and a line generally eastward therefrom, and if thereafter the Chinese Communists mass large forces against your positions with an evident capability of forcing us out of Korea, it then would be necessary under these conditions to direct you to commence a withdrawal to Japan.

MacArthur, wrote General Whitney, "read the message in utter dismay." That night he composed a long reply, setting down the arguments and objections expressive of his conviction that the war against China should be extended. He wrote:

Any estimate of relative capabilities in the Korean campaign appears to be dependent upon political-military policies yet to be formulated vis-à-vis Chinese military operations being conducted against our forces. It is quite clear now that the entire military resource of the Chinese nation, with logistic support from the Soviet, is committed to a maximum effort against the United Nations command. In implementation of this commitment a major concentration of Chinese force in the Korean-Manchurian area will increasingly leave China vulnerable in areas whence troops to support Korean operations have been drawn. Meanwhile, under existing restrictions, our naval and air potential are being only partially utilized and the great potential of Chinese Nationalist force on Formosa and guerrilla action on the mainland are being ignored. Indeed, as to the former, we are preventing its employment against the common enemy by our own naval force.

Should a policy determination be reached by our government or through it by the United Nations to recognize the stage of war which has been forced upon us by the Chinese authorities and to take retaliatory measures within our capabilities, we could: (1) blockade the coast of China; (2) destroy through naval gunfire and air bombardment China's industrial capacity to wage war; (3) secure reinforcements from the Nationalist garrison in Formosa to strengthen our position in Korea if we decided to continue the fight for that peninsula; and (4) release existing restrictions upon the Formosan garrison for diversionary action (possibly leading to counterinvasion) against vulnerable areas of the Chinese mainland.

I believe that by the foregoing measures we could severely cripple and largely neutralize China's capability to wage aggressive war and thus save Asia from the engulfment otherwise facing it. I believe furthermore that we could do so with but a small part of our overall military potential committed to the purpose. There is no slightest doubt but that this action would at once release the pressure upon our forces in Korea, whereupon determination could be reached as to whether to maintain the fight in that area or to effect a strategic displacement of our forces with the view to strengthening our defense of the littoral island chain while continuing our naval and air pressure upon China's military potential. I am fully conscious of the fact that this course of action has been rejected in the past for fear of provoking China into a major war effort, but we must now realistically recognize that China's commitment thereto has already been fully and unequivocably made and that nothing we can do would further aggravate the situation as far as China is concerned.

Whether defending ourselves by way of military retaliation would bring in Soviet military intervention or not is a matter of speculation. I have always felt that a Soviet decision to precipitate a general war would depend solely upon the Soviet's own estimate of relative strengths and capabilities with little regard to other factors. . . . If we are forced to evacuate Korea without taking military measures against China proper as suggested in your message, it would have the most adverse affect upon the people of Asia, not excepting the Japanese, and a material reinforcement of the forces now in this theater would be mandatory if we are to hold the littoral defense chain against determined assault.

Moreover, it must be borne in mind that evacuation of our forces from Korea under any circumstances would at once release the bulk of the Chinese forces now absorbed by that campaign for action elsewhere—quite probably in areas of far greater importance than Korea itself. . . .

I understand thoroughly the demand for European security and fully concur in doing everything possible in that sector, but not to the point of accepting defeat anywhere else—an acceptance which I am sure could not fail to ensure later defeat in Europe itself. The preparations for the defense of Europe, however, by the most optimistic estimate are aimed at a condition of readiness two years hence. The use of forces in the present emergency in the Far East could not in any way prejudice this basic concept. To the contrary, it would ensure thoroughly seasoned forces for later commitment in Europe synchronously with Europe's own development of military resources.

The last paragraph contained the core of MacArthur's criticism of the policies recommended by the National Security Council and approved by President Truman. The *immediate* threat, he was saying, was in the Far East—not Europe. This estimate, however, ignored the American-British position best expressed by Winston Churchill when he told Parliament: "It is one of the most well known—almost hackneyed—strategical and tactical methods to draw your opponents' reserves to one part of the field and then, at the right moment, to strike in another." The Truman Administration, with its UN allies, believed the immediate Far East threat to be just such a feint. Thus the Joint Chiefs' reply brushed aside MacArthur's criticism of policy:

> . . . There is little possibility of policy change or other eventuality justifying the strengthening of our effort in Korea. Blockade of China coast, if undertaken, must await either stabilization of our position in Korea or our evacuation from Korea. However, a naval blockade off the coast of China would require negotiations with the British in view of the extent of British trade with China through Hong Kong; naval and air attacks on objectives in Communist China probably can be authorized only if the Chinese Communists attack United States forces outside of Korea and decision must wait that eventuality. Favorable action cannot be taken on the proposal to obtain Korean reinforcements from the Chinese Nationalists garrison on Formosa, in view of improbability of their decisive effect on the Korean outcome and their probable greater usefulness elsewhere. . . .
>
> . . . In the light of the foregoing and after full consideration of all pertinent factors you are directed to defend in successive positions . . . inflicting maximum damage to hostile forces in Korea, subject to primary consideration of the safety of your troops and your basic mission of protecting Japan. Should it become evident in your judgment that evacuation is essential to avoid severe losses of men and material, you will at that time withdraw from Korea to Japan.

This message, dispatched January 9, added to the Supreme Commander's dismay. Talk of evacuation and the new emphasis suddenly placed upon the defense of Japan—evident in both messages—seemed to him an attempt to put the onus of a possible evacuation on him. At this point, evacuation of Korea had been generally accepted, not as possible but as probable. General Ridgway's crumbling center and collapsing right had caused general loss of faith in the South Koreans' ability to continue fighting. On January 5 Senator Taft had openly called for evacuation, advancing the theory that "foreigners" should do the free world's fighting on land while the United States supplied air and sea support: the gentleman's war for us, the dirty work for them. To this end, the Joint Chiefs had asked MacArthur if he thought rearming and equipping 200,-000 to 300,000 more South Koreans feasible. But MacArthur, already mindful of the renewed emphasis on Japan, evacuation-minded himself, had replied he would prefer to give the arms to the Japanese National Police Reserve. And so, having had his plea for what was tantamount to a change in national policy brushed aside, having had his arguments for extending the war against China countered—with the infuriating suggestion, at least to him, that British profits in Hong Kong precluded a naval blockade—being again reminded that his "primary mission" was defense of Japan and, seemingly, having had the distasteful decision as to whether or not to accept evacuation—defeat, that is—once more thrown in his own lap, General MacArthur angrily demanded "clarification" of the entire Korean situation.

In view of the self-evident fact that my command as presently constituted is of insufficient strength to hold a position in Korea and simultaneously protect Japan against external assault, strategic dispositions taken in the present situation must be based upon overriding political policy establishing the relativity of American interests in the Far East. There is no doubt but that a beachhead line can be held by our existing forces for a limited time in Korea, but this could not be accomplished without losses. Whether such losses were regarded as "severe" or not would to a certain extent depend upon the connotation one gives the term.

... The troops are tired from a long and difficult campaign, embittered by the shameful propaganda which has falsely condemned their courage and fighting quality in misunderstood retrograde maneuver, and their morale will become a serious threat to their battle efficiency unless the political basis on which they are asked to trade life for time is quickly delineated, fully understood and so impelling that the hazards of battle are cheerfully accepted.

The issue really boils down to the question whether or not the United States intends to evacuate Korea, and involves a decision of highest national and international importance, far above the competence of a theater commander guided largely by incidents affecting the tactical situation developing upon a very limited field of action. Nor is it a decision which should be left to the initiative of enemy action, which in effect would be the determining criteria under a reasonable interpretation of your message. My query therefore amounts to this: is it the present objective of United States political policy to maintain a military position in Korea indefinitely, for a limited time, or to minimize losses by the evacuation as soon as it can be accomplished?

This query, together with the first message critical of national policy, had the effect of producing another special session of the National Security Council. It was held on January 13, and resulted in President Truman's decision to write a long and personal message to MacArthur.

I want you to know that the situation in Korea is receiving the utmost attention here and that our efforts are concentrated upon finding the right decisions on this matter of the gravest impor tance to the future of America and to the survival of free peoples everywhere.

I wish in this telegram to let you have my views as to our basic national and international purposes in continuing the resistance to aggression in Korea. We need your judgment as to the maximum effort which could reasonably be expected from the United Nations forces under your command to support the resistance to aggression which we are trying rapidly to organize on a worldwide basis. This present telegram is not to be taken in any sense as a directive. Its purpose is to give you something of what is in our minds regarding the political factors.

1. A successful resistance in Korea would serve the following important purposes:

(a) To demonstrate that aggression will not be accepted by us or by the United Nations and to provide a rallying point around which the spirits and energies of the free world can be mobilized to meet the world-wide threat which the Soviet Union now poses.

(b) To deflate the dangerously exaggerated political and military prestige of Communist China which now threatens to undermine the resistance of non-Communist Asia and to consolidate the hold of Communism on China itself.

(c) To afford more time for and to give direct assistance to the organization of non-Communist resistance in Asia, both outside and inside China.

(d) To carry out our commitments of honor to the South Koreans and to demonstrate to the world that the friendship of the United States is of inestimable value in time of adversity.

(e) To make possible a far more satisfactory peace settlement for Japan and to contribute greatly to the post-treaty security position of Japan in relation to the continent.

(f) To lend resolution to many countries not only in Asia but also in Europe and the Middle East who are now living within the shadow of Communist power and to let them know that they need not now rush to come to terms with Communism on whatever terms they can get, meaning complete submission.

(g) To inspire those who may be called upon to fight against great odds if subjected to a sudden onslaught by the Soviet Union or by Communist China.

(h) To lend point and urgency to the rapid build-up of the defenses of the western world.

(i) To bring the United Nations through its first great effort on collective security and to produce a free-world coalition of incalculable value to the national security interests of the United States.

(j) To alert the peoples behind the Iron Curtain that their masters are bent upon wars of aggression and that this crime will be resisted by the free world.

2. Our course of action at this time should be such as to consolidate the great majority of the United Nations. This majority is not merely part of the organization but is also the nations whom we would desperately need to count on as allies in the

event the Soviet Union moves against us. Further, pending the build-up of our national strength, we must act with great prudence in so far as extending the area of hostilities is concerned. Steps which might in themselves be fully justified and which might lend some assistance to the campaign in Korea would not be beneficial if they thereby involved Japan or Western Europe in large-scale hostilities.

3. We recognize, of course, that continued resistance might not be militarily possible with the limited forces with which you are being called upon to meet large Chinese armies. Further, in the present world situation, your forces must be preserved as an effective instrument for the defense of Japan and elsewhere. However, some of the important purposes mentioned above might be supported, if you should think it practicable, and advisable, by continued resistance from off-shore islands of Korea, particularly from Cheju-do, if it becomes impracticable to hold an important portion of Korea itself. In the worst case, it would be important that, if we must withdraw from Korea, it be clear to the world that that course is forced upon us by military necessity and that we shall not accept the result politically or militarily until the aggression has been rectified.

4. In reaching a final decision about Korea, I shall have to give constant thought to the main threat from the Soviet Union and to the need for a rapid expansion of our armed forces to meet this great danger.

5. I am encouraged to believe that the free world is getting a much clearer and realistic picture of the dangers before us and that the necessary courage and energy will be forthcoming. Recent proceedings in the United Nations have disclosed a certain amount of confusion and wishful thinking, but I believe that most members have been actuated by a desire to be absolutely sure that all possible avenues to peaceful settlement have been fully explored. I believe that the great majority is now rapidly consolidating and that the result will be an encouraging and formidable combination in defense of freedom.

6. The entire nation is grateful for your splendid leadership in the difficult struggle in Korea and for the superb performance of your forces under the most difficult circumstances.

(Signed) HARRY TRUMAN

Although Harry Truman has said, "I wasn't one of the great Presidents, but I had a good time trying to be one," there was greatness in that message, if only in its patience and its sincere attempt to clarify a difficult situation for a military commander who was himself difficult. In the first portion dealing with the national purpose in Korea he was masterly, and in his concluding sentence of praise he was magnanimous. He would not be so again.

That "confusion and wishful thinking" in the United Nations to which the President alluded had gone a fair way down the road toward appeasement of Red China. The peace-at-any-price mood which Peiping's intransigence had apparently destroyed for good in December had been revived by the seemingly inexorable advance of the Chinese Communist Forces' "third phase offensive." On January 13, the same day on which Truman wrote MacArthur, the General Assembly voted on a new peace plan which offered, in effect, complete capitulation to Red China on the questions of Formosa and United Nations membership, if Peiping would agree to a satisfactory Korean settlement. It directly contradicted United States policy, but the United States, already pledged to go along with the UN majority, voted for it—once it became clear that the majority of the members favored it. By a vote of 50 to 7, the General Assembly called for:

1. An immediate cease-fire in Korea with guarantees that the truce would not be used to screen military buildups.

2. Decisions during the truce which would provide a permanent Korean settlement.

3. Withdrawal of all "non-Korean" troops by "appropriate stages."

4. United Nations-approved administration of all Korea during the truce.

5. Creation of a special United Nations agency, including Russia, Red China, Britain and the United States, to settle Far Eastern issues such as the future of Formosa and Chinese membership in the United Nations.

A storm of outrage, both in press and Congress, burst upon Truman's head after Ambassador Warren Austin had voted in support of this proposal. Demands for the resignation of Secretary of State Dean Acheson were widespread, even though Acheson had constantly fought against adoption of just such a course. The fact that Austin's affirmative vote had been cast only to be consistent with the U. S. policy of working through the United Nations was not accepted as justification by many powerful American leaders, among them Democrats as well as Republicans. Senator Taft called Point Five "the most complete surrender to which the United States has ever agreed." But the Truman Administration rode out the storm—with the President himself issuing an angry refusal to dismiss Acheson—and then, on January 17, Red China overplayed her hand.

Chou En-lai replied to the Assembly's offer with a proposal which Acheson described as "complete rejection" of the UN terms. Chou asked for a seven-nation conference on Korea and other Far Eastern problems to be held without a cease-fire. In other words, the conference would be bullied into line by a Chinese war club. Actually, it need not be bullied, for Red China's list of nations included herself, Russia, India, Egypt, Britain, France and the United States—an alignment of two Communist states, India, and Egypt, still nursing a grudge against the United States because of American support for Israel, against the three Western powers. More, the conference would be held in China but not until after Red China had been admitted to the United Nations. Elated, Secretary Acheson declared: "We must face squarely and soberly the fact that the Chinese Communists have no intention of ceasing their defiance of the United Nations."

The United States began working to obtain a United Nations vote branding Communist China as an aggressor in Korea, a charge which had already been made by the UN Commission on Korea. However, Britain and an Arab-Asian block led by India still clung to the hope that Red China would modify her terms. Peiping did retreat to the extent of agreeing to accept a cease-fire as the first item on the agenda of a Far East conference, but insisted on membership in the United Nations as her price for attending it. As had happened in December, the intransigence of a Red China confident in her military strength had squelched the second and likeliest movement to appease her. Then, in Korea, General Ridgway's forces doomed the conciliatory moves forever. The lull already described had come upon the battlefront. On January 20, General MacArthur declared: "No one is going to drive us into the sea. This command intends to maintain a military position in Korea just as long as the statesmen of the United Nations decide we should do so." About the same time, General Collins came to Korea and told newsmen: "As of now, we are going to stay and fight." There was no more talk of evacuation. Soon, Ridgway's patrols were punching north, finding the enemy vanished or withdrawing. By January 25 the United Nations armies in Korea were poised for full-scale offensive. On February 1, with the Asian countries still reluctant, with some of the NATO nations acting only on U. S. assurance that the Korean War would not be extended, the General Assembly formally branded Communist China as an aggressor in Korea.

Chapter Three

THE reversal of military fortunes in Korea was the result of rapid and bold United Nations reaction to the discovery that Lin Piao's New Year's offensive had quite literally run out of gas.

By mid-January action along the Pyongtaek-Samchok line held by the United Nations forces had generally slackened. The western sector was completely quiet. Anxious to know more about the enemy in the west, General Ridgway gave the 27th Wolfhounds armor, artillery and engineers, and sent them probing north toward Osan on a scouting expedition. The Wolfhounds set out on January 15, moving up the Seoul road and passing through a frozen and desolated countryside. The only signs of life were solitary civilians moving across frozen fields or an occasional wisp of smoke rising from a hut which had escaped destruction. Below Osan, the column exchanged rifle shots with the first enemy soldiers encountered,

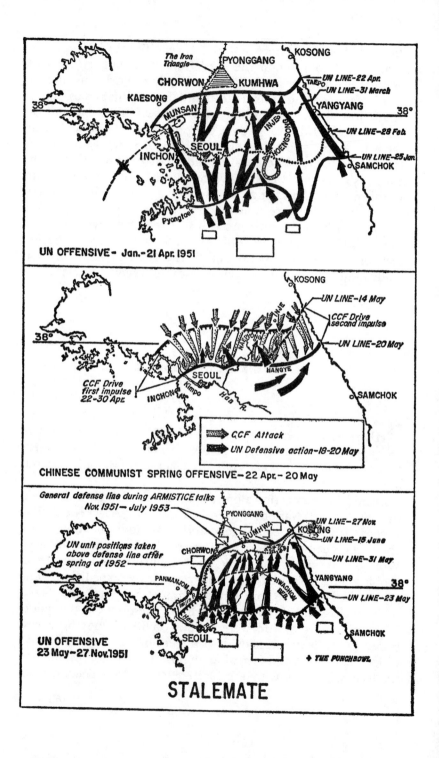

UN OFFENSIVE – Jan.–21 Apr. 1951

CHINESE COMMUNIST SPRING OFFENSIVE – 22 Apr. – 20 May

UN OFFENSIVE
23 May – 27 Nov. 1951

STALEMATE

but the next day, moving on, the Wolfhounds reached the southern edge of Suwon before being fired upon. Having discovered what Ridgway suspected—the absence of large forces of Chinese Communists between Pyongtaek and Suwon—they were ordered to withdraw.

During the next few days pressure against the center and east continued to fall off, and though the 1st Marine Division in the south was still active cleaning out guerrillas, all signs pointed to a general abatement of enemy operations. This did not mean that Lin Piao's drive for Pusan had been called off. It meant only that the bulk of his forces was being withdrawn to a staging area for a new and heavier stroke. Light screening troops had been left behind to cover this movement. United Nations air reconnaissance had already reported the movement of large stocks of supplies to the battle area, along with thousands of troops replacements. Ridgway decided to strike the enemy before he could reorganize.

He ordered his commanders to use everything they had—armor, artillery, infantry, close air support—to disrupt the enemy buildup. Meanwhile, Eighth Army's staff began planning offensive operations, and its commander turned to the vital problem of renewing its fighting spirit. On January 21, Ridgway issued a bulletin which he hoped would end Eighth Army's apprehensive habit of "looking over the shoulder" as well as clear up the bewilderment caused by the continuing debate between President Truman and his conservative opposition. The message said:

> To me the issues are clear. It is not a question of this or that Korean town or village. Real estate is, here, incidental. It is not restricted to the issue of freedom for our South Korean Allies, whose fidelity and valor under the severest stresses of battle we recognize; though that freedom is a symbol of the wider issues, and included among them.
>
> The real issues are whether the power of Western civilization, as God has permitted it to flower in our own beloved lands, shall defy and defeat Communism; whether the rule of men who shoot their prisoners, enslave their citizens, and deride the dignity of man, shall displace the rule of those to whom the individual and his individual rights are sacred; whether we are to survive with

God's hand to guide and lead us, or to perish in the dead exist-ence of a Godless world.

If these be true, and to me they are, beyond any possibility of challenge, then this has long since ceased to be a fight for free-dom for our Korean Allies alone and for their national survival. It has become, and it continues to be, a fight for our own free-dom, for our own survival, in an honorable, independent na-tional existence.

The sacrifices we have made, and those we shall yet support, are not offered vicariously for others, but in our own direct de-fense.

In the final analysis, the issue now joined right here in Korea is whether Communism or individual freedom shall prevail; whether the flight of fear-driven people we have witnessed here shall be checked, or shall at some future time, however distant, engulf our own loved ones in all its misery and despair.

These are the things for which we fight. Never have members of any military command had a greater challenge than we, or a finer opportunity to show ourselves and our people at their best —and thus to do honor to the profession of arms, and to those brave men who bred us.

Though Ridgway was eager to attack, he still had to con-sider the possibility that the Chinese withdrawal might be a trap. He removed these doubts on January 24, when he recon-noitered the battlefield from a two-seater training plane flown by Lieutenant General Earle Partridge, commander of the Fifth Air Force.

For two hours we flew over that lonely, empty land, skimming the ridge tops, ducking into the valleys, circling over the little dead villages. Over all this snowy land, which covered our entire battlefront, we saw no sign of life or movement. No smoke came from the chimneys, and nothing moved either on or off the roads, neither vehicles, men nor animals. In only one little village, that lay at the head of a valley, did I see faint signs that troops were there. From this huddle of thatched houses a thin line of car tracks led from the outskirts of the village into the dense pine woods on the hills above. It was clear that here, in this village, the enemy was taking shelter against the bitter cold by night, moving out before sun-up to hide in the woods, for with our bomber aircraft hunting targets like hungry hawks hunting mice, a village was no safe place to be by day. I flew back to my headquarters pondering what I had seen. The information I had gathered was negative. But I was satisfied in my own mind that, if I should order an attack, I would not be sending Eighth Army into a trap in which it could be destroyed.[1]

That attack was ordered forward the following day, January 25, 1951. Seven columns struck north from the two-corps western front, moving warily, relying heavily on aerial support, methodically destroying enemy pockets while maintaining an unbroken front across the hills and thereby avoiding the error of roadbound fighting which left the enemy free to infiltrate down the ridgelines at night. Meanwhile, the left flank was guaranteed against amphibious surprise by U. S. warships patrolling the west coast. Gradually, Ridgway fed more power into the advance, putting the 3rd Infantry Division into line on January 27, sending armored spearheads probing boldly toward Seoul, massing his artillery and striking the enemy with aerial bombs and napalm.

Gradually, the Chinese began to counterattack, and the advance slowed. It became obvious that the Chinese Communist 50th Army was fighting a delaying action. The last day of January the United Nations advance was held to a mile, but it continued throughout early February, inexorably slugging its way up to the south banks of the Han River. In the center, meanwhile, the town of Wonju had been recaptured, and Ridgway had ordered the U. S. X and the ROK III Corps to advance in the same manner as the U. S. I and IX in the west. The movement was begun, but intense opposition suggested that the Chinese were unwilling to retreat as easily in the center. On the west, again, the advance approached Inchon and Kimpo Airfield to the west of Seoul. On February 9, enemy resistance collapsed there, Inchon and Kimpo were taken without a shot the next day, and U. S. soldiers once more looked across the frozen Han into the blackened desolation that was the city of Seoul.

At this point the Communists made their most determined effort to wreck the United Nations offensive. The advance in the central sector had been scattered because of the mountainous terrain. Five columns had fanned out west, north and east of the town of Hoengsong, about 15 miles north of Wonju. They were overextended, and the Communists, who had been steadily sideslipping east since the United Nations advance began, quickly cut them off. Two Chinese armies and one North Korean corps attacked out of the mountains, and again their victims were the U. S. 2nd and the ROK 8th Divisions. One battalion of the 2nd's 38th Regiment was caught in a dreadful trap known as "Massacre Valley," while the ROK 8th was all but annihilated. The ROK 5th was also mauled. The Dutch Battalion attached to the 2nd Division was struck savagely at Hoengsong and its commander, Lieutenant Colonel M. P. A. den Ouden, was killed in his command post. Hoengsong was finally abandoned and what seemed a general retreat on Wonju began. Once more, United Nations troops found themselves forced to fight to the rear, for the enemy had set up the customary roadblocks behind them.

Then the Chinese threw their main blow at Chipyong-ni, a road junction 20 air miles northwest of Wonju and midway between Ridgway's west and center. Breakthrough here would place the entire UN assault in jeopardy. But there was no breakthrough. A 4,000-man combat force from the 2nd Division's 38th Regiment and the French Battalion fell back to a ring of low hills and set up defensive perimeters. The French and American soldiers fought valiantly for three days, holding off three Chinese divisions which had surrounded them, receiving their food and ammunition by air, until an armored relief column from the U. S. 5th Cavalry Regiment broke through the Chinese on the 15th. Then the enemy attack melted away. Lin Piao's most serious counterstroke had failed.

To the east, Lin's secondary one was also blunted. Here the North Koreans moving southeast from Hoengsong had punched to within 10 miles of Chechon, a town 30 air miles southeast of Wonju, but Ridgway dispatched a force of Americans and ROKs to contain them. And so, his line was preserved intact, while to the rear the Marines were whittling North Korean guerrillas by surrounding them, band by band, pounding them with mortars and artillery, and then moving in for the kill.

By mid-February, the Chinese and their North Korean allies

were in full retreat. Ridgway, hot to pursue, began another advance called Operation Killer. Its purpose was described by its name, although Ridgway was criticized for using such a word. It was said, "with many holiday and lady terms," that the word was bloodthirsty and its use would offend Asian sensibilities. Such criticism came, not from President Truman's conservative opposition, but from the extreme liberal group who supported Truman's limited war, but seemed to wish it could be won on the sly. However, "Killer" went forward throughout the final two weeks of February, 1951. Most of the fighting was done in the western zone, extended somewhat farther east to allow the 1st Marine Division to enter the line opposite Hoengsong. It was successful, though unspectacular. An early spring had thawed the hills and the men fought in heavy rains, crossing swollen streams or stumbling calf-deep in the stinking muck of melting rice paddies. On February 24, the Marines took Hoengsong and the last enemy footholds south of the Han River began to crumble all along the line. By the end of the month, they had collapsed—and the United Nations soldiers had begun to find evidence of how cruelly the winter and American firepower had treated the armies of Red China. The hills were littered with their dead; shallow, mass graves were uncovered everywhere around Wonju and Chechon. The "People's Volunteers" who had been fresh and strong and close to home when they attacked the Eighth Army in the hills near Manchuria, had not been able to withstand the climate and the failures of a supply line running back 260 miles to the Yalu. Many of these dead had perished of cold or hunger, or of inadequate treatment for their wounds. From Chinese prisoners came reports of typhus epidemics. In the main, though, the vast majority of enemy bodies discovered south of the Han River were battle casualties, and Eighth Army was quick to make psychological capital of this fact. Retreating enemy soldiers were showered with leaflets which said:

COUNT YOUR MEN!

Among the hundreds of thousands of casualties suffered in the Communists' unsuccessful "third phase offensive" and subsequent counterattacks was General Lin Piao. He was relieved of command of the Fourth Field Army in early March, either for wounds or for illness, it is not known which. General Peng Teh-huai took complete charge of Communist forces in Korea. His first order to the Fourth Field Army was to hold the 38th Parallel "at all costs" until another major offensive—supplied and supported by Russia—could be launched in May. A North Korean corps was to defend Seoul, while roughly six Chinese armies held the mountains east of the city. Behind this line new forces would be assembled.

To disrupt this buildup, to continue the attrition of the enemy and thus to carry out American policy of "deflating" Red China's newly won military prestige, General Ridgway extended his January-February offensives with a new attack called Operation Ripper. The U. S. IX and X Corps were to advance in the center on Chunchon, about 30 miles north of the existing positions, while the right flank was guarded by ROK units and the left remained in place west and south of Seoul. A good gain northward would expose Seoul's eastern flank, and thus, in the eloquent Ridgway phrase, by "imposing a threat against the mind of the enemy commander" there, a withdrawal from Seoul might also be forced. Operation Ripper began on March 7 and was successful from the beginning. The first day of the advance, Eighth Army claimed an enemy casualty toll of 11,400 men, exclusive of the results of aerial attacks. Substantial gains were made all along the two-corps front, except at a point 15 miles east of Seoul. Here the soldiers of the U. S. 25th Division crossed the Han in rubber assault boats. Though they had been helped by feints made to the west and south of Seoul, they ran into stubborn resistance. By March 10, however, enemy opposition to the Han bridgehead had also collapsed, and it became apparent that the Communists were falling back all along the west-central front.

On the night of March 14 foot patrols of the ROK 1st Division probed into the southern outskirts of Seoul and found the city deserted. United Nations troops commenced movement into the city and the Republic of Korea's red-and-blue flag was hauled up the mast above the National Assembly Building. For the fourth time, Seoul had changed hands—although this time there was very little left to exchange. The city was without light or power, water and food were scarce, very few buildings of height remained standing, and of the original population of 1,500,000 persons only 200,000 ragged civilians—chiefly women, children and old men—remained to welcome the United Nations on its second liberating entry. By the end of March, however, a city government was again functioning in Seoul.

Meanwhile, Operation Ripper was pressed forward on all fronts. To the east, four ROK regiments had at last polished off the North Korean guerrillas who had been a problem since the breakout from the Pusan Perimeter in September, 1950, and the two ROK corps in that sector were free to strike north. In the center, the U. S. IX and X Corps advanced steadily, entering Chunchon on March 19. To the west, an attempt was made to trap an estimated 20,000 North Korean soldiers between Seoul and Kaesong. On March 23 the 187th Airborne Regiment and two Ranger companies were dropped over Munsan while an armored column drove up from Seoul 20 miles to the southeast. But the North Koreans had already withdrawn and the gathering net caught very few fish. The enemy retreat, however, allowed a near-bloodless advance to the Imjin River. By the end of the month, supported by United Nations air and the increased bombardment of both coasts by the United Nations navy—notably the U. S. Navy's protracted siege of Wonsan—Operation Ripper had brought the United Nations land forces to a line generally approximating the 38th Parallel. For the second time the Korean War was back where it had started. For the second time, the United Nations forces prepared to cross the 38th Parallel, not to "unify Korea" or in pursuit of "complete victory," but only, following the new Truman policy of fighting to force the Red Chinese to negotiate, to inflict maximum damage on the enemy as well as to prevent him from organizing a new offensive unmolested.

These were General Ridgway's purposes, when, in the streaming spring rains of late March and early April, his units punched into North Korea for depths of from six to eight miles. And then Ridgway was ordered to proceed to Tokyo. The collision course on which Douglas MacArthur and Harry Truman had been running since August of 1950 had produced the inevitable crash. On April 11, President Truman relieved General MacArthur of all his commands and replaced him with Ridgway.

Chapter Four

THE letter of clarification which President Truman sent to General MacArthur on January 13 had produced only a temporary lull in the conflict between the President's policy of containment and the general's desire to extend the war. Indeed, MacArthur's reply on that date had been only a terse: "We will do our best." Actually, he seems to have regarded the Truman letter more as assurance that there would be no evacuation in Korea, as then seemed likely, than as a policy statement to which he should adhere.

For the next two months, General MacArthur, while continuing to struggle for a freer hand in Korea, was less explosive in public. His protests against the enemy's "privileged sanctuary" were generally addressed to the Joint Chiefs only. On February 21 he asked for permission to bomb Racin, a port 35 miles below the Siberian border which the Chinese Communists were using for a supply center. It was denied on the ground that Racin was too close to Soviet territory, causing MacArthur to complain of the "unparalleled conditions of restraint and handicap" imposed on him by the government's policies. His subsequent request to bomb the generating plants on China's Yalu frontier was also disapproved.

Meanwhile, the general's friends among the American conservatives had been beating out a drumfire of criticism of "Mr. Truman's war." On February 12, Representative Joseph Martin, Republican minority leader in the House, renewed the call for "opening a second front in Asia" by using Chiang Kaishek's soldiers against Communist China. He said there was "good reason to believe that General MacArthur favors such an operation," and delivered this judgment on the morality of limited war:

264

"If we are not in Korea to win, then this Administration should be indicted for the murder of thousands of American boys."

Three weeks later, on March 7, the day General Ridgway's Operation Killer was launched, General MacArthur himself delivered a dramatic battlefield statement which reopened the entire controversy. Having flown into Suwon Airfield, MacArthur gathered the war correspondents in a tent and read to them, with gravity and great deliberation, from a penciled manuscript. He said:

> Progress of the campaign continues to be satisfactory, with all three services—army, navy and air—performing well their completely co-ordinated tactical missions. Designed to meet abnormal military inhibitions, our strategic plan, involving constant movement to keep the enemy off balance with a correspondent limitation upon his initiative, remains unaltered.
>
> Our selection of the battle area, furthermore, has forced him into the military disadvantage of fighting far from his base and permitted greater employment of our air and sea arms against which he has little defense. There has been a resultant continuing and exhausting attrition upon both his manpower and supplies. There should be no illusions in this matter, however. In such a campaign of maneuver, as our battle lines shift north the supply position of the enemy will progressively improve, just as inversely the effectiveness of our air potential will progressively diminish, thus in turn causing his numerical ground superiority to become of increasing battlefield significance.
>
> Assuming no diminution of the enemy's flow of ground forces and material to the Korean battle area, a continuation of the existing limitation upon our freedom of counteroffensive action, and no major additions to our organizational strength, the battle lines cannot fail in time to reach a point of theoretical military stalemate. Thereafter our further advance would militarily benefit the enemy more than it would ourselves.
>
> The exact place of stabilization is of necessity a fluctuating variable dependent upon the shifting relative strengths of forces committed and will constantly move up or down. Even now there are indications that the enemy is attempting to build up from China a new and massive offensive for the Spring. These

are the salient factors which must continue to delimit strategical thinking and planning as the campaign proceeds.

This does not alter the fact, however, that the heavy toll we have taken of the enemy's military power since its commitment to war in Korea cannot fail to weaken his hold upon the Chinese nation and people and materially dampen his ardor for engaging in other aggressive adventure in Asia.

Even under our existing conditions of restraint it should be clearly evident to the Communist foes now committed against us that they cannot hope to impose their will in Korea by military force. They have failed twice—once through North Korean forces, and now through the military might of the army of Communist China. Theirs was the aggression in both cases. Theirs has been the double failure. That they should continue this savage slaughter despite an almost hopeless chance of ultimate military success is a measure of their wanton disregard of international decencies and restraints and displays a complete contempt for the sanctity of human life.

No longer is there even a shallow pretense of concern for the welfare of the Korean nation and people, now being so ruthlessly and senselessly sacrificed. Through endless bloodshed it is apparently hoped to enforce either international banditry or blackmail or both.

Vital decisions have yet to be made—decisions far beyond the scope of the authority vested in me as the military commander, decisions which are neither solely political nor solely military, but which must provide on the highest international levels an answer to the obscurities which now becloud the unsolved problems raised by Red China's undeclared war in Korea.

Here was the opening gun of MacArthur's renewed drive for a freer hand in Korea. Newsmen called it MacArthur's "Die-for-a-Tie" statement, and that very suggestion that American lives were being sacrificed in Korea for something less than victory was considered so dangerous to Eighth Army morale that Ridgway himself called a press conference five days later to say:

We didn't set out to conquer China. We set out to stop Communism. We have demonstrated the superiority on the battlefield of our men. If China fails to throw us into the sea, that is a defeat for her of incalculable proportions. If China fails to drive us from Korea, she will have failed monumentally. . . .

The things for which we are fighting here are of such overwhelming importance I can't conceive of any member of our fighting forces feeling that there lies ahead any field of indefinite or indeterminate action.

This war is positive from beginning to end, and the potentialities are positive.

Ridgway's remarks, indicating his acceptance of stalemate as one of the "victories" possible in limited war, was well received in the United Nations, where the United States Government had already begun to move among its allies for support of a new Presidential statement of peace aims in Korea. By March 19 a draft of this proposal had already been made, saying in part:

A prompt settlement of the Korean problem would greatly reduce international tension in the Far East and would open the way for the consideration of other problems in that area by the processes of peaceful settlement envisaged in the Charter of the United Nations.

Until satisfactory arrangements for concluding the fighting have been reached, United Nations military action must be continued.

Both Truman and Secretary Acheson hoped that this announcement of a willingness to talk, being calm and without threats, might obtain a favorable reply. On March 20 General MacArthur was notified that it was pending and was asked for his recommendations. His reply requested only that no further restrictions be placed on his command. In the meantime, the State Department began conferring with nations having troops in Korea, hoping to secure approval of the announcement. But it was never made. On March 24, MacArthur issued this statement:

Operations continue according to schedule and plan. We have now substantially cleared South Korea of organized Communist forces. It is becoming increasingly evident that the heavy destruction along the enemy's lines of supply, caused by our "round-the-clock" massive air and naval bombardment, has left his troops in the forward battle area deficient in requirements to sustain his operations.

. . . Of even greater significance than our tactical success has been the clear revelation that this new enemy, Red China, of such exaggerated and vaunted military power, lacks the industrial capacity to provide adequately many critical items essential to the conduct of modern war.

. . . These military weaknesses have been clearly and definitely revealed since Red China entered upon its undeclared war in Korea. Even under inhibitions which now restrict activity of the United Nations forces and the corresponding military advantages which accrue to Red China, it has been shown its complete inability to accomplish by force of arms the conquest of Korea.

The enemy therefore must by now be painfully aware that a decision of the United Nations to depart from its tolerant effort to contain the war to the area of Korea through expansion of our military operations to his coastal areas and interior bases would doom Red China to the risk of imminent military collapse.

These basic facts being established, there should be no insuperable difficulty arriving at decisions on the Korean problem if the issues are resolved on their own merit without being burdened by extraneous matters not directly related to Korea, such as Formosa and China's seat in the United Nations.

The Korean nation and people which have been so cruelly ravaged must not be sacrificed. That is the paramount concern. Apart from the military area of the problem where the issues are resolved in the course of combat, the fundamental questions continue to be political in nature and must find their answer in the diplomatic sphere.

Within the area of my authority as military commander, however, it should be needless to say I stand ready at any time to confer in the field with the commander-in-chief of the enemy forces in an earnest effort to find any military means whereby the realization of the political objectives of the United Nations in Korea, to which no nation may justly take exceptions, might be accomplished without further bloodshed.

The effect of this extraordinary statement was enormous, both in Washington and among the United Nations allies.

The State Department felt that the "MacArthur pronunciamento," as the Norwegian Ambassador called it, was a deliberate attempt to scuttle a cease-fire offer by presenting Red China an ultimatum she must reject. The inevitable rejection came on March 29 when Peiping Radio called the statement an "insult to the Chinese people" and "nothing but a demand for the Chinese and Korean forces to yield to the so-called United Nations forces, [as well as] a threat that the aggressors will advance on our homeland."

President Truman has written: "By this act MacArthur left me no choice—I could no longer tolerate his insubordination." Perhaps so, but the President did not act at all rapidly. He merely instructed the Joint Chiefs of Staff to silence MacArthur for good with this message:

FROM JCS PERSONAL FOR MAC ARTHUR

The President has directed that your attention be called to his order transmitted 6 December 1950. In view of the information given you 20 March 1951 any further statements by you must be coordinated as prescribed in the order of 6 December.

The President has also directed that in the event Communist military leaders request an armistice in the field, you immediately report that fact to the JCS for instructions.

Unfortunately, the gag was applied too late. On March 20, 1951, General MacArthur had written to Representative Joseph Martin in response to Martin's request for comment on his February 12 speech which attacked President Truman's policy of limited war and demanded "opening a second front in Asia" by sending Chiang Kai-shek's Nationalist troops into battle on the Chinese mainland. On April 5, MacArthur's reply was read by Martin on the floor of the House of Representatives. It said:

I am most grateful for your note of the eighth forwarding me a copy of your address of February 12. The latter I have read with much interest, and find that with the passage of years you have certainly lost none of your old-time punch.

My views and recommendations with respect to the situation created by Red China's entry into war against us in Korea have been submitted to Washington in most complete detail. Generally, these views are well known and generally understood, as they follow the conventional pattern of meeting force with maximum counterforce as we have never failed to do in the past. Your view with respect to the utilization of the Chinese forces in Formosa is in conflict with neither logic nor this tradition.

It seems strangely difficult for some to realize that here in Asia is where the Communist conspirators have elected to make their play for global conquest, and that we have joined the issue thus raised on the battlefield; that here we fight Europe's war with arms, while the diplomats there still fight it with words; that if we lost the war to Communism in Asia the fall of Europe is inevitable; win it, and Europe most probably would avoid war and yet preserve freedom. As you point out, we must win. There is no substitute for victory.

In this letter, the commander who wished to cross the military Yalu had crossed his political Rubicon. Defiance had been shifted to open challenge, and the politician to whom this gauntlet had been flung down, President Truman, has written of his reaction:

The time had come to draw the line. MacArthur's letter showed that the general was not only in disagreement with the policy of the government but was challenging this policy in open insubordination to his Commander in Chief.

I asked Acheson, Marshall, Bradley, and Harriman to meet with me on Friday morning, April 6, to discuss MacArthur's action. I put the matter squarely before them. What should be done about General MacArthur? . . .

Averell Harriman was of the opinion that I should have fired MacArthur two years ago. In the spring of 1949, as in 1948, MacArthur had pleaded that he could not come home because of the press of business in Tokyo, and it had been necessary for the Secretary of the Army, Kenneth Royall, to intervene urgently from Washington in order to get MacArthur to withhold his approval from a bill of the Japanese Diet which was completely contrary to the economic policy for the occupation as prescribed by the governmental authorities in Washington.

Secretary of Defense Marshall advised caution, saying he wished to reflect further. He observed that if I relieved Mac-

Arthur it might be difficult to get the military appropriations through Congress.

General Bradley approached the question entirely from the point of view of military discipline. As he saw it, there was a clear case of insubordination and the general deserved to be relieved of command. He did wish, however, to consult with the Chiefs of Staff before making a final recommendation.

Acheson said that he believed that General MacArthur should be relieved, but he thought it essential to have the unanimous advice of the Joint Chiefs of Staff before I acted. He counseled that the most careful consideration be given to this matter since it was of the utmost seriousness. He added, "If you relieve MacArthur, you will have the biggest fight of your administration."

. . . [After a meeting of the Cabinet] I suggested to Marshall that he go over all the messages in the Pentagon files that had been exchanged with General MacArthur in the past two years. . . .

The next morning Saturday, April 7, we met again in my office. . . . General Marshall stated that he had read the messages and that he had now concluded that MacArthur should have been fired two years ago. . . .

At nine o'clock Monday morning I again met with Marshall, Bradley, Acheson, and Harriman. General Bradley reported that the Joint Chiefs of Staff had met with him on Sunday, and it was his and their unanimous judgment that General MacArthur should be relieved.

General Marshall reaffirmed that this was also his conclusion. Harriman restated his opinion of Friday. Acheson said he agreed entirely to the removal of MacArthur.

It was only now that I answered that I had already made up my mind that General MacArthur had to go when he made his statement of March 24.[1]

According to Truman, notice of dismissal was to be delivered to MacArthur personally by Secretary of the Army Pace, who was then in Korea, but a report that the story had "leaked out" and was to be printed by a Chicago newspaper the morning of April 11 forced him to forego this courtesy. This, says the President, is why a press conference was hastily scheduled for the bizarre hour of one o'clock in the morning of April 10, at which time newsmen were handed the following Presidential statement:

> With deep regret I have concluded that General of the Army Douglas MacArthur is unable to give his wholehearted support to the policies of the United States Government and of the United Nations in matters pertaining to his official duties. In view of the specific responsibilities imposed upon me by the Constitution of the United States and the added responsibility which has been entrusted to me by the United Nations, I have decided that I must make a change of command in the Far East. I have, therefore, relieved General MacArthur of his commands and have designated Lieutenant General Matthew B. Ridgway as his successor.
>
> Full and vigorous debate on matters of national policy is a vital element in the constitutional system of our free democracy. It is fundamental, however, that military commanders must be governed by the policies and directives issued to them in the manner provided by our laws and Constitution. In time of crisis, the consideration is particularly compelling.
>
> General MacArthur's place in history as one of our greatest commanders is fully established. The Nation owes him a debt of gratitude for the distinguished and exceptional service which he has rendered his country in posts of great responsibility. For that reason I repeat my regret at the necessity for the action I feel compelled to take in his case.

The order which President Truman dispatched to General MacArthur stated: "I deeply regret that it becomes my duty as President and Commander in Chief of the United States military forces to replace you as Supreme Commander, Allied powers; Commander-in-Chief, United Nations Command; Commander-in-Chief, Far East; and Commanding General, U. S. Army, Far East. You will turn over your commands effective at once to Lt. Gen. Matthew B. Ridgway. You are authorized to have issued such orders as are necessary to complete desired travel to such place as you select. . . ." Unfortunately, because of transmission delays, the Presidential announcement to the press beat the formal order to Tokyo by twenty minutes, and General MacArthur learned of his having been stripped of all his commands as he was finishing lunch in the U. S. Embassy at about three o'clock the afternoon of April 11.

... The MacArthurs had two luncheon guests, Senator Warren Magnuson of Washington and William Sterns of Northwest Airlines. The meal was proceeding quietly and the conversation was still devoted to the amenities, when from her end of the table Mrs. MacArthur looked over the General's shoulder and through the door to see the anguished face of a MacArthur aide-de-camp, Colonel Sidney Huff. She excused herself quietly, rose from the table, and left the room. There were tears in Huff's eyes when she came up to him. He told her quickly and simply the news that he had just heard on the radio. MacArthur was abruptly ... removed from his command. ...

The General was laughing heartily at a remark made by one of his guests when she walked into the room behind him and touched his shoulder. He turned and she bent down and told him the news in a voice so low that it was not heard across the table. ...

MacArthur's face froze. Not a flicker of emotion crossed it. For a moment, while his luncheon guests puzzled on what was happening, he was stonily silent. Then he looked up at his wife, who still stood with her hand on his shoulder. In a gentle voice audible to all present, he said:

"Jeannie, we're going home at last."[2]

In such cruelly casual fashion was a great military career brought to its close. No argument, except one of national security, could excuse such incivility—and there was no security involved. President Truman's explanation that the courtesy of personal notice by Secretary Pace was canceled so as to get the announcement to the press before a single newspaper could print its own "unofficial" report of his decision is hard to accept, unless, of course, it is accepted that in the Age of Publicity even the American President must behave rudely in the interests of "getting there first with our side of the story." Nor do the transmission delays excuse that scene in the U. S. Embassy, for the simple reason that the press was informed before MacArthur was. And Mr. Truman's order was itself a model of graceless brevity. No, much as the President's act was within his rights as Commander in Chief, ample as had been his provocation, his execution of his decision was badly handled. And because of it, the storm already breaking over the country clapped more thunderously about his own political head.

Some Republicans, while reiterating demands for Acheson's head, went as far as to call for the impeachment of President Truman. MacArthur was hailed as a martyr who had sacrificed his career rather than betray his country to "the State Department crowd," while Truman was castigated as a mean and vengeful little man who had dismissed the general either while "full of brandy and bourbon," in the phrase of Senator Joseph McCarthy, or to placate "British interests." The storm's opening gusts of anger seemed to blow heavily against the President and in favor of the general, and so hostile were the numerous telegrams which began flooding the White House that the President decided he had better act quickly to defend himself in what Acheson had accurately forecast as the fight of his Presidential life. He broadcast his side of the dispute to the nation, saying:

> In the simplest terms, what we are doing in Korea is this: We are trying to prevent World War III. So far, by fighting a limited war in Korea, we have prevented aggression from succeeding and bringing on a general war. . . .
>
> We do not want to see the conflict in Korea extended. We are trying to prevent a world war—not to start one. The best way to do that is to make it plain that we and the other free countries will continue to resist the attack.
>
> But you may ask why can't we take the other steps to punish the aggressor? Why don't we bomb Manchuria, and China itself? Why don't we assist Chinese Nationalist troops to land on the mainland of China?
>
> If we were to do these things we would be running a very grave risk of starting a general war. If that were to happen, we would have brought about the exact situation we were trying to prevent. If we were to do these things we would become entangled in a vast conflict on the continent of Asia and our task would become immeasurably more difficult all over the world. What would suit the ambitions of the Kremlin better than for our military forces to be committed to a full-scale war with Red China?

A number of events have made it evident that General Mac-Arthur did not agree with that policy. I have therefore considered it essential to relieve General MacArthur so that there would be no doubt or confusion as to the real purpose and aim of our policy. It was with the deepest personal regret that I found myself compelled to take this action. General MacArthur is one of the greatest military commanders. . . .

We are ready at any time to negotiate for a restoration of peace in the area. But we will not engage in appeasement. We are only interested in peace. . . .

In the next few days, the President detailed the provocations General MacArthur had given him by releasing to the press his order concerning the clearance of public statements with the Joint Chiefs; the message asking MacArthur's opinion on the arming of the ROKs, together with MacArthur's reply stating his preference for arming the Japanese National Police Force; the notification given MacArthur of the impending Presidential announcement; MacArthur's own subsequent statement which made the announcement impracticable; the message to MacArthur reminding him of the clearance-of-statements order; and, finally, the letter to Congressman Martin. In effect, President Truman was fighting his battle in the court of public opinion—and yet, with so much evidence to justify his action, he was not winning it.

The return which General Douglas MacArthur made to the United States after fourteen years of absence was nothing less than a Roman triumph. In Honolulu, in San Francisco, in New York, in Washington, he was received and hailed as a conquering hero, and his movements and words were relayed by radio and television to nationwide audiences. To the Democrats' charges that he had been guilty of "meddling in politics," he replied: "The only politics I have is contained in the simple phrase known well by all of you: God bless America." On April 19, granted the unusual privilege of addressing a joint session of Congress, General MacArthur defended his conduct with all his high eloquence, sense of drama and force of argument. In part, he said:

I stand on this rostrum with a deep sense of humility and great pride—humility in the wake of those great American architects of our history who have stood here before me, and pride in the reflection that this forum of legislative debate represents human liberty in the purest form yet devised. Here are centered the hopes and aspirations and faith of the entire human race. . . .

I address you with neither rancor nor bitterness, in the fading twilight of life, with but one purpose in mind: to serve my country. . . .

The issues are global, and so interlocked that to consider the problems of one sector oblivious to those of another is to court disaster for the whole. While Asia is commonly referred to as the gateway to Europe, it is no less true that Europe is the gateway to Asia, and the broad influence of one cannot fail to have its impact upon the other. . . . There are those who claim our strength is inadequate to protect on both fronts, that we cannot divide our effort. I can think of no greater expression of defeatism. . . .

Any major breach [of the American chain of island defenses in the western Pacific] would render vulnerable to determined attack every other major segment. This is a military estimate as to which I have yet to find a military leader who will take exception. For that reason I have strongly recommended in the past, as a matter of military urgency, that under no circumstances must Formosa fall under Communist control. . . .

While I was not consulted prior to the President's decision to intervene in support of the Republic of Korea, that decision, from a military standpoint, proved a sound one . . . as we hurled back the invader and decimated his forces. Our victory was complete, and our objectives within reach, when Red China intervened with numerically superior ground forces. This created a new war and an entirely new situation, a situation not contemplated when our forces were committed against the North Korean invader; a situation which called for new decisions in the diplomatic sphere to permit the realistic adjustment of military strategy. Such decisions have not been forthcoming. . . .

. . . Military necessity in the conduct of the war made necessary:

1. The intensification of our economic blockade against China.

2. The imposition of a naval blockade against the China Coast.

3. Removal of restrictions on air reconnaissance of China's

coastal area and of Manchuria [and action to] neutralize the sanctuary protection given the enemy north of the Yalu.

4. Removal of restrictions on the forces of the Republic of China on Formosa with logistical support to contribute to their effective operations against the Chinese mainland.

. . . [It is] my understanding that from a military standpoint the above views have been fully shared in the past by practically every military leader concerned with the Korean campaign, including our own Joint Chiefs of Staff.

It has been said, in effect, that I am a warmonger. Nothing could be further from the truth. . . .

But once war is forced upon us, there is no other alternative than to apply every available means to bring it to a swift end. War's very object is victory, not prolonged indecision. . . .

In war, indeed, there can be no substitute for victory. . . . Why, my soldiers asked me, surrender military advantages to an enemy in the field? I could not answer.

In concluding, MacArthur spoke his farewell to the profession of arms in a moving passage which has since entered history. He said: "I am closing my fifty-two years of military service. When I joined the Army, even before the turn of the century, it was the fulfillment of all my boyish hopes and dreams. The world has turned over many times since I took the oath on the Plain at West Point, and the hopes and dreams have all since vanished. But I still remember the refrain of one of the most popular barracks ballads of that day, which proclaimed most proudly that old soldiers never die; they just fade away. And like the old soldier of that ballad, I now close my military career and just fade away, an old soldier who tried to do his duty as God gave him the light to see that duty. Good-by."

But the general did not fade away. His farewell was but a prelude to the angry and emotional months of May and June, the days of the Great Debate, as the Truman-MacArthur dispute has been called, a period when the American people were divided in an internal controversy which, both for the volume of words poured out as well as for the strident bitterness with which they were spoken or written, has not been equaled before or since. Although the chief and official arena of the Great Debate was the hearing room of the Senate Armed Services and

Foreign Relations Committees, which jointly heard more than two million words of testimony, the controversy raged all over the land, quickly assuming, as such debates often do, the indelible outlines of partisanship. Many of the commentators who fed its fires did not understand the issues; indeed, a good part of the nation seemed to believe that the dispute was over President Truman's right to dismiss General MacArthur, even though this was unquestionable and has been described as such by MacArthur's most sympathetic biographer, Courtney Whitney. To the public confusion was added the additional hurt of public disclosure of almost every detail of American strategy in the cold war against Soviet Russia and her satellites. With both these large Senatorial committees assembled together, with all other Senators invited to attend their meetings, it was impossible to keep from the press testimony which was to have been deleted from the record for reasons of security. In this atmosphere, General MacArthur defended the actions which had brought about his dismissal. He said the Administration's policy in Korea, or "lack of policy," would result in "perpetuating a slaughter such as I have never heard of in the history of mankind," to which the Administration replied by saying that during the world war which MacArthur's policies would provoke, a single atomic bomb dropped on an American city would cause more casualties than the 60,000 which America had already suffered in Korea.

Thereafter MacArthur, with conservative Senators rallying behind him, concentrated on attacking the entire concept of limited war. He began this by saying: "I am just one hundred per cent a believer against war. . . . It is a form of mutual suicide." But, he added, if it came, the choices during war were, "either to pursue it to victory; to surrender to an enemy and end it on his terms; or what I think is the worst of all choices, to go on indefinitely and indefinitely, neither to win nor to lose in that stalemate." Limited war, he said, had introduced "a new concept into military operations—the concept of appeasement, the concept that when you use force, you can limit that force. . . ." He continued:

"If that is the concept of a continued and indefinite campaign in Korea, with no definite purpose of stopping it until the enemy gets tired or you yield to his terms, I think that introduces into the military sphere a political control such as I have never known in my life or ever studied. . . . If you hit soft, if you practice appeasement in the use of force, you are doomed to disaster. . . .

"I do unquestionably state that when men become locked in battle, that there should be no artifice, under the name of politics, which should handicap your own men, decrease their chances for winning and increase their losses."

Many high-ranking officers either supported MacArthur or, like Admiral Sherman, Navy member of the Joint Chiefs, or Lieutenant General Albert Wedemeyer, the Army's chief planner, expressed repugnance for a stalemate. Among those more openly approving MacArthur's testimony were General Carl Spaatz, retired chief of the Air Force; Major General O'Donnell, the former Far East Bomber Command chief; and Major General Claire Chennault, for many years on the staff of Generalissimo Chiang Kai-shek.

The Administration's leading defenders were Secretary Marshall, General Bradley, chairman of the Joint Chiefs, and General Hoyt Vandenberg, Air Force Chief of Staff. Marshall said:

> There can be, I think, no quick and decisive solution to the global struggle short of resorting to another world war. The cost of such a conflict is beyond calculation. It is, therefore, our policy to contain Communist aggression in different fashions in different areas without resorting to total war, if that be possible to avoid. This policy may seem costly, if maintained over a period of years, but those costs would not be comparable at all to what happens if we get involved in what you might call an atomic war. . . . The application of this policy has not always been easy or popular.

A more detailed military exposition of the policy of containment was made by General Bradley, speaking for the Joint Chiefs in his famous "wrong war" statement:

> . . . From a global viewpoint . . . our military mission is to support a policy of preventing Communism from gaining the manpower, the resources, the raw materials, and the industrial capacity essential to world domination. If Soviet Russia ever controls the entire Eurasian land mass, then the Soviet satellite imperial-

ism may have the broad base upon which to build the military power to rule the world.

Korea must be looked upon with proper perspective. It is just one engagement, just one phase. . . . As long as we keep the conflict within its present scope we are holding to a minimum the forces we must commit and tie down. The strategic alternative, enlargement of the war in Korea to include Red China, would probably delight the Kremlin more than anything else we could do. It would necessarily tie down additional forces, especially our sea power and our air power, while the Soviet Union would not be obliged to put a single man into the conflict. . . .

Red China is not the powerful nation seeking to dominate the world. Frankly, in the opinion of the Joint Chiefs of Staff, this strategy would involve us in the wrong war, at the wrong place, at the wrong time, and with the wrong enemy.

The most practical argument against extension of the war, and therefore perhaps the most telling among some of the Republican Senators, was General Vandenberg's simple—though overly pessimistic—estimate that the United States had not the power to do it. He said:

Air power, and especially the application of strategic air power, should go to the heart of the industrial centers to become reasonably efficient. Now, the source of the material that is coming to the Chinese Communists and the North Koreans is from Russia. Therefore, hitting across the Yalu, we could destroy or lay waste all of Manchuria and the principal cities of China if we utilized the full power of the United States Air Force. . . . In doing that, however, we are bound to get attrition. If we utilize less than the full power of the United States Air Force, in my opinion it might not and probably would not be conclusive.

And even if we utilized it and laid waste to it there is a possibility that it would not be conclusive. But the effect on the United States Air Force, with our start from approximately 40 groups, would fix it so that, should we have to operate in any other area with full power of the United States Air Force, we would not be able to . . . [and the defenses of the United States would be] naked for several years to come.

The fact is that the United States is operating a shoestring air force in view of its global responsibilities. . . .

> In my opinion, the United States Air Force is the single potential that has kept the balance of power in our favor. It is the one thing that has, up to date, kept the Russians from deciding to go to war. . . .
>
> While we can lay the industrial potential of Russia today to waste, in my opinion, or we can lay the Manchurian countryside to waste, as well as the principal cities of China, we cannot do both, again because we have got a shoestring air force.

To the sobering effect of such testimony was added the announcement that the United States was resuming large-scale military aid to Chiang Kai-shek and was sending a large military mission to Formosa. Secretary Marshall also said that Formosa would never be allowed to fall into Communist hands. The Asia First group was thus mollified and Chiang and Formosa were taken out of the argument. Insinuations of treachery or outright charges of "sellout" were silenced by what seemed to be a stiffening Administration attitude toward Red China, and, more important, attention was gradually brought to focus on the true issue: the policy of containment through limited war, based on the theory that time worked against the unwieldy monolithic Communist empire, versus that of saving Asia from the Communist conspiracy before it was too late, by extending the war to include Manchuria or even Red China itself. Gradually, it became clear that the MacArthur program was not even the opposite of the Administration's "containment." It would, by extending the war to Red China alone—on the hopeful premise that Soviet Russia would not join the conflict—become a limited war itself. It would only be larger, but it would not be total. It would only be costlier, while running the dreadful risk of touching off the nuclear holocaust in which humanity itself might perish. And as much as General MacArthur was hailed, as often as he was quoted that "there is no substitute for victory," there was never, in those controversial days, the slightest indication that large numbers of Americans were standing ready to enlist in the armed forces or pay higher taxes or send their sons out to fight the bigger and costlier war that General MacArthur was advocating. Because of this, gradually, even grudgingly, public opinion shifted to the Administration. It never shifted to President Truman, for "the mess in Korea" would never make him popular; it never departed General MacArthur, for he was still a figure of heroic martyrdom, little as anyone wanted to follow him into the Asian heartland. The Great Debate ended in victory for the Administration's policy of containment through collective security, with General MacArthur entering private life entertaining political ambitions which were to be dashed by his onetime aide, Dwight Eisenhower, in the Republican Convention of 1952, and with "Mr. Truman's war" still tasting as bitter as ever on the public palate.

Actually, it tasted worse. Too much had been said against it during the Great Debate. General MacArthur had called it an "accordion war" in which fortunes went "up and down" with mounting and "staggering" losses. "It isn't just dust that is settling in Korea, Senator—it is American blood." Senator William Knowland had called for replacing Occidental troops with Orientals and Senator Harry Cain had demanded the withdrawal of all Americans from Korea if some of America's NATO allies, chiefly Britain, did not stop trading with Communist China. The Republican minority report on the hearings said: "We believe a policy of victory must be announced to the American people in order to restore unity and confidence. It is too much to expect that our people will accept a limited war." Such remarks appealed to nationalist and isolationist groups, already incensed at the truly enormous and disproportionate commitment of American men and money in Korea. The fact that some of America's allies were continuing to trade with the enemy could not help but add to their discontent, as well as make the Administration more unpopular for being unable to prevent it. All this had the effect of increasing President Truman's eagerness to obtain a cease-fire in Korea, and this, as will be seen, would result in unfortunate and unseemly haste to accept Red China's cries for truce talks, once the Eighth Army in Korea had beaten her armies in Korea and driven them well back of the 38th Parallel.

Chapter Five

COMMAND of the Eighth Army in Korea, as well as of the ROK Army which its orders controlled, passed from General Ridgway to Lieutenant General James Van Fleet on April 14, after which Ridgway assumed General MacArthur's duties in Tokyo and Van Fleet took charge at Eighth Army headquarters in Taegu.

The changeover occurred during a critical phase of the war, just before the end of Ridgway's last drive on April 18, and the renewal of the Chinese Communist onslaught on April 22. Fortunately, Van Fleet needed no briefing on the situation. Like Ridgway, he had been chosen as next-in-line for Eighth Army command and had been keeping abreast of Korean developments. More, it was Van Fleet—"Big Jim" as he was called—who had successfully directed a similar peninsular civil war in Greece when, as chief of the Joint United States Military Advisory and Planning Group, he rebuilt the Greek Army and led the fight which in two and one-half years thwarted the attempt of Communist guerrillas to seize power.

Few commanders in U. S. Army history have had as much combat experience as had Van Fleet at the time of his appearance in Korea (he is the only one eligible to wear the Combat Infantryman's Badge), and few had a career so notable for its early frustrations and its later successes. Van Fleet had been graduated from West Point in 1915, a member of the "Class of the Generals" which included Omar Bradley and Dwight Eisenhower. He had been famous as a fullback on the undefeated Army football team, but thereafter he spent nearly thirty years in obscurity. Though he had served on the Mexican Border and had been a machine-gun captain in France, being wounded in the Meuse-Argonne a few days before the Armistice, his promotions came very slowly and his assignments were not calculated to excite hopes of rapid rise. He spent most of the years between wars with Reserve Officer Training Corps units at several state colleges, among them the University of Florida, where he also coached the football team. His chance did not come until 1944, when he led a regiment of the 4th Infantry Division onto Omaha Beach during the invasion of Normandy. Thereafter, his leadership and canniness in combat brought him swift promotion, to assistant commander and then commander of the 4th Division, and eventually to command of the Third Corps as it spearheaded First Army's crossing of the Rhine. After his success in Greece, which gave world Communism its first postwar setback, Van Fleet commanded the First Army. Greece, however, had most aptly fitted him for Korea. There, as in Korea, he had faced an enemy able to reinforce and supply overland, while his own forces lay at the end of a long sea supply route. There, as in Korea, he had learned to value the vast possibilities of sea power in peninsular warfare, either for coastal or flanking bombardment or for the amphibious threat it posed. But there was one new worry which confronted Van Fleet on his arrival in Korea, and that was the fact that his United Nations forces were in danger of losing control of the air.

This fact, generally ignored in the popular assumption that Korea's skies were always American, was so compelling a consideration among UN commanders that Lieutenant General Partridge could warn his Fifth Air Force wing commanders on March 31: "Present world tension indicates that all possible action be taken in preparation for air attack without warning." Official Washington was so well aware of the Red air buildup in Manchuria and Red China that it had quietly informed nations with troops in Korea that in the event of massed Red air attacks in Korea, American airmen would be authorized to attack across the Yalu. Intelligence reports calculated Russian deliveries of planes would raise the Red air potential in Korea from 650 combat planes in December, 1950, to 1,050 by June of 1951. What was not known, but suspected, was the Communist Chinese displeasure with the aerial support given the ignominious "third phase offensive" in January. The Special Aviation Group sent out from Peiping to supervise the aerial buildup had complained: "If we had a strong air support, we could have driven the enemy into the sea. . . ." And so, sometime after January, 1951, General Liu Ya-lou, commander in chief of the Chinese Communist Air Force, went to work on a plan to support the ground troops in the big offensive scheduled for spring. Like the famous American who had commanded the enemy, General Douglas MacArthur, General Liu was hampered by political restrictions. Peiping, fearing American air retaliation, forbade him to use Manchurian bases for attacks against United Nations troops or installations, a prohibition which caused the Special Aviation Group, in language somewhat similar to General MacArthur's, to raise the lamentation: "The conservative policy adopted by China has apparently ensued from the high-handed policy of threats of the enemy." And so, as a U. S. Air Force historian has written:

> Recognizing the limitations and capabilities of the Chinese Communist Air Force, General Liu Ya-lou drew up a forward-looking air war plan which outlined several phases for accomplishment prior to the initiation of an air offensive against the United Nations. Using bases at Antung and MIG fighters, the Reds intended to effect a zone of air superiority over northwestern Korea. During this phase the Reds would give their pilots badly needed combat training. Having established a working air superiority, the Communists meant to repair and to construct airfields in the defended area. They would also seek to build or repair many other "secret" airfields immediately north of the 38th Parallel. As work progressed, the Reds would move in automatic weapons and flak batteries to protect the new airfields. When the forward airfields were operational, the Chinese Communist Air Force would garrison them with MIGs and ground-attack planes and commence the full-scale air offensive against the United Nations.[1]

Since the United Nations second retreat from Seoul had caused abandonment of Kimpo Airfield, and later of Suwon Airfield, as well as the subsequent withdrawal to Japan of the Fifth Air Force, the first part of this plan, seizure of the skies above northwestern Korea, was quickly effected. The territory between the Chongchon and Yalu Rivers became known as "MIG Alley." Reconnaissance pilots flying in that area counted themselves lucky to escape the swarming formations of MIGs. On March 1, the Far East Bomber Command decided to send Superfortresses back into MIG Alley and systematic bombardment began. Then, Suwon Airfield, recaptured by Ridgway's offensive, was restored to UN use. Sabrejets once more began to operate as far north as the Yalu, but found the MIG pilots vastly improved in flying and fighting ability. The second phase of General Liu's plan—training—seemed successful. By April the third phase, airfield repair and construction, was under way on bases at Sinuiju, Sinanju, Sunan, Pyongyang, Yonpo, Wonsan, Ongjin, Anak, Sinmak and Kangdong in North Korea. Obviously, the Communists were planning to give their spring ground offensive its required air support. General Stratemeyer informed Brigadier General James Briggs, Bomber Command's new chief, that these airstrips must be destroyed.

Briggs reasoned that to seek their destruction before the Communist offensive began would be foolish, for the Communists' abundance of manpower would make possible rapid repair of the installations. Briggs therefore requested permission to hold off his bombing attacks until the Reds were almost ready to operate their airfields. In the meantime, the Sabres and other American jets flashed north to the Yalu to recover air superiority and thus prepare the way for the Superforts. Then, between April 17 and 23, the Superforts began working over the airfields, and until mid-June, interdiction of the Red aerial network in North Korea was constant, with Naval and Marine aircraft joining the attack. Fighter-bombers also struck, as well as B-26 night intruders. General Liu's air force was effectively wrecked, and on July 12, the Special Aviation Inspection Group reported that it had "spent two months on the battlefield supervising the repair of 69 airfields which in the end only helped facilitate the operations of 30 planes." Such costly effort, it concluded, "was far beyond the financial power of Red China."

Thus, the Communist offensive that began on April 22 had to be launched without the promised air support. Only desultory air strikes were flown, although the "Bedcheck Charlies"—those little wood-and-canvas 80-knot biplanes which sneaked down moonlit valleys to heckle the Seoul area at night—remained a thorn in the flesh of the Eighth Army.

By the time of the Communist offensive, the Eighth Army had become one of the finest military forces ever put in the field by the United States; General Ridgway had made it so, and Van Fleet would keep it that way. Its seven American divisions, reinforced by the United Nations battalions and brigades, all contained 20,000 men or more; their commanders were combat-wise, and they were armed with big Patton and Pershing tanks—plus mammoth Centurians for the British—and heavy guns. Numerous artillery battalions, some of them U. S. National Guard units, had reached Korea with 240mm howitzers, 155mm rifles—the famous "Long Toms" of World War II —self-propelled 155s and smaller howitzers. The 3.5-inch rocket launchers were in abundance, as were antitank mines, although the "yo-yo" or up-and-down nature of the war had made mine warfare hazardous: troops returning to positions abandoned during retreats blundered into their own uncharted minefields. Morale in the Eighth Army was also at its peak, and the men were as cocky as men can be when fighting, as it seemed to them, without a cause. Their renewed spirit was manifested by the joke: "I was attacked by two hordes, sir, and I killed them both." The enemy order of battle was derisively tabled as three "swarms" to one "horde," two hordes to a "human flood" and a number of human floods to one "inexhaustible reservoir of Chinese manpower." Morale had also been improved by sending men to Japan for five days of "Rest and Rehabilitation." Men became eligible for "R & R" after six months in Korea. A rotation system had also been announced, and soon men who had foreseen no future but the inevitable bullet in the belly knew that after a year of duty in Korea they would be eligible to be rotated home.

The ROK Army had also been revitalized, although its enormous casualties—170,000 men—suffered since June 25, 1950, had seriously weakened it. Green recruits filled the ranks of its 10,000-man divisions and heavy losses among junior officers and NCOs left squads and platoons virtually leaderless. Many of the ROK Army's regimental and divisional commanders still failed to comprehend the complications of large-scale operations or the value of communications. In fairness to the ROKs, it must be pointed out that their divisions rarely had more than police-force armament. They had no organic artillery, depending on corps artillery when they needed it, and American armor was only assigned them during special missions. When the lightly armed ROKs fought lightly armed Chinese or North Koreans one-for-one, they performed well. But when they were outgunned or outnumbered they did not. As a consequence, the ROK divisions—with the exception of General Paik Sun Yup's dependable 1st—were usually spotted in sectors where terrain made enemy attack difficult or, in critical open areas, wedged in between the American divisions of the Eighth Army. By April 21, the ROK Army in the east held perhaps one quarter of General Van Fleet's front, the other three quarters being defended, from west to east, by the U. S. I, IX and X Corps and those ROK divisions attached to them.

Van Fleet's line began at Munsan below the 38th Parallel—to take advantage of the natural barrier of the Imjin River—proceeded northeast to Yonchon about ten miles above the Parallel and then ran virtually due east to Taepo-ri on the Sea of Japan. In the late afternoon of April 22, it was struck by enemy artillery concentrations. Four hours later, by the light of a full moon, the Communists attacked.

An estimated half of the 700,000 Chinese and North Korean troops in Korea were committed in a three-pronged assault which, said Radio Pyongyang, would utterly destroy the United Nations. The first thrust, a secondary one, came in the center; a second and larger drive was mounted in the east, while in the west, the biggest blow of all was delivered in an attempt to encircle Seoul by enveloping the city from both sides. Surprisingly, after the opening barrage, the enemy used little artillery, and had very few tanks: Russia had again failed to come through with shells and gasoline.

Although the UN lines generally held firm in most sectors, the center was cracked when the ROK 6th Division was driven back, thus exposing the flanks of the U. S. 24th and 1st Marine Divisions to either side of it. The Americans quickly refused their flanks, that is, bent them back inward, and hung on. At this point, Van Fleet began to roll with the punch. He instructed the I and IX Corps to fall back, surrendering all the ground gained in the Ridgway offensives, while artillery and air hammered the pursuing Communists. Enemy attempts to outflank Seoul were beaten back on both sides, and by April 29 the highly heralded Communist offensive had been stopped cold. Once again the poorly supported Communist Chinese Army had demonstrated its inability to sustain an offensive for more than a few days. General Van Fleet, not yet aware of his enemy's immobility, decided to hold at a new line, rather than to gather his reserves and strike. This was designated No-Name Line, beginning at a point north of Seoul, gently rising northeast to Sabangu in the center, then slanting sharply northeast to Taepo-ri, still above the Parallel.

As it became clear that the enemy had halted to regroup and bring new forces forward, Van Fleet decided to take a limited initiative designed to recover Ridgway's old Kansas Line eight to ten miles above the Parallel. Regimental patrol bases were set up eight miles north of No-Name Line and armored patrols began ranging north. The ROK 1st Division drove to Munsan and Uijongbu was recaptured by the 1st Cavalry Division. On May 7 the 1st Marine Division evicted North Koreans from Chunchon at bayonet point, and a 2nd Division French-American task force fought northeast of Chaun-ni in the center. On the right or east the ROK III and I Corps also surged forward. Then Communist resistance stiffened. All the signs pointed to renewal of their assault. American patrols began falling back on No-Name Line, a position now formidable with mines, registered artillery, interlocking lanes of machine-gun fire, and barbed-wire networks made more menacing with 55-gallon drums of gasoline and napalm to be fired electrically and thus allow the Americans to see, as well as burn, the enemy. General Van Fleet, meanwhile, had called for an unprecedented volume of artillery, which, in the proportion of five times the normal output, would become famous as "the Van Fleet load."

"We must expend steel and fire, not men," Van Fleet said. "I want so many artillery holes that a man can step from one to the other."

The night of May 15–16 the ground shook and the air howled with the myriad shells of the "Van Fleet load" as twenty-one Chinese divisions, flanked by three North Korean divisions in the west, and six in the east, struck down the center of the peninsula. The brunt of the attack was received by the U. S. X Corps in the center-east and the ROK III Corps on its right, and the Chinese quickly drove a deep salient into the ROK lines.

After the ROKs had been hurled back, the U. S. 2nd and 1st Marine Divisions attacked to the right or east out of the X Corps zone to fill the gap, while the IX Corps in the center also shifted east to fill the hole left by the Marines. Van Fleet then sent the 15th Infantry from the U. S. 3rd Division to bolster the western edge of the gap, while rushing its 7th and 65th Regiments to blocking positions at the southern end of the salient. In this way, and with the 38th Field Artillery Battalion alone firing 12,000 rounds of 105mm shells in twenty-four hours, the Chinese breakthrough in the center-east was contained. Though the entire eastern quarter of No-Name Line had been forced back below the 38th Parallel, the renewed Chinese Communist offensive had failed as utterly as the April 22 drive. By May 19 it had petered out. By May 20 it was at a standstill and the United Nations forces were stabilizing their lines. Three days later, with men of the 1st Marine Division still holding the No-Name Line positions they had never lost, the 2nd Infantry Division began driving north to join them. The United Nations, having handed the Chinese Communist Forces the bloodiest and most decisive beating in their history,* were striking north again, crossing the Parallel for the third time, stabbing into the enemy's supply routes in the Hwachon Reservoir area and threatening the logistics nerve center in the Iron Triangle.

Throughout the end of May the United Nations forces attacked along a four-corps, 140-mile front—and the enemy withdrew rapidly before them. By the end of the month most of the positions on the old Kansas Line eight to ten miles north of the Parallel had been reached. The offensives kept going, urged on by Van Fleet's remark: "The 38th Parallel has no significance in the present tactical situation. . . . The Eighth Army will go wherever the situation dictates in hot pursuit of the enemy." During early June the Iron Triangle in the west-center was brought under concerted attack by Americans, Filipinos, ROKs and Turks, and its Chorwon-Kumhwa base fell on June 10. Three days later armored patrols entered the triangle's apex at Pyonggang, withdrawing after being fired upon from

---

*Exact casualty figures are not available for the totality of these actions, but an indication of their extent can be gained from the 2nd Infantry Division's report of having suffered 900 killed and wounded while inflicting an estimated 35,000 casualties on the Chinese.

high ground to the north. But the gains all the way up to Chor-won-Kumhwa had extended the center of Van Fleet's line to a point 20 miles north of the Parallel. In the center-east, mean-while, the 1st Marine Division and the ROK 7th and 5th had fought into the Punchbowl, a circular depression in the moun-tains at the eastern rim of the Kansas Line. With its capture on June 16, Van Fleet now held a line beginning west of Mun-san ten miles below the Parallel, running 40 air miles northeast to the Chorwon-Kumhwa base of the Iron Triangle, then run-ning on a southeast gradient to the Punchbowl and the east coast. It was at this moment that Van Fleet proposed his blue-print for victory: a series of amphibious landings on the east coast, coupled with a breakout drive northeast from the Kansas Line. Though his plan was turned down, Van Fleet has since said of it:

> I had the 1st Marine Division and some Korean Marines set for a shore-to-shore operation, leapfrogging up the east coast—almost administrative [unopposed] landings. At that time the east coast did not have a big buildup of defensive forces, and we could easily have made landings there. The Navy could have shot us ashore and kept us ashore as we built up. We could have built up faster than the enemy could have managed.
>
> With those landings, the Chinese couldn't have met it. They're not flexible enough. The Chinese armies had no conception of fast moves; they had no communication system; they had no logistical support.
>
> In fact, there have been only two armies in the history of the world that have been able to move any direction at any time. That's the American Army and the German Army.
>
> So in June 1951, we had the Chinese whipped. They were defi-nitely gone. They were in awful shape. During the last week of May we captured more than 10,000 Chinese prisoners.[2]

Without doubt, the Communists were ready for destruction by mid-June of 1951. In one year of warfare, the North Korean Army had suffered an estimated 600,000 casualties (including 100,000 men who had surrendered) and was virtually de-stroyed. In only eight months, the Chinese Communists had lost an estimated half million men. The April and May of-fensives had subjected the Red Army to a frightful pounding and the May assault had clearly revealed its inability to support large bodies of men moving against modern firepower. Communist Korea was a shambles, its railroads ruined, its communications crippled, its industry close to nonexistent. At Wonsan and the adjacent Hungnam-Songjin steel complex, the United States Navy was continuing the siege which had begun on February 16 and which, maintained until war's end, would be the longest in American naval history. All Communist supply now came from the Soviet Union, and Russia had already shown, in the disastrous May offensive, how she could fail to deliver the goods. Moreover it would be some time before the Chinese received the Russian artillery which would give them a fighting chance against United Nations firepower. Truly enough, the Communists were reeling and a bold move such as Van Fleet proposed might have dealt them a knockout blow.

Van Fleet's plan was nevertheless shelved, chiefly because the notion of complete victory was by then already in disfavor. In mid-June, the MacArthur hearings were coming to a close, and the Administration had at last spelled out its policy of limited war. The Eighth Army's very victories had already renewed hopes of obtaining a satisfactory cease-fire somewhere along the 38th Parallel. A new amphibious attempt, which might bring the Communist Air Force out of Manchuria again, which might bring fresh Chinese Communist armies south of the Yalu River, which might raise the specter of a second Hungnam, ran counter to all these hopes. And so, the Joint Chiefs of Staff ordered Van Fleet not to proceed beyond the general vicinity of his Kansas Line, though Ridgway granted him permission to conduct local advances to seize better ground. Ridgway himself later wrote of this decision:

> Military men, and statesmen, too, will long debate the wisdom of stopping that proud Army in its tracks at the first whisper that the Reds might be ready to sue for peace. To my mind it is fruitless to speculate on what might have been. If we had been ordered to fight our way to the Yalu, we could have done it—if our government had been willing to pay the price in dead and wounded that action would have cost. From the purely military standpoint the effort, to my mind, would not have been worth

the cost. A drive to the line of the Yalu and the Tumen would have cleared Korea of the Chinese enemy. But he would have still been facing us in great strength beyond those rivers. The seizure of the land between the truce line and the Yalu would have merely meant the seizure of more real estate. It would have greatly shortened the enemy's supply lines by pushing him right up against his main supply bases in Manchuria. It would have greatly lengthened our own supply routes, and widened our battlefront from 110 miles to 420. Would the American people have been willing to support the great army that would have been required to hold that line? Would they have approved our attacking on into Manchuria? On into the heart of the great mainland of Asia, a bottomless pit into which all the armies of the whole free world could be drawn and be ground to bits and destroyed? I doubt it.[3]

On the positive side, the United Nations could consider that the Eighth Army and the ROKs had won a victory. Collective security had, in fact, stopped aggression—and both "aggressor" states had been driven back beyond the pre-war border. Communism *had* been shown that it would not be allowed to consume the world piecemeal. The United Nations *had* met the test the League of Nations had failed: whether a world body can prevent the use of force as a means to political end. And, more important, that "deflation" of the military prestige of Red China which President Truman so earnestly desired had been accomplished without committing additional American forces, to the possible detriment of NATO. The opportunity to end the unpopular war which had already caused 80,000 American casualties—including 12,000 dead and 10,000 missing—seemed to be at hand.

In the meantime, the political front was alive with maneuver. Neutral diplomats in Peiping made the U. S. position known to Premier Mao and Foreign Minister Chou En-lai. At the United Nations, Secretary-General Trygve Lie said that the time to talk peace had come and that the Security Council's resolutions on Korea would be fulfilled with a cease-fire somewhere along the Parallel followed by "restoration of peace and security" by peaceful means. Lie appealed to the Russians to "say the one word the world is waiting for."

The word came on June 23. Soviet Delegate Jacob Malik appeared on the weekly United Nations radio broadcast and spent fifteen minutes denouncing the United States and NATO. Then, running overtime, he said:

"The Soviet peoples further believe that the most acute problem of the present day—the problem of the armed conflict in Korea—could also be settled. This would require the readiness of the parties to enter on the path of peaceful settlement of the Korean question. The Soviet peoples believe that as a first step discussions should be started between the belligerents for a cease-fire and an armistice providing for the mutual withdrawal of forces from the 38th Parallel."

Two days later the Peiping newspaper, *People's Daily*, endorsed Malik's proposal, and President Truman directed Ambassador Alan Kirk in Moscow to contact the Russians for additional information. Kirk learned from Soviet Foreign Minister Andrei Gromyko that the proposed armistice would not involve "political or territorial matters" but would be strictly military; that is, would discuss only the cease-fire which would provide for later political settlements. On this basis, on June 29, the following message was sent to General Ridgway by the National Security Council:

> The President has directed that at 0800 Saturday (the 31st) Tokyo Daylight Saving Time you send following message by radio in clear addressed to Commander in Chief Communist Forces in Korea and simultaneously release to press:
>
> "As Commander in Chief of the United Nations Command I have been instructed to communicate to you the following:
>
> "I am informed that you may wish a meeting to discuss an armistice providing for the cessation of hostilities and all acts of armed force in Korea, with adequate guarantees for the maintenance of such armistice.
>
> "Upon the receipt of word from you that such a meeting is desired I shall be prepared to name my representative. I propose that such a meeting could take place aboard a Danish hospital ship (*Jutlandia*) in Wonsan Harbor."

Ridgway broadcast the message, and the following night came a reply from Premier Kim Il Sung and General Peng Teh-huai. They agreed to the meeting, but they rejected the meeting place. Rather than the decks of *Jutlandia,* they suggested the town of Kaesong about a mile below the Parallel and ten miles northwest of the United Nations west flank at Munsan. Ridgway sent patrols into Kaesong. They reported finding "little enemy activity," whereupon Ridgway decided that Kaesong would be an acceptable neutral site.

And the talks began.

Part IV

The Talking War

Chapter One

THE war-weary world held high hopes for the meeting that began at Kaesong on July 10. Diplomats, and especially the free world press, were optimistic over the outcome, so much so, according to correspondent Rutherford Poats, that the "pessimists" among the numerous newsmen who had converged on Korea were saying that it might be "as long" as six weeks before an armistice was signed.

The United Nations truce team, led by its senior delegate, Vice-Admiral Joy, felt no such optimism. Joy refused to make predictions on the outcome, for in two days of preliminary negotiations he had received too many earnests of Communist insincerity to believe a speedy solution of the Korean conflict possible.

On July 8, Air Force Colonel Andrew Kinney had led a party to Kaesong and found that the "neutral site" was in fact an armed camp. Kinney's officers, come to make preliminary arrangements for the July 10 meeting, were required to fly white flags from their jeeps and were surrounded by Communist soldiers brandishing burp guns. The spectacle of the imperialist "paper tigers" come to sue for peace was duly recorded by crowds of Communist newsmen and photographers. Communist liaison officers also sought to detain the Americans at Kaesong overnight, thus completing the picture of defeated Americans in the grip of the victorious Red Chinese Army, but Kinney refused and returned to Joy's headquarters at Munsan.

Unknown to Kinney, he had accidentally upset part of the Communists' elaborate propaganda stage set. Entering the Korean teahouse where the meetings were to be held, he had casually taken over the north end of a long conference table, unaware that Oriental custom assigns the north side to the victors. His Communist counterparts were flustered and dismayed, but it was not until the talks began, with the United Nations delegates firmly barred from the north end of the table, that he was able to understand their consternation. As the English Communist correspondent, Alan Winnington, later told free world newsmen: "This is the first time Oriental Communists have ever sat down at a conference table on terms of equality with Americans, and they intend to make the most of it."

Kinney's reports, indicating that General Ridgway's acceptance of Kaesong as a meeting ground—made in the interests of speed and sincerity—was the first of many United Nations miscalculations of the enemy's character and purpose, were at the root of Admiral Joy's deep misgivings when he led his United Nations Command to the Kaesong teahouse on July 10. With him were Major General L. C. Craigie, vice-commander of the Far East Air Force; Major General Henry Hodes, deputy chief of staff of the Eighth Army; Rear Admiral Arleigh ("31-Knot") Burke, the famous destroyer commander of World War II and now commander of a cruiser division; and the youthful Major General Paik Sun Yup, whose distinguished record with the ROK 1st Division had already brought him quick promotion. General Paik, however, was no more than an observer for President Rhee. He had little voice in the ensuing truce talks which, from the United Nations side, were invariably governed by decisions made in Washington or Tokyo.

The Communist delegation included Lieutenant General Nam Il, Major General Chang Pyong San and Major General Lee Sang Cho of the North Korean Army, and Major General Hsieh Fang and Major General Tung Hua of the Red Chinese Army, or "Chinese People's Volunteers" as they continued to call themselves. The chief spokesmen in this group were General Hsieh, acting as deputy for General Peng Teh-huai, and General Nam, acting in the same capacity for Premier Kim Il Sung.

The thirty-eight-year-old Nam was the nominal chief of the delegation. Like his friend and mentor, Premier Kim, Nam was the product of the strictest Russian tutelage. He had been born in Asiatic Russia of Korean parents and had been educated in Soviet Union schools. During World War II he fought in the Red Army as a captain, coming to North Korea with the Soviets at the end of the war and assuming high posts in Stalin's puppet state. In 1948 he was Vice-Minister of Education of the Democratic People's Republic of Korea and in 1950, just before the invasion of South Korea, he was promoted to the National Defense Ministry. At the time of his appointment to the Kaesong delegation he was chief of staff of the North Korean Army. According to Admiral Joy:

> Nam Il was short in stature, slender, and gave the impression of considerable nervous energy. He spoke forcefully in Korean, seeming to spit out his words. At no time did he ever exhibit the least tendency to humor. If he laughed, it was in a sarcastic vein. His smooth Oriental face rarely revealed emotion, and if so the emotion was anger or feigned astonishment. He dressed nattily in the Russian type of uniform of the North Korean Army. His military boots were highly polished at all times.[1]

General Nam, however, was restless during the brief proceedings at Kaesong and those that were to drag on for two more years at Panmunjom, to the disgust of a disillusioned world. He fiddled with pencils, shuffled papers, whispered to his colleagues and chain-smoked constantly. Colonel Kinney has described his uneasiness during the first conference: "At one point he vainly attempted to light one of his Russian cigarettes with Chinese matches. None fired, although he struck perhaps a dozen. Embarrassed and desperate, he brought out an American cigarette lighter. It clicked and flared brightly. He took one deep drag and then, apparently feeling that somehow he had been disloyal to things Communistic, he tossed the American lighter out the window behind him!" Nam's nervousness, of course, was due to his position as a figurehead. Actual power in the Communist delegation was held by Major General Hsieh Fang, to whom Nam always deferred, whose approving nod was sought before anyone spoke.

Hsieh Fang was born in Manchuria in 1904, spending his youth studying in Japan, where he had been sent by the "Young Marshal" Chang Hsueh-liang. He was graduated from the Japanese Military Academy in 1923, thereafter studying in Moscow. In 1940, at the instruction of the Chinese Communists, he joined the Japanese puppet government at Peking (Peiping), remaining there until 1945. During Oriental Communism's war on Chiang Kai-shek he was credited with persuading large numbers of Nationalist troops to join the Communist cause. He was serving as General Peng's chief of staff and political commissar at the time of his appointment to the armistice delegation. In the estimate of Admiral Joy, he was a formidable opponent:

> Hsieh Fang was thin and angular. His nondescript uniform folded about his spare frame gracelessly. He gave me the impression of Shakespeare's "Yon Cassius has a lean and hungry look ... such men are dangerous." Hsieh was indeed dangerous. He possessed a bitterly sharp mind, and used it effectively. His head was radically close-cropped, giving the impression of a high forehead. Sharp eyes flicked restlessly as he watched proceedings. Hsieh Fang rarely spoke from prepared material as Nam Il did invariably. His remarks were extemporaneous and fluent.
>
> Hsieh Fang was markedly the mental superior among the Communist delegation. He conducted himself in a self-assured manner at all times, never bothering to check his intended remarks with other Communists before making them. He was the only member of the Communist delegation who seemed to be confident of his position with his Communist superiors in Peking. On the many occasions when it became obvious that no progress could be made in the day's meeting, any Communist spokesman but Hsieh Fang would feel compelled to deliver a long-winded harangue praising Communist objectives and damning those of the United Nations Command. Not so Hsieh Fang. If there was nothing more to be accomplished, he simply shut up his brief case and departed....[2]

The only other active member of the delegation was Major General Lee Sang Cho, short, chunky, given to long discursive speech, as well as to impressing imperialists with his iron self-control by permitting flies to crawl over his face as he spoke. Lee, only thirty-seven, was born in Korea but educated at China's Whampoa Military Academy. He became a member of the Communist Party in 1940, fought with the Korean Volunteer Army on the side of Red China and came to Korea in 1945 with the Soviet Army. His last post had been chief of staff for the North Korean National Defense Minister, Vice-Marshal Choe Yong Gun.

Staff officers who accompanied the Communist negotiators to the truce talks were Colonel Chang Chun San and Lieutenant Colonel Lee Soo Young of North Korea, and Colonel Tsai Chen Wen of China. Their counterparts were Colonel Kinney and Colonel Raymond Murray, who had commanded the Fifth Marines during the Pusan Perimeter and Chosin breakout days.

Such were the men who were to negotiate the armistice and make recommendations for the eventual settlement of the Korean conflict. Judging from the record, they disliked each other at sight, or at least grew to despise each other. From the outset, hostility—which would later erupt into flashes of outright hatred—characterized the truce talks in the teahouse at Kaesong and the tent at Panmunjom, even though at the beginning Admiral Joy suggested that "success or failure of the negotiations begun here today depends directly upon the good faith of the delegations here present," and General Tung Hua, making one of his rare speeches, declared that "peoples of all countries bitterly hate war and desire peace ardently." Thereafter, language was to be either coldly formal or hotly insulting.

On that first day, July 10, it became plain that the Communists hoped to put over a loaded agenda and discuss more than military matters—in violation of Soviet Foreign Minister Gromyko's assurance to Admiral Kirk—and that the United Nations Command was not going to give up its gains north of the Parallel and send its troops home. Although Admiral Joy's original proposal contained eight points, the conflict which developed immediately between the rival proposals were these:

Communist

1. Establishment of the 38th Parallel as the military demarcation line between both sides, and establishment of a demilitarized zone, as *basic conditions* for the cessation of hostilities in Korea.
2. Withdrawal of all armed forces of foreign countries from Korea.

3. Cessation of hostilities and of acts of armed force in Korea under conditions that would assure against resumption of hostilities and acts of armed force in Korea.
4. Agreement on a demilitarized zone across Korea.

In his first two points, Nam Il merely wanted to restore Korea's *status quo ante bellum*. With foreign troops withdrawn —a political, not military matter—he would presumably be free to launch a new invasion. By stating that these two points formed a basic condition for a cease-fire, he offered not an issue to be discussed, but a conclusion to be confirmed. Selection of the 38th Parallel also pretended that the Chinese Communist Forces had not been decisively defeated and ignored their present position, except for the Kaesong area, about twenty miles north of the line where they were still subjected to attrition from air and sea. Nam's insistence on the Parallel was so illogical and absurd, even for Communists whose force of logic is the logic of force, who are embarrassed only by failure, that he and his colleagues must have been impressed by Secretary of State Acheson's remark on June 7 that the 38th Parallel would be a satisfactory demarcation line. A week earlier UN Secretary-General Trygve Lie had said that a cease-fire could be arranged at a line approximating the Parallel, and no one in the United Nations had challenged Jacob Malik's phrase in his June 23rd speech calling for "mutual withdrawal of forces from the 38th Parallel." Nam must have thought, then, that he could get away with it, and he was angry and frustrated when, on that first day of negotiation, Admiral Joy insisted that adoption of an agenda must precede any discussion of a truce line. Nam became angrier when Joy pointed out that the 38th Parallel was not the *only* line possible for an armistice. This dispute was continued the next day:

> *ADMIRAL JOY: We do not believe you understand yet what we mean by an agenda. We wish to specifically define it again. An

*The quotations used throughout this book are taken verbatim from the official transcripts of the meetings. The remarks of the Communists were translated into English by their own interpreters and recorded by the conference stenographers. They have not been altered or corrected for reasons of grammar or usage.

agenda is merely a list, in order, of subjects to be discussed. Is that your understanding of an agenda?

GENERAL NAM IL: We know fully what an agenda means.

The senior delegate of the other party asked me if I clearly understood the term "agenda." By agenda it is meant the items that will be discussed at a meeting, ordered items which will be discussed at a meeting and which must be considered first when the agenda is being formed. What are the important problems to be discussed at a meeting? Then the important problems must be discussed first. That is to say what kind of problems should be discussed and what are the central problems; then the central problems are discussed first.

ADMIRAL JOY: When I use the term "agenda," I am referring to a group of items which are general questions—general items such as the demilitarized zone. You, however, are in fact talking about one line [the 38th Parallel] when as a matter of fact there are many many lines—many possible lines.

GENERAL NAM IL: We have showed you our line. What are the possible lines for you?

ADMIRAL JOY: We do not suggest any line yet because that is getting into the substance of that item of the agenda.

GENERAL NAM IL: As for a line, we proposed a concrete line.

ADMIRAL JOY: As I understand it, you do not wish to broaden the question of a demilitarized zone.

GENERAL NAM IL: May I ask what you imply by "broaden"?

ADMIRAL JOY: To make it more general.

GENERAL NAM IL: Our proposal is general.

ADMIRAL JOY: Referring again to your item on the agenda, we cannot agree to have any specific line on the agenda as you propose.

GENERAL NAM IL: You do not agree?

ADMIRAL JOY: We will agree to place on the agenda an item calling for the establishment of some demilitarized zone. The location and limits of that zone can be discussed later when the substance of the item is taken up. I would like to re-emphasize that the work of this meeting on the agenda is not to determine solutions of problems, lines, etc., but to formulate an agenda—in other words, to state the problems to be discussed at later meetings.

GENERAL NAM IL: We cannot consider the 38th Parallel line as an imaginary line. The 38th Parallel line had existed and the war broke out right on that line. Therefore, it is the principle that the question of the cease fire must be concluded also on the 38th Parallel line. Therefore, this must be on the agenda.

So it continued for ten bitter meetings, during which tempers were sharpened by a subsidiary quarrel over equal press representation at Kaesong. The first day, July 10, Admiral Joy had asked that twenty selected free world newsmen be admitted to the conference site, although not to the conference room itself. Nam Il agreed. The next day he recanted, saying he would need confirmation from Premier Kim Il Sung. Meanwhile, crowds of Communist correspondents and cameramen continued to roam Kaesong, even bursting into the conference room to take pictures the moment a little United Nations flag on the conference table was dwarfed by a big North Korean flag placed alongside it. Of similar incidents, Admiral Joy has written:

At the first meeting of the delegates, I seated myself at the conference table and almost sank out of sight. The Communists had provided a chair for me which was considerably shorter than a standard chair. Across the table . . . General Nam Il protruded a good foot above my cagily diminished stature. This had been accomplished by providing stumpy Nam Il with a chair about four inches higher than usual. Chain-smoking Nam Il puffed his cigarette in obvious satisfaction as he glowered down on me, an apparently torpedoed admiral. . . . Such devices by the Communists may seem childish when each is considered in isolation. It should be borne in mind, however, that a great multitude of these maneuvers can add up to a propaganda total of effective magnitude.

Not the least of the stage setting employed by the Communists was their legion of armed guards. These heavily armed sentinels were everywhere, governing each step taken by the United Nations Command delegation. During a recess of the first meeting of delegates I was directly threatened by a Communist guard who pointed a burp gun at me and growled menacingly. My messenger, dispatched to convey an interim report to General Ridgway, was halted and turned back by Communist armed force.

One sentinel posted conspicuously beside the access doorway to the conference room wore a gaudy medal which he proudly related to Colonel Kinney was for "killing forty Americans." . . .[3]

With so many propaganda incidents created in the four days since Colonel Kinney had met the Communist liaison officers, Joy decided to use the issue of the banned newsmen to call a halt to the proceedings. On July 11, he announced: "If by tomorrow morning the newsmen are still unacceptable at the site of the conference, it is requested that we be informed by 0730 hours tomorrow on what date it will be possible to resume the conference with newsmen present at the conference site." The Communists replied the next day that the problem of the newsmen should be delayed, although their own press remained present at Kaesong, whereupon General Ridgway, ruefully admitting the lost opportunity of "the completely neutral atmosphere" of the Danish hospital ship, sent a strong message to both Kim and Peng denouncing the incidents and demanding that Kaesong be made truly neutral. Kim and Peng replied that the newsmen would be admitted and requested the United Nations to return to the talks, although their own propaganda broadcasts in Japanese and Chinese "demanded" the return. Ridgway would not allow them even that. He branded their reply evasive and himself "demanded" absolute equality and neutrality at Kaesong. The Communist resistance collapsed. It was still in their interest to keep the truce talks going, if only, as will be seen, to continue strengthening their forces in Korea. Thus, on July 14, the conference was resumed, as was the endless haggling over Nam Il's demands for withdrawal of all foreign troops and selection of the 38th Parallel as a truce line. Finally, on July 25, General Nam withdrew his demands and the next day, July 26, the historic agenda was adopted with these points:

1. Adoption of agenda.
2. Fixing of military demarcation line between both sides so as to establish a demilitarized zone as a basic condition for the cessation of hostilities in Korea.
3. Concrete arrangements for the realization of cease-fire and armistice in Korea, including the composition, authority,

and functions of a supervisory organ for carrying out the terms of cease-fire and armistice.

4. Arrangements relating to prisoners of war.
5. Recommendation to governments of countries concerned on both sides (toward the post-armistice political conference).

To the world it seemed that the squabbling and bickering at the Kaesong teahouse were now about to end. Not so. They had just begun.

The United Nations Command, always acting on instructions from the United States, had made a major mistake in allowing the truce line to be the first item to be settled once the agenda had been adopted. To specify a line on the map before hostilities ceased would, in effect, freeze the battle line and relieve the Communists of the military pressure still being maintained by the Eighth Army. In order to avoid this result, the United Nations Command sought to establish the principle that the truce line would be the line of contact between the belligerents *at the time the armistice was signed.* Thus, either side would be free to exert military pressure until the cease-fire was ordered. And military pressure—the success of Van Fleet's forces —it must be remembered, was the only factor that had induced the Communist world to agree to truce talks.

The Communists, having been beaten on the field, now sought to win back lost ground at the conference table. Their proposal of a cease-fire along the 38th Parallel would guarantee them against United Nations offensives while the truce talks continued, for any ground gained in such attacks would, of course, have to be surrendered when the armistice was signed. Van Fleet, then, would be in the position of asking his men to die for hills they could not keep. Furthermore, the Communists, aware of the Westerner's impatience to settle things, adopted delaying tactics designed to gain concessions. On August 10, General Nam Il showed how well he understood the power of silence. When Admiral Joy spoke of discussing a truce line "generally in the area of the 38th Parallel," Nam's reply was a cold stare that lasted for two hours and eleven minutes. The men of both delegations sat in silence, doodling, passing notes to one another, until Joy finally called a recess and walked out.

Such was the atmosphere of this peace meeting. Not once did these men betray the slightest courtesy to one another. It was always "your side" or "our side" or "I have a question to ask" or "Yesterday you said." Here, from the meeting of August 11, 1951, is an example of this mutual malevolence:

GENERAL NAM IL: In order to support your proposal of pushing the military demarcation line to the north of the 38th Parallel, deep into our positions, you have persistently emphasized the so-called superiority of your naval and air forces and that, therefore, you must be compensated on the ground.

Yet, today you have presented a new and strange argument that since our army is already superior at present, it will be more so after armistice and, therefore, you should be again compensated for reasons of security. In using these self-contradictory arguments in support of your proposal, do you not feel ridiculous?

You said that because your air and naval forces were strong you should be compensated, and now you admit that your army is weak, but again you claim that you should be compensated. Just imagine, you need compensation no matter whether you are strong or weak. Is that not completely without reason, and wholly nonsense?

It has been proved that your proposal is untenable and that our proposal is based on reason. Therefore, whatever novel and ridiculous arguments you should fabricate, they would never bolster up your proposal.

I can tell you frankly that as long as you do not abandon your unreasonable proposal, it will not be possible for our conference to make any progress.

As for our proposal, its reasons are irrefutable; therefore it is unshakable. We insist on our proposal of making the 38th Parallel the military demarcation line.

ADMIRAL JOY: Yesterday you used the word "arrogant" in connection with a proposal the United Nations Command delegation now has before this conference. The United Nations Command delegation has been in search of an expression which conveys the haughty intransigence, the arbitrary inflexibility, and the unreasoning stubbornness of your attitude. Arrogance is indeed the word for it.

From the first day of these conferences your arguments have

reflected the very essence of arrogance. You stated, in your opening remarks, that your view in regard to a military line of demarcation had to be accepted. You have made the same statement over and over again. Once more yesterday, you stated that your solution of the question of a demarcation line "must be accepted." Your attitude has been that of an arrogant dictator, not that of a negotiator seeking in good faith an end of hostilities.

By your obdurate and unreasoning refusal to negotiate you have brought these meetings to a standstill. You have slammed every door leading to possible progress. By trying to deceive the world into believing that you have defeated the United Nations Command, you have delayed and stalled these meetings. You refuse to negotiate except on your own terms, thus seeking to falsely portray yourself as a victor dictating to the vanquished.

. . . Ruthlessly, arrogantly, and with the assumed air of a victor, you baldly assert that your demands must be met. The record of these proceedings has become your unanswerable accuser. You did not come here to stop the fighting. You did not come here to negotiate an armistice. You came here to state your price—your political price—for which you are willing to sell the people of Korea a temporary respite from pain. You have tried to camouflage your purpose in words cleverly designed to trap the unwary. You are failing. Your arrogance and your bad faith stain through every attempted deception. The immutable facts hold you guilty of having delayed, and of continuing to delay, the end of hostilities in Korea. I do not envy you the place to which Truth assigns you.

. . . I propose a recess until 1100 hours our time tomorrow.

GENERAL NAM IL: There is nothing new in your statement. Your statement does not frighten us and cannot change our stand. As our proposal of making the 38th Parallel the military demarcation line and our proposal of establishing a demilitarized zone is fair, reasonable, and proper, we will continue to insist upon it.

We agree to your proposal of recessing until tomorrow, 1000 our time, and 1100 your time.

The resumption of talks the next day failed to break the deadlock, nor did four more sessions of the full delegations, or six additional meetings subsequently held by subdelegations attempting to clear the way. Meanwhile, the Communists began creating new "incidents" designed to discredit the United Nations, as well as to recover prestige lost when Ridgway forced the admission of the newsmen and the actual neutralization of Kaesong. On August 19, Chinese Communist liaison officers charged that one of their "security patrols" in now-neutral Kaesong had been ambushed by UN forces and the patrol leader killed. Investigation showed that the assailants had not worn steel helmets, or uniforms, and the United Nations Command concluded that the attack had been the work of anti-Communist partisans known by both sides to be operating in the area. The Communists insisted it was a "wanton attack" by United Nations forces and so proclaimed it to the world. Then, on August 22, they followed with a charge that the United Nations had "bombed" Kaesong in an attempt to murder their delegation. At midnight of that date, Colonel Chang Chun San called upon Colonel Kinney to examine the "evidence" of the attack. Kinney set out immediately, his haste to respond prompted by the realization that United Nations aircraft were active around the Parallel and might have mistakenly bombed Kaesong.

At Kaesong, Kinney, an aviator himself, was unimpressed by the "evidence." He was shown a twisted piece of metal covered with oil which the Communists claimed was a napalm bomb dropped by the attacking aircraft, but Kinney saw no napalm jelly about, no scorched earth and no other visible proof of an explosion. The piece of metal was identified by Kinney as the wing tip of a crashed aircraft. Shown next a small unexploded rocket, Kinney pointed out that the United Nations air forces had not been issued such a rocket in nearly a year. Kinney's comments on the "evidence," particularly his barbed allusion to the fact that there had been no damage and no casualties—not a normal consequence of UN aerial strikes— had no effect on the voluble Chang, who continued to expostulate angrily in the rain, until, at three in the morning, Kinney suggested suspending the investigation until daylight. Chang refused, demanding, instead, that Kinney make instant acknowledgment of United Nations guilt. When Kinney refused, Chang announced the immediate and indefinite suspension of the armistice conference.

And so an obscure North Korean colonel brought to an end the truce talks begun at the instance of the most powerful men in the world. Obviously, Chang had been granted this enormous responsibility before Kinney was called to Kaesong, and equally obvious is the fact that nothing Kinney could do, short of agreeing to dishonor his country and the United Nations, could prevent Chang from dashing the hopes of the world. Why was this done?

Until more is known of the policy which produced Communist China's decisions during the Korean War, no final answer can be given to the question. Military men believed that the Communists broke the truce because they knew that the United Nations was not going to launch any new large-scale offensive. They could rearm and reinforce unmolested and return to the talks in a better military position. Diplomats believed that the breakoff was effected to score a propaganda victory. Blame for any resumption of hostilities, as well as for delay in reaching an armistice, could be fixed on the United Nations "murderers" who had "bombed" Kaesong. It is also significant that a week after the Kaesong affair, the Chinese Communists made another attempt to gain air superiority in North Korea.

Beginning September 1, as many as 90 MIGs at a time flew across the Yalu to attack the U. S. Sabrejets. They flew in a wide variety of formations suggesting that some of the flight leaders had learned a few lessons from the German *Luftwaffe* of World War II. Sabre pilots, still far more skillful than their Communist adversaries, often found that the men parachuting from burning MIGs were blond Caucasians. Russian pilots, or Russian pilots together with other white men from Soviet satellite states, were helping Asiatic Communism in its bid for aerial supremacy. Even so, fighting with all the advantages of altitude, speed and position, the Russian aviators attained the same end as had their Chinese predecessors. They were badly beaten. United Nations control of the skies was maintained, while on the ground General Van Fleet's post-truce assaults drove the Communists back.

In August of 1951, Lieutenant General James Van Fleet commanded a force of 586,000 men, divided between the

Eighth Army's 229,000 men and 357,000 ROKs. With the arrival of the Canadian 25th Brigade and the Colombian Battalion, the United Nations Command now included forces from the Republic of Korea, the United States, Australia, Belgium, Canada, Ethiopia, France, Great Britain, Greece, India, the Netherlands, New Zealand, Norway, the Philippines, Sweden, Thailand, Turkey, and the Union of South Africa. Opposing them were General Peng Teh-huai's sixty divisions. On the night of August 27–28, troops from this force counterattacked the ROK 5th Division at Bloody Ridge just west of the Punchbowl in the center-east sector held by the U. S. X Corps. The Chinese broke through the line, but were eventually contained.

Van Fleet thereupon decided to renew his offensive to drive the enemy back from the Hwachon Reservoir area, which was Seoul's source of water and electricity. On August 31, the U. S. 1st Marine Division began attacking the northern rim of the Punchbowl, and two days later, the U. S. 2nd Infantry Division on the Marine left or west advanced north against Bloody and Heartbreak Ridges. Fierce fighting developed in both sectors, but the American infantrymen drove the Chinese before them. By the 19th of September, Van Fleet's line had been pushed north of the Punchbowl, later to be stabilized by fighting distinguished by the Marines' introduction of helicopters as a means of moving troops in combat zones. In the east, meanwhile, the ROK I Corps moved up the coast toward Kosong, an advance of about ten miles. In the west and west-center, five divisions—the 1st British Commonwealth, the 1st ROK and the U. S. 1st Cavalry, 3rd and 25th Infantry—struck north along a 40-mile front from Kaesong to Chorwon, advancing the front from three to four miles, jumping halfway up the Iron Triangle, and establishing a new Jamestown Line above the old Kansas Line. By the second week in October, the Communists, having been beaten once more, came back to the conference table.

Chapter Two

AMONG the nations of the free world there persists a popular notion that the record of the United Nations Command in Korea was one long succession of blunders. This is not so. The Communists also made their share of wrong moves, and chief among them was the decision to break off the truce talks at Kaesong.

As has been seen, the decision was not followed by continued relaxation of hostilities, for the Eighth Army attacked anew, and the "Kaesong bombing" story not only had a short propaganda life but the entire propaganda circus at Kaesong was lost for good. Kaesong became what it had been in fact: the headquarters of the Red delegation. Once the talks had been suspended, General Ridgway had no intention of renewing them against a Red backdrop. In late August he radioed the Communist leaders:

> When you decide to terminate the suspension of armistice negotiations, I propose that our liaison officers meet immediately at the bridge at Panmunjom to discuss selection of a new site.

The Communist reply was silence, until Van Fleet's September–October assaults struck them. Then, on October 8, liaison officers from both sides met at Panmunjom, a deserted village of four mud huts two-thirds of the way along the ten-mile road from Munsan to Kaesong. After two weeks of meetings which produced elaborate precautions for making Panmunjom neutral, the delegations met again at a green-topped table set in the middle of a simple military tent. Once again the world turned hopeful, for the Communists had left their demands for a truce line at the 38th Parallel behind them. And so a fresh attempt was made to settle Item Two, that is, to fix a truce line. This was to be handled by one of the numerous subdelegations which were constituted to work out the details of general agreements. And then, once again, the world was disillusioned by dialogue such as this between Major General Lee Sang Cho and Major General Henry Hodes:

GENERAL LEE: Now we will open the meeting.

GENERAL HODES: OK.

GENERAL LEE: Do you have any idea about the military demartation line?

GENERAL HODES: We ended the last conference before the suspension by asking for your proposal. Do you have one?

GENERAL LEE: We would like your opinion first.

GENERAL HODES: We gave our opinion many times, and asked for your proposal based on our proposal. As it was your proposal to have the Sub-Delegation meeting, we expected you to have a proposal. Let's have it.

GENERAL LEE: You said you had made a new proposal, but we have heard nothing new which would break the deadlock.

GENERAL HODES: That's right. You haven't.

[*Fifty minutes more of this, and a quarter-hour recess later:*]

GENERAL HODES: Were you able to find some proposal to solve the problem while you were out?

GENERAL LEE: Did you?

GENERAL HODES: Is the answer that you didn't?

GENERAL LEE: We haven't thought of one.

So it continued for another week, with the United Nations still insisting that the line of contact between forces be the truce line, but with the important proviso that the truce line be the line of contact *at the time the armistice was signed.* On October 31, the Communists finally agreed to the present line of contact as the demarcation line. But they insisted that it be made permanent. This, of course, meant a *de facto* cease-fire, for if the line were to be made final, who would then try to change it on the battlefield? In effect, the only real change in the Communist position was that they had given up a few North Korean hills. Their true objective, a *de facto* cease-fire with subsequent easing of military pressure, had not been changed. If they obtained it, they could build up their forces unmolested, either to renew an offensive or to be at peak strength while dragging out settlement of all the other armistice points to the ultimate disillusionment of United Nations countries with troops in Korea. Those troops, it will be recalled, were at the end of a long and therefore costly sea supply route, while Red China was still fighting in her own backyard. In fairness to the Communists, the fixing of a demarcation line *had* been designated as the first matter to be settled. The United Nations attempt to make it the line of contact *at the time the armistice was signed* looked like welshing. More, the Communist call for an immediate cease-fire could not fail to be popular, among United Nations troops as well as among the Communists, to say nothing of the peoples of the world who cared to hear nothing of Korea but that the mess was at last cleaned up. Admiral Joy's position was difficult and unpopular, and it was no wonder that by late November he had been ordered by Washington to agree to give the Communist *de facto* cease-fire a thirty-day trial—a move which came to be known as the Little Armistice. The fact that the Communists would use the Little Armistice to reinforce and resupply was made clear to Admiral Joy by the delaying tactics which the Reds employed even while marking out the demarcation line.

> . . . Staff officers labored for weeks to reach an agreed version of where this line of contact lay. After seemingly interminable haggling by the Communists, a line was finally marked out, mile by tortured mile, on a huge map of Korea. Each point on the line was disputed, until finally one side or the other conceded the position. After long days and nights of such crawling progress, at last a line existed on the map that had been accepted in all parts by both groups of staff officers. No sooner had the last section been drawn in, completing the line to the sea, than the Communist staff officers began welshing on their agreements. Colonel Tsai turned to previously agreed sections of the map and announced that he would not accept the positions marked thereon. The first point he indicated as unacceptable was contained in a section of the line that he himself had marked in with a red pencil. . . . Colonel Murray, our United Nations Command staff officer who had developed the line along with Tsai, slammed down his fist on the conference table and grated at the Chinese: "Why, you damned buffoon! You deny agreements you entered into not an hour ago, in fact one you yourself offered!" This outburst by Murray, a formidable-looking Marine officer, caused

Tsai to retire to the far corner of the tent muttering that he could not be bullied.[1]

By November 27 the disputed points were settled and a thirty-day demarcation line was agreed upon. The Little Armistice was in effect, the front became quiet, optimism was back in fashion throughout the world and once more the troops spoke aloud of being home for Christmas. Then came the greatest disillusionment of the Korean War.

December 27 passed without the slightest agreement on the issues at Panmunjom. Artillery boomed once more and combat patrolling recommenced. The war was on again, but with a big difference: the Chinese *had* used the October–November delays at Panmunjom and the thirty days of the Little Armistice to rebuild their battered army. They had dug in with an energy equaling the burrowing abilities of the Japanese during World War II, suggesting that they, too, were not the great offensive fighters they thought themselves, but actually defensive fighters of the first order. By the spring of 1953, the Chinese main line of resistance would be among the most formidable fortifications in the history of the world. Its key feature was the tunnel, which was dug into the reverse or protected slope of a hill and emerged facing the American lines. The tunnel was then expanded into a honeycomb of corridors and gun positions large enough for companies or battalions, and protected from air attack by the natural cover of the undisturbed hill crest. Into this mushrooming defensive line during the months of Communist stalling at Panmunjom, the Chinese had fed great numbers of well-equipped troops, and by the end of the year, Lieutenant General James Van Fleet found himself facing an enemy army of 850,000 men, rearmed, resupplied and already receiving shipments of excellent Russian artillery with which to carry on trench warfare. Communist diplomacy, assisted by American naïveté, had done Communist arms a great service. Equally disturbing to Van Fleet—and to General Ridgway—was the realization that Chinese doggedness and ingenuity had frustrated the United Nations attempt to isolate the battle field.

In the early summer of 1951, General Ridgway had ordered an aerial campaign to cut off the enemy from his sources of supply in Manchuria. The plan was to paralyze movement along the highways which ran south to the battlefield from enemy railheads situated along the 39th Parallel. There were eight such highways and it was reasoned that if they could be interdicted, the forces of Premier Kim and General Peng would be isolated. The three western routes were assigned to the Fifth Air Force, the two central ones to the carriers of Task Force 77, and the three eastern ones to the First Marine Air Wing. This interdiction campaign, widely publicized as Operation Strangle, commenced in early June.

For about a month, American airmen and their allies flew all types of aircraft against the highway routes, firing rockets into tunnels, destroying highway bridges and passes, cratering the roadbeds, searching out and rocketing the numerous enemy trucks that hid by day, dropping delayed-action and "butterfly" bombs at all the choke points, flying on from dusk—when night hecklers took off to harry enemy truck movements—until dawn, when the same aircraft surprised trains pulling out of tunnel hideouts with dawn attacks.

And yet, the Fourth Field Army Logistical Command under General Tao Chu continued to keep the Communists on the battle line supplied, to the annoyance as well as open admiration of the Americans. "How he has kept supplies moving in the face of all the obstacles is a real mystery," Brigadier General Darr Alkire of the Far East Air Force said of General Tao. "He has done it against air superiority, fire superiority, guts, and brawn." And so, at the end of the summer, the United Nations decided to extend Operation Strangle to include the enemy's railroad system as well as his highway network. This was done after intelligence had concluded that the Communists depended far more heavily on direct rail transport to the front than had been suspected. It had been ascertained that while the UN airmen were busy trying to interdict the roads, the Communists had been moving supplies by rail into such southern terminals as Sariwon and Pyongyang. The North Korean rail system also possessed a load-hauling capacity larger than the motor transport organization, which depended on gasoline imported from China or Russia, and there were also abundant supplies of coal available in North Korea. So the attack on the railroads began, with some United Nations aviation experts confident that it would force the Communists to withdraw closer to their Manchurian base. But after ten months of day and night bombardment, during which even untouchable Racin was stripped of its immunity and attacked and the Navy's siege of Wonsan tightened, Operation Strangle resulted in failure. The Communists got the supplies through. More, they increased the flow in a remarkable demonstration of how tenacity and ingenuity can take advantage of manpower to thwart the firepower of a modern air force.

To the North Korean Department of Military Highway Administration had fallen the task of keeping the road networks passable. This agency consisted of 20,000 troops divided into 12 regiments of three 500-man battalions each. Each battalion was assigned to a section of North Korea. Platoons of men were stationed along the roads at two-mile intervals. Sometimes local labor would be drafted into service, and as many as 1,000 people might be put to work repairing a damaged choke point. The regular road platoons, however, did most of the work. Using only picks, axes, shovels, sandbags and wicker baskets, they could fill in a road crater or clear a blocked tunnel within a matter of hours.

A similar though slightly larger organization handled railroad repair. This, the North Korean Railroad Recovery Bureau, consisted of three brigades of about 9,000 men each. The brigades were broken down into 300-man repair teams, equipped like the highway battalions with simple tools, but also issued horses and wagons for hauling rails and timbers. Special equipment such as welding and surveying gear, levers and cranes or building materials were assembled near the key bridges or rail junctions most often attacked, and hidden in North Korea's numerous caves and tunnels.

Korea's shallow rivers helped the Communists immensely. When bridges over such streams were bombed out, the damaged span would be ignored and a temporary bridge thrown across the riverbed itself. Where rivers ran deep or the terrain would not permit temporary constructions, the Communists built bypasses to circumvent the break entirely.

Train shuttling was widely used. At night trains would come as far south as possible until a blown bridge, blocked tunnel or railway cut was reached. Then the train's load would be removed, usually by truck but sometimes by hand, and carried to another train waiting below the obstacle. The new train would then run farther south to shift its load to another waiting below the next break. In daylight the trains hid out in tunnels, resuming movement with darkness, moving as little as a dozen miles in a single night, but crawling inexorably south to the battle line. Meanwhile, the Communists made extensive use of camouflage.

Trucks were never left exposed. In wintertime they were covered with white canvas, in summer with straw and foliage, and whenever possible they were hidden in woods or driven into caves or beneath bridges. Many of the highways were dotted with revetments into which a truck could be driven almost on the instant of attack, and in North Korea's hundreds of railway tunnels there was room enough for 8,000 railroad cars, or sufficient space for every locomotive and boxcar in the country.

In the arts of deception the Communists had no peer. Damaged trains and trucks were left in plain view, often brightly painted, to invite attack; truck drivers carried oily rags which they were to light upon attack to simulate destruction; trucks were hidden in bombed-out buildings or their hoods were left open and their wheels removed to give the impression of being crippled—until nightfall, whereupon they were quickly made serviceable—or they were parked alongside churches, schools, hospitals and all other such structures which the UN flyers would not deliberately bomb. Enemy trucks also used UN flags and marks or painted the Red Cross on their cabin roofs. The trucks moved in convoys, sometimes with as many as twenty in a column. Surprise attack by day was prevented by spotters who were stationed along the roads at mile intervals and instructed to fire their rifles on the approach of a United Nations airplane. At night, lights were flashed from mountaintops.

Railway deception included such dodges as placing a locomotive in the center of a train rather than at the front or back, and railroad breaks were simulated by strewing debris across sections of track. Like the trucks, the cars and locomotives were never left uncovered. Wide dispersal and small stockpiles were standard procedure, while all the storage areas were heavily defended by automatic radar-controlled guns.

Flak traps were also numerous in North Korea, and unwary UN pilots were often lured into deadly concentrations of anti-aircraft fire by dummy airmen dangling from parachutes hung in trees, or by dummy trains and tanks, or troops made of straw and cardboard. Steel cables were stretched across the narrow valleys into which the UN planes had to fly.

The Communists were also ingenious in making bridges and railway lines that were operable at night appear to be destroyed during daylight. Just before dawn, a crane would lift out a portable span from a serviceable bridge and deposit it in a nearby tunnel. At night, the section went back in place. Or else a bridge section would be floated downstream and camouflaged, to be hauled upstream at dusk. Sometimes piles of construction materials would be left visible beside such "damaged" bridges to enhance the impression of repairs-in-progress. Tracks were made to seem destroyed simply by having laborers tear up sections and carry them into the nearest tunnel.

Meanwhile, as the Communists successfully thwarted United Nations airpower—always with great loss of that human life for which they had little respect—the truce talks at Panmunjom were growing increasingly acrimonious. Such recrimination began when the delegates from both sides discussed Item Three of the agenda, which called for: "Concrete arrangements for the realization of cease-fire and armistice in Korea, including the composition, authority, and functions of a supervisory organ for carrying out the terms of cease-fire and armistice."

The "supervisory organ" was to be known as the Neutral Nations Supervisory Commission, to be composed of six nations, three to be proposed by each side. Its job would be to oversee the armistice; that is, to make sure that neither side was secretly building up its forces. Admiral Joy proposed Sweden, Switzerland and Norway for membership, while General Nam Il proposed Poland, Czechoslovakia, and—with no trace of embarrassment—the Soviet Union.

Admiral Joy objected. He himself might as well have proposed America as a "neutral." But his protests, directed by Washington, were on the basis that the Soviet Union was a neighbor of North Korea's. Premier Stalin's role as the probable instigator and the certain supplier of the Communist invasion was not to be mentioned. It may have been that the United States still feared that formal denunciation of Russia as an aggressor might wreck the United Nations. Whatever the reason, it made negotiations painful for Admiral Joy and his officers, and pleasant for the Communists, who gleefully repeated taunts such as this:

> Why do you give no logical reason for opposing the great, peace-loving U.S.S.R. as a member of the Neutral Nations? You give no reason because you have none. You are unable to deny that the U.S.S.R. is a true neutral in the Korean conflict.

The Americans had to sit and take it, red-faced, and their embarrassment was increased after Washington offered the lamer excuse that the Soviet Union had helped liberate Korea from Japan at the end of World War II, and was therefore not neutral. Eventually, the impasse was removed when the United Nations Command dropped Norway from its candidates and the Communists dropped the Soviet Union. The commission, when formed, would include only four members and a referee. And the net result of the limping American attitude was that the Reds had reaped a propaganda harvest and had also been reminded of the Soviet Union's part in the war against Japan, a role which had been described with enormous exaggeration during the earlier truce line squabble. Then, seeking to deride the United States' military strength, Nam II had remarked:

> You said that in the last war Japan was defeated as a result of blows inflicted by your naval and air forces. . . . Your forces fought Japan for nearly four years without being able to defeat them. It was only by the Soviet Army that a crushing blow was dealt and Japan was finally defeated.

Russia, it will be remembered, did not declare war against Japan until two days after the first atomic bomb was dropped on Hiroshima by the U. S. Army Air Corps. Thereafter Russia "fought" for one week against a Japan already crushed by American military might and suing for peace. But the Communists were not at Panmunjom to give and take points of debate. They were shopping for bargains—which was why they objected so heatedly to the Item Three proposals of the United Nations which would freeze both sides, in strength as well as position, once the armistice was signed.

It should be remembered that the Panmunjom conference was begun to obtain a *truce,* not *peace.* Once the *truce* was called, *peace* talks could begin. But it would be absurd for either side to agree to a truce by which it would grow weaker while the other side grew stronger. If this happened, the chances would be good that there would be no peace talks at all—only an end to the truce and renewal of battle by the side which had grown stronger. All the United Nations arguments on the Item Three controversy were to gain an armistice which would freeze the strength of both sides at the time of its signing. All the Communist arguments were aimed at an agreement which would either weaken the United Nations or allow themselves to strengthen their own forces during the truce. The fact that they eventually retreated from most of their early positions does suggest, however, that they might have merely been seeking to stall the talks, either to make good use of Panmunjom as a propaganda platform, or to gain time while they continued a military buildup. Also, both sides naturally presented excessive demands at the outset, hoping, like haggling merchants, to provide themselves bargaining room.

Both sides, it was agreed, would need to replace troops and equipment during the truce or else wither away in the field. But when the United Nations proposed a troop replacement figure of 35,000 men a month—the rate reached during the rotation policy of replacing each man after a year's service—the Communists replied that 5,000 men a month ought to suffice. Then the United Nations proposed that each side be allowed ten ports of entry through which to effect a man-for-man, item-by-item replacement of troops and equipment. Each port was to be inspected by neutral observation teams to see that neither side put more into Korea than it took out. The Communists replied that one port apiece was enough, and this, as they well knew, was a logistics absurdity. The United Nations forces alone had estimated that their bare minimum need was five ports. Could the Communists, twice their size, do it with one? The United Nations delegation at Panmunjom concluded that the Communists did not want ten teams of neutral observers stationed in their camp—a camp, incidentally, most conveniently close to home—and from this they drew the inevitable additional conclusion that the Communists intended to violate an agreement which the United Nations, exposed to the full glare of publicity at the end of its long sea supply line, could not dishonor if it wanted to. So the haggling went on, becoming a hopeless deadlock when the Communists refused to accept the prohibition against building new airfields during the truce. This they called an attempt to interfere in their internal affairs. The Communist viewpoint was expressed by General Nam Il:

> The question of the military facilities is an internal question, and is not a question to be discussed at the armistice conference. As to the observation question, too, you want to have a freedom of movement in observing in the rear of our side, but that is also an interference in the internal affairs of our side. Outside of the demilitarized zone agreed upon by both sides, you have no right to observe freely in the rear of our side. You said that we, too, could make observation in your rear, but we do not make any such demand and we are not accustomed to doing so.

It was not, however, the United Nations which was to observe the Communist rear as Nam charged, but neutral observation teams, as the Communists themselves had proposed. The Communists blithely ignored this point, completely rejecting the UN plan with the statement:

> As long as your side insists upon your unilateral and unreasonable demands of introduction into Korea of military forces under the pretext of rotation and replenishment, while, on the other hand, insisting upon interfering in the internal sovereign state, the negotiations can have no progress at all.

The most masterful exposition of the United Nations stand was delivered by Major General Henry Turner, a U. S. Air Force officer who had replaced Major General Craigie on the delegation. Turner said:

> You have made a number of statements attempting to show that principles advocated by the UNC are unfair, unreasonable,

and unwarranted. You condemn our insistence on prohibiting the rehabilitation and reconstruction of airfields as being interference in your internal affairs. You object to our intention to rotate and replenish our forces in Korea. You complain that our retention of islands threatens your rear. You object to aerial surveillance as being more interference in your internal affairs.

On the other hand, we defend these principles as insuring against an increase of military capabilities during the armistice. Let's look at the situation as it is today. You are not threatening our rear in any way. You are not preventing us from rehabilitating airfields or building new ones. You are not conducting aerial surveillance of our communication centers. You are not preventing unlimited rotation and replenishment of our forces. You do not interfere in the internal affairs of our side in any way. Under conditions as they exist today, you do none of these things. You do none of these things because you cannot—you lack the military capability to do them.

On the other hand, we do hold islands which threaten your rear. We do keep your airfields unusable by constantly attacking them. We do conduct aerial surveillance throughout your rear. We do limit the extent to which you can replenish your forces by our air interdiction program. We do interfere in your so-called "internal affairs" by disrupting your internal communications systems and by destroying communications centers in your rear. We do these things today because we have the military capability to do them. Until the armistice is signed we will keep on doing them.

. . . We propose only that during the armistice you shall not gain a military capability which you do not now possess. We go even further. We agree to apply the same restrictions to ourselves, even though you lack the military capability today to implement these restrictions by force of arms. But you complain this is unfair—you who are unable to impose any of these military restrictions upon our side by your own strength. You complain that it is unfair for us to insist on continuing restrictions through armistice terms which we are fully able to impose, and are imposing on you by military means during hostilities.

In short, you seek to gain, through negotiation, what you could not win through fighting. You seek to avoid, through negotiation, what you could not avoid through fighting.

But once again neither logic nor acceptance of reality had any influence on the Communist position. The Item Three deadlock dragged on, concurrent with a similar stalemate over the Item Two or prisoner exchange issue. Here was the true powder keg of the armistice negotiations, though its fuse had longer to burn. Here the United Nations firmly refused to repatriate prisoners who said they did not wish to return to Communism, while the Communists insisted that their men be returned, forcibly if need be. Meanwhile, with an illogic characteristic of Panmunjom, the rival delegations agreed on Item *Five*, that is, "Recommendations to the governments of the countries concerned." On February 17, 1952, an agreement to be entered into an eventual armistice pact as Article Four was adopted. It provided:

> In order to insure the peaceful settlement of the Korean question, the military commanders of both sides hereby recommend to the governments of the countries concerned on both sides that within three months after the armistice agreement is signed and becomes effective, a political conference of a higher level of both sides be held by representatives appointed respectively to settle through negotiation the questions of the withdrawal of all foreign forces from Korea, the peaceful settlement of the Korean question, et cetera.

Admiral Joy had agreed to this recommendation with the qualification that the United Nations members "do not construe the word 'et cetera' to relate to matters outside of Korea." This brief show of harmony was succeeded by other signs of agreement when, on February 23, the Communists finally accepted the figure of 35,000 men for rotation and, on March 25, agreed that each side should have at least five ports of entry. But there was no agreement to be reached on the building of airfields. Here the Communists were adamant, and the UN Command, having been informed by its intelligence that crated aircraft were already stored near wrecked North Korean airfields, was equally unbending. The impasse was cleared by an official directive from Washington instructing Admiral Joy to allow the Communists to build airfields during the truce. On April 28, Admiral Joy presented the United Nations' "final offer" with the remark:

In the interest of reaching an early armistice agreement, we are willing to accede to your stand that no restriction be placed on the rehabilitation and construction of airfields. I must make it absolutely clear, however, that our acceptance of your positions regarding airfields is contingent upon your acceptance of our position regarding prisoners of war [i.e., voluntary repatriation of prisoners] and the composition of the Neutral Nations Supervisory Commission [i.e., omission of Norway and the Soviet Union]. . . . I wish to emphasize that the United Nations command offer . . . is our final and irrevocable effort.

And so, President Truman's eagerness to end an unpopular war during the Presidential election year of 1952 had resulted in contradicting the basic premise of the United Nations stand: that no power should use the truce to make itself stronger. When the armistice did come, fourteen months after Admiral Joy had made his final offer, and based, in fact, on that proposal, the Communists quickly began building twenty airfields, equipping them with jet aircraft secretly brought into North Korea in violation of the armistice agreement. They had never had any intention of honoring that agreement, as Admiral Joy knew, as the Truman Administration must have suspected. It may have been that President Truman hoped to gain more throughout the world by his popular stand against forcible repatriation of prisoners than by maintenance of a purely military stance. It is also true that, apart from the psychological victory to be won by holding out for voluntary repatriation, Truman also considered this a moral responsibility. More, 1952 was a Presidential election year and the Democrats were anxious to remove the Korean albatross from their necks. And President Truman had himself learned during the steel strike of that year how unpopular the war still was.

In April, 1952, President Truman seized the steel mills the day a nationwide strike was to shut down steel production in America. The seizure was intended to keep the plants producing while labor and management worked out their differences. Truman explained his action in a radio broadcast, saying: "If steel production stops, we will have to stop making shells and bombs that are going to Korea. . . . With American troops facing the enemy on the field of battle, I would not be living up to my oath of office if I failed to do whatever is required to provide them with the weapons and ammunition they need for their survival." But neither American management, labor, press, legislature or judiciary seemed to consider Korea that critical. In six different opinions, the U. S. Supreme Court agreed that President Truman had not the power to seize the steel mills—to the satisfaction of most of the newspapers which had denounced the seizure from the start—Congress refused to grant Truman such power when he requested it, the plants were returned to the steel industry, were promptly struck by the United Steelworkers, were shut down for fifty-three days, and were finally reopened after an agreement which had the effect of raising the price of steel as much as $5.65 a ton—thus sending the inflation spiral galloping still higher. Such was the power of Korea to inflame hearts with the pure fire of patriotism, and such may have had much to do with President Truman's eagerness to get the mess cleaned up before the election booths opened in November.

In the meantime, the Presidential election campaign had its own effect on the conduct of the Korean War. General Dwight Eisenhower came back to the United States that April to begin his successful drive for the Republican nomination. His place as Supreme Commander of NATO was taken by General Ridgway, while Ridgway was relieved as United Nations Supreme Commander by General Mark Clark.

Clark, tall, angular, hawk-faced, whom Winston Churchill had once called "the American eagle," was at that time Chief of Army Field Forces. He had had wide battle command experience in World War II—though he was frequently criticized for the costliness of his campaign in Italy—and was also a veteran of negotiating with the Russians. He came to Tokyo on May 6, 1952, just the day before the prisoner repatriation powder keg blew up with the loudest explosion of the armistice negotiations.

Chapter Three

D EBATE on exchange of prisoners formally commenced December 11, 1951. At that time, the United Nations casualties stood at 305,000 dead, wounded, missing or captured, of which 192,000 were ROKs, 104,000 Americans and 9,000 other United Nations troops. Eighteen months later an agreement on prisoner exchange was finally reached, during which period the United Nations and South Korea suffered an additional 140,000 casualties on the battlefield, of which some 32,000 were Americans, 9,000 of whom were killed.

Those 140,000 additional casualties, with their 9,000 American dead, were suffered to uphold a principle new in the history of warfare: that a prisoner who does not wish to return to his homeland should not be made to go home. Like any other novel principle, it was new because the conditions requiring its definition were new: never before had great masses of prisoners refused repatriation. In Korea more than 60,000 of 132,000 North Korean and Chinese prisoners refused to return home, and thus caused the eighteen-month deadlock with its consequent bloodshed.

The United Nations principle of "voluntary repatriation," later changed to "no forced repatriation," was given dramatic expression in President Harry Truman's vow: "We will not buy an armistice by turning over human beings for slaughter or slavery." It was both a moral stand and a political one, charitable in its intent to protect prisoners who did fear punishment or did detest Communism, self-serving in its desire to inflict a propaganda defeat on the enemy. But it was enunciated with no calculation of how fiercely it would be resisted by the Communists, even though Americans, so fond of publicity themselves, should have realized that no Communist power will take a propaganda defeat lightly. The fact is that the Communists did resist, with anger and vigor, and they made absolute repatriation—at bayonet point, if necessary—a *sine qua non* of any armistice agreement. They took this position arbitrarily from the outset, without suspecting that nearly half their captured soldiers wanted to escape their rule. Later, when this appalling fact was made known to them, they reacted to their impending propaganda defeat with a swift and vicious propaganda counterattack that left the United Nations staggered and embarrassed. After this event, in midsummer of 1952, repatriation ceased to be an issue and became a symbol. The free world could not retreat; the Communists could not lose face. By then too much was at stake, and the men on the battlefield had to continue to kill one another.

This, however, was the situation *in rigor mortis*. It seemed much more flexible in December, 1951, when Admiral Joy asked General Nam to exchange prisoner lists. On December 18, the United Nations reported the names of 132,000 prisoners out of a total of 176,000 captives. The seeming discrepancy resulted from a screening conducted by the International Committee of the International Red Cross which showed that 38,000 "North Korean soldiers" were in fact citizens of South Korea whom the Communists had impressed into ranks. Another 6,000 had been lost through death and escapes. Nor did the Communists object to this figure. They were too busy defending themselves against angry and piercing questioning about their own list.

The Communist list contained the names of 11,559 UN and ROK prisoners, despite the fact that Pyongyang radio, at the end of nine months of war, had claimed capture of 65,000 men. But on December 18, 1951, they reported holding only 7,142 South Koreans, 3,198 Americans, 919 British, 234 Turks, 40 Filipinos, 10 French, 6 Australians, 4 South Africans, 3 Japanese, and one each from Canada, Greece and Holland. Of 10,000 Americans known to be missing, only a third were reported. Of 110 prisoners whose names had been reported to the Red Cross before the Communists stopped all such reporting, only 44 appeared on the list. Of 585 prisoners, mostly Americans, who were known to have reached Communist prison camps, only 135 were listed. Not one of 1,056 prisoners named at one time or another in Communist broadcasts and publications was mentioned. Worst of all, what had happened to the more than 50,000 missing South Koreans? They had "been released at the front," answered Major General Lee Sang Cho, meaning that the prisoners had been brought to within sight of their own lines and told they were free to return. The North Koreans had, in fact, used this technique at the beginning of the war, chiefly for propaganda purposes, but no more than 177 such prisoners had ever been released. The United Nations believed that the 50,000 missing South Koreans had been dragooned into the North Korean Army at pistol point, as Rear Admiral R. E. Libby, chief of the United Nations prisoner subdelegation, told General Lee:

ADMIRAL LIBBY: The United Nations Command knows, and your side knows that we know, that you have captured many more soldiers of the Republic of Korea than the 7,142 listed in your data. Where are all those soldiers now? Some of them who have succeeded in making their way back to our lines have told us of having been forced to fight against their own army until they managed to escape. But thousands of others are still serving in your army. You say they are all volunteers. We are by no means convinced that this is so, in the light of what those returned soldiers have told us. In any case, these captured soldiers are, and always have been, entitled to the status of prisoners of war. This means that they should never have been used to do work directly connected with military operations. This means that you should have shielded them and protected them from the effects of military action. . . .

GENERAL LEE: You want to know where, when, and how many prisoners we released. I think your insistence is more than an insistence on not trying to solve the question but trying to continue the useless arguments. You again make such groundless statement that we should possess about twenty times as much as we actually possess at present. The fact is certain that of a large amount of prisoners of war released, some may be in your army and some may be living their family life at home. To release all the prisoners of war directly at the front during hostilities is possible only for an army which fights only for the people; that you may find it hard to understand.

But this dispute over what had happened to more than 70 percent of the Communists' prisoners soon faded into obscurity when the United Nations Command began pressing for the "voluntary repatriation" principle ordered by Washington. Replying with anticipated invective, the Communists also seized upon the Geneva Conventions—which they had refused to sign —and quoted these pertinent sections:

> Article 7: Prisoners of war may in no circumstances renounce in part or in entirety the rights secured to them by the present convention.
> Article 118: Prisoners of war shall be released and repatriated without delay after the cessation of active hostilities.

Admiral Libby retorted that the Communists were insisting upon the letter rather than the spirit of the Geneva Conventions, and thus were trying to "convert a document designed to aid the individual into one completely negating his rights. You are saying that the prisoner of war has a right to be handed over to you, and since he has that right he has the obligation to go back whether or not he wishes to. We cannot believe that the framers of the convention had any such purpose in mind."

The ensuing deadlock continued into 1952, until, on February 17, agreement was reached on another issue: the calling of a political conference three months after an armistice. At the prisoner subdelegation meetings, then held in secrecy to take the dispute off the news pages of the world, the Communists cautiously asked the number of prisoners who sought asylum in United Nations countries. Then they agreed to the screening of prisoners, perhaps because by this time their agents ruled many of the massive prison compounds on Koje Island—the UN Command's main prisoner-of-war camp—and seemingly could control the results by continuing the brutal and murderous intimidation which had put them in power. The Communists also agreed to issue this statement to the prisoners:

> We wholeheartedly welcome the return of all of our captured personnel to the arms of the motherland; we have further guaranteed, in an agreement reached with the other side, that all cap-

tured personnel shall, after their repatriation, rejoin their families to participate in peaceful construction and live a peaceful life.

The screening began, and continued despite bloody riots which broke out in the Communist-controlled compounds. Prisoners were carefully informed that in refusing repatriation they were choosing a life of hardship and would probably not see their homes or families again. To the amazement of the United Nations, as much as to the consternation of the Communists, only 70,000 of the 132,000 prisoners held by the UN chose repatriation. This figure was later raised to 75,000, once the same brutal control of *anti*-Communist compounds was broken down, for the soft American attitude toward prisoners had also permitted Syngman Rhee to send his agents into Koje Island. But a gain of 5,000 was no solace to the shocked Communists, who angrily repudiated their screening agreement, denying, even, that it had been made.

GENERAL NAM IL: We absolutely do not recognize any of the so-called screening and its results conducted by your side. Our side absolutely cannot agree to any such course of action taken by your side. This figure, which does not in the least represent actual facts, is meaningless and our side absolutely cannot consider it. . . .

ADMIRAL JOY: You furnished our side for use in our screening process a statement of amnesty from your official sources. In short, you knew that screening was to take place; you acquiesced in its accomplishment; and only when its result was not to your liking and expectation did you decide to object to it. Had the results been to your liking, you would have enthusiastically welcomed the product of the screening.

GENERAL NAM IL: Our side has always been opposed to your screening of our captured personnel. Our side opposed it in the past, opposes it now, and will oppose it in the future.

Communist denunciation of the screening process continued, seeming to dash again all hopes for an armistice. But then came the Communist concessions on the troop rotation figure and ports of entry, to be followed, on April 28, by Admiral Joy's concession in the building of airfields during the truce.

In that concession, Admiral Joy laid down his final offer relative to prisoners, requiring Communist acceptance of the principle of voluntary repatriation. Also the United Nations would then drop its demand for recovery and repatriation of the thousands of ROK captives in the North Korean Army. If the Communists still doubted the fairness of UN screening, they could observe a second screening to be carried out by a neutral agency such as the International Red Cross, and if any prisoners changed their minds then, they would be repatriated.

On May 2 the Communists flatly rejected Joy's offer. General Nam Il, in once more denouncing the villainy of the United Nations, was playing for time. For on Koje Island the stage had been set for the kidnaping of the American general who commanded the prison camp. When this happened, the Communists would deliver their propaganda counterstroke.

Lieutenant General Nam Il was confident of the outcome of the Koje kidnaping because it was he who had ordered it, as it had been he who had secretly controlled the organization of United Nations prison compounds into Communist armed camps. Nor is the latter an exaggeration. Nam was in command, and his orders were carried out not only beneath the noses of the American administration of Koje-do, and the smaller islands of Cheju and Pongam, but while that administration, in full knowledge of what was taking place, deliberately looked the other way in consonance with a policy of "lenient" treatment of prisoners. The holy grail of America's quest for "good propaganda," coupled with the Joint Chiefs of Staff's desire for economy in Korea, had made Koje a setup for General Nam's agents.

Koje is a cross-shaped island off the southern tip of Korea, about 20 miles southwest of Pusan. No more than 20 miles at its longest, about 12 at its broadest, it is a jumble of barren rocky hills, fit to be only what the Koreans had made of it: a fishing center. Early in the Korean War the island became a reception center for approximately one million refugees who had been driven down to Pusan by the Communist invasion. Then, in 1951, the United Nations Command decided to use Koje as a prison base for the thousands of soldiers captured in the Inchon-Pusan envelopment and later imprisoned in numerous small camps throughout South Korea. By mid-1951, following the savage spring fighting of that year, Koje held a total of 150,000 men: 130,000 Koreans and 20,000 Chinese.

Koje did have obvious advantages. Lying only five miles off the mainland, transportation would be cheap; its rocky wastes could easily be converted into prison camps by the prisoners themselves; and it could be guarded by a single small force, thus releasing numerous other guard units for line duty. Its drawbacks were not so obvious. Koje's very closeness to the mainland over a five-mile strait filled with some 4,000 fishing boats enabled Communist agents to observe the island and communicate with it. Its unscreened and constantly swelling refugee population offered an anonymous mass in which agents or escaped prisoners might hide themselves. Koje's other defects were the fault of the UN Command: one, to save money, huge compounds which could house up to 5,000 men, and in some, more than 6,000; two, to save troops, a guard of only 7,000 men, or perhaps 25 sentries to one compound; three, to gain face, an order that neither force nor disciplinary action was to be used against prisoners. Therefore, at Koje there was no bed check, no roll call, no inspection of quarters. The guards, in the main raw recruits and misfit officers—the discard of line outfits —were jittery and terrified by tales of Oriental cruelty. And so, when a prisoner walked into one of the Koje compounds he actually passed out of the control of his captors.

One such prisoner was Senior Colonel Lee Hak Koo, the former chief of staff of the North Korean 13th Division. Colonel Lee, it will be remembered, had gently and obligingly surrendered to sleeping U. S. soldiers on the morning of September 21, 1950, just at the beginning of the breakout from the Pusan Perimeter.* It may seem absurd to suggest that the Communists were planning to organize their captured soldiers as early as September, 1950, at a time when they were not yet beaten, or were at least unaware of impending defeat. Nonetheless, the Communists do have a record for planting agents who await with great patience the day of their usefulness. Colonel Lee did emerge as Koje's chief organizer and is currently, in 1962, chief of security for the People's Republic of

*See page 145.

North Korea. Most indicative of all, Lee was unusually co-operative with his captors, and it was this pleasant and youthful enemy colonel who spoke such good English who was put in charge of construction crews on Koje.* Whereupon he set prisoners to mixing rice with the cement in which the compound posts would be set. Once the wet and bloated grains had shriveled, the cement became air-pocketed and crumbly. A charging man could easily knock over the posts when the day of breakout dawned. Soon, hammers, pliers, and metal shears vanished inside the compounds, and strips of barbed wire from the compound fences were also cut away. With these Colonel Lee's men built an arsenal of crude weapons. Oil drums supplied as garbage cans were converted into forges, and crude but effective knives, swords, hatchets and bayonets were made. Steel arch supports from GI shoes were fashioned into spear-heads. Barbed-wire strips were fitted with handles to be used as flails. Later, after General Nam Il had trained his agents in prison subversion and instructed them to surrender, black powder was manufactured from wood ashes and nitrates crudely extracted from urine. The powder was stuffed in C-ration cans to make hand grenades. Stolen gasoline was also poured into bottles for Molotov cocktails. Meanwhile, other prisoners cut camouflaged gates in the barbed wire or dug tunnels to connect the compounds. Inside Compound 76, the big center for enemy officers, Colonel Lee began to organize his end of the communications link with General Nam Il in North Korea.

Nam had been training agents to surrender and get inside the compounds as well as to operate in and around Koje. They were given two months of instruction in Communist theory and organization techniques. They were instructed to tell the prisoners that the North Korean Army was getting modern equipment from Russia and China, that the life of North Korean soldiers had become much less harsh, that their country was concerned about them, and that if they held firm they would be treated as heroes when they returned home. The agents were also ordered to collect the names of those soldiers

*The author does not intend to convey the impression that Colonel Lee *was* planted. The author means only that he *could* have been. There is not enough evidence to conclude either way, only enough to make conclusion impossible. R. L.

who had voluntarily surrendered or deserted or who were co-operating with the United Nations. To counteract their own propaganda, the Communists told the agents they need not fear captivity because the advent of an armistice had caused the United Nations to stop murdering prisoners.

Assisted by these specially trained men, Colonel Lee set up a communications system with its "message center" based in the 64th Field Hospital inside the prison camp, and the Koje village outside of it. Men with messages feigned illness to enter the hospital, passing along their reports from ward to ward, either by word of mouth or by wrapping a note around a rock and throwing it. By this means, a man from one compound could pass information to a man in another compound. To transmit messages north to the Communist High Command, the prisoners on work details outside the compounds carried notes which they dropped in preassigned places where the village agents would find them. Mainland runners carried them north to General Nam Il. All directives from Nam Il were sent south by radio and received by highly trained teams of communications experts equipped with Russian portable receiving sets. Then the village agents passed notes to work-detail prisoners.

By December, 1951, Koje was effectively, though still secretly, organized. In that month, UN intelligence captured a South Korean Communist Party document which said:

> According to information from the party in Kyongsang Namdo, South Korea, approximately thirty thousand to sixty thousand North Korean Army soldiers interned in the Koje-do prisoner-of-war camp have been organized and the Kyongsang Namdo Branch of the Korean Labor Communist Party will start activities in their behalf.

Inside Koje, Colonel Lee issued this statement:

> We are reborn members of the Party and will sacrifice our lives and display all our ability for the Party so that the North Korean People's Republic may win the final victory.

As organization became more efficient, the tone of such proclamations became sharper and more detailed:

We must consider the possible rupture of the cease-fire negotiations which are now underway and be ready to liberate ourselves in accordance with orders from Kim Il Sung. The prisoners of war should educate themselves and surround themselves with Party members. All types of units must be organized to rise in revolt simultaneously in order to liberate all the prisoners of war and attack the ROK and American forces that now occupy Koje-do. After we win autonomous rights we will keep in touch with the commanding officer of the North Korean People's Army by wireless and will land on Korea proper. After that we will join the NKPA together with the Chiri Mountain guerrillas.

Thereafter Colonel Lee, perhaps emboldened by the number of ineffectual American commandants who came and went at Koje—there were thirteen in all—began to rule by terror. Kangaroo courts were established to try deviationists. Victims were brought before these "People's Courts" with their hands tied behind their backs and were beaten to their knees while "charges" were read against them. The sentence was pronounced on the spot. If it was death, the sentence was carried out immediately while the prisoners howled Communist songs to drown out the victim's cries. Here, from United Nations intelligence files, are some reports of such executions:

> A 1,000-man "jury" (250 men from each battalion) on June 6, 1952, conducted a "self-criticism" of prisoners and sentenced one to death. The prisoner who received the death sentence was a member of an anti-Communist group which, it was alleged, had plotted to kill the Communist leaders and take control of Compound 85.
>
> In December, 1951, three prisoners were stoned to death on orders of the Communist "people's court."
>
> A prisoner accused of being anti-Communist refused to speak before the Chief of the Political Committee in Compound 66 on November 11, 1951. All platoon members kicked or struck the prisoner. Two of them took a section of a tent pole and beat him to death.

Once, as the guard was being changed at Compound 78, a mob of prisoners dragged one of their terrified captives into view and shouted: "Yankees, see and beware. This is what we do to the traitors who oppose us." Whereupon they cut off the man's tongue, allowed him to stumble about for a few moments, uttering terrible muted cries of pain, and then beat him to death—jeering at the Americans who were sickened at the sight. With such tactics did Colonel Lee gain control of about half of Koje's prisoners, and by early 1952, having staged a number of demonstrations, he was openly training his men within the compounds he controlled and openly flying the Red flag from the tops of compound buildings.

And the American commandants of Koje sat still.

Then, in January, 1952, a stupid and bearded private named Jeon Moon Il was brought to Koje. A few days later he turned up in Compound 76, where, no longer bearded or stupid but shaven and superior, he was introduced to the officers as Brigadier General Pak Sang Hyon, the chief of North Korea's Political Committee and another one of those thirty-six Koreans whom Stalin had sent to Pyongyang to build his puppet state. General Pak was also the new "commandant" of Koje, relieving Colonel Lee. His arrival signaled a rise in the reign of terror, and was also followed by improved organization among Communist prisoners. The General Leading Headquarters, as Pak's prison command was called, was divided into four sections: Political Security, Organization and Planning, Guard Unit, and Agitation and Propaganda. The Political Security Section planted trusted Party members in as many of Koje's squads and platoons as possible, instructing them to be on the lookout for "spies and agents to include agents of the Republic of Korea Army, civil interpreters, Christian ministers, Party members with bad qualities, religionists, former security chiefs, draft evaders, reactionary groups and those who associated with reactionary elements." So thorough was Organization and Planning that one of its subsections, External Liaison and Reconnaissance, was given detailed instructions on its mission during the breakout.

> Whenever the time is appropriate for an uprising or break, the members dispatched to the outside will assist the basic fighting units to get out of the compound by occupying stationary firing posts and guard posts by surprise attack, [and will] light signal fires on the hills, capture weapons and destroy United Nations

ammunition and armory storehouses. This sub-section will be organized from Party members experienced in guerrilla fighting in China and South Korea, those who have a thorough knowledge of enemy weapons and those who served in the North Korean Army in engineering and reconnaissance.

... After extrication [they will] construct a partisan base and set fire to the camp's headquarters petroleum dump, food storage and other supply areas and destroy the transportation route. After completion of this duty, they will get to the mainland and report to an officer higher than a major and join the partisans. Extrication or escape will be accomplished before dawn, while on work details or during foggy weather.

One of the Guard Unit's chief duties was to prevent the escape from Koje of anti-Communist prisoners—an irony if ever there was one—while Agitation and Propaganda worked to provoke incidents or riots which would be useful to General Nam during his propaganda tirades at Panmunjom.

And so, in February, 1952, when the United Nations began screening prisoners, the organization controlled by General Pak and Colonel Lee was prepared to act. Repatriation teams coming into the Communist compounds faced the assembled prisoners and asked, with hopeful naïveté, for a simple show of hands. Hardly a hand went up. The Communists were openly triumphant, and the United Nations decided that it would need to control the Communist compounds if individual screening beyond the coercive stare of Communist *hanchos,* or leaders, was to be carried out. On February 18 a battalion from the famous 27th Wolfhound Regiment attempted to seize Compound 62 in a pre-dawn, bloodless coup, but as Major John Klein led one company inside the gate, Communist sentries screamed, "Yankees! Yankees!" and the American soldiers were showered with stones. "For God's sake, don't shoot!" Major Klein cried, but then a mob of Communist prisoners was upon his men with spears, knives and flails. Homemade grenades boomed among them. Klein had to call for rifle fire from the companies stationed outside the gate, and this was followed by a bayonet charge. The prisoners fell back, and the riot ended with American casualties of one dead and 39 wounded, as opposed to 75 prisoners dead and 139 wounded. This riot, and another on March 13, gave General Nam at Panmunjom the "incidents" he required for an increasingly vituperative propaganda tirade.

GENERAL NAM IL: Everybody knows that for a long period of time you have been using Chiang Kai-shek's gangsters and Syngman Rhee's agents to take all kinds of barbarous measures to coerce our captured personnel into refusing repatriation. You have not hesitated to use methods of bloodshed and murder to gain your infamous aim. You have not yet made an account for the incidents of February 18th and March 13th, when your side twice massacred our captured personnel.

In order to assist you to gain the aim of retaining our captured personnel, the Chiang Kai-shek ring repeatedly directed their agents to force our captured personnel to start the so-called movement of refusing repatriation by writing blood petitions, making appeals, and even by announcing collective suicide. For all these facts, our side is in possession of incontestable evidence. Your activities in employing barbarous methods in an attempt to retain our captured personnel by force have already reached such an extent as makes it impossible for you to hide or deny them.

To strengthen your rule of bloodshed and violence over our captured personnel, your side recently moved large amounts of reinforcing forces to the locality of your prisoner-of-war camp, for further suppression of the just resistance of our captured personnel. The fact now placed before the people of the whole world is that in spite of your such barbarous measures, you violated the will of the captured personnel of our side. Thousands of them would rather die than yield to your forcible retention. Your side dares not face this fact. In order to cover up this fact, your side has invented the myth that our captured personnel were not willing to be repatriated.

And so into April and Admiral Joy's April 28th proposal.* The next day, at Koje-do itself, came a dress rehearsal for the kidnaping of Brigadier General Francis Dodd, the prison base

*The so-called "final offer," which, conceding the Communists the right to build airfields after the truce, insisted on an armistice based upon the principle of voluntary repatriation. See pages 326–27.

commander. On April 29, Dodd's assistant, Lieutenant Colonel Wilbur Raven, boldly strode alone into Compound 76 in unwise reply to a demand from Colonel Lee. He was surrounded by a mob of chanting prisoners, and when the mob dispersed, Colonel Raven had vanished from view. The Communists held him for three hours, striking him, throwing soup on him, and then releasing him, having used him to practice for the bigger kidnaping to come while testing the camp command's reaction to deliberate insult. Evidently they thought it meek, for on May 7 Colonel Lee demanded that General Dodd come to Compound 76. Incredibly enough, the American general answered the summons of the enemy colonel who was his prisoner. Here is General Dodd's own report of what happened:

On the morning of May 7, I received a message that the spokesman of Compound 76 requested an interview with me. At 2 o'clock I proceeded to the compound gate where the interview was held. The outer gate was opened and the compound spokesman and leader were permitted to step just outside the gate for the conference. The interview consisted of the usual Communist complaints concerning their needs for additional food, clothing, medical supplies, etc., as well as a number of demands concerning forced repatriation, acceptance of Russia as a neutral nation, and other matters not appropriate for such an interview.

As the interview proceeded, additional members from the leaders group within the compound gathered around inside the gate to listen to the discussion. At about 3:15 I had decided that the interview was at an end, and turned to depart; whereupon I was rushed by some 20 leaders, dragged into the compound and quickly carried to a building where I was searched and my personal possessions removed.

According to witnesses, Dodd was rushed by men returning to the compound after having emptied buckets of latrine sewage. The "honey bucket detail," as it came to be known, had been carefully planned and timed. Nor had Dodd or Colonel Raven, who was with him, gone to their interview armed. Raven, by now a veteran of such indignity, saved himself by clinging to a gatepost until American guards rescued him. Dodd was hustled off with one final hoarse shout indicative of his state of mind: "I'll court-martial any man who fires a gun!" In a few minutes the jubilant Communists hoisted signs which they had painted on blankets beforehand. They said: WE CAPTURE GENERAL DODD. IF OUR PROBLEMS ARE RESOLVED HIS SECURITY IS GUARANTEED. IF THERE IS BRUTAL ACT OR SHOOTING HIS LIFE IS IN DANGER.

That night, General Mark Clark learned that the day of his arrival to relieve Ridgway as U. S. Far East and United Nations chief had coincided with the execution of one of the boldest and most successful propaganda plots in history. And the situation on Koje would deteriorate further, even though Lieutenant General James Van Fleet had acted quickly, appointing Brigadier General Charles Colson to take Dodd's place and dispatching tanks to Koje. For Colson, a supply officer, seems to have had his judgment impaired by his anxiety to rescue Dodd, his close friend, from the clutches of the Communists. On the morning of May 10, from "The PW Representative Group of North Korean Peoples Army and Chinese Peoples Volunteer Army," General Colson received an ultimatum which, hastily and poorly translated, made these demands:

1. Immediate ceasing the barbarous behavior, insults, torture, forcible protest with blood writing, threatening, confine, mass murdering, gun and machine-gun shooting, using poison gas, germ weapons, experiment object of A-bomb by your command. You should guarantee PW human rights and individual life with the base on the International Law.

2. Immediate stopping the so-called illegal and unreasonable voluntary repatriation of North Korean Peoples Army and Chinese Peoples Volunteer Army PW.

3. Immediate ceasing the forcible investigation [screening] which thousands of PW of North Korean Peoples Army and Chinese Peoples Volunteer be rearmed and falled in slavery, permanently and illegally.

4. Immediate recognition of the PW Representative Group [Commission] consisted of North Korean Peoples Army and Chinese Peoples Volunteer Army PW and close cooperation to it by your command.

This Representative Group will turn in Brig Gen Dodd, USA, on your hand after we receive the satisfactory written declaration to resolve the above items by your command. We will wait for your warm and sincere answer.

Colson signed. He did not sign the document quoted above, but rather a ransom note which he had written himself and which underwent several changes which General Dodd has described:

They studied this answer until noon. They then came to my tent and reported to me that the answer was entirely unsatisfactory. Actually, General Colson had agreed to their demands, but from their translation from English into [Korean] it was obvious that they did not understand this.

I then modified General Colson's letter to their liking, and asked them if such a modified statement would be satisfactory. They informed me that it would. General Colson signed this statement and returned it to them promptly. However they then found minor corrections necessary, to which they attached considerable importance. It was therefore, necessary to prepare a third statement. Colonel Lee Hak Koo (leader of the prisoners' association) had sent a written statement to General Colson that as soon as they had received a satisfactory statement signed by him and had an opportunity to read and understand it they would release me unharmed.

The final statement signed by Colson said:

1. With reference to your Item 1 of that message, I do admit that there have been instances of bloodshed where many prisoners of war have been killed and wounded by UN Forces. I can assure you that in the future the prisoners of war can expect humane treatment in this camp according to the principles of International Law. I will do all within my power to eliminate further violence and bloodshed. If such incidents happen in the future, I will be responsible.

2. Reference your Item 2 regarding voluntary repatriation of NKPA and CPVA prisoners of war, that is a matter which is being discussed at Panmunjon. I have no control or influence over the decisions at the Peace Conference.

3. Regarding your Item 3 pertaining to forcible investigation [screening], I can inform you that after Gen. Dodd's release, unharmed, there will be no more forcible screening or any rearm-

344

ing of prisoners of war in this camp, nor will any attempt be made at nominal screening.

4. Reference your Item 4, we approve the organization of a PW Representative Group or Commission consisting of NPKA and CPVA prisoners of war, according to the details agreed by Gen Dodd and approved by me.

I am furnishing this reply in writing over my signature as requested by you, through Gen Dodd with the understanding that upon the receipt of this reply you will release Gen Dodd, unharmed, as soon as possible, but under no circumstances later than 8 o'clock P.M. this date. Signed Charlie F. Colson, Brig Gen USA, Command General.

Even with this, Dodd was not released as quickly as he had hoped. The Communists thought they might humiliate their captors a bit further, as Dodd himself reported:

I then discovered that they had prepared another letter to General Colson informing him of the arrangements for the release ceremony. Apparently I was to be decorated in flowers and escorted to the gate between formed lines of PWs.

I was to be met at the gate by General Colson where I would be delivered into his custody. I informed them that we could call the whole matter off, that they had not lived up to their promises, that they had admitted that General Colson's statement was satisfactory and now they wished to place other unacceptable conditions upon my release.

I informed them that if they could not live up to their promise we would not live up to ours. By this time it was 9 o'clock. They immediately agreed that I was right and requested that I inform General Colson that I would be released at 9:30. There was some further discussion about the possibility of the removal of the troops in order that I might depart in a peaceful atmosphere. This I refused to discuss. They then agreed to arrange for my release at 9:30 and at this time I was delivered to the gate by the principal leaders and released.

Thus, capitulation by the captor to his captives. Not even the "incidents" of February 18 or March 13, nor the "germ warfare" charge which the Communists were then attempting to hang around America's neck, had given General Nam a propaganda stick so thick with which to beat the United Nations. Here is General Nam Il at Panmunjom:

> The former commandant of your prisoner-of-war camp openly admitted that your side used all sorts of violence to screen our captured personnel by force in an attempt to retain them as your cannon fodder. The newly appointed commandant of your prisoner-of-war camp openly implied to our captured personnel that no *further* criminal activities in violation of the Geneva Conventions would be perpetrated. Is it not a fact that your side, in order to carry out forcible screening, committed all kinds of atrocities, even including mass massacre against our captured personnel in disregard of the Geneva Conventions and repudiating the minimum standard of human behavior? Is it not a fact that the commandant of your prisoner-of-war camp promised our captured personnel that: "There will be no more forcible screening"? You cannot deny these facts.
>
> Is it a sign of your good faith to continue to slaughter war prisoners in open repudiation of the pledge of no further maltreatment or murder of war prisoners made by Colson before the whole world as well as before all the war prisoners?
>
> The series of cowardly acts of persecuting and slaughtering our captured personnel carried out by your side for the purpose of retaining them proves conclusively the utter bankruptcy of every fraudulent proposition of retaining war prisoners.

Henceforth, until the second breakoff of truce talks in September of 1952, the Communists came to the conference table chiefly to denounce or inveigh, to spread on the record in scurrilous language those charges which would be trumpeted throughout the world by Communist propaganda media. General Mark Clark's statement repudiating Colson's ransom note as one "made under duress," while citing the testimony of the International Red Cross as proof that no prisoners on Koje had been harmed, was of little countervailing propaganda value. The Communists had the world's ear and they were shouting too loud for anyone else to be heard. One result was that Admiral Joy, certain now that his final offer was doomed for at least another year, asked to be relieved at Panmunjom. On May 22 his place was taken by Major General (later Lieutenant

General) William Harrison, the tall, stern Army officer who had been serving under Joy for some months. And in the meantime the Communist hold on Koje was broken by Brigadier General Haydon Boatner, a seasoned infantry commander with a record of long service in the Orient.

Boatner decided to destroy Communist power by scattering it, and began building smaller compounds to hold 500 men each. His tanks and soldiers, meanwhile, trained openly outside the tough Compounds 76 and 77. General Pak and Colonel Lee ordered their men to drill also, but the disparity between their own broom-bayonets and the American tanks was doubtless not lost on them. On June 10, Boatner was ready to move against Compound 76. He told his soldiers: "Use the bayonet, your rifle butt, or a knee in the groin. Don't shoot unless you have to, but if you have to, shoot to kill." To Colonel Lee he sent this message: "Have all prisoners ready to be escorted to new compounds in exactly 30 minutes. Failure to obey will necessitate the use of force."

Half an hour later, Boatner told his men: "Go in and roust them out." A red flare shot up, the big tanks battered down the compound fences, and American soldiers in gas masks went in, hurling only tear-gas and concussion grenades. No shots were fired, though the prisoners launched a single fierce charge and closed with their homemade weapons. In the end, Compound 76 was reduced and Colonel Lee and General Pak captured. Compound 77 fell without a fight, as did the other Communist compounds. A search of Compound 76 uncovered an arsenal of 3,000 tent-pole spears, 1,000 Molotov cocktails, 4,500 knives and uncounted quantities of clubs, hatchets, hammers and flails. Inside Compound 77 were found the bodies of 16 prisoners murdered on orders of the "People's Courts." Both compounds were connected by a tunnel, and trenches had been dug around the huts of each. A complete battle plan for defense of the compounds was also discovered. But the fight to break the Communist hold had not been bloodless. One American was killed and 13 wounded, while 41 prisoners died and 274 were wounded, and the Communist press redoubled its vilification of "the American Fascists." Here are two samples from articles in *Pravda*:

Koje Island! Again the gloomy shadow of Maidenek has come upon the world, again the stench of corpses . . . again the groans of the tormented. . . . We have learned that "civilized" Americans can be yet more inhuman, yet more infamous than the bloody Hitlerites. Dachau was a death camp, Maidenek was a death factory. Koje is a whole island of death. . . . The American hangmen are torturing, tormenting, and killing unarmed people here. They are trying out their poisons on them. They have surpassed the Hitlerites; they have turned POWs into guinea pigs and are testing on them the strength of their germ "soldiers"— microbes.

The speeches of orators exhale wrath . . . noble wrath against these bandits in generals' uniforms, the butchers in white gloves, the bloody bigots and traders in death who have unleashed the most inhuman carnage in history, warfare with the assistance of microbes, fleas, lice, and spiders. . . . The Koje butchers will not escape!

The "inhuman carnage" here alleged was the "germ warfare" which the United States was supposedly waging against the civilian population of North Korea. This hoax, one of the most grandiose in history, was the other of the two great propaganda offensives which the Communists mounted against the free world during the stalled truce talks at Panmunjom.

Chapter Four

IT HAS been argued that Red China did not invent the germ warfare hoax merely to smear the free world but had made her accusations to escape blame for having brought typhus into North Korea from Manchuria. Unfortunately, as with so much else in the Korean War, this theory cannot be upheld until more is known about what the Communists actually planned or did not plan. All that is known is that in December, 1951, typhus appeared in North Korea, a land which had not known it since the Japanese occupation in 1904. Manchuria, however, had been plagued by typhus for centuries. Moreover, it will be recalled that in January–February of 1951 captured Chinese soldiers spoke of typhus ravaging their units.* The only other point which might be cited in support of the shift-of-guilt theory is that hoaxes or smear campaigns rarely spring fully formed from someone's brain. They usually grow, meaning that a seed already exists. Thus, according to the shift-of-guilt theory, Red China, anxious to avoid reproach for having brought a deadly disease into Korea, decided to kill two birds with one stone by fixing blame on the United States.†

Germ warfare itself, or bacteriological warfare or biological warfare, is nearly as old as war itself. Loathsome weapon though it is, it has been used—as has every other weapon devised by man. In ancient times, bodies thrown over the walls of besieged towns were intended to spread infection. Napoleon flooded the flats around Mantua, hoping to afflict its people with malaria-bearing mosquitoes rising from the new marsh. Traders in colonial America infected blankets to spread smallpox among the Indians. The Germans of World War I infected Rumanian horses, as well as American livestock to be shipped to the Allies. One of the bizarre "uses" of germ warfare occurred during the Russian invasion of Finland just prior to World War II, when, to explain why the bodies of her fallen soldiers had been left to freeze in the snow, Russia said that they would fester during the spring thaw and epidemics or plagues would result.

The purposes of systematic and organized germ warfare are to infect a civil population and thus cripple arms production and lower the will to fight, to infect crops and achieve the same results through famine, or to infect large masses of reserve troops. Germ warfare has no use at the front for the obvious reason that it might infect friendly as well as enemy troops. It has to be waged in the enemy's rear, either by spraying bacteria from airplanes or by dropping germs in canisters. Nor would it be of any great value in a poor country such as Korea,

*See page 261.
†Admittedly, this is an attractive speculation, since it makes the enemy doubly dastardly. But it cannot be proven, and since the Communists showed themselves unscrupulous enough in their lies and torture of American fliers throughout the germ warfare hoax, it is in any case superfluous.

where disease is constant and various, where there is frequent contact with animals, where there is no sanitation, and where, as a consequence, fear of disease is low and immunity is high. But in sanitary countries such as America, where the populace is not used to disease and is dependent on medication, where people dread disease and have low resistance to it, the use of germ warfare might cause panic as well as plague. In America, germ warfare would introduce a new and fearful thing, whereas in Korea it would not. Finally, apart from the moral considerations which ought to inhibit the use of such weapons anywhere, the waging of germ warfare in North Korea would have been of no benefit. The country was a wasteland. To infect it would be like poisoning a dying enemy just to see him squirm. And this, of course, is just the villainous image of America which the germ warfare hoax attempted to parade through the world. America, rich, powerful, sated and glutted, deriving a new thrill sensation from tormenting a poor and tiny land.

Though the first blast was made by a North Korean, Foreign Minister Pak Hen, on February 22, 1952, the germ warfare cacophony was trumpeted chiefly by Communist China with the Soviet Union and her satellites supplying the chorus. On February 25, Peiping denounced the American "atrocity" to the (Communist) World Peace Committee in Oslo. Two days later Dr. Istvann Florian, chief of the Communist Hungarian Red Cross, sent the following cable to the International Red Cross in Switzerland:

> American troops have again seized the bacteriological arm! They have hurled from their planes sickened insects upon the Korean People's Army, the Chinese Volunteers and the rear territorities. ... The International Red Cross must raise its voice against these inhuman atrocities.

Two more days and the Red Cross of Communist Poland made a similar protest, concluding that "all inactivity in this matter signifies solidarity with the criminals." On March 6 the Rumanian Red Cross demanded immediate action "to stop this bacteriological war of mass extermination."

Against the background of these official protests, world Communism's vast propaganda apparatus had taken up the "germ war" outcry. Riots and demonstrations against America were staged, in free world countries as well as in Communist ones. Peiping radio thundered ceaselessly. Civilians in North Korea and Manchuria were organized into "germ-hunting parties" and they were photographed using chopsticks to pick black specks off snow. A "germ war exhibit" was held in Peiping. How the germ warfare charges were used to fan the flames of Mao Tse-tung's "Hate-America" campaign throughout China itself, has been described by the Australian journalist Denis Warner:

> ... The population was mobilized to take preventive measures to kill flies, mosquitoes, fleas and rats, to clean up garbage, to destroy everything that might be a carrier or a breeding ground for America's filthy pestilences. In the first year of this campaign Peking listed the destruction of 120 million rats, and nearly 1½ million pounds weight of flies, mosquitoes and fleas. A hundred and sixty million tons of garbage, including some that had been there since Ming times, was carted away from the streets: 280,000 kilometers of drains and ditches were filled; 40 million cubic meters of earth were used to fill up stagnant pools. Big contingents of Chinese scientists went to Korea and came back laden with U. S.-made containers and "contaminated" insects. . . . It was the greatest propaganda hoax in history; but that it succeeded in its purpose in China there is no doubt.[1]

The hoax, moreover, was to have a long run. When Paul Ruegger, president of the International Red Cross, queried both sides on the matter, U. S. Secretary of State Acheson replied on March 7:

> Despite categorical denials . . . Communists continue to charge [that] biological warfare by the UN Command has caused an epidemic in Communist-held areas of Korea. I repeat the United States has not engaged in any form of bacteriological warfare. [I] would like to suggest that the International Red Cross make . . . an investigation [and be] given free access to all sources of possible information behind the United Nations lines.

The Communists sent no reply, although Ruegger had set April 20 as a deadline for response, but they did make public their attitude by having delegates to the Committee for World

Peace in Oslo explain that they "did not consider the IRC sufficiently free from political influence" and that the World Health Organization was also tainted. So the International Red Cross suspended its plans to investigate, and was promptly called an American lackey by the Communists. Of this, Ruegger said: "The IRC has been accused of being a 'depraved lackey' of the American government since, when the U. S. asked that an investigation be opened, the IRC declared itself ready to organize one. It might just as well be claimed that the IRC was in the pay of North Korea, since it was sufficient for this government to refuse an investigation for the IRC to abandon it."

There was nothing puzzling about Communism's abrupt end of appeals to the International Red Cross. Impartial investigation had not been wanted. What had been desired was the preparation of propaganda window dressing while Communist interrogators wore down the wills of captured American airmen with that wearying technique which the world has called "brainwashing." The object was to obtain "confessions" of having waged germ warfare. By the middle of May, 1952, four months of brainwashing had broken down the resistance of two U. S. Air Force lieutenants. They "confessed" to having dropped infected insects on North Korea. Their "confessions," usually written for them by the British Communist reporter, Alan Winnington, and his Australian associate, Wilfred Burchett, were read before newsreel cameras and distributed throughout the world. Others followed. One American airman told the sound cameras: "I was coward enough to do as I was told. Why are we using this barbarous weapon when peace talks go on? When I think of my future, how can I tell my son, how can I tell my family, that I am a criminal?" Another declared: "A shower may clean my body, but my soul will never be clean!"

And so the world was deluged with the maudlin *mea culpas* of thirty-eight American airmen who were either tortured into "confessing," or lacking strength of will, "confessed" under threats.* The prize "confession" of all was the 6,000-word

---

*Some fliers later repatriated said they had encouraged Winnington and Burchett to be melodramatic, hoping the free world would "see how corny it was." They also stated that most of their interrogators seemed to believe that germ warfare *had* been waged.

document extorted from Colonel Frank Schwable, a graduate of the Naval Academy and chief of staff of the First Marine Air Wing at the time he was shot down. Schwable, like all the seventy-eight airmen selected for interrogation, was kept apart from other prisoners. The Communists charged him with germ warfare and ordered him to confess. For five months he was held incommunicado, left to languish in his own filth within an unheated 3x7-foot hole, constantly subjected to the hammer-like reiterations of his interrogators.

"It was the last couple of days in November that I gave up," Schwable explained after his repatriation. "I was cold. I was damn cold. My hand was frozen. There was no question in my mind. I knew they weren't going to let me stand up in front of a firing squad. They were going to leave me there all winter. I knew I'd never make it. I think slow mental torture over a long period of time is worse than quick physical torture. You sit there day in and day out, day in and day out. Your choices are very limited. You either confess or you stay there."

For three months, Schwable was forced to write and rewrite his "confession" until his captors found it suitable, and of this he explained: "Once you do this thing you've got to play it both ways. You've got to make it both realistic and ridiculous. I hope to God—I pray to God—I achieved that aim. I knew military people would understand. I don't know about the public. . . . But it is fantastic that anyone can believe that anything of that sort was used. I once told my interrogator that I would stand before God and swear it was never used. I told him that in our religion that's a pretty strong oath. But they never tried to make me swear it was true."

Not all of the thirty-eight airmen who "confessed" held out as long. The most pathetic case was that of the pilot who said: "They fed me fish soup. Good God, *fish soup!* Then I knew they really meant to get what they wanted, so I said just what they asked me to." On the other hand, among the forty who refused to confess there were men of heroic toughness of will, officers such as Captain Theodore Harris of the U. S. Air Force, who was handcuffed and placed in a small thatched hole and kept there for fourteen months. Harris said: "If I can't go back with my self-respect, I won't go back at all." Another Air

Force lieutenant refused to "confess" after the Communists did this to him:

> . . . After being classified as a war criminal [he] was interrogated and pressured for four months by the Chinese Communists. Eight times he was ordered to confess, offered relief if he did, death if he didn't. Eight times he refused. He was stood at attention for five hours at a time, was confined eight days in a doorless cell less than six feet long, held to the ground by two guards while a third kicked and slapped him, stood at attention another time for twenty-two hours until he fell and was then hit while lying down with the side of a hatchet and stood up for two hours. He was interrogated for three hours with a spotlight six inches from his face. He was ordered to confess while a pistol was held at the back of his head. He was placed under a roof drain all night during a rainstorm. He was left without food for three days. He was put before a firing squad and given a last chance, hung by hands and feet from the rafters of a house. When he still refused, the Chinese Communists let him alone. They had apparently given him up as an impossible case. He came back alive.

Still, the thirty-eight "confessions" obtained between February, 1952, and March of the following year provided the Communists with the necessary "authentication" of their accusations, and the germ warfare charge was made to stick for a good part of that time. It was also expanded to include atrocities. On July 9, 1952, the North Korean newspaper *Nodong Sinmun* charged that the United States planned to use 500 prisoners to test new weapons and that "last year Americans and British took one thousand prisoners of war from Korea . . . to an island in the Atlantic for atom bomb tests." Meanwhile, all ills within their own camp were blamed on the Americans. According to the testimony of a captured Chinese Communist soldier, printed in *The Korean Republic* of March 15, 1954:

> The Communists sent us out to the mountains to find bugs. They wanted flies, mosquitoes, and fleas. We had a hard time finding them. When we brought the bugs back, the Communist

officers exhibited them. They told the men that they had been dropped from American planes. They said they carried germs and were intended to wipe out the Communist forces. Whenever a man became sick, the Communists blamed it on these germs that the Americans allegedly had dropped. Regardless of whether it was a cold, fever, or something else, they declared that it was caused by the American germ warfare.

In China, the tons of insects collected, as well as a few pounds of clams found after the suspicious passage of American planes, were held for the arrival of the International Scientific Commission, an organization made up of scientists from Communist countries or Communist sympathizers from other lands. The Commission found that one "insuperable difficulty was the fact that . . . classification of many groups of insects in the Chinese sub-continent remains unknown." More, the only "perfect proof" would be an American airplane "forced down with its biological cargo intact, and its crew prepared to admit their proceedings forthwith." So the International Scientific Commission, though suggesting that the Americans might be using a new germ warfare technique by clam-bombing North Korea—the mouth of the clam is an ideal place for breeding cholera organisms—was not entirely successful. But the overall germ warfare campaign still was, especially in its purpose of portraying America as the new nest of the Fascists. Of this latter aim General Clark has written:

> A basic objective of all [the Communist] propaganda in Korea as elsewhere was to plant the idea in men's minds that Americans were the new Nazis. American airmen were "butchers," American bombardiers aimed at hospitals and schools and reveled in a blood bath. Cartoons of our generals in Korea, from MacArthur on, showed us in caps shaped like the exaggerated military caps the Nazi generals used to wear. The term "new Nazis" was a cliché in the Communist doggerel. Talking with Communist agents at Panmunjom our people heard this doggerel and became familiar with it. The FBI was the "Gestapo," Senator McCarthy was a "Himmler." America was ruled by "Chicago gangsters" in the service of "Wall Street." America, like Hitler Germany, could not exist economically without war.

Fascist! Fascist! Fascist! That was the theme, the constant, pounding refrain of the Communists as they battled to turn men's minds against America.[2]

In the end, the germ warfare hoax collapsed. It fell apart in the one place where it was expected to do most harm: the United Nations. After the Soviet Union introduced the charges there, the U. S. delegate Dr. Charles Mayo, in an empassioned summing up, described the brainwashing technique which had extorted the thirty-eight "confessions":

> It is a method obviously calculated by the Communists to bring a man to the point where a dry crust of bread or a few hours' uninterrupted sleep is a great event in his life. All the prisoners victimized were subjected to the same pattern of intimidation, deprivation of basic physical needs, isolation and physical and mental torture.... The techniques varied only in detail.... The total picture presented is one of human beings reduced to a status lower than that of animals, filthy, full of lice, festered wounds full of maggots, their sickness regulated to a point just short of death, unshaven, without haircuts or baths for as much as a year, men in rags, exposed to the elements, fed with carefully measured minimum quantities and the lowest quality of food and unsanitary water served often in rusty cans, isolated, faced with squads of trained interrogators, bulldozed, deprived of sleep and browbeaten with mental anguish....

The United States then proposed that the United Nations set up a commission to investigate both American charges of Communist atrocities and Communist charges of American germ warfare. With that, the Russians on the UN General Assembly's Political Committee changed the subject.

Chapter Five

A S AN unforeseen result of the Red propaganda war, the United Nations adopted a firmer attitude at Panmunjom, while increasing that military pressure which the Communists seemed to understand more clearly than words. Much of this action was ordered by General Clark on his own initiative, though it was later approved and even intensified by the Joint Chiefs of Staff on the recommendations of the State Department.

In June, 1952, Clark ordered Major General William Harrison to break off the Panmunjom talks for a few days without advance warning. At the close of proceedings on June 7, Harrison told General Nam Il: "We are not coming back tomorrow. We are coming back on June 11."

> The effect [wrote General Clark] was startling. Nam Il, usually an unruffled, deadly calm operator, came very close to losing control. Harrison, obviously pleased, reported the scene to me in detail. Nam Il was so shocked and upset that he pleaded with Harrison to sit down and talk the thing over a little. Harrison said he never saw such a change in a man, change wrought by a single, simple sentence. He was flabbergasted. Obviously his instructions were to keep the talks going so that he could put Communist propaganda on the record for the world press every day. The Communists at this stage were emphasizing the war of words and Panmunjom was the main battleground. And now Harrison had made it impossible for him to carry out his instructions to the letter. Harrison had taken away the propaganda platform, even though for only three short days.[1]

357

Clark's next move was to release 27,000 North Korean civilian internees who had refused repatriation, an event which Syngman Rhee organized into a national holiday. On June 21, after General Clark had issued a strong statement denying the charge of germ warfare, while warning the Communists they would be held responsible for their treatment of captive UN troops, Harrison read into the Panmunjom record a long account of the Soviet Union's disposition of prisoners during World War II. At that time, Russia demanded the right of asylum for captured Axis soldiers, and this, said Harrison, sharply pressing the embarrassed Nam, was ample justification of the UN principle of voluntary repatriation.

On the military front, the Joint Chiefs of Staff authorized Clark to bomb the vast Suiho Dam hydroelectric complex on the North Korean side of the Yalu River. Suiho, which supplied power to all of North Korea's industry and much of Manchuria's, had heretofore been untouchable. But on June 23, 1952, it was battered by some 500 United Nations aircraft, most of them American. The Suiho raid produced another storm of protest from the British, for it had been carried out without prior consultation with U. S. allies. But on June 24, 200 more American bombers returned to Suiho to finish the job, and the protests in the House of Parliament, based on the fear that American patience had been exhausted and the war was about to be extended, at last subsided.

The air war against the Communists did not abate. On August 8, the Joint Chiefs stated: "While we consider it probable that the Communist wish to conclude an armistice, we see little or no indication that various factors exerting pressure on the Communists are sufficient to make an armistice a matter of urgency." One of those insufficient "factors" was U. S. air power, and accordingly, the Joint Chiefs ordered Clark to step up the aerial war in North Korea. On August 29 an even larger raid than Suiho was flown against the Red capital at Pyongyang. It was called the "All United Nations Air Effort." Carrier-based air joined the strike, during which 1,403 sorties were flown, with particular attention paid to government buildings, Radio Pyongyang, and the Ministry of Rail Transportation headquarters. The attack was renewed the next night by Superforts and Pyongyang was left smoldering. Out of the ruins came

the failing voice of Radio Pyongyang explaining that the Ameɪ-
cans had attacked at night because they were afraid to risk the
MIGs by day. In truth, the MIGs had been swept clear of
North Korea except for their sallies into MIG Alley from their
sanctuary bases at Antung, Manchuria. Figures for air-to-air
combat showed that at the end of 1952, the United Nations
fliers had shot down 365 MIGs and 145 propeller-driven craft,
at a loss of 79 planes of their own. This high proportion increased until the war's end, by which time the U. S. Sabrejets
had established a 14-to-1 ratio of kills to losses. How it was done
has been described by the U. S. Air Force jet ace, Colonel Harrison Thyng:

For you combat has become an individual "dogfight." Flight
integrity has been lost, but your wing man is still with you,
widely separated but close enough for you to know that you are
covered. Suddenly you go into a steep turn. Your Mach drops
off. The MIG turns with you, and you let him gradually creep
up and outturn you. At the critical moment you reverse your
turn. The hydraulic controls work beautifully. The MIG cannot
turn as readily as you and is slung out to the side. When you pop
your speed brakes, the MIG flashes by you. Quickly closing the
brakes, you slide onto his tail and hammer him with your "50s."
Pieces fly off the MIG, but he won't burn or explode at that high
altitude. He twists and turns and attempts to dive away but you
will not be denied. Your "50s" have hit him in the engine and
slowed him up enough so that he cannot get away from you. His
canopy suddenly blows and the pilot catapults out, barely missing your airplane. Now your wing man is whooping it up over
the radio, and you flash for home very low on fuel. At this point
your engine is running very rough. Parts of the ripped MIG have
been sucked into your engine scoop, and the possibility of it
flaming out is very likely. Desperately climbing for altitude you
finally reach forty thousand feet. With home base now but eighty
miles away, you can lean back and sigh with relief for you know
you can glide your ship back and land, gear down, even if your
engine quits right now. You hear over the radio, "Flights re-
forming and returning—the last MIGs chased back across the
Yalu." Everyone is checking in, and a few scores are being discussed. The good news of no losses, the tension which gripped

you before the battle, the wild fight, and the "G" forces are now being felt. A tired yet elated feeling is overcoming you, although the day's work is not finished. Your engine finally flames out, but you have maintained forty thousand feet and are now but twenty miles from home. The usual radio calls are given, and the pattern set up for a deadstick landing. The tower calmly tells you that you are number three deadstick over the field, but everything is ready for your entry. Planes in front of you continue to land in routine and uninterrupted precision, as everyone is low on fuel. Fortunately this time there are no battle damages to be crash landed. Your altitude is decreasing, and gear is lowered. Hydraulic controls are still working beautifully on the pressure maintained by your windmilling engine. You pick your place in the pattern, land, coast to a stop, and within seconds are tugged up the taxi strip to your revetment for a quick engine change.[2]

Such destruction of the enemy aircraft had been expressly requested by the U. S. State Department shortly after the appearance of signs of cracks in the façade of Sino-Soviet solidarity. The first occurred August 17 when Chou En-lai and a delegation of military, political, and economic leaders arrived in Moscow on a visit which surprised the world, since it had not been preceded by the customary publicity or pronouncements on its purpose. From the latter, and because of the military and economic specialists accompanying Chou, U. S. Ambassador to Moscow George Kennan deduced that Communist China might be hastily seeking increased military and economic help from Russia. He suggested to Washington that anything the United Nations Command could do "to frighten" Red China into asking for more military aid might be of value. "Something in the nature of an increased military threat or feint might come to good effect," advised Kennan, suggesting that it also be accompanied by a conciliatory move toward Russia, thus providing Stalin with a cease-fire as an alternative to giving more assistance to China. So the aerial war was stepped up, for this, said General Clark, was all he could do while all-out offensives were still prohibited by the U. S. policy to limit the war. It was the Chinese Communist Forces themselves who had to provide the means of punishing themselves on the ground, when, in September–October of 1952, apparently unfrightened by the

United Nations air war, they sent their ground troops smashing into the United Nations lines again.

The objective of the Chinese Communist Forces and their North Korean allies in the fall of 1952 was to seize high ground overlooking the United Nations defense line. That battle line, it will be remembered, had been pushed high above the 38th Parallel in General Van Fleet's fall offensive of the preceding year. It began in the west at Munsan just below the Parallel, ran northeast to its center at the Iron Triangle and the Punchbowl about 20 miles above the line, and thence northeast to Kosong on the Sea of Japan still 20 miles farther above it. North of this battle line, guarding it like sentries, were a number of hill outposts which Van Fleet's men had seized.

In the summer and fall of 1952, after a long military stalemate, the Communists attempted to seize these heights. Stubborn fighting resulted, during which mountain peaks given fanciful names by the troops and newspapermen changed hands frequently. In these battles, the 1st Marine Division fought for Bunker Hill; the 3rd Infantry Division, with attached Greek and Belgian Battalions, defended Big Nori and Kelly Hill; the 2nd Infantry Division and its French Battalion held Old Baldy and Arrowhead Hill; the 7th Infantry Division was on Triangle Hill, the ROK 2nd Division on Sniper Ridge, the ROK Capitol Division on Finger Ridge and Capitol Hill, and the 25th Infantry Division with the Turkish Brigade on Heartbreak Ridge, while the ROK 8th Division was brought to battle in the Punchbowl area. During the summer assaults around these hill bastions the Communists were only moderately successful, but they continued to exert pressure on the United Nations troops until the torrential rains of July–August turned the battle field into the customary mire.

In September the rains stopped and Communist artillery began to fire with remarkable force and accuracy. The Russians had finally delivered the guns and shells, removing one of the enemy's chief defects. On a single day in September alone, a record high of 45,000 shells fell on the United Nations front. Enemy infantrymen were now able to attack behind barrages which kept the United Nations troops pinned down in their trenches and bunkers. But the Communist renewal of battle in September–October came to the same futile end as had previous offensives. Van Fleet's line held fast during fighting distinguished by the efforts of the French Battalion and the U. S. 2nd and 7th Infantry and 1st Marine Divisions. The U. S. 45th Infantry Division—the first National Guard division to come to Korea—also saw action, after relieving the 1st Cavalry Division, which returned to Japan. Most important, the ROK Army emerged as a dependable force. The ROKs held firm in the face of many Chinese attacks and also counterattacked frequently. Thus, after the descent of winter brought an end to the Communist assaults, Van Fleet turned nearly 75 percent of the line over to the South Koreans.

By year's end, Van Fleet had sixteen divisions manning a line resembling the old bunker-and-trench battlefronts of World War II. This force consisted of eleven ROK divisions, one British Commonwealth division and one U. S. Marine and three U. S. Army divisions, with one ROK and three U. S. Army divisions in reserve. Attached to the American divisions were all those battalions and brigades from the other United Nations members with troops in Korea, and there was a regiment of South Korean Marines attached to the U. S. Marine division.

In addition to having his South Koreans well trained and equipped, Van Fleet also possessed one of the finest communications systems ever built in the field. U. S. Army Signal Corps men had overcome the initial handicap of South Korea's shattered communications, building an extensive wire system—supplemented by very high-frequency radio—which ran from Pusan to the front. South Korea's roads and railways were also improved, and the problem of caring for the uprooted civilian population was being met by the United Nations Civil Assistance Command. And so, with the United Nations ground forces holding excellent ground, with the Communists again faltering in their assaults and still being struck by UN air power, General Mark Clark decided that he might as well put an end to the truce-talk travesty at Panmunjom. The conferences were hopelessly stalled by the prisoner exchange deadlock, and each Plenary Session of the full delegations produced its foaming quota of vilification. Here is the Communist statement for September 20, 1952:

It is solely in the interest of a handful of munitions merchants and warmongers of your side that the soldiers of seventeen nations have been driven by your side to come far from their native countries and carry out inhuman destruction and murder against the innocent people of Korea at the cost of their own lives, although people throughout the world who uphold peace and justice, unanimously condemn your side for launching and carrying on this unjust war and demand an early stop to the bloodshed in Korea. And your side has for the interest of that handful of men consistently delayed and even prevented the realization of an armistice in Korea.

The facts of the past fourteen months of the Korean Armistice Negotiations have already inexorably proved and exposed the ferocity and cruelty of an imperialist aggressor which are the true colors of your side.

When your outrageous proposition of forceful retention of war prisoners has gone bankrupt and you can no longer use it as a camouflage to play deceit, your side cannot but resort to vituperation and distortion in these conferences. This only shows how desperate and disreputable—how childish and ridiculous your side has become. . .

To this Major General Harrison replied: "Some of your language this morning is what we civilized countries associate with common criminals or persons who through ignorance or stupidity are unable to speak logically or convincingly."

Eight days later Harrison laid on the table three different plans to guarantee prisoners the freedom of choice in accepting or refusing repatriation. One of these would bring prisoners to the demilitarized zone, where they would be told the position of the Communist and United Nations lines. Then they would be released, free to move in either direction. This was what the Communists said they had done to those 50,000 South Koreans "released at the front." But they rejected this plan, too, and on October 8, Harrison broke off the talks with the remark: "We will meet with you whenever you indicate that you are willing to accept one of our proposals or have presented in writing the text of any constructive proposals, designed to achieve an armistice, which you may desire to make. The plenary sessions now stand in recess."

Six months passed before another meeting was held, and in the meantime, the United States elected its first Republican President since 1932.

Chapter Six

ALTHOUGH the unpopular Korean War did not play as large a part in the defeat of the Democratic candidate, Adlai Stevenson, as did the enormous popularity of the man who defeated him, General Dwight Eisenhower, there certainly was no other issue to characterize the difference between the candidates. Eisenhower, while critical of "the mess in Washington," proposed no radical changes in policy at home or abroad. Stevenson did not repudiate the Administration of Harry Truman, who had decided not to seek re-election. The difference, then, was Eisenhower's popularity aided and abetted by Korea's unpopularity, a distinction made apparent when Eisenhower, acting on the suggestion of his speech writer, Emmett John Hughes, told an audience that if elected: "I will go to Korea." The effect was astonishing. The audience literally erupted with delight. The remark, "I will go to Korea," became the most famous of the campaign, even though the Republican candidate did not say that by going there he expected to end the war or solve the peninsula's problems. More, the American press—almost solidly behind candidate Eisenhower—played endlessly on the theme of the cost of Korea. The New York *World-Telegram and Sun,* for example, began printing the weekly American casualty lists as its leading headline, using "scareheads" eight columns wide and of the size usually reserved for momentous news events.

The damage done the Democrats by the attacks of Senator

Joseph McCarthy, charging the Truman Administration was "soft on Communism," even treasonable, was directly related to the war against Communism in Korea. The slow buildup of the ROK Army also became a campaign issue after the wife of General Van Fleet allowed one of her husband's embittered private letters on the subject to get into the hands of candidate Eisenhower, who accused the Truman Administration of failing to exploit all opportunities in Korea. The Joint Chiefs of Staff replied, on the eve of the November election, with an order to Van Fleet calling for activation of two more ROK divisions. And yet, as much as the Korean War was an issue in the 1952 Presidential election, there were very few voices raised in support of General MacArthur's policy of extending the war to the Chinese mainland. The theme, "In war there is no substitute for victory," was quietly buried in the Republican Convention, along with one of its outstanding proponents and Eisenhower's chief opponent, Senator Robert Taft.

After his election—by a vote of 33,936,252 to 27,314,992—President-elect Eisenhower did go to Korea, but only to fulfill his campaign promise; not, as he repeatedly warned, to find a "trick solution" to the problem. He arrived there on December 2, 1952, and spent three days conferring with Generals Clark and Van Fleet, reviewing ROK troops, visiting American and UN units, and talking with President Rhee. At the end of his visit, Eisenhower said: "How difficult it seems to be in a war of this kind to work out a plan that would bring a positive end and definite victory without possibly running the grave risk of enlarging the war."

Plainly, he had rejected the MacArthur alternative, and had decided to follow the Truman Administration's policy of seeking an honorable truce, and later full peace, while standing firm against forcible repatriation of prisoners. On this issue, he would later say: ". . . To force those people to go back to a life of terror and persecution is something that would violate every moral standard by which America lives. Therefore, it would be unacceptable to the American code, and it cannot be done."

Still, wrote Robert Donovan, the chronicler of Eisenhower's first term in the White House, "The President wanted to liquidate the war. He wanted to halt the drain of American power in a peripheral conflict that offered no hope of decision in the struggle against Communism." To do so, the new President decided to harden the stiffening U. S. attitude toward Communist China. On December 14, 1952, he said: ". . . We face an enemy whom we cannot hope to impress by words, however eloquent, but only by deeds—executed under the circumstances of our own choosing." Talking informally to reporters, he expanded on this theme: "Because you know, my friends, just because one side wants peace doesn't make peace. We must go ahead and do things that induce the others to want peace also."

The things which Eisenhower planned to do could not be done until he assumed office in early January of 1953. Enunciation of them did not begin until his first State of the Union message on February 3. Before then, what was perhaps the queerest war in history had entered another new phase.

Between the onset of winter in November–December of 1952 and the arrival of the spring of 1953, the Korean battlefront was characterized by artillery exchanges, sporadic small-scale fighting, constant patrolling, and a propaganda war carried on through loudspeakers set up at the front by both sides. On one side, the Chinese and North Koreans occupied their honeycombed hillsides, on the other United Nations troops sat out the winter in bunkers or in the trenches of the outposts. Both sides sent out patrols to see what the other side was doing, but sometimes the men of these patrols were more interested in listening to the other side's loudspeakers. Such scouting parties have been described by a Marine rifleman, Martin Russ, in his book *The Last Parallel.*

> We blackened our faces and hands and departed 1 A.M. . . .
> . . . We were halfway between check point two and the base of Old Bunker when a loudspeaker began blaring. It was located far to the east probably on the hill known as Siberia in front of the Charlie company sector. As usual, we only heard parts of the program but it was so interesting that we halted and lay down close beside the dike and listened. One isolated phrase sticks in my mind as one of the typical comic-book phrases: "Ike is one of the leaders who could bring about peace in Korea; but, like the rest of the big-money boys, he is not interested in peace."

A woman sang a song, a very sentimental one but quite moving. "The Last Rose of Summer." I looked back at the other three men and could see the outline of their brush-covered helmets. They were listening, too, not aware of each other, and maybe for a moment unaware of the surroundings. When the song ended, a woman said, "Did you enjoy my song, marine? If so, then fire your rifle twice and I will sing another." A wag on the MLR fired an extremely long burst from a machine gun. It echoed for several seconds. A few miles to the east, in the Army sector, five or six parachute flares hovered above the mountains. Artillery rumbled in the distance, a kind of muffled thunder. . . .[1]

The war had become so stabilized that many of the units began to regard their own positions on the line with a proprietary eye. The rights of possession were proclaimed on signs springing up everywhere. A visitor to Korea, perhaps one of those junketing Congressmen who seemed to proliferate as the war dragged on, would enter this sector "by courtesy" of this division, cross this bridge "by courtesy" of this engineering battalion, or even enter this latrine "by courtesy" of some rear-rank private with the good rifleman's earthy sense of humor. Congressmen rarely reached the ultimate sign, on which, beneath a macabre skull and crossbones, was printed the warning:

CAUTION
THIS IS THE M.L.R.
THE REDS DIRECT TRAFFIC FROM THIS POINT.

Sometimes huge billboards were used to drive home a point of safety to the troops, who were still reluctant to wear the new —and heavy—bulletproof vests, to say nothing of the armored shorts. The 25th Division tacked up a torn armored vest over the words:

THIS VEST SAVED A MAN'S LIFE. WEAR YOURS!

In the Marine sector, the risky habit of walking against the skyline in silhouette for enemy snipers was discouraged by a bullet-riddled helmet hung on a cross above the epitaph:

HERE LIES THE BODY OF CORPORAL JOE BLOW
HE WALKED ON THE SKYLINE. HAVA NO.

In such dull, yet apprehensive times, the men naturally talked of home, of Rest and Rehabilitation in Japan, or of the Big R—rotation home. Frequently, elaborate precautions would be taken to protect a man about to reach the year of combat duty which would put him on the homebound ship. One night Corporal Charles Gordon of Liberty, Mississippi, led a patrol into enemy territory. Halfway out, his radioman overtook him and said: "I just talked to the CO. He says for you to lay down right where you are and wait for the patrol to come back. That's orders. You're going home tomorrow."

Even with rotation, the strength of the United Nations forces rose to 768,000 men. The arrival of the U. S. 40th Infantry Division—another National Guard unit—increased the American contribution to seven 20,000-man U. S. Army divisions and one even larger U. S. Marine division. The South Koreans had twelve 10,000-man divisions, the British Commonwealth Nations one 15,000-man division, the Turks one 5,000-man brigade, and the remaining nations from 1,000 to 1,500 men apiece, distributed among the U. S. divisions. The thousands upon thousands of service, supply and security troops which kept this force in the field were American.

Opposing the UN force of three-quarters of a million was a Communist Army of well over a million men. Of these, 270,000 soldiers manned the first line of defense, while an estimated 531,000 were deployed in reserve behind them. The rest were logistics and security troops. More than three-fourths of this force was Chinese, and the Chinese Communists occupied a similar proportion of the entire Communist line. The North Koreans held only the eastern quarter from the Kum River to the Sea of Japan.

Lieutenant General James Van Fleet still thought he could defeat this Communist host, when, after twenty-two months in Korea, he was relieved of his command to go into retirement. The new commander was Lieutenant General Maxwell Taylor, then U. S. Deputy Chief of Staff for Operations and Administration. Taylor, tall, handsome, a paratrooper and an aggressive leader like Ridgway and Van Fleet, had been assistant commander of the 82nd Airborne in Italy and later commanded the 101st Airborne Division in France. Taylor took charge of Eighth Army and the ROKs on February 11, 1953,

while Van Fleet, by then a supporter of the bellicose Syngman Rhee, announced to reporters that his forces had been
strong enough to wage a successful offensive against the Communists. This statement angered General Mark Clark in
Tokyo, who declared that the UN Command had never possessed sufficient strength to wage such a campaign. But Van
Fleet's remarks found support in the United States, chiefly
among those Republican conservatives who had been President
Truman's chief critics, and whose demands that the United
States "get tough with Red China" were not silenced by the
presence of a fellow Republican in the White House.

But the United States had already gotten "tough with Red
China," and this, coupled with the death of Premier Joseph
Stalin, had wrought a great change in the Communist camp.

One of the Truman Administration's last acts on the world
stage was to warn Red China that its patience in Korea was
not inexhaustible. During the fall of 1952, U. S. Ambassador
to India Chester Bowles told Indian diplomats that extension
of the war was inevitable unless a solution was reached soon.
Bowles suggested that India take the lead in finding an end to
the problem, and so India sought to end the prisoner exchange
deadlock by introducing a compromise proposal in the United
Nations.

The Indian plan upheld the American principle of no forced
repatriation, while accepting the Communist notion that the
fate of those who refused to go home should be decided at
the peace conference to be held after an armistice. India proposed:

1. All prisoners held by both sides would be taken to the
   Demilitarized Zone and released to a neutral commission
   of five nations.
2. All prisoners who told the commission they wanted to go
   home would be immediately repatriated.
3. Decision on those still in the commission's custody after
   ninety days would be referred to the peace conference,
   which, as both sides already had agreed, was to be held
   ninety days after the armistice. The peace conference would
   therefore get the prisoner issue as soon as it began.

4. If, after thirty days, the peace conference had not settled the problem of non-repatriates, the prisoners would be turned over to the United Nations for resettlement. Meanwhile, the United Nations would always have the power to block any attempt at the peace conference to impose forcible repatriation.

Neither side thought highly of the proposal. The Communists still held out for forcible repatriation, while the United States thought that to refer the prisoner matter to the peace conference would be futile, to say nothing of the cruelty of forcing non-repatriates to wait four months to learn their fate. Still, the United States said it would vote for the plan. On December 1, 1952, despite the violent opposition of the Communist bloc, the UN Political Committee adopted India's proposal. But this was merely an empty formality. All hope of Communist acceptance had already been doomed by Andrei Vishinsky's denunciation of India for having "joined" the free world camp by accepting the principle of no forced repatriation. Peiping and Pyongyang Radio followed suit, and official rejection of any proposal which did not include forced repatriation was quick in coming.

It was after this that President-elect Eisenhower returned from Korea, openly determined to continue the rebuilding of the ROK Army, making broad hints at increased use of force. On February 2, 1953, President Eisenhower delivered his famous State of the Union message in which he said:

> In June, 1950, following the aggressive attack on the Republic of Korea, the United States Seventh Fleet was instructed both to prevent attack upon Formosa and also to insure that Formosa should not be used as a base of operations against the Chinese Communist mainland.
>
> This has meant, in effect, that the United States Navy was required to serve as a defensive arm of Communist China. Regardless of the situation in 1950, since the date of that order the Chinese Communists have invaded Korea to attack the United Nations forces there. They have consistently rejected the proposals of the United Nations Command for an armistice. They recently joined Soviet Russia in rejecting the armistice proposal sponsored in the United Nations by the Government of India. This

proposal has been accepted by the United States and fifty-three other nations.

Consequently, there is no longer any logic or sense in a condition that required the United States Navy to assume defensive responsibilities on behalf of the Chinese Communists, thus permitting those Communists, with greater impunity, to kill our soldiers and those of our United Nations allies in Korea.

I am, therefore, issuing instructions that the Seventh Fleet no longer be employed to shield Communist China. Permit me to make crystal clear this order implies no aggressive intent on our part. But we certainly have no obligation to protect a nation fighting us in Korea.

There were unexpected reactions to Eisenhower's decision. Britain's Foreign Secretary Anthony Eden said "it might have very unfortunate political repercussions" and India's Prime Minister Nehru thought it intensified "the fear psychosis of the world." Many American conservatives, however, were delighted at the description of the U. S. Seventh Fleet as "a defensive arm of Communist China," just as many Democrats were outraged by it. Actually the Seventh Fleet had been helping Chiang Kai-shek maintain contact with guerrillas on the mainland. Apart from this artful dig, suggesting that Eisenhower was not at all the amateur politician he professed himself to be, it would seem that the President's real intention was to make the Chinese Communists fear invasion from Formosa. Both Eisenhower and Dulles believed that the Chinese Communists would come to terms in Korea if they became convinced that the alternative to stalemate there would be increased American military action against them on other fronts. It was also hoped that the "de-neutralizing" of the Seventh Fleet would cause Peiping to deploy opposite Formosa units which might otherwise be used in Korea.

This last result was achieved, for there is evidence that the Communist Chinese did siphon off men and arms to the mainland opposite Formosa. How successful it was psychologically is another of those questions which only Communists themselves can answer.

On the diplomatic front, the new American Administration made one last effort to break the deadlock by taking advantage of a two-month-old resolution adopted by the Executive Committee of the League of Red Cross Societies, which called for an exchange of sick and wounded prisoners in Korea. The U. S. State Department, planning to have a similar resolution introduced in the United Nations, asked the Joint Chiefs of Staff to put this proposition to the Communists, and on February 22, 1953, General Mark Clark addressed such an offer to Premier Kim Il Sung and General Peng Teh-huai.

The Communist reply was silence. It seemed that the American effort to renew negotiations had failed, until, on March 5, the Moscow radio made this simple announcement:

> The heart of the comrade and inspired continuer of Lenin's will, the wise leader and teacher of the Communist Party and the Soviet People—Josef Vissarionovich Stalin—has stopped beating.

The Communist world was turned upside down. The death of its leader removed from the world the man who had probably ordered the invasion of South Korea and may also have coaxed or coerced Communist China into opposing the United Nations on the battlefield. In his place stood Georgi Malenkov, apparently supported by the eventual power in Soviet Russia, Nikita Khrushchev. And just as Malenkov did not have Stalin's appetite for foreign lands, so Nikita Khrushchev was to be the author of the revolutionary theory of peaceful coexistence which was to divide the Communist world. Standing senior to Malenkov in Communist history was China's Mao Tse-tung. Now, the rest of the world asked itself, would Mao continue to waste his treasure in Korea for Malenkov? Would Malenkov continue a blunder which had succeeded in uniting the Western world, as well as fulfilling, along with the formation of NATO, the old Russian dread of being ringed by hostile bases? The answer—if answer it was—came on March 28. On that date, Premier Kim and General Peng replied to General Clark's forgotten proposal for an exchange of sick and wounded. They agreed unconditionally, and said:

> At the same time, we consider that the reasonable settlement of the question of exchanging sick and injured prisoners of war of both sides during the period of hostilities should be made to lead to the smooth settlement of the entire question of prisoners

of war, thereby achieving an armistice in Korea for which people throughout the world are longing. Therefore, our side proposes that the delegates for armistice negotiations of both sides immediately resume the negotiations at Panmunjom.

On March 30, Foreign Minister Chou En-lai, returning from Stalin's funeral in Moscow—where it is believed he argued China's case for ending the war—announced that men who refused repatriation might "be handed over to a neutral state and that explanations be given them by the parties concerned, thus ensuring that the question of their repatriation will be justly settled and will not obstruct the realization of an armistice in Korea." Although Chou insisted that Red China did not recognize the fact that any prisoners had actually refused repatriation, his remarks were the most encouraging yet made on the prisoner issue. More encouragement came after Soviet Foreign Minister V. M. Molotov endorsed Chou's statement on April 10. And so, on April 16, Rear Admiral John Daniel met Major General Lee Sang Cho at Panmunjom to begin liaison talks. Relations were unusually cordial, or at least comparatively so, the single, slight outburst coming when Admiral Daniel called the Communist figure of about 600 ailing UN troops "incredibly small."

Still, on April 11 it was agreed that each side exchange sick and wounded prisoners, and on April 20, the exchange known as Operation Little Switch began, lasting until April 26. During it the United Nations handed over 5,194 North Koreans, 1,030 Chinese and 446 North Korean civilian internees, or a total of 6,670 sick and wounded prisoners. The Communists returned 684 United Nations prisoners, among them 471 South Koreans, 149 Americans, 32 British, 15 Turks, 6 Colombians, 5 Australians, 2 Canadians, and 1 Greek, 1 South African, 1 Filipino, and 1 Netherlander. From tales told by the American soldiers released, the U. S. Army was able to confirm an unpleasant suspicion which had been held since the days around Pusan. This was that a shocking number of American prisoners had been cooperating with their Communist captors. But details of this were to be withheld until the Army could make its own investigations following the final Operation Big Switch which occurred three months later.

In the meantime, armistice negotiations were renewed at Panmunjom on April 27. The Communists appeared to be retreating slightly from their heretofore unbudging stand on forcible repatriation, although General Nam Il repeated Chou's proposal that non-repatriates be handed over to a neutral state for "explanation." Hope for peace rose again throughout the world, only to be shattered once more by the spectacular revolt of South Korea's President Syngman Rhee.

Chapter Seven

THE single passionate purpose of Syngman Rhee was to build a free and democratic state in Korea. It had inspired him as a radical young republican in the days before the Japanese occupation, it had nourished him during the long years of exile, and it had burned even more fiercely within him when, in 1945, he returned to Korea to lead the southern half of his now-partitioned homeland. For partition meant to Syngman Rhee that before he built his free and democratic Korea, he must first unify the country.

From 1945 onward, Rhee had made it clear that he considered force the only means of unifying Korea. Communism and freedom had collided in Korea and war between them was inevitable. For this reason, he had opposed the unsuccessful unification talks between the United States and the Soviet Union in 1946. After his election as president of the Republic of Korea in 1948, he spoke openly of "liberating" the North from Communism. It was because the United States feared that Rhee might touch off World War III that heavy weapons and planes had been withheld from the ROK Army, while the repeated rattling of Rhee's saber had given North Korea the pretext for its invasion.

When the armistice talks began, Rhee had sent an observer,

but he had publicly predicted failure. He did not believe that "peaceful political means" employed after an armistice would do anything but harden the military stalemate and continue the division of his country, and in this history has surely demonstrated his acumen. Throughout the truce talks, President Rhee insisted that the Communists must be fought to the finish and no Chinese allowed to remain in Korea. He was happiest when the talks were in recess or deadlocked because, finally, an armistice was abhorrent to him. This was why, amid the hope renewed by Operation Little Switch and the impending resumption of talks at Panmunjom, President Syngman Rhee made his last desperate effort to block a truce.

On April 24, three days before the return of both sides to Panmunjom, the Korean Ambassador in Washington advised President Eisenhower that President Rhee would withdraw the ROK Army from the UN Command if any armistice was signed permitting Chinese Communist troops to remain in Korea. Rhee's move brought General Clark to Seoul from Tokyo. Clark tried to convince Rhee of the futility of trying to get the Chinese out of Korea by demanding it, after having spent two and a half years unsuccessfully seeking to force them out at gunpoint. But Clark's visit was inconclusive. Rhee, in effect, promised nothing. Three days later Rhee wrote to Clark that he would agree to an armistice if the United Nations set up a buffer strip of land *north* of the Yalu and Tumen Rivers—in other words, in Chinese and Russian territory. Rhee, of course, knew how impossible such an outrageous demand was, but, like the Communists, he knew that an impossible price had bargaining value. At the same time, Rhee opened his public campaign against an armistice, calling a press conference to say:

> ... We feel that so long as the Chinese Communists remain in Korea we cannot survive. For the last five months we have been receiving information that strongly advises us that unless the Chinese leave we should never accept any armistice or peace. . . . Any armistice or truce that fails to force the Chinese to leave the country is unthinkable and cannot be accepted by us.
>
> According to the Indian resolution [in the United Nations] those prisoners—Korean and Chinese who do not wish to return —should be sent to a third country like Sweden or Switzerland

and kept there pending a final decision of their fate. But we have to insist that Korean war prisoners be kept in Korea.

These, then, were Rhee's two main objections: that the Chinese Communists would remain in North Korea during the armistice and that North Korean prisoners refusing repatriation would be shipped to a neutral country where Communists would "explain" to them why they should return to Communism.

On May 7, the Communists at Panmunjom offered an eight-point armistice plan that resembled the Indian Resolution which they had flatly rejected more than five months earlier. It dropped insistence on shipping prisoners from Korea to a neutral nation, thus removing one of Rhee's objections to the armistice. But it differed from the Indian Resolution in other ways which Rhee might find even more repugnant.

First, the Neutral Nations Repatriation Commission was to include India in addition to Sweden and Switzerland, already proposed by the United Nations, and the Communist nations of Poland and Czechoslovakia. Rhee detested India as a pro-Communist state parading as a "neutral."

Second, these nations were to furnish troops of their own to guard the non-repatriate prisoners at existing prison camps within *South Korea.*

Third, political agents from Red China and North Korea, as well as the Communist Czech and Polish members from the Commission, were to be allowed to visit the prisoners to persuade them to return. With them would go Communist newsmen, that is, agents themselves, such as Winnington and Burchett.

Finally, it rejected the Indian Resolution's point that if the post-armistice political conference did not settle a prisoner's destiny, the United Nations should be allowed to. The Communist plan insisted that the Political Conference was the final authority.

Nevertheless, the Communist offer *had* dropped insistence on shipping the prisoners out of Korea and it was absolutely devoid of such phrases as "irrevocable opposition" to voluntary repatriation. The United Nations Command did not reject it, rather subjecting the Communist negotiators to a series of

376

questions intended to discover how much closer the Communists might come to the Indian Resolution, which was now the official U. S. stand. Syngman Rhee was enraged, and his anger has been described by General Clark:

> On May 12 I called on President Rhee again and explained my government's position. I found him angrier and more anti-Armistice than ever. He declared he would never let this crowd of potential spies, saboteurs and agitators into his rear areas, and I couldn't blame him. As UN Commander, they were my rear areas, too.
>
> Then he brought up another objection which was to be most troublesome in the hectic weeks to follow. He said he would not permit any Indian troops on ROK soil as neutrals or anything else. He said that rather than countenance the presence of Indian troops in his country he might, on his own, release the non-repatriates "without involving the UN Command." This was the first positive storm warning of what was to come. I reminded Rhee that the ROK security troops guarding the prisoners were under my command and that for him to take such unilateral action would be contrary to his pledge, even though I previously had recommended the release of the non-repatriates.[1]

Nevertheless, Clark was impressed. He notified Washington that Rhee was determined both to release the non-repatriates if need be, and to prevent the entry of Communists or Indians into South Korea. Clark recommended that the United Nations Command insist that non-repatriates be discharged as civilians at the time of the armistice, giving as his reasons Rhee's determination to do that himself and the Communists' own "release at the front" of 50,000 South Korean soldiers now impressed in their own forces.

Washington replied that the United Nations Command could insist on this only as an *initial* position from which to bargain. Obviously, Washington wanted to do two things: beat down objectionable demands in the Communist offer with an objectional demand of its own, that same demand to serve double duty by placating Syngman Rhee. But the placation was to be *temporary*. It was to be, as the soldiers on the line in Korea would say, a "sympathy card."

On May 13 General Harrison presented a lengthy counter-proposal to the Communist offer, suggesting that only Indian troops be used to guard the non-repatriates while refusing to accept the Political Conference as the final arbiter of a prisoner's destiny. But it also made that *initial* demand that only 22,-000 Chinese prisoners be turned over to the Repatriation Commission. The 35,000 North Koreans would be released as civilians, free to choose either South or North Korea.

General Nam Il angrily branded this as "a step backward," and so it must have seemed. He resumed his tirades, and after three days of them Harrison recessed the talks until May 20. Another five-day recess was obtained, at the direction of Washington, while the United States and its allies in the United Nations worked out their final stand. This withdrew the demand that 35,000 North Koreans be discharged as civilians, and agreed that they, too, should be handed over to the Neutral Nations Repatriation Commission. On May 24, while General Harrison read the new proposal to the Communists at Panmunjom, General Clark came to Seoul to persuade Rhee to accept it.

What we offered Rhee was this: early announcement by the sixteen United Nations that had fought against Communism in Korea of a joint policy which guaranteed that all sixteen nations would band together against the Reds should the Communists violate the truce in Korea. Included in this proposed policy statement was the most important proviso that if the Communists broke the truce the sixteen nations might not confine their retaliatory efforts to Korea.

Unilaterally the United States promised to build up the ROK Army to twenty divisions, with appropriate air and naval strength. This was quite a promise, for it costs between 150 and 200 million dollars to equip a ROK division and supply it in combat for one year. The United States also promised Rhee economic rehabilitation of his country, a billion-dollar project at least, and further assured him that American troops would be kept on the alert in and near Korea until peace was established firmly.

In return for this we asked Rhee to co-operate with the armistice negotiations, refrain from agitation against the talks and go along with the agreement once it was signed.

378

Above all, Rhee was asked to leave his armed forces in my UN Command.

The emotional effect of this on Rhee was profound. I had never seen him so disturbed. He sat bolt upright in his chair, the muscles of his face twitched occasionally and he kept rubbing the ends of his fingers, which, I had heard, had been burned by Japanese secret police in the early days of his fight for Korean independence. Once he broke into our recital of our plans and promises and said:

"I am deeply disappointed. Your government changes its position often. You pay no attention to the view of the ROK Government."

As it became increasingly clear that an armistice was a distinct probability and that Rhee's lifelong goal of an independent and undivided Korea had to be pushed into a future he might not live to see, the President became overwrought.

"One thing we must insist upon is the withdrawal of Chinese Communists from our territory," he said. "There can be no peaceful settlement without that. Your threats have no effect upon me. We want to live. We want to survive. We will decide our own fate. Sorry, I cannot assure President Eisenhower of my co-operation under the circumstances."[2]

Thereafter Rhee informed the United States Government that he would cooperate with the armistice in return for: (1) An irrevocable pledge that the United States would help South Korea unify Korea by force if the Political Conference failed to do so. (2) An agreement to renew the war if the Political Conference failed to make a settlement after ninety days. Such terms were impossible, more so if it was believed in Washington—as would seem likely—that the Political Conference would fail and the armistice would ossify the division of Korea and perpetuate an armed truce. On June 6, President Eisenhower wrote to Rhee:

The moment has now come when we must decide whether to carry on by warfare a struggle for the unification of Korea or whether to pursue this goal by political and other methods.

The enemy has proposed an armistice which involves a clear abandonment of the fruits of aggression. The armistice would leave the Republic of Korea in undisputed possession of substantially the territory which the Republic administered prior to the aggression, indeed this territory will be somewhat enlarged.

The proposed armistice, true to the principle of political asylum, assures that the thousands of North Koreans and Communist Chinese prisoners in our hands, who have seen liberty and who wish to share it, will have the opportunity to do so and will not be forcibly sent back into Communist areas. . . .

It is my profound conviction that under these circumstances acceptance of the armistice is required of the United Nations and the Republic of Korea. We would not be justified in prolonging the war with all the misery that it involves in the hope of achieving by force the unification of Korea.

The unification of Korea is an end to which the United States is committed, not once but many times. . . . Korea is, unhappily, not the only country which remains divided after World War II. We remain determined to play our part in achieving the political union of all countries so divided.

But we do not intend to employ war as an instrument to accomplish the world-wide political settlements to which we are dedicated. . . . It was indeed a crime that those who attacked from the North invoked violence to unite Korea under their rule. Not only as your official friend but as a personal friend I urge that your country not embark upon a similar course.

In exchange for Rhee's cooperation, Eisenhower offered these commitments:

1. The United States will not renounce its efforts by all peaceful means to effect the unification of Korea. . . .

2. I am prepared promptly after the conclusion and acceptance of an armistice to negotiate with you a mutual defense treaty along the lines of the treaties heretofore made between the United States and the Philippines, and the United States and Australia and New Zealand. You may recall that both of these treaties speak of "the development of a more comprehensive system of regional security in the Pacific area." A security pact between the United States and the Republic of Korea would be a further step in that direction. . . .

3. The United States Government, subject to requisite Congressional appropriations, will be prepared to continue economic

aid to the Republic of Korea which will permit in peace a restoration of its devastated land.

Rhee rejected these as well, declaring: "A truce on the present terms simply means death to us. We have consistently demanded that Chinese Communist forces should be driven out of our territory [meaning all Korea], even if in so doing, we have to fight by ourselves." Rhee's representative at Panmunjom, Major General Choe Duk Shin, had already boycotted the truce talks, and now the South Korean National Assembly voted unanimously against the truce terms, while antitruce demonstrations were held in Seoul and other cities.

Nevertheless, with all of South Korea seemingly chanting "Never! Never! Never!" the delegations of both sides met secretly at Panmunjom and signed the agreement on prisoner exchange. It proposed, in substance:

1. All prisoners who sought repatriation would be returned home immediately.
2. Those who refused repatriation would be taken to the Demilitarized Zone between the two sides and placed in custody of the Neutral Nations Repatriation Commission, of which India was to be the umpire and sole provider of troops for the custodial force.
3. For the next ninety days "explanation teams" from the nations involved would be allowed to talk to the prisoners—under the eyes of the Neutral Nations members and representatives of both sides—in an attempt to persuade them to come home. Those who changed their minds would be repatriated immediately.
4. After this the Political Conference would try to settle the question of those still refusing repatriation.
5. If the Political Conference failed to settle this in thirty days, the Neutral Nations would discharge the non-repatriate prisoners as free civilians, as well as help them to settle in homelands of their choice.

Thus, four months after the armistice, men who still refused repatriation would not have to accept it. By this agreement, the dispute of eighteen months' duration was at an end, and the United States' principle of voluntary repatriation had triumphed. All that remained after June 8 was to work out the details and to establish a Demilitarized Zone by instructing both sides to withdraw two kilometers (about a mile and a quarter) from their present positions. Peace in Korea, it seemed, was a few details away.

But Syngman Rhee did not drop his agitation against the truce terms, and his reiterated threats to "go it alone" against the Communist Chinese began to disturb both sides. General Clark visited Rhee again and wrote to him frequently, meanwhile taking steps to guard against the possibility of Rhee's withdrawing the ROK Army from his command, though he believed that Rhee was bluffing in his other threat to release the North Korean prisoners on his own. The Chinese Communists responded on the night of June 13–14 by throwing their strongest attack in two years against the center-east sector of the line held by the ROK 5th and 8th Divisions, driving them back and thereby seeming to demonstrate to Rhee what would happen to his forces if he tried to carry out his threats. President Eisenhower, meanwhile, made the supreme gesture by secretly inviting Rhee to the White House to talk things over. Rhee declined. Eisenhower was prepared for the next-best offer, the dispatch of Secretary of State John Foster Dulles to Seoul, until Dulles persuaded him that Walter Robertson, Assistant Secretary of State for Far Eastern Affairs, should go in his place. On June 17, Rhee agreed to receive Robertson. Slowly, official Washington let out its breath. At Panmunjom that June 17, the truce line had been fixed and the details now to be handled were those of the ceremony at which the armistice agreement was to be signed.

The following day [wrote General Clark] all hell broke loose, by Rhee's order. It was June 18. At six o'clock in the morning I was awakened with the news that what we had feared was happening. During the night, on orders from Rhee, ROK guards at anti-Communist prison camps all over South Korea had opened the gates and some 25,000 prisoners walked out and lost themselves among the civilian population. During the following few nights another 2,000 were released, boosting the total to 27,000 Korean POWs freed in a dramatic, well-planned operation.

Everyone concerned in the mass release was well briefed. The prisoners knew when they would go, what to take, where to shed and burn their prison garb, where to get civilian clothing and where to hide. South Korean police were instructed on what they were to do to help the fugitives. As the break was under way high ROK officials broadcast the news to the country. The people were told to take care of the men from the prison camps. The people did. They took them into their homes. South Korean police stood watch to warn of the approach of American soldiers on a manhunt for the prisoners.

There were many stories of the reception the South Korean people gave the prisoners, stories that supported the idea that although the ROKs ordered demonstrations, the demonstrators more often than not believed in the slogans they were instructed to chant. The South Koreans welcomed the prisoners as heroes, brought out the best in food, drink and tobacco. Even South Koreans who disagreed with Rhee and were fearful of the consequences expressed great pride in the daring of the release. All signs indicated Rhee reached a new high of popularity among his people the day of the big release.[3]

But throughout the world the popularity of Syngman Rhee reached its nadir. Denunciations arrived from every quarter, while in Washington, Dulles was dumfounded and the President astonished and upset. Washington's first reaction was to cancel Walter Robertson's visit to Seoul, while Dulles issued a statement designed to placate the infuriated Communists by saying:

> This action was in violation of the authority of the United Nations Command to which the Republic of Korea agreed. On behalf of the United Nations we have conducted our negotiations for an armistice in good faith and we have acted and are acting in good faith.

The Chinese Communists reacted exactly as had been anticipated. On June 20, they broke off the armistice talks with this letter from Premier Kim Il Sung and General Peng Teh-huai to General Clark:

> In view of the extremely serious consequences of this incident, we cannot but put the following questions to your side: Is the United Nations Command able to control the South Korean government and army? If not, does the armistice in Korea include the Syngman Rhee clique? If it is not included, what assurance

is there for the implementation of the Armistice Agreement on the part of South Korea? If it is included, then your side must be responsible for recovering immediately all . . . prisoners of war who are now "at liberty," that is, those who are "released" and retained under coercion and to be press-ganged into the South Korean Army.

On June 29, in a letter proposing resumption of the armistice talks, General Mark Clark replied that "you undoubtedly realize that the recovery of all these prisoners would be as impossible for us as it would be for your side to recover the fifty thousand South Korean prisoners 'released' by your side during the course of hostilities."

And so the Communists made a propaganda harvest of the incident, while Rhee, appealed to personally by Eisenhower, informed by an indignant Mark Clark that he would get no U. S. military help in a loner attack on the Communists, bereft of support among the American conservatives, gradually began to soften his opposition to the truce. The Robertson mission to Seoul was rescheduled and the tall, soft-spoken American diplomat arrived in the South Korean capital on June 26.

Robertson conferred with Rhee daily until July 11, patiently hearing the passionate old man out, but returning again and again to his purpose of gaining the South Korean president's agreement to the armistice. Finally, Rhee agreed, but on these conditions:

1. Promise of an American-ROK Mutual Security Pact after the armistice (such a pact having to be ratified by the U. S. Senate).
2. Long-term economic aid with a first installment of $200,-000,000, plus distribution of $9,500,000 in food to the Korean people immediately with the signing of the armistice.
3. Agreement that if the Political Conference produced no results in ninety days, the United States and South Korea would withdraw to discuss plans of their own for unifying the country.
4. Agreement to expand the ROK Army to 20 divisions.
5. Agreement to hold high-level American-ROK talks before the Political Conference.

In return, Syngman Rhee promised that he would no longer obstruct the armistice.

Meanwhile, the Communists, having carefully followed the Rhee-Robertson talks, had replied favorably to Clark's letter of June 29, saying on July 8:

> ... Although our side is not entirely satisfied with the reply of your side, yet in view of the indication of the desire of your side to strive for an early armistice and in view of the assurances given by your side, our side agrees that the delegations of both sides meet at an appointed time to discuss the question of implementation of the Armistice Agreement and the various preparations prior to the signing of the Armistice.

On July 10, 1953, the second anniversary of the start of truce talks in the teahouse at Kaesong, the plenary sessions were resumed. They proceeded without hindrance, although on July 13, in what General Mark Clark called a "politically inspired" offensive, five Chinese Communist armies struck savagely at three ROK Divisions holding the Kumsong Bulge between the Iron Triangle and the Punchbowl. It was a far larger attack than the assault of June 13–14, and the purpose was to show Rhee again how futile any South Korean fight against Red China would be. To make their point, the Communists were willing to lose 72,000 men, 25,000 of them killed. The ground gained was useless and had almost no effect on the military position when the armistice was finally signed.

The historic signing took place on July 27, 1953, at Panmunjom. Once again, there was discord. The Communists attempted to nail blue-and-white Picasso "peace doves"—a familiar Communist propaganda symbol—over the entrances to the building in which the signing was to take place. Colonel Murray demanded that the doves be taken down. Then it turned out that Premier Kim Il Sung, like his deceased mentor, Joseph Stalin, had qualms about public appearances. He would not come to Panmunjom to sign with General Mark Clark unless all South Koreans and Chinese Nationalists were barred from the village and all newsmen kept away from the signing ceremony. The United Nations refused. So neither Kim nor Clark came to Panmunjom.

At ten in the morning of July 27, 1953, Lieutenant General William Harrison and Lieutenant General Nam Il silently led their delegations into the "peace pagoda" made of tar paper and straw mat. They sat behind a straight row of tables. They signed eighteen copies of the armistice agreement, nine of which were covered in United Nations blue, nine in Communist red. Ten minutes later they arose and walked out.

They had spoken not a word to each other.

Twelve hours later, with the silencing of the guns, the Korean War was over.

Chapter Eight

THE end of fighting in Korea at ten o'clock on the night of July 27, 1953, did not cause rejoicing throughout the world. There was only relief. It was as though a man, having had a boil lanced, felt suddenly soothed, in the next moment forgetting the boil and all its aching history. More, if such relief had given way to fresh irritation at the discovery that another boil was on the way, the analogy would still hold—for the mounting conflict between the free world and the Communists in Indo-China was indeed producing a second sore spot on the surface of the world. The beginning of the climactic fight in Indo-China —the Battle of Dienbienphu—was only four months away from the cease-fire in Korea.

No, there was neither joy nor sorrow in either camp, for there had been neither victory nor defeat. Even the Communists, having made a feeble attempt to proclaim the armistice as a triumph, shortly afterward lapsed into silence. And the mood of the free world was best expressed by President Eisenhower's remark: "The war is over and I hope my son is going to come home soon."

Many, many sons were not coming home, for the Korean War

was not, as is sometimes supposed, a small brush-fire war. An estimated total of nearly 1,820,000 men were killed and wounded in Korea, of which the Communists suffered about 1,420,000. According to U. S. Defense Department estimates, the Chinese Communists lost 900,000 dead and wounded, while the North Koreans lost 520,000 dead and wounded. Of the United Nations losses of 150,000 dead and 250,000 wounded, the South Koreans suffered the most. These figures, too, have to be estimated, inasmuch as the Republic of Korea Defense Ministry has not issued military casualty figures. The combined ROK civilian-military losses were 415,004 dead and 428,568 wounded, with no figures for missing soldiers such as the 50,-000 known to have been impressed into the Communist forces. Of these totals, it can be estimated that between one-fifth and one-quarter were military, or about 100,000 dead and 100,000 wounded. American battle losses in Korea were 33,629 dead and 103,284 wounded. No other nation among the United Nations allies suffered as many as 1,000 dead.

The actual cost of the war is not known, and it would be absurd to try to estimate it. Suffice it to say that the North Korean countryside was laid waste, South Korea was shattered, and Seoul alone suffered the ruin befalling any great city unfortunate enough to be conquered and liberated twice. In South Korea there were 3,700,000 people made fugitive by the war, 400,000 of whom had fled North Korea. Something like 400,000 homes were destroyed up and down the peninsula. And to all this must be added the treasure which Soviet Russia and the United States, and to a lesser degree her United Nations allies, poured out on Korea's bloody soil.

The aftermath of this melancholy war was as sorrowful and dispiriting as had been the waging of it. During Operation Big Switch—the mass exchange of prisoners which followed the armistice—it was found that on the one hand the Communists had been guilty of widespread atrocities and brutal treatment of prisoners, and on the other many United Nations troops, chiefly U. S. soldiers, had collaborated with the enemy in order to gain privileged treatment.

Big Switch began on August 5 and lasted through the first week of September. The United Nations returned to the Communists 70,159 North Koreans and 5,640 Chinese seeking repatriation, a total of 75,799. The Communists sent back 12,757 prisoners, or 3,597 Americans, 1,312 other UN troops and 7,848 of the 65,000 South Koreans whom Pyongyang had once boasted of capturing. These troops were brought to Freedom Village constructed near Panmunjom, given delousing treatment, food and new clothes, and then subjected to extensive questioning about life in Communist prison camps.

Their replies provided the evidence from which the U. S. Defense Department concluded that more than 6,000 American troops and 5,500 other soldiers—most of the latter ROKs—had perished after falling into Communist hands. Half of these 11,500 men were the victims of Communist atrocities, and the other half died in imprisonment. The U. S. Army alone was able to prove that 1,036 of its soldiers had been murdered after capture. It was also proven that 2,370 Americans had died after reaching the prison camps. True enough, many of these men perished because they were not accustomed, as were their Communist captors, to the intense cold and coarse food of the Korean north. But there were others who died because the Communists were either indifferent to their responsibilities toward them as prisoners or had brutally refused them food or medical care in an attempt to force them to collaborate.

Collaboration in the Communist prison camps took the form of writing for Communist publications, participating in Communist plays or oratorical contests—all denunciatory of American ways—praising the Communists in broadcasts to the world, signing Communist peace appeals or petitions or helping the work of the Communist propaganda agency, the Central Peace Committee. Collaboration was extorted from the prisoners either by a very much milder form of the brainwashing techniques used on fliers during the "germ warfare" hoax, by denying them necessities or leaving them to wallow in filth and discomfort, by refusing to allow their relatives to know that they were alive, or by attempting to exploit racial or economic discontent, as evidenced by the Communist concentration on American Negroes or youths from poor families. The Communists were also skillful in playing the men off against each other, and there was not only frequent dissension among the American prisoners but also instances of outright hostility culminating in killing. Sergeant James Gallagher was later convicted of having killed two of his fellow prisoners by throwing them out in the snow to die. In all, the tales of collaboration compiled after the return of a total of 4,435 American prisoners six months after the end of the Korean War added up to a dismaying image which made the unpopular war even less palatable.

Collaboration was not, however, as widespread as the 33 percent average reported in some exaggerated accounts. Many of the men in captivity feigned collaboration by attending the Communist meetings and listening to the Marxist line without comment, thus appearing as "progressives"—as the Communists called the collaborators—in the eyes of those men of stronger will and character whom their captors scornfully called "reactionaries." U. S. Army figures show that only 15 percent of its men collaborated with the enemy, but that only 5 percent actively resisted. This left a vast middle ground of 80 percent, most of whom never went beyond signing a "peace petition" to let their relatives know they were alive.

The Communists, having fought the principle of voluntary repatriation on the grounds of the Geneva Convention, which they had never signed, had consistently refused to report the names of all prisoners as that Convention requires. A prisoner could ease the agonizing doubts of his wife or parents only by signing a "peace petition" or making a falsely cheerful broadcast. Such mental cruelty is sometimes more subtle and effective than the rack or the iron maiden.

And yet, apart from the airmen who were tortured to "confess" to germ warfare, none of the Americans held in captivity was subjected to physical torment, or at least not to the extent which the U. S. Army defines as torture. This is: "Application of pain so extreme that it causes a man to faint or lose control of his will."* It is true enough that it was their minds, not their bodies, on which torture was inflicted, but even so, these prisoners were generally not exposed to hardships greater than those being met by their comrades on the battlefield, where the constant fear of death can be a persistent form of mental torment. Worse, not a single American attempted to escape from captivity, a record of apathy which surely reached its ludicrous

*In Every War But One, Eugene Kinkead, Norton, 1959, p. 112.

389

nadir in the explanation given by one soldier: "Well, there was trouble if you left camp, because you had to find a Chinese soldier to bring you back. They wouldn't let you back inside the lines unless a Chinese soldier brought you. And sometimes you couldn't find a Chinese soldier." Probably a more likely reason for this failure to attempt escape was given by the correspondent Philip Deane quoting a North Korean officer: "Don't you realize you cannot possibly escape with your big nose and your red skin?" Finally, the most wounding blow to American self-esteem came with the discovery that something like 75 U. S. soldiers had agreed to spy for the Communists or act as their agents after repatriation to America, and 23 more did not want to return home at all.*

One result of this sorry record—the worst in American history —was the realization that the Communists made war against the minds of their prisoners, most of whom were youths little able to resist mature men trained in the waging of such warfare. And so, after lengthy study of the testimony of repatriated prisoners, President Eisenhower promulgated, on August 17, 1955, the new Code of Conduct for Members of the Armed Forces of the United States. The Code of Conduct, to be memorized by all U. S. servicemen, declares:

I

I am an American fighting man, I serve in the forces which guard my country and our way of life. I am prepared to give my life in their defense.

II

I will never surrender of my own free will. If in command I will never surrender my men while they have the means to resist.

III

If I am captured I will continue to resist by all means available. I will make every effort to escape and aid others to escape. I will accept neither parole nor special favors from the enemy.

---

*Among the 196 U. S. Marines returned from captivity there were no active collaboraters and only 14 signed peace petitions. None of the 229 imprisoned Turks signed, but the Turks were generally left alone by the Communists, who neither spoke their language nor needed them for propaganda purposes. All non-American troops of the United Nations received better treatment.

IV

If I become a prisoner of war I will keep faith with my fellow prisoners. I will give no information or take part in any action which might be harmful to my comrades. If I am senior, I will take command. If not, I will obey the lawful orders of those appointed over me and will back them up in every way.

V

When questioned, should I become a prisoner of war, I am bound to give only name, rank, service number, and date of birth. I will evade answering further questions to the utmost of my ability. I will make no oral or written statements disloyal to my country and its allies or harmful to their cause.

VI

I will never forget that I am an American fighting man, responsible for my actions, and dedicated to the principles which made my country free. I will trust in my God and in the United States of America.

Unhappily, this rather starry-eyed vow is likely to cause any serviceman patient enough to understand it, let alone memorize it, to ask the pertinent question: "How come all the talk about surrendering?" For surrender, like objects suitable for stuffing the noses of children, is one of those subjects best not mentioned. A man thinking of adaptation may eventually come to adoption. It would have been far better if the United States, instead of lamenting the American performance in captivity and typically overreacting to it, had occupied its energies in describing the record of the Communist soldiers in United Nations prisons —for in comparison to that record, the conduct of the American soldiers emerges as a triumph.

Though there had been American collaboration, though 23 Americans—and about 350 South Koreans and one Briton—initially seemed to prefer Communism, there were about 22,000 North Koreans and Chinese who still preferred not to return home. Add to these the 27,000 North Koreans already set free by Syngman Rhee and the total climbs close to 50,000. Of the approximately 22,000 prisoners who were taken to the Demilitarized Zone for "explanations" in October of 1953, 15,000 were Chinese. Since only 5,600 Chinese prisoners had been repatriated, three of every four Chinese soldiers taken prisoner, then, did not wish to return to Communism. The propaganda blow which this struck against world Communism was staggering, and every effort was made to reverse this proportion when the North Korean and Chinese Communist "explainers" came to the Demilitarized Zone.

Explanations themselves took place inside rooms under the eyes of the Swedish, Swiss, Polish and Czechoslovakian members of the Neutral Nations Repatriation Commission, as well as the Indian umpire and representatives from both sides. Prisoners entered the tent, were greeted by the "explainers," heard their arguments in favor of coming home, and rejected or accepted repatriation by going out doors plainly marked with such destinations as "South Korea" or "North Korea." Explanation, of course, was not nearly that orderly, for those Communist soldiers who hated Communism did so with a startling vehemence. Colonel William Robinette, one of the United Nations representatives at the explanations, has described some of these confrontations:

> Each prisoner would be brought in by guards, in half the cases dragged in kicking, biting, and flailing his arms. This first compound manufactured masks to avoid identification by the Communists. The Pole of course objected to this, but was overruled by the Indian chairman—they could come nude or in suits of armor, as they pleased. But the Indian guard usually would handle the prisoner so that his mask would fall off.
>
> Often the press of both sides was in my tent, but generally they were roaming the area looking for violence, which was easy to find, because every quarter-hour or so a prisoner would throw a chair, upset the explainer's table or start chanting or reciting poetry at the top of his lungs.
>
> Presently they brought in a particularly violent prisoner—it took two guards to hold him down on his heavy bench. Gradually he seemed to relax. When he could see that his guards had done likewise, quick as a cat he was up, grabbed his bench, and had sent it sailing through the air at the explainers.
>
> Naturally the Pole protested. So, maybe to accommodate him, the prisoner began to spit at the explainer. We quickly saw he

was no mere gentleman amateur spitter, but a professional. For he began digging up solid hunks of phlegm, and aiming them well.

But the Pole, who seemed hard to please, also objected to this, and wanted the man court-martialed.

So I, as the American representative, asked if it wasn't true that the prisoner had just been promised that if he returned to Communism, he would get no punishment?

They said it was.

So then I asked that if the man did go back, would he be court-martialed as the Pole was now demanding?

The Pole said no, he would not. But he demanded that he be court-martialed now, while still in the hands of the Indians. It was all very confusing.

While the Indians ruled out spitting and throwing benches at the explainers, they allowed the prisoners to call them any names they could think up, and the one most frequently used is a Korean litany which goes:

> Your father is a man of no brains—
> Your mother, a woman of no shame—
> And you are a fat slob![1]

Some prisoners feigned deep interest in what the explainers said, encouraging them to continue, and then, grinning, arose to go out the "South Korea" door with the remark, "You have wasted your time." Others teased the explainers, saying: "Why don't you come south with *us*?" In the end, the Communist explanations were a failure: 21,805 soldiers of Communist North Korea and Red China still refused repatriation. Add these to those freed by Rhee and the figure remains at close to 50,000, as opposed to the United Nations' final total of 327 non-repatriates, of whom 305 were South Korean, 21 were American (3 of whom later changed their minds and came home) and one Briton. It was no contest, and if it is argued that the United Nations also waged war against the minds of its prisoners, the answer is yes, but with different methods. Though there were Rhee agents in the prison compounds and the Indians did discover radio equipment supplied by the United Nations Command, there was no brutality, no brainwashing, no denial of necessities; in effect, none of the means by which Communists attain their ends. The United Nations, on balance, carried on its campaign for its prisoners' allegiance with compassion, the Communists with cruelty. The objectives may have been the same, but the methods were different, and since few, if any, political systems have ever deliberately pursued evil objectives, it becomes obvious that the only difference possible is one of method.

So these 21,805 anti-Communists were eventually set free in January–February of 1954, most of the Chinese choosing to renew life under Chiang Kai-shek on Formosa, for the Political Conference which was to have settled their fate was never held.

On July 27, 1953, the day the armistice was signed in Korea, the sixteen United Nations allies who fought there worked out a joint statement which, as it was made public two weeks later, declared:

> We affirm in the interest of the world peace that if there is a renewal of the armed attacks, challenging again the principles of the United Nations, we should again be united and prompt to resist. The consequences of such a breach of the armistice would be so grave that in all probability it would not be possible to confine hostilities within the frontiers of Korea.

One month later, the United Nations General Assembly adopted a resolution limiting participation in the Political Conference to these sixteen nations and South Korea on one side, the Soviet Union, Communist China and North Korea on the other. Neutral nations were to be excluded. During January–February of 1954, the foreign ministers of the United States, the United Kingdom, France and the Soviet Union met in Berlin and upheld this resolution. It was also agreed that settlement of the Korean question, along with the war in Indo-China, would be made at a conference to begin in Geneva, Switzerland, on April 26, 1954.

But the Geneva Conference produced nothing on Korea, as President Syngman Rhee had predicted. The Communists, led by Red China's Chou En-lai, would accept no formula which gave the United Nations any authority in Korea or which proposed genuinely free elections to unify the unhappy peninsula.

This fact was reported to the United Nations by the sixteen allies. On December 11, 1954, the United Nations General Assembly declared that its purpose remained "achievement by peaceful means of a unified, independent and democratic Korea under a representative form of government, and the full restoration of international peace and security in the area." Meanwhile, the General Assembly hoped that some progress to this end would soon be made.

But there was no hope and there never was a Political Conference. It is doubtful if any of the leaders of the sixteen United Nations allies—as well as the Communist leaders—ever seriously anticipated that it would be held, or, being held, would achieve anything. How could Korea be unified peacefully? By an election? If so, if it was to a Communist-controlled vote the result would be a Communist Korea, and this would be unacceptable to the United Nations. If the United Nations held elections the result would be a free Korea, which the Communists would not accept. What then?

Nothing, and the military stalemate and partition of Korea still exists nearly a decade after the cease-fire. As Admiral Joy feared, the Communists have violated the Armistice Agreement by building their forces. United Nations protests against these violations have unvaryingly been rejected by the Neutral Nations Supervisory Commission members from Communist Poland and Czechoslovakia. As of February 7, 1955, there were sixty-one of them, and the Swiss member of the Commission remarked at the agency's 179th meeting: "I think the hand of the honorable Polish member must shake every month when he signs the evaluation stating that we have established that both sides have remained within the limits of the Armistice Agreement." The violations have continued until the Communists in Korea now have a navy and air force and an army of approximately 1,500,000 men.

Opposite this force, on the south side of the 2½ mile Demilitarized Zone which still separates both sides, is a ROK Army of 500,000 men, reinforced by two U. S. Army divisions. The American air and sea power which had been so decisive against the Communists has dwindled or vanished.

Even passionate old Syngman Rhee—one of the tragic figures of this century—has been forced to flee his beloved country again. In 1960, at eighty-five years of age, a student revolution drove him to Hawaii. Nor did Rhee's successor, Premier John Chang, remain long in office. An army revolt of 1961 deposed Chang's government, and Korea, as of mid-1962, remains under the rule of a military junta led by General Chung Hee Park.

And so, a dozen years after the Communist invasion of June 25, 1950, the situation then prevailing has been restored, with the exception that South Korea is now better armed and occupies a better defense line. This is the result of three years, one month and two days of war, during which the attempt of Stalinist North Korea to unify the peninsula by force was blocked by the United Nations, the United Nations attempt to unify Korea by force was stopped by the intervention of Communist China, and the Communist Chinese attempt was thwarted by the United Nations, after which a stalemate obtained while both sides struggled for propaganda or diplomatic victories at Panmunjom, the stalemate then settling down to eighteen months of positional warfare until the United Nations principle of voluntary repatriation was finally upheld. But had so much marching and countermarching produced only a *status quo ante bellum?*

No.

One result of the Korean War is that the People's Liberation Army is no longer an unwieldy mass composed mainly of peasant foot soldiers, but a modern striking force of balanced arms and a good logistics system. Mao Tse-tung and Marshal Chu Teh may have been beaten in Korea, but they learned about their weaknesses and took steps to remove them. Another result not intended by Communism—certainly not Stalinist Communism—is that North Korea is now a Red Chinese puppet rather than a Red Russian puppet—a shift which became apparent in the open break in Sino-Soviet relations occurring at the Twenty-second Congress of the Soviet Communist Party at Moscow in October, 1961. When Russia's Premier Khrushchev denounced the Communist Party of Albania for opposing his theory of peaceful coexistence based on economic rather than military defeat of the free world, only three Communist leaders present refused to join him. These were Chou En-lai of Communist China, Ho Chi Minh of the state of North Vietnam which Red China had helped create in Indo-China, and Premier Kim Il Sung of North Korea. Kim Il Sung, one of Russian Communism's prized pupils, had thrown in his lot with Red China. Russia, having thwarted Japan in Korea and installed herself, seems now to have been ousted by the old suzerain of Korea, China. But Russia still abuts both Korea and China through her province of Siberia. Moreover, the power that supplanted Japan in the Far East's triangular struggle—the United States of America—stands entrenched in South Korea, firmly, however reluctantly, committed to a mutual defense treaty with the ROK government. Thus, three great powers again confront one another on the Korean peninsula. They may still be there, confronting one another, long after the ideological conflict which now divides them has vanished or been replaced by a new one, with, possibly, a new alignment—for power politics have a way of surviving creeds and crusades.

Among those results intended in Korea which failed to materialize was the American hope of scoring a propaganda victory by enforcing the principle of voluntary repatriation. It had been supposed that the sight of the free world continuing to protect thousands of Communist soldiers who had sought political sanctuary would cause widespread defections from the ranks of Asiatic Communism. It did not happen, not even during the Indo-Chinese fighting which continued after the Korean armistice. Nor was India impressed, as some Americans had hoped. What India saw during the "explanations" given Communist soldiers in Korea did not deter India from rescuing Communist prestige from the severe criticism which might have overtaken it in late 1961 when, after having broken the moratorium on the testing of nuclear weapons, the Soviet Union set off a series of massive nuclear explosions in the atmosphere. India, in effect, equated this with simple possession of nuclear weapons. It was probably too much to hope that America's decision not to use atomic weapons against Red China, together with its compassion toward its prisoners as well as toward the Korean refugees it cared for, would ever make Asian nations forget the cloud that rose over Hiroshima.

But Korea's successes outnumber its failures. The Korean War did halt Communist armed aggression and it has not been tried since. In fact, the end of the Korean War may have brought about that shift to economic warfare and the struggle for the allegiance of rising young nations which, with its attendant characteristic of subversive or guerrilla warfare, has already been called World War III. Korea also saved the United Nations from the fate of the League of Nations, while encouraging small nations to resist the Communists and keeping Japan outside the orbit of Asiatic Communism. And Korea renewed in the free world mind that concept of limited war which the total wars of 1914–1918 and 1939–1945 had obliterated from memory.

Before these two great wars, with their indiscriminate bombing of cities and civilians, war had usually been limited. It had been pursued to obtain an objective of foreign policy, and more than one premier or chancellor had been forced to check-rein generals eager to exceed the limit of that policy. Unfortunately, or fortunately as some think, the totality of these two wars so accelerated weapons development that the atomic bomb resulted, and in the shadow of the mushroom cloud, as Korea seems to have proved, total war became unthinkable. It is probable—granting that Red China does not acquire the atomic bomb before her evangelical fervor cools—that any shooting conflict of the future will be fought along the lines of the limited war in Korea. Another important result of the Korean War was that collective security worked. To the aid of the tottering Republic of Korea came the men of sixteen nations, putting aside their national pride and forming, despite their disparate races, religions, customs and culture, a single army under the single command furnished by the United States. A lesser result, perhaps only important in the United States, was the reaffirmation, during the Truman-MacArthur controversy, of the principle of civilian control of the military. And the theory dividing Truman and MacArthur—that Europe, not Asia, was the prize—seems to have been supported by the events of the decade succeeding the Armistice, though it has not been proved or disproved, if such broad concepts are ever susceptible of proof.

Finally, the Korean War again showed that the difference between the Communists and the democracies is the difference of means. By the "germ warfare" hoax and the torture of those who "confessed" to it; by the Koje reign of terror; by the murder of prisoners, or the impressment or kidnaping of them, or by the brutal war against the minds of prisoners; by the "Kaesong bombing" and the windy stall at Panmunjom, or by systematic violations of the Armistice Agreement premeditated before it was signed—by all of this, and by the invasion of Korea itself, the Communists showed that they will use any means to attain their ends. They believe that a posterity comfortable in their gift of a classless society will forgive them their sins. Their ends lie somewhere in the future, as did those of their arch-opponent, Syngman Rhee, who said: "If there must be trouble, let it be in my day, that my children may have peace." And Syngman Rhee also chose means incompatible with this high end, unaware that no grandfather can achieve peace for his grandchildren, nor fight for them nor impose an order or tranquillity on the future. The fiercest tormentors of mankind have been those idealists seeking to build invincible utopias on earth. All had high ends, but then, finding complex, turbulent human nature noncompliant, turned to the whip and the goad.

But the democracies know, as Secretary of State Dean Acheson has said, that "the means we choose to overcome the obstacles in our path must be consonant with our deepest moral sense." Because of this, the United Nations made no attempt to deceive the world, did not torture or murder or brainwash or remain indifferent to human suffering. There might have been lapses in this direction, as there are in every army, but they were in contradiction to a policy of compassion. The free world chose means compatible with its purpose of political freedom, a purpose, incidentally, which does not lie in the future and therefore command religious zeal, but which remains forever present. Because the United Nations did not betray themselves, they gained a victory which historians may place on a level higher than the battlefield. Most magnificent of all, these sixteen states of the United Nations fought on for eighteen months, exposing their soldiers to that much more misery and suffering, to uphold a man's right to refuse to be a slave.

And though Korea was neither that marvelous victory nor miserable defeat to which a half century of total war had accustomed the world, it was, nonetheless, a triumph for the United Nations. In Korea invasion was repelled, and in such manner as to remind the world that an invader need not be destroyed to be repulsed. To gnash one's teeth because the invader escaped destruction is to revert to that concept of "total war" which is no longer possible without mutual total destruction. Of Korea, then, it is enough to say: It was here that Communism suffered its first defeat.

That was the only victory possible.

Appendix

Appendix

Armistice Agreement

VOLUME I

TEXT OF AGREEMENT

AGREEMENT BETWEEN THE COMMANDER-IN-CHIEF, UNITED NA-
TIONS COMMAND, ON THE ONE HAND, AND THE SUPREME COM-
MANDER OF THE KOREAN PEOPLE'S ARMY AND THE COMMANDER
OF THE CHINESE PEOPLE'S VOLUNTEERS, ON THE OTHER HAND,
CONCERNING A MILITARY ARMISTICE IN KOREA

PREAMBLE

The undersigned, the Commander-in-Chief, United Nations Command, on the
one hand, and the Supreme Commander of the Korean People's Army and the
Commander of the Chinese People's Volunteers, on the other hand, in the interest of stopping the Korean conflict, with its great toll of suffering and bloodshed
on both sides, and with the objective of establishing an armistice which will insure a complete cessation of hostilities and of all acts of armed force in Korea
until a final peaceful settlement is achieved, do individually, collectively, and
mutually agree to accept and to be bound and governed by the conditions and
terms of armistice set forth in the following Articles and Paragraphs, which said
conditions and terms are intended to be purely military in character and to per-
tain solely to the belligerents in Korea.

ARTICLE I

MILITARY DEMARCATION LINE AND
DEMILITARIZED ZONE

1. A Military Demarcation Line shall be fixed and both sides shall withdraw
two (2) kilometers from this line so as to establish a Demilitarized Zone between
the opposing forces. A Demilitarized Zone shall be established as a buffer zone to
prevent the occurrence of incidents which might lead to a resumption of hostilities.

2. The Military Demarcation Line is located as indicated on the attached map
(Map 1).

3. The Demilitarized Zone is defined by a northern and a southern boundary
as indicated on the attached map (Map 1).

4. The Military Demarcation Line shall be plainly marked as directed by the Military Armistice Commission hereinafter established. The Commanders of the opposing sides shall have suitable markers erected along the boundary between the Demilitarized Zone and their respective areas. The Military Armistice Commission shall supervise the erection of all markers placed along the Military Demarcation Line and along the boundaries of the Demilitarized Zone.

5. The waters of the Han River Estuary shall be open to civil shipping of both sides wherever one bank is controlled by one side and the other bank is controlled by the other side. The Military Armistice Commission shall prescribe rules for the shipping in that part of the Han River Estuary indicated on the attached map (Map 2). Civil shipping of each side shall have unrestricted access to the land under the military control of that side.

6. Neither side shall execute any hostile act within, from, or against the Demilitarized Zone.

7. No person, military or civilian, shall be permitted to cross the Military Demarcation Line unless specifically authorized to do so by the Military Armistice Commission.

8. No person, military or civilian, in the Demilitarized Zone shall be permitted to enter the territory under the military control of either side unless specifically authorized to do so by the Commander into whose territory entry is sought.

9. No person, military or civilian, shall be permitted to enter the Demilitarized Zone except persons concerned with the conduct of civil administration and relief and persons specifically authorized to enter by the Military Armistice Commission.

10. Civil administration and relief in that part of the Demilitarized Zone which is south of the Military Demarcation Line shall be the responsibility of the Commander-in-Chief, United Nations Command; and civil administration and relief in that part of the Demilitarized Zone which is north of the Military Demarcation Line shall be the joint responsibility of the Supreme Commander of the Korean People's Army and the Commander of the Chinese People's Volunteers. The number of persons, military or civilian, from each side who are permitted to enter the Demilitarized Zone for the conduct of civil administration and relief shall be as determined by the respective Commanders, but in no case shall the total number authorized by either side exceed one thousand (1,000) persons at any one time. The number of civil police and the arms to be carried by them shall be as prescribed by the Military Armistice Commission. Other personnel shall not carry arms unless specifically authorized to do so by the Military Armistice Commission.

11. Nothing contained in this Article shall be construed to prevent the complete freedom of movement to, from, and within the Demilitarized Zone by the Military Armistice Commission, its assistants, its Joint Observer Teams with their assistants, the Neutral Nations Supervisory Commission hereinafter established, its assistants, its Neutral Nations Inspection Teams with their assistants, and of any other persons, materials, and equipment specifically authorized to enter the Demilitarized Zone by the Military Armistice Commission. Convenience of movement shall be permitted through the territory under the military control of either side over any route necessary to move between points within the Demilitarized Zone where such points are not connected by roads lying completely within the Demilitarized Zone.

ARTICLE II

CONCRETE ARRANGEMENTS FOR CEASE-FIRE AND ARMISTICE

A. GENERAL

12. The Commanders of the opposing sides shall order and enforce a complete cessation of all hostilities in Korea by all armed forces under their control, including all units and personnel of the ground, naval, and air forces, effective twelve (12) hours after this Armistice Agreement is signed. (See Paragraph 63 hereof for effective date and hour of the remaining provisions of this Armistice Agreement.)

13. In order to insure the stability of the Military Armistice so as to facilitate the attainment of a peaceful settlement through the holding by both sides of a political conference of a higher level, the Commanders of the opposing sides shall:

a. Within seventy-two (72) hours after this Armistice Agreement becomes effective, withdraw all of their military forces, supplies, and equipment from the Demilitarized Zone except as otherwise provided herein. All demolitions, minefields, wire entanglements, and other hazards to the safe movement of personnel of the Military Armistice Commission or its Joint Observer Teams, known to exist within the Demilitarized Zone after the withdrawal of military forces therefrom, together with lanes known to be free of all such hazards, shall be reported to the Military Armistice Commission by the Commander of the side whose forces emplaced such hazards. Subsequently, additional safe lanes shall be cleared; and eventually, within forty-five (45) days after the termination of the seventy-two (72) hour period, all such hazards shall be removed from the Demilitarized Zone as directed by and under the supervision of the Military Armistice Commission. At the termination of the seventy-two (72) hour period, except for unarmed troops authorized a forty-five (45) day period to complete salvage operations under Military Armistice Commission supervision, such units of a police nature as may be specifically requested by the Military Armistice Commission and agreed to by the Commanders of the opposing sides, and personnel authorized under Paragraphs 10 and 11 hereof, no personnel of either side shall be permitted to enter the Demilitarized Zone.

b. Within ten (10) days after this Armistice Agreement becomes effective, withdraw all of their military forces, supplies, and equipment from the rear and the coastal islands and waters of Korea of the other side. If such military forces are not withdrawn within the stated time limit, and there is no mutually agreed and valid reason for the delay, the other side shall have the right to take any action which it deems necessary for the maintenance of security and order. The term "coastal islands," as used above, refers to those islands which, though occupied by one side at the time when this Armistice Agreement becomes effective, were controlled by the other side on 24 June 1950; provided, however, that all the islands lying to the north and west of the provincial boundary line between HWANG-HAE-DO and KYONGGI-DO shall be under the military control of the Supreme Commander of the Korean People's Army and the Commander of the Chinese People's Volunteers, except the island groups of PAENGYONG-DO (37°58′N, 124°40′E), TAECHONG-DO (37°50′N, 124°42′E), SOCHONG-DO (37°46′N,

124°46′E), YONPYONG-DO (37°38′N, 125°40′E), and U-DO (37°36′N, 125°58′E), which shall remain under the military control of the Commander-in-Chief, United Nations Command. All the islands on the west coast of Korea lying south of the above-mentioned boundary line shall remain under the military control of the Commander-in-Chief, United Nations Command. (See Map 3.)

c. Cease the introduction into Korea of reinforcing military personnel; provided, however, that the rotation of units and personnel, the arrival in Korea of personnel on a temporary duty basis, and the return to Korea of personnel after short periods of leave or temporary duty outside of Korea shall be permitted within the scope prescribed below. "Rotation" is defined as the replacement of units or personnel by other units or personnel who are commencing a tour of duty in Korea. Rotation personnel shall be introduced into and evacuated from Korea only through the ports of entry enumerated in Paragraph 43 hereof. Rotation shall be conducted on a man-for-man basis; provided, however, that no more than thirty-five thousand (35,000) persons in the military service shall be admitted into Korea by either side in any calendar month under the rotation policy. No military personnel of either side shall be introduced into Korea if the introduction of such personnel will cause the aggregate of the military personnel of that side admitted into Korea since the effective date of this Armistice Agreement to exceed the cumulative total of the military personnel of that side who have departed from Korea since that date. Reports concerning arrivals in and departures from Korea of military personnel shall be made daily to the Military Armistice Commission and the Neutral Nations Supervisory Commission; such reports shall include places of arrival and departure and the number of persons arriving at or departing from each such place. The Neutral Nations Supervisory Commission, through its Neutral Nations Inspection Teams, shall conduct supervision and inspection of the rotation of units and personnel authorized above, at the ports of entry enumerated in Paragraph 43 hereof.

d. Cease the introduction into Korea of reinforcing combat aircraft, armored vehicles, weapons, and ammunition; provided, however, that combat aircraft, armored vehicles, weapons, and ammunition which are destroyed, damaged, worn out, or used up during the period of the armistice may be replaced on the basis of piece-for-piece of the same effectiveness and the same type. Such combat aircraft, armored vehicles, weapons, and ammunition shall be introduced into Korea only through the ports of entry enumerated in Paragraph 43 hereof. In order to justify the requirement for combat aircraft, armored vehicles, weapons, and ammunition to be introduced into Korea for replacement purposes, reports concerning every incoming shipment of these items shall be made to the Military Armistice Commission and the Neutral Nations Supervisory Commission; such reports shall include statements regarding the disposition of the items being replaced. Items to be replaced which are removed from Korea shall be removed only through the ports of entry enumerated in Paragraph 43 hereof. The Neutral Nations Supervisory Commission, through its Neutral Nations Inspection Teams, shall conduct supervision and inspection of the replacement of combat aircraft, armored vehicles, weapons, and ammunition authorized above, at the ports of entry enumerated in Paragraph 43 hereof.

e. Insure that personnel of their respective commands who violate any of the provisions of this Armistice Agreement are adequately punished.

406

f. In those cases where places of burial are a matter of record and graves are actually found to exist, permit graves registration personnel of the other side to enter, within a definite time limit after this Armistice Agreement becomes effective, the territory of Korea under their military control, for the purpose of proceeding to such graves to recover and evacuate the bodies of the deceased military personnel of that side, including deceased prisoners of war. The specific procedures and the time limit for the performance of the above task shall be determined by the Military Armistice Commission. The Commanders of the opposing sides shall furnish to the other side all available information pertaining to the places of burial of the deceased military personnel of the other side.

g. Afford full protection and all possible assistance and cooperation to the Military Armistice Commission, its Joint Observer Teams, the Neutral Nations Supervisory Commission, and its Neutral Nations Inspection Teams, in the carrying out of their functions and responsibilities hereinafter assigned; and accord to the Neutral Nations Supervisory Commission, and to its Neutral Nations Inspection Teams, full convenience of movement between the headquarters of the Neutral Nations Supervisory Commission and the ports of entry enumerated in Paragraph 43 hereof over main lines of communication agreed upon by both sides (see Map 4), and between the headquarters of the Neutral Nations Supervisory Commission and the places where violations of this Armistice Agreement have been reported to have occurred. In order to prevent unnecessary delays, the use of alternate routes and means of transportation will be permitted whenever the main lines of communication are closed or impassable.

h. Provide such logistic support, including communications and transportation facilities, as may be required by the Military Armistice Commission and the Neutral Nations Supervisory Commission and their Teams.

i. Each construct, operate, and maintain a suitable airfield in their respective ports of the Demilitarized Zone in the vicinity of the headquarters of the Military Armistice Commission, for such uses as the Commission may determine.

j. Insure that all members and other personnel of the Neutral Nations Supervisory Commission and of the Neutral Nations Repatriation Commission hereinafter established shall enjoy the freedom and facilities necessary for the proper exercise of their function, including privileges, treatment, and immunities equivalent to those ordinarily enjoyed by accredited diplomatic personnel under international usage.

14. This Armistice Agreement shall apply to all opposing ground forces under the military control of either side, which ground forces shall respect the Demilitarized Zone and the area of Korea under the military control of the opposing side.

15. This Armistice Agreement shall apply to all opposing naval forces, which naval forces shall respect the waters contiguous to the Demilitarized Zone and to the land area of Korea under the military control of the opposing side, and shall not engage in blockade of any kind of Korea.

16. This Armistice Agreement shall apply to all opposing air forces, which air forces shall respect the air space over the Demilitarized Zone and over the area of Korea under the military control of the opposing side, and over the waters contiguous to both.

17. Responsibility for compliance with and enforcement of the terms and pro-

visions of this Armistice Agreement is that of the signatories hereto and their successors in command. The Commanders of the opposing sides shall establish within their respective commands all measures and procedures necessary to insure complete compliance with all of the provisions hereof by all elements of their commands. They shall actively cooperate with one another and with the Military Armistice Commission and the Neutral Nations Supervisory Commission in requiring observance of both the letter and the spirit of all of the provisions of this Armistice Agreement.

18. The costs of the operations of the Military Armistice Commission and of the Neutral Nations Supervisory Commission and of their Teams shall be shared equally by the two opposing sides.

B. MILITARY ARMISTICE COMMISSION

1. COMPOSITION

19. A Military Armistice Commission is hereby established.

20. The Military Armistice Commission shall be composed of ten (10) senior officers, five (5) of whom shall be appointed by the Commander-in-Chief, United Nations Command, and five (5) of whom shall be appointed jointly by the Supreme Commander of the Korean People's Army and the Commander of the Chinese People's Volunteers. Of the ten members, three (3) from each side shall be of general or flag rank. The two (2) remaining members on each side may be major generals, brigadier generals, colonels, or their equivalents.

21. Members of the Military Armistice Commission shall be permitted to use staff assistants as required.

22. The Military Armistice Commission shall be provided with the necessary administrative personnel to establish a Secretariat charged with assisting the Commission by performing record-keeping, secretarial, interpreting, and such other functions as the Commission may assign to it. Each side shall appoint to the Secretariat a Secretary and an Assistant Secretary and such clerical and specialized personnel as required by the Secretariat. Records shall be kept in English, Korean, and Chinese, all of which shall be equally authentic.

23. a. The Military Armistice Commission shall be initially provided with and assisted by ten (10) Joint Observer Teams, which number may be reduced by agreement of the senior members of both sides on the Military Armistice Commission.

b. Each Joint Observer Team shall be composed of not less than four (4) nor more than six (6) officers of field grade, half of whom shall be appointed by the Commander-in-Chief, United Nations Command, and half of whom shall be appointed jointly by the Supreme Commander of the Korean People's Army and the Commander of the Chinese People's Volunteers. Additional personnel such as drivers, clerks, and interpreters shall be furnished by each side as required for the functioning of the Joint Observer Teams.

2. FUNCTIONS AND AUTHORITY

24. The general mission of the Military Armistice Commission shall be to supervise the implementation of this Armistice Agreement and to settle through negotiations any violations of this Armistice Agreement.

25. The Military Armistice Commission shall:

a. Locate its headquarters in the vicinity of PANMUNJOM (37°57'29"N, 126°40'00"E). The Military Armistice Commission may relocate its headquarters at another point within the Demilitarized Zone by agreement of the senior members of both sides on the Commission.

b. Operate as a joint organization without a chairman.

c. Adopt such rules of procedure as it may, from time to time, deem necessary.

d. Supervise the carrying out of the provisions of this Armistice Agreement pertaining to the Demilitarized Zone and to the Han River Estuary.

e. Direct the operations of the Joint Observer Teams.

f. Settle through negotiations any violations of this Armistice agreement.

g. Transmit immediately to the Commanders of the opposing sides all reports of investigations of violations of this Armistice Agreement and all other reports and records of proceedings received from the Neutral Nations Supervisory Commission.

h. Give general supervision and direction to the activities of the Committee for Repatriation of Prisoners of War and the Committee for Assisting the Return of Displaced Civilians, hereinafter established.

i. Act as an intermediary in transmitting communications between the Commanders of the opposing sides; provided, however, that the foregoing shall not be construed to preclude the Commanders of both sides from communicating with each other by any other means which they may desire to employ.

j. Provide credentials and distinctive insignia for its staff and its Joint Observer Teams, and a distinctive marking for all vehicles, aircraft, and vessels, used in the performance of its mission.

26. The mission of the Joint Observer Teams shall be to assist the Military Armistice Commission in supervising the carrying out of the provisions of this Armistice Agreement pertaining to the Demilitarized Zone and to the Han River Estuary.

27. The Military Armistice Commission, or the senior member of either side thereof, is authorized to dispatch Joint Observer Teams to investigate violations of this Armistice Agreement reported to have occurred in the Demilitarized Zone or in the Han River Estuary; provided, however, that not more than one half of the Joint Observer Teams which have not been dispatched by the Military Armistice Commission may be dispatched at any one time by the senior member of either side on the Commission.

28. The Military Armistice Commission, or the senior member of either side thereof, is authorized to request the Neutral Nations Supervisory Commission to conduct special observations and inspections at places outside the Demilitarized Zone where violations of this Armistice Agreement have been reported to have occurred.

29. When the Military Armistice Commission determines that a violation of this Armistice Agreement has occurred, it shall immediately report such violation to the Commanders of the opposing sides.

30. When the Military Armistice Commission determines that a violation of this Armistice Agreement has been corrected to its satisfaction, it shall so report to the Commanders of the opposing sides.

3. GENERAL

31. The Military Armistice Commission shall meet daily. Recesses of not to exceed seven (7) days may be agreed upon by the senior members of both sides; provided, that such recesses may be terminated on twenty-four (24) hour notice by the senior member of either side.

32. Copies of the record of the proceedings of all meetings of the Military Armistice Commission shall be forwarded to the Commanders of the opposing sides as soon as possible after each meeting.

33. The Joint Observer Teams shall make periodic reports to the Military Armistice Commission as required by the Commission and, in addition, shall make such special reports as may be deemed necessary by them, or as may be required by the Commission.

34. The Military Armistice Commission shall maintain duplicate files of the reports and records of proceedings required by this Armistice Agreement. The Commission is authorized to maintain duplicate files of such other reports, records, etc., as may be necessary in the conduct of its business. Upon eventual dissolution of the Commission, one set of the above files shall be turned over to each side.

35. The Military Armistice Commission may make recommendations to the Commanders of the opposing sides with respect to amendments or additions to this Armistice Agreement. Such recommended changes should generally be those designed to insure a more effective armistice.

C. NEUTRAL NATIONS SUPERVISORY COMMISSION

1. COMPOSITION

36. A Neutral Nations Supervisory Commission is hereby established.

37. The Neutral Nations Supervisory Commission shall be composed of four (4) senior officers, two (2) of whom shall be appointed by neutral nations nominated by the Commander-in-Chief, United Nations Command, namely, SWEDEN and SWITZERLAND, and two (2) of whom shall be appointed by neutral nations nominated jointly by the Supreme Commander of the Korean People's Army and the Commander of the Chinese People's Volunteers, namely, POLAND and CZECHOSLOVAKIA. The term "neutral nations" as herein used is defined as those nations whose combatant forces have not participated in the hostilities in Korea. Members appointed to the Commission may be from the armed forces of the appointing nations. Each member shall designate an alternate member to attend those meetings which for any reason the principal member is unable to attend. Such alternate members shall be of the same nationality as their principals. The Neutral Nations Supervisory Commission may take action whenever the number of members present from the neutral nations nominated by one side is equal to the number of members present from the neutral nations nominated by the other side.

38. Members of the Neutral Nations Supervisory Commission shall be permitted to use staff assistants furnished by the neutral nations as required. These staff assistants may be appointed as alternate members of the Commission.

39. The neutral nations shall be requested to furnish the Neutral Nations Supervisory Commission with the necessary administrative personnel to establish a Secretariat charged with assisting the Commission by performing necessary record-

keeping, secretarial, interpreting, and such other functions as the Commission may assign to it.

40. a. The Neutral Nations Supervisory Commission shall be initially provided with, and assisted by, twenty (20) Neutral Nations Inspection Teams, which number may be reduced by agreement of the senior members of both sides on the Military Armistice Commission. The Neutral Nations Inspection Teams shall be responsible to, shall report to, and shall be subject to the direction of, the Neutral Nations Supervisory Commission only.

b. Each Neutral Nations Inspection Team shall be composed of not less than four (4) officers, preferably of field grade, half of whom shall be from the neutral nations nominated by the Commander-in-Chief, United Nations Command, and half of whom shall be from the neutral nations nominated jointly by the Supreme Commander of the Korean People's Army and the Commander of the Chinese People's Volunteers. Members appointed to the Neutral Nations Inspection Teams may be from the armed forces of the appointing nations. In order to facilitate the functioning of the Teams, sub-teams composed of not less than two (2) members, one of whom shall be from a neutral nation nominated by the Commander-in-Chief, United Nations Command, and one of whom shall be from a neutral nation nominated jointly by the Supreme Commander of the Korean People's Army and the Commander of the Chinese People's Volunteers, may be formed as circumstances require. Additional personnel such as drivers, clerks, interpreters, and communications personnel, and such equipment as may be required by the Teams to perform their missions, shall be furnished by the Commander of each side, as required, in the Demilitarized Zone and in the territory under his military control. The Neutral Nations Supervisory Commission may provide itself and the Neutral Nations Inspection Teams with such of the above personnel and equipment of its own as it may desire; provided, however, that such personnel shall be personnel of the same neutral nations of which the Neutral Nations Supervisory Commission is composed.

2. FUNCTIONS AND AUTHORITY

41. The mission of the Neutral Nations Supervisory Commission shall be to carry out the functions of supervision, observation, inspection, and investigation, as stipulated in Sub-paragraphs 13c and 13d and Paragraph 28 hereof, and to report the results of such supervision, observation, inspection, and investigation to the Military Armistice Commission.

42. The Neutral Nations Supervisory Commission shall:

a. Locate its headquarters in proximity to the headquarters of the Military Armistice Commission.

b. Adopt such rules of procedure as it may, from time to time, deem necessary.

c. Conduct, through its members and its Neutral Nations Inspection Teams, the supervision and inspection provided for in Sub-paragraphs 13c and 13d of this Armistice Agreement at the ports of entry enumerated in Paragraph 43 hereof, and the special observations and inspections provided for in Paragraph 28 hereof at those places where violations of this Armistice Agreement have been reported to have occurred. The inspection of combat aircraft, armored vehicles, weapons, and ammunition by the Neutral Nations Inspection Teams shall be such as to enable them to properly insure that reinforcing combat aircraft, armored vehicles, weapons, and ammunition are not being introduced into Korea; but this shall not be construed as authorizing inspections or examinations of any secret designs or characteristics of any combat aircraft, armored vehicle, weapon, or ammunition.

d. Direct and supervise the operations of the Neutral Nations Inspection Teams.

e. Station five (5) Neutral Nations Inspection Teams at the ports of entry enumerated in Paragraph 43 hereof located in the territory under the military control of the Commander-in-Chief, United Nations Command; and five (5) Neutral Nations Inspection Teams at the ports of entry enumerated in Paragraph 43 hereof located in the territory under the military control of the Supreme Commander of the Korean People's Army and the Commander of the Chinese People's Volunteers; and establish initially ten (10) mobile Neutral Nations Inspection Teams in reserve, stationed in the general vicinity of the headquarters of the Neutral Nations Supervisory Commission, which number may be reduced by agreement of the senior members of both sides on the Military Armistice Commission. Not more than half of the mobile Neutral Nations Inspection Teams shall be dispatched at any one time in accordance with requests of the senior member of either side on the Military Armistice Commission.

f. Subject to the provisions of the preceding Sub-paragraph, conduct without delay investigations of reported violations of this Armistice Agreement, including such investigations of reported violations of this Armistice Agreement as may be requested by the Military Armistice Commission or by the senior member of either side on the Commission.

g. Provide credentials and distinctive insignia for its staff and its Neutral Nations Inspection Teams, and a distinctive marking for all vehicles, aircraft, and vessels, used in the performance of its mission.

43. Neutral Nations Inspection Teams shall be stationed at the following ports of entry:

Territory under the military control of the United Nations Command		Territory under the military control of the Korean People's Army and the Chinese People's Volunteers	
INCHON	(37°28'N, 126°38'E)	SINUIJU	(40°06'N, 124°24'E)
TAEGU	(35°52'N, 128°36'E)	CHONGJIN	(41°46'N, 129°49'E)
PUSAN	(35°06'N, 129°02'E)	HUNGNAM	(39°50'N, 127°37'E)
KANGNUNG	(37°45'N, 128°54'E)	MANPO	(41°09'N, 126°18'E)
KUNSAN	(35°59'N, 126°43'E)	SINANJU	(39°36'N, 125°36'E)

These Neutral Nations Inspection Teams shall be accorded full convenience of movement within the areas and over the routes of communication set forth on the attached map (Map 5).

3. GENERAL

44. The Neutral Nations Supervisory Commission shall meet daily. Recesses of not to exceed seven (7) days may be agreed upon by the members of the Neutral

Nations Supervisory Commission; provided, that such recesses may be terminated on twenty-four (24) hour notice by any member.

45. Copies of the record of the proceedings of all meetings of the Neutral Nations Supervisory Commission shall be forwarded to the Military Armistice Commission as soon as possible after each meeting. Records shall be kept in English, Korean, and Chinese.

46. The Neutral Nations Inspection Teams shall make periodic reports concerning the results of their supervision, observations, inspections, and investigations to the Neutral Nations Supervisory Commission as required by the Commission and, in addition, shall make such special reports as may be deemed necessary by them, or as may be required by the Commission. Reports shall be submitted by a Team as a whole, but may also be submitted by one or more individual members thereof; provided, that the reports submitted by one or more individual members thereof shall be considered as informational only.

47. Copies of the reports made by the Neutral Nations Inspection Teams shall be forwarded to the Military Armistice Commission by the Neutral Nations Supervisory Commission without delay and in the language in which received. They shall not be delayed by the process of translation or evaluation. The Neutral Nations Supervisory Commission shall evaluate such reports at the earliest practicable time and shall forward their findings to the Military Armistice Commission as a matter of priority. The Military Armistice Commission shall not take final action with regard to any such report until the evaluation thereof has been received from the Neutral Nations Supervisory Commission. Members of the Neutral Nations Supervisory Commission and of its Teams shall be subject to appearance before the Military Armistice Commission, at the request of the senior member of either side on the Military Armistice Commission, for clarification of any report submitted.

48. The Neutral Nations Supervisory Commission shall maintain duplicate files of the reports and records of proceedings required by this Armistice Agreement. The Commission is authorized to maintain duplicate files of such other reports, records, etc., as may be necessary in the conduct of its business. Upon eventual dissolution of the Commission, one set of the above files shall be turned over to each side.

49. The Neutral Nations Supervisory Commission may make recommendations to the Military Armistice Commission with respect to amendments or additions to this Armistice Agreement. Such recommended changes should generally be those designed to insure a more effective armistice.

50. The Neutral Nations Supervisory Commission, or any member thereof, shall be authorized to communicate with any member of the Military Armistice Commission.

ARTICLE III

ARRANGEMENTS RELATING TO PRISONERS OF WAR

51. The release and repatriation of all prisoners of war held in the custody of each side at the time this Armistice Agreement becomes effective shall be effected

in conformity with the following provisions agreed upon by both sides prior to the signing of this Armistice Agreement.

a. Within sixty (60) days after this Armistice Agreement becomes effective, each side shall, without offering any hindrance, directly repatriate and hand over in groups all those prisoners of war in its custody who insist on repatriation to the side to which they belonged at the time of capture. Repatriation shall be accomplished in accordance with the related provisions of this Article. In order to expedite the repatriation process of such personnel, each side shall, prior to the signing of the Armistice Agreement, exchange the total numbers, by nationalities, of personnel to be directly repatriated. Each group of prisoners of war delivered to the other side shall be accompanied by rosters, prepared by nationality, to include name, rank (if any) and internment or military serial number.

b. Each side shall release all those remaining prisoners of war, who are not directly repatriated, from its military control and from its custody and hand them over to the Neutral Nations Repatriation Commission for disposition in accordance with the provisions in the Annex hereto: "Terms of Reference for Neutral Nations Repatriation Commission."

c. So that there may be no misunderstanding owing to the equal use of three languages, the act of delivery of a prisoner of war by one side to the other side shall, for the purposes of this Armistice Agreement, be called "repatriation" in English, "song hwan" in Korean, and "ch'ien fan" in Chinese, notwithstanding the nationality or place of residence of such prisoner of war.

52. Each side insures that it will not employ in acts of war in the Korean conflict any prisoner of war released and repatriated incident to the coming into effect of this Armistice Agreement.

53. All the sick and injured prisoners of war who insist upon repatriation shall be repatriated with priority. Insofar as possible, there shall be captured medical personnel repatriated concurrently with the sick and injured prisoners of war, so as to provide medical care and attendance en route.

54. The repatriation of all the prisoners of war required by Sub-paragraph 51a hereof shall be completed within a time limit of sixty (60) days after this Armistice Agreement becomes effective. Within this time limit each side undertakes to complete the repatriation of the above-mentioned prisoners of war in its custody at the earliest practicable time.

55. PANMUNJOM is designated as the place where prisoners of war will be delivered and received by both sides. Additional place(s) of delivery and reception of prisoners of war in the Demilitarized Zone may be designated, if necessary, by the Committee for Repatriation of Prisoners of War.

56. a. A Committee for Repatriation of Prisoners of War is hereby established. It shall be composed of six (6) officers of field grade, three (3) of whom shall be appointed by the Commander-in-Chief, United Nations Command, and three (3) of whom shall be appointed jointly by the Supreme Commander of the Korean People's Army and the Commander of the Chinese People's Volunteers. This Committee shall, under the general supervision and direction of the Military Armistice Commission, be responsible for coordinating the specific plans of both sides for the repatriation of prisoners of war and for supervising the execution by both sides

of all of the provisions of this Armistice Agreement relating to the repatriation of prisoners of war. It shall be the duty of this Committee to coordinate the timing of the arrival of prisoners of war at the place(s) of delivery and reception of prisoners of war from the prisoner of war camps of both sides; to make, when necessary, such special arrangements as may be required with regard to the transportation and welfare of sick and injured prisoners of war; to coordinate the work of the joint Red Cross teams, established in Paragraph 57 hereof, in assisting in the repatriation of prisoners of war; to supervise the implementation of the arrangements for the actual repatriation of prisoners of war stipulated in Paragraphs 53 and 54 hereof; to select, when necessary, additional place(s) of delivery and reception of prisoners of war; and to carry out such other related functions as are required for the repatriation of prisoners of war.

b. When unable to reach agreement on any matter relating to its responsibilities, the Committee for Repatriation of Prisoners of War shall immediately refer such matter to the Military Armistice Commission for decision. The Committee for Repatriation of Prisoners of War shall maintain its headquarters in proximity to the headquarters of the Military Armistice Commission.

c. The Committee for Repatriation of Prisoners of War shall be dissolved by the Military Armistice Commission upon completion of the program of repatriation of prisoners of war.

57. a. Immediately after this Armistice Agreement becomes effective, joint Red Cross teams composed of representatives of the national Red Cross Societies of the countries contributing forces to the United Nations Command on the one hand, and representatives of the Red Cross Society of the Democratic People's Republic of Korea and representatives of the Red Cross Society of the People's Republic of China on the other hand, shall be established. The joint Red Cross teams shall assist in the execution by both sides of those provisions of this Armistice Agreement relating to the repatriation of all the prisoners of war specified in Sub-paragraph 51a hereof, who insist upon repatriation, by the performance of such humanitarian services as are necessary and desirable for the welfare of the prisoners of war. To accomplish this task, the joint Red Cross teams shall provide assistance in the delivering and receiving of prisoners of war by both sides at the place(s) of delivery and reception of prisoners of war, and shall visit the prisoner of war camps of both sides to comfort the prisoners of war and to bring in and distribute gift articles for the comfort and welfare of the prisoners of war. The joint Red Cross teams may provide services to prisoners of war while en route from prisoner of war camps to the place(s) of delivery and reception of prisoners of war.

b. The joint Red Cross teams shall be organized as set forth below:

(1) One team shall be composed of twenty (20) members, namely, ten (10) representatives from the national Red Cross Societies of each side, to assist in the delivering and receiving of prisoners of war by both sides at the place(s) of delivery and reception of prisoners of war. The chairmanship of this team shall alternate daily between representatives from the Red Cross Societies of the two sides. The work and services of this team shall be coordinated by the Committee for Repatriation of Prisoners of War.

(2) One team shall be composed of sixty (60) members, namely, thirty

(30) representatives from the national Red Cross Societies of each side, to visit the prisoner of war camps under the administration of the Korean People's Army and the Chinese People's Volunteers. This team may provide services to prisoners of war while en route from the prisoner of war camps to the place(s) of delivery and reception of prisoners of war. A representative of the Red Cross Society of the Democratic People's Republic of Korea or of the Red Cross Society of the People's Republic of China shall serve as chairman of this team.

(3) One team shall be composed of sixty (60) members, namely, thirty (30) representatives from the national Red Cross Societies of each side, to visit the prisoner of war camps under the administration of the United Nations Command. This team may provide services to prisoners of war while en route from the prisoner of war camps to the place(s) of delivery and reception of prisoners of war. A representative of a Red Cross Society of a nation contributing forces to the United Nations Command shall serve as chairman of this team.

(4) In order to facilitate the functioning of each joint Red Cross team, sub-teams composed of not less than two (2) members from the team, with an equal number of representatives from each side, may be formed as circumstances require.

(5) Additional personnel such as drivers, clerks, and interpreters, and such equipment as may be required by the joint Red Cross teams to perform their missions, shall be furnished by the Commander of each side to the team operating in the territory under his military control.

(6) Whenever jointly agreed upon by the representatives of both sides or any joint Red Cross team, the size of such team may be increased or decreased, subject to confirmation by the Committee for Repatriation of Prisoners of War.

c. The Commander of each side shall cooperate fully with the joint Red Cross teams in the performance of their functions, and undertakes to insure the security of the personnel of the joint Red Cross team in the area under his military control. The Commander of each side shall provide such logistic, administrative, and communications facilities as may be required by the team operating in the territory under his military control.

d. The joint Red Cross teams shall be dissolved upon completion of the program of repatriation of all the prisoners of war specified in Sub-paragraph 51a hereof, who insist upon repatriation.

58. a. The Commander of each side shall furnish to the Commander of the other side as soon as practicable, but not later than ten (10) days after this Armistice Agreement becomes effective, the following information concerning prisoners of war:

(1) Complete data pertaining to the prisoners of war who escaped since the effective date of the data last exchanged.

(2) Insofar as practicable, information regarding name, nationality, rank, and other identification data, date and cause of death, and place of burial, of those prisoners of war who died while in his custody.

b. If any prisoners of war escape or die after the effective date of the supplementary information specified above, the detaining side shall furnish to the other side, through the Committee for Repatriation of Prisoners of War, the data pertaining thereto in accordance with the provisions of Sub-paragraph 58a hereof.

Such data shall be furnished at ten-day intervals until the completion of the program of delivery and reception of prisoners of war.

c. Any escaped prisoner of war who returns to the custody of the detaining side after the completion of the program of delivery and reception of prisoners of war shall be delivered to the Military Armistice Commission for disposition.

59. a. All civilians who, at the time this Armistice Agreement becomes effective, are in territory under the military control of the Commander-in-Chief, United Nations Command, and who, on 24 June 1950, resided north of the Military Demarcation Line established in this Armistice Agreement shall, if they desire to return home, be permitted and assisted by the Commander-in-Chief, United Nations Command, to return to the area north of the Military Demarcation Line; and all civilians who, at the time this Armistice Agreement becomes effective, are in territory under the military control of the Supreme Commander of the Korean People's Army and the Commander of the Chinese People's Volunteers, and who, on 24 June 1950, resided south of the Military Demarcation Line established in this Armistice Agreement shall, if they desire to return home, be permitted and assisted by the Supreme Commander of the Korean People's Army and the Commander of the Chinese People's Volunteers to return to the area south of the Military Demarcation Line. The Commander of each side shall be responsible for publicizing widely throughout territory under his military control the contents of the provisions of this Sub-paragraph, and for calling upon the appropriate civil authorities to give necessary guidance and assistance to all such civilians who desire to return home.

b. All civilians of foreign nationality who, at the time this Armistice Agreement becomes effective, are in territory under the military control of the Supreme Commander of the Korean People's Army and the Commander of the Chinese People's Volunteers shall, if they desire to proceed to territory under the military control of the Commander-in-Chief, United Nations Command, be permitted and assisted to do so; all civilians of foreign nationality who, at the time this Armistice Agreement becomes effective, are in territory under the military control of the Commander-in-Chief, United Nations Command, shall, if they desire to proceed to territory under the military control of the Supreme Commander of the Korean People's Army and the Commander of the Chinese People's Volunteers, be permitted and assisted to do so. The Commander of each side shall be responsible for publicizing widely throughout the territory under his military control the contents of the provisions of this Sub-paragraph, and for calling upon the appropriate civil authorities to give necessary guidance and assistance to all such civilians of foreign nationality who desire to proceed to territory under the military control of the Commander of the other side.

c. Measures to assist in the return of civilians provided for in Sub-paragraph 59a hereof and the movement of civilians provided for in Sub-paragraph 59b hereof shall be commenced by both sides as soon as possible after this Armistice Agreement becomes effective.

d. (1) A Committee for Assisting the Return of Displaced Civilians is hereby established. It shall be composed of four (4) officers of field grade, two (2) of whom shall be appointed by the Commander-in-Chief, United Nations Command, and two (2) of whom shall be appointed jointly by the Supreme Commander of the

Korean People's Army and the Commander of the Chinese People's Volunteers. This Committee shall, under the general supervision and direction of the Military Armistice Commission, be responsible for coordinating the specific plans of both sides for assistance to the return of the above-mentioned civilians, and for supervising the execution by both sides of all of the provisions of this Armistice Agreement relating to the return of the above-mentioned civilians. It shall be the duty of this Committee to make necessary arrangements, including those of transportation, for expediting and coordinating the movement of the above-mentioned civilians; to select the crossing point(s) through which the above-mentioned civilians will cross the Military Demarcation Line; to arrange for security at the crossing point(s); and to carry out such other functions as are required to accomplish the return of the above-mentioned civilians.

(2) When unable to reach agreement on any matter relating to its responsibilities, the Committee for Assisting the Return of Displaced Civilians shall immediately refer such matter to the Military Armistice Commission for decision. The Committee for Assisting the Return of Displaced Civilians shall maintain its headquarters in proximity to the headquarters of the Military Armistice Commission.

(3) The Committee for Assisting the Return of Displaced Civilians shall be dissolved by the Military Armistice Commission upon fulfillment of its mission.

ARTICLE IV

RECOMMENDATION TO THE GOVERNMENTS CONCERNED ON BOTH SIDES

60. In order to insure the peaceful settlement of the Korean question, the military Commanders of both sides hereby recommend to the governments of the countries concerned on both sides that, within three (3) months after the Armistice Agreement is signed and becomes effective, a political conference of a higher level of both sides be held by representatives appointed respectively to settle through negotiation the questions of the withdrawal of all foreign forces from Korea, the peaceful settlement of the Korean question, etc.

ARTICLE V

MISCELLANEOUS

61. Amendments and additions to this Armistice Agreement must be mutually agreed to by the Commanders of the opposing sides.

62. The Articles and Paragraphs of this Armistice Agreement shall remain in effect until expressly superseded either by mutually acceptable amendments and additions or by provision in an appropriate agreement for a peaceful settlement at a political level between both sides.

63. All of the provisions of this Armistice Agreement, other than Paragraph 12, shall become effective at   hours on   1953.

Done at Panmunjom, Korea, at   hours on the   day of 1953, in English, Korean, and Chinese, all texts being equally authentic.

KIM IL SUNG	PENG TEH-HUAI	MARK W. CLARK
Marshal, Democratic People's Republic of Korea Supreme Commander, Korean People's Army	Commander, Chinese People's Volunteers	General, United States Army Commander-in-Chief, United Nations Command

PRESENT

NAM IL	WILLIAM K. HARRISON, JR.
General, Korean People's Army Senior Delegate, Delegation of the Korean People's Army and the Chinese People's Volunteers	Lieutenant General, United States Army Senior Delegate, United Nations Command Delegation

ANNEX

TERMS OF REFERENCE
FOR
NEUTRAL NATIONS REPATRIATION
COMMISSION
(See Sub-paragraph 51b)

I

GENERAL

1. In order to ensure that all prisoners of war have the opportunity to exercise their right to be repatriated following an armistice, Sweden, Switzerland, Poland, Czechoslovakia and India shall each be requested by both sides to appoint a member to a Neutral Nations Repatriation Commission which shall be established to take custody in Korea of those prisoners of war who, while in the custody of the detaining powers, have not exercised their right to be repatriated. The Neutral Nations Repatriation Commission shall establish its headquarters within the Demilitarized Zone in the vicinity of Panmunjom, and shall station subordinate bodies of the same composition as the Neutral Nations Repatriation Commission at those locations at which the Repatriation Commission assumes custody of prisoners of war. Representatives of both sides shall be permitted to observe the operations of the Repatriation Commission and its subordinate bodies to include explanations and interviews.

2. Sufficient armed forces and any other operating personnel required to assist the Neutral Nations Repatriation Commission in carrying out its functions and responsibilities shall be provided exclusively by India, whose representative shall be the umpire in accordance with the provisions of Article 132 of the Geneva Convention, and shall also be chairman and executive agent of the Neutral Nations Repatriation Commission. Representatives from each of the other four powers shall be allowed staff assistants in equal number not to exceed fifty (50) each.

When any of the representatives of the neutral nations is absent for some reason, that representative shall designate an alternate representative of his own nationality to exercise his functions and authority. The arms of all personnel provided for in this Paragraph shall be limited to military police type small arms.

3. No force or threat of force shall be used against the prisoners of war specified in Paragraph 1 above to prevent or effect their repatriation, and no violence to their persons or affront to their dignity or self-respect shall be permitted in any manner for any purpose whatsoever (but see Paragraph 7 below). This duty is enjoined on and entrusted to the Neutral Nations Repatriation Commission. This Commission shall ensure that prisoners of war shall at all times be treated humanely in accordance with the specific provisions of the Geneva Convention, and with the general spirit of that Convention.

II

CUSTODY OF PRISONERS OF WAR

4. All prisoners of war who have not exercised their right of repatriation following the effective date of the Armistice Agreement shall be released from the military control and from the custody of the detaining side as soon as practicable, and, in all cases, within sixty (60) days subsequent to the effective date of the Armistice Agreement to the Neutral Nations Repatriation Commission at locations in Korea to be designated by the detaining side.

5. At the time the Neutral Nations Repatriation Commission assumes control of the prisoner of war installations, the military forces of the detaining side shall be withdrawn therefrom, so that the locations specified in the preceding Paragraph shall be taken over completely by the armed forces of India.

6. Notwithstanding the provisions of Paragraph 5 above, the detaining side shall have the responsibility for maintaining and ensuring security and order in the areas around the locations where the prisoners of war are in custody and for preventing and restraining any armed forces (including irregular armed forces) in the area under its control from any acts of disturbance and intrusion against the locations where the prisoners of war are in custody.

7. Notwithstanding the provisions of Paragraph 3 above, nothing in this agreement shall be construed as derogating from the authority of the Neutral Nations Repatriation Commission to exercise its legitimate functions and responsibilities for the control of the prisoners of war under its temporary jurisdiction.

III

EXPLANATION

8. The Neutral Nations Repatriation Commission, after having received and taken into custody all those prisoners of war who have not exercised their right to be repatriated, shall immediately make arrangements so that within ninety (90) days after the Neutral Nations Repatriation Commission takes over the custody, the nations to which the prisoners of war belong shall have freedom and facilities to send representatives to the locations where such prisoners of war are in custody to explain to all the prisoners of war depending upon these nations their rights and to inform them of any matters relating to their return to their homelands,

particularly of their full freedom to return home to lead a peaceful life, under the following provisions:

a. The number of such explaining representatives shall not exceed seven (7) per thousand prisoners of war held in custody by the Neutral Nations Repatriation Commission; and the minimum authorized shall not be less than a total of five (5);

b. The hours during which the explaining representatives shall have access to the prisoners shall be as determined by the Neutral Nations Repatriation Commission, and generally in accord with Article 53 of the Geneva Convention Relative to the Treatment of Prisoners of War;

c. All explanations and interviews shall be conducted in the presence of a representative of each member nation of the Neutral Nations Repatriation Commission and a representative from the detaining side;

d. Additional provisions governing the explanation work shall be prescribed by the Neutral Nations Repatriation Commission, and will be designed to employ the principles enumerated in Paragraph 3 above and in this Paragraph;

e. The explaining representatives, while engaging in their work, shall be allowed to bring with them necessary facilities and personnel for wireless communications. The number of communications personnel shall be limited to one team per location at which explaining representatives are in residence, except in the event all prisoners of war are concentrated in one location, in which case, two (2) teams shall be permitted. Each team shall consist of not more than six (6) communications personnel.

9. Prisoners of war in its custody shall have freedom and facilities to make representations and communications to the Neutral Nations Repatriation Commission and to representatives and subordinate bodies of the Neutral Nations Repatriation Commission and to inform them of their desires on any matter concerning the prisoners of war themselves, in accordance with arrangements made for the purpose by the Neutral Nations Repatriation Commission.

IV

DISPOSITION OF PRISONERS OF WAR

10. Any prisoner of war who, while in the custody of the Neutral Nations Repatriation Commission, decides to exercise the right of repatriation, shall make an application requesting repatriation to a body consisting of a representative of each member nation of the Neutral Nations Repatriation Commission. Once such an application is made, it shall be considered immediately by the Neutral Nations Repatriation Commission or one of its subordinate bodies so as to determine immediately by majority vote the validity of such application. Once such an application is made to and validated by the Commission or one of its subordinate bodies, the prisoner of war concerned shall immediately be transferred to and accommodated in the tents set up for those who are ready to be repatriated. Thereafter, he shall, while still in the custody of the Neutral Nations Repatriation Commission, be delivered forthwith to the prisoner of war exchange point at Panmunjom for repatriation under the procedure prescribed in the Armistice Agreement.

11. At the expiration of ninety (90) days after the transfer of custody of the prisoners of war to the Neutral Nations Repatriation Commission, access of repre-

sentatives to captured personnel as provided for in Paragraph 8 above, shall terminate, and the question of disposition of the prisoners of war who have not exercised their right to be repatriated shall be submitted to the Political Conference recommended to be convened in Paragraph 60, Draft Armistice Agreement, which shall endeavor to settle this question within thirty (30) days, during which period the Neutral Nations Repatriation Commission shall continue to retain custody of those prisoners of war. The Neutral Nations Repatriation Commission shall declare the relief from the prisoner of war status to civilian status of any prisoners of war who have not exercised their right to be repatriated and for whom no other disposition has been agreed to by the Political Conference within one hundred and twenty (120) days after the Neutral Nations Repatriation Commission has assumed their custody. Thereafter, according to the application of each individual, those who choose to go to neutral nations shall be assisted by the Neutral Nations Repatriation Commission and the Red Cross Society of India. This operation shall be completed within thirty (30) days, and upon its completion, the Neutral Nations Repatriation Commission shall immediately cease its functions and declare its dissolution. After the dissolution of the Neutral Nations Repatriation Commission, whenever and wherever any of those above-mentioned civilians who have been relieved from the prisoner of war status desire to return to their fatherlands, the authorities of the localities where they are shall be responsible for assisting them in returning to their fatherlands.

V

RED CROSS VISITATION

12. Essential Red Cross service for prisoners of war in custody of the Neutral Nations Repatriation Commission shall be provided by India in accordance with regulations issued by the Neutral Nations Repatriation Commission.

VI

PRESS COVERAGE

13. The Neutral Nations Repatriation Commission shall insure freedom of the press and other news media in observing the entire operation as enumerated herein, in accordance with procedures to be established by the Neutral Nations Repatriation Commission.

VII

LOGISTICAL SUPPORT FOR PRISONERS OF WAR

14. Each side shall provide logistical support for the prisoners of war in the area under its military control, delivering required support to the Neutral Nations Repatriation Commission at an agreed delivery point in the vicinity of each prisoner of war installation.

15. The cost of repatriating prisoners of war to the exchange point at Panmunjom shall be borne by the detaining side and the cost from the exchange point by the side on which said prisoners depend in accordance with Article 118 of the Geneva Convention.

16. The Red Cross Society of India shall be responsible for providing such general service personnel in the prisoner of war installations as required by the Neutral Nations Repatriation Commission.

17. The Neutral Nations Repatriation Commission shall provide medical support for the prisoners of war as may be practicable. The detaining side shall provide medical support as practicable upon the request of the Neutral Nations Repatriation Commission and specifically for those cases requiring extensive treatment or hospitalization. The Neutral Nations Repatriation Commission shall maintain custody of prisoners of war during such hospitalization. The detaining side shall facilitate such custody. Upon completion of treatment, prisoners of war shall be returned to a prisoners of war installation as specified in Paragraph 4 above.

18. The Neutral Nations Repatriation Commission is entitled to obtain from both sides such legitimate assistance as it may require in carrying out its duties and tasks, but both sides shall not under any name and in any form interfere or exert influence.

VIII

LOGISTICAL SUPPORT FOR THE NEUTRAL NATIONS REPATRIATION COMMISSION

19. Each side shall be responsible for providing logistical support for the personnel of the Neutral Nations Repatriation Commission stationed in the area under its military control, and both sides shall contribute on an equal basis to such support within the Demilitarized Zone. The precise arrangements shall be subject to determination between the Neutral Nations Repatriation Commission and the detaining side in each case.

20. Each of the detaining sides shall be responsible for protecting the explaining representatives from the other side while in transit over lines of communication within its area, as set forth in Paragraph 23 for the Neutral Nations Repatriation Commission, to a place of residence and while in residence in the vicinity of but not within each of the locations where the prisoners of war are in custody. The Neutral Nations Repatriation Commission shall be responsible for the security of such representatives within the actual limits of the locations where the prisoners of war are in custody.

21. Each of the detaining sides shall provide transportation, housing, communication, and other agreed logistical support to the explaining representatives of the other side while they are in the area under its military control. Such services shall be provided on a reimbursable basis.

IX

PUBLICATION

22. After the Armistice Agreement becomes effective, the terms of this agreement shall be made known to all prisoners of war who, while in the custody of the detaining side, have not exercised their right to be repatriated.

X

MOVEMENT

23. The movement of the personnel of the Neutral Nations Repatriation Commission and repatriated prisoners of war shall be over lines of communication as determined by the command(s) of the opposing side and the Neutral Nations Repatriation Commission. A map showing these lines of communication shall be furnished the command of the opposing side and the Neutral Nations Repatriation Commission. Movement of such personnel, except within locations as designated in Paragraph 4 above, shall be under the control of, and escorted by, personnel of the side in whose area the travel is being undertaken; however, such movement shall not be subject to any obstruction and coercion.

XI

PROCEDURAL MATTERS

24. The interpretation of this agreement shall rest with the Neutral Nations Repatriation Commission. The Neutral Nations Repatriation Commission, and/or any subordinate bodies to which functions are designed or assigned by the Neutral Nations Repatriation Commission, shall operate on the basis of majority vote.

25. The Neutral Nations Repatriation Commission shall submit a weekly report to the opposing Commanders on the status of prisoners of war in its custody, indicating the numbers repatriated and remaining at the end of each week.

26. When this agreement has been acceded to by both sides and by the five powers named herein, it shall become effective upon the date the Armistice becomes effective.

Done at Panmunjom, Korea, at 1400 hours on the 8th day of June 1953, in English, Korean, and Chinese, all texts being equally authentic.

NAM IL
General, Korean People's Army
Senior Delegate,
Delegation of the Korean People's
   Army and the Chinese People's
   Volunteers

WILLIAM K. HARRISON, JR.
Lieutenant General, United
   States Army
Senior Delegate,
United Nations Command
   Delegation

Medal of Honor Winners in Korea

SUMMARY

U. S. Army	78
U. S. Marine Corps	42
U. S. Navy	7
U. S. Air Force	4
TOTAL	131

Abrell, Charles G.	Terre Haute, Ind.	USMC	Cpl.
Adams, Stanley T.*	Olathe, Kans.	USArmy	Sgt. 1/c
Barber, William E.*	West Liberty, Ky.	USMC	Capt.
Barker, Charles H.*	Pickens, S. C.	USArmy	Pvt.
Baugh, William B.	Harrison, O.	USMC	Pfc.
Benfold, Edward C.	Philadelphia, Pa.	USN	HM3
Bennett, Emory L.	Cocoa, Fla.	USArmy	Pfc.
Bleak, David B.*	Shelley, Idaho	USArmy	Sgt.
Brittin, Nelson V.	Audubon, N. J.	USArmy	Sgt. 1/c
Brown, Melvin L.	Mahaffey, Pa.	USArmy	Pfc.
Burke, Lloyd L.*	Stuttgart, Ark.	USArmy	1 Lt.
Burris, Tony K.	Blanchard, Okla.	USArmy	Sgt. 1/c
Cafferata, Hector A., Jr.*	Montville, N. J.	USMC	Pvt.
Champagne, David B.	Wakefield, R. I.	USMC	Cpl.
Charette, William R.*	Ludington, Mich.	USN	HM3
Charlton, Cornelius H.	New York, N. Y.	USArmy	Sgt.
Christianson, Stanley R.	Mindoro, Wis.	USMC	Pfc.
Collier, Gilbert G.	Tichnor, Ark.	USArmy	Cpl.
Collier, John W.	Worthington, Ky.	USArmy	Cpl.
Commiskey, Henry A.*	Hattiesburg, Miss.	USMC	2 Lt.
Coursen, Samuel S.	Madison, N. J.	USArmy	1 Lt.
Craig, Gordon M.	Elmwood, Mass.	USArmy	Cpl.
Crump, Jerry K.*	Forest City, N. C.	USArmy	Cpl.
Davenport, Jack A.	Mission, Kans.	USMC	Cpl.
Davis, George A.	Lubbock, Tex.	USAF	Lt. Col.
Davis, Raymond G.*	Goggins, Ga.	USMC	Lt. Col.
Dean, William F.*	Berkeley, Calif.	USArmy	M/Gen.
Desiderio, Reginald B.	El Monte, Calif.	USArmy	Capt.
DeWert, Richard D.	Taunton, Mass.	USN	HM

425

Dewey, Duane E.*	South Haven, Mich.	USMC	Cpl.
Dodd, Carl H.*	Kenvir, Ky.	USArmy	2 Lt.
Duke, Ray E.	Whitwell, Tenn.	USArmy	Sgt. 1/c
Edwards, Junior D.	Indianola, Iowa	USArmy	Sgt. 1/c
Essebagger, John, Jr.	Holland, Mich.	USArmy	Cpl.
Faith, Don C., Jr.	Washington, D. C.	USArmy	Lt. Col.
Garcia, Fernando L.	Utado, P. R.	USMC	Pfc.
George, Charles	Whittier, N. C.	USArmy	Pfc.
Gilliland, Charles L.	Yellville, Ark.	USArmy	Cpl.
Gomez, Edward	Omaha, Nebr.	USMC	Pfc.
Goodblood, Clair	Burnham, Me.	USArmy	Cpl.
Gullen, Ambrosio	El Paso, Tex.	USMC	S/Sgt.
Hammond, Francis C.	Alexandria, Va.	USN	HM
Hammond, Lester, Jr.	Quincy, Ill.	USArmy	Cpl.
Handrich, Melvin O.	Manawa, Wis.	USArmy	M/Sgt.
Hanson, Jack G.	Escatawpa, Miss.	USArmy	Pfc.
Hartell, Lee R.	Danbury, Conn.	USArmy	1 Lt.
Harvey, Raymond*	Pasadena, Calif.	USArmy	Capt.
Henry, Frederick F.	Clinton, Okla.	USArmy	1 Lt.
Hernandez, Rodolfo P.*	Fowler, Calif.	USArmy	Cpl.
Hudner, Thomas J., Jr.*	Fall River, Mass.	USN	Lt. JG
Ingman, Einar H.*	Tomahawk, Wis.	USArmy	Cpl.
Jecelin, William R.	Baltimore, Md.	USArmy	Sgt.
Johnson, James E.	Pocatello, Idaho	USMC	Sgt.
Jordan, Mack A.	Collins, Miss.	USArmy	Pfc.
Kanell, Billie G.	Poplar Bluff, Mo.	USArmy	Pvt.
Kaufman, Loren R.	The Dalles, Ore.	USArmy	Sgt. 1/c
Kelly, John D.	Homestead, Pa.	USMC	Pfc.
Kelso, Jack W.	Fresno, Calif.	USMC	Pvt.
Kennemore, Robert S.*	Greenville, S. C.	USMC	S/Sgt.
Kilmer, John Edward	San Antonio, Tex.	USN	Hn
Knight, Noah O.	Jefferson, S. C.	USArmy	Pfc.
Koelsch, John K.	Scarborough, N. Y.	USN	Lt. JG
Kouma, Ernest R.*	Dwight, Nebr.	USArmy	M/Sgt.
Krzyzowski, Edward C.	Cicero, Ill.	USArmy	Capt.
Kyle, Darwin K.	S. Charleston, W. Va.	USArmy	2 Lt.
Lee, Hubert L.*	Leland, Miss.	USArmy	M/Sgt.
Libby, George D.	Casco, Me.	USArmy	Sgt.
Littleton, Herbert A.	Nampa, Idaho	USMC	Pfc.
Long, Charles R.	Kansas City, Mo.	USArmy	Sgt.
Lopez, Baldomero	Tampa, Fla.	USMC	1 Lt.
Loring, Charles J., Jr.	Portland, Me.	USAF	Maj.
Lyell, William F.	Old Hickory, Tenn.	USArmy	Cpl.
McGovern, Robert M.	Washington, D. C.	USArmy	1 Lt.
McLaughlin, Alford L.*	Leeds, Ala.	USMC	Pfc.
Martinez, Benito	Fort Hancock, Tex.	USArmy	Cpl.
Matthews, Daniel P.	Van Nuys, Calif.	USMC	Sgt.
Mausert, Frederick W., III	Dresher, Pa.	USMC	Sgt.

Mendonca, Leroy A.	Honolulu, T. H.	USArmy	Sgt.
Millett, Lewis L.*	S. Dartmouth, Mass.	USArmy	Capt.
Mitchell, Frank N.	Roaring Spr., Tex.	USMC	1 Lt.
Miyamura, Hiroshi H.*	Gallup, N. M.	USArmy	Sgt.
Mize, Ola L.*	Gadsden, Ala.	USArmy	M/Sgt.
Monegan, Walter C., Jr.	Seattle, Wash.	USMC	Pfc.
Moreland, Whitt L.	Austin, Tex.	USMC	Pfc.
Moyer, Donald R.	Keego Harbor, Mich.	USArmy	Sgt. 1/c
Murphy, Raymond G.*	Pueblo, Colo.	USMC	1 Lt.
Myers, Reginal R.*	Boise, Idaho	USMC	Maj.
Obregon, Eugene A.	Los Angeles, Calif.	USMC	Pfc.
O'Brien, George H., Jr.,*	Big Spring, Tex.	USMC	2 Lt.
Ouellette, Joseph R.	Lowell, Mass.	USArmy	Pfc.
Page, John U. D.	St. Paul, Minn.	USArmy	Lt. Col.
Pendleton, Charles F.	Fort Worth, Tex.	USArmy	Cpl.
Phillips, Lee H.	Ben Hill, Ga.	USMC	Cpl.
Pililaau, Herbert K.	Waianae, T. H.	USArmy	Pfc.
Pittman, John A.*	Tallula, Miss.	USArmy	Sgt.
Pomeroy, Ralph E.	Quinwood, W. Va.	USArmy	Pfc.
Porter, Donn F.	Ruxton, Md.	USArmy	Sgt.
Poynter, James I.	Downey, Calif.	USMC	Sgt.
Ramer, George H.	Lewisburg, Pa.	USMC	2 Lt.
Red Cloud, Mitchell, Jr.	Friendship, Wis.	USArmy	Cpl.
Reem, Robert D.	Elizabethtown, Pa.	USMC	2 Lt.
Rodriguez, Joseph C.*	San Bernardino, Calif.	USArmy	Pfc.
Rosser, Ronald E.*	Crooksville, O.	USArmy	Cpl.
Schoonover, Dan D.	Boise, Idaho	USArmy	Cpl.
Schowalter, Edward R., Jr.	Metairie, La.	USArmy	1 Lt.
Sebille, Louis J.	Harbor Beach, Mich.	USAF	Maj.
Shea, Richard T., Jr.	Portsmouth, Va.	USArmy	1 Lt.
Shuck, William E., Jr.	Ridgeley, West Va.	USMC	S/Sgt.
Simanek, Robert E.*	Detroit, Mich.	USMC	Pfc.
Sitman, William S.	Bedford, Pa.	USArmy	Sgt.
Sitter, Carl L.*	Pueblo, Colo.	USMC	Capt.
Skinner, Sherrod E., Jr.	East Lansing, Mich.	USMC	2 Lt.
Smith, David M.	Livingston, Ky.	USArmy	Pfc.
Speicher, Clifton T.	Gray, Pa.	USArmy	Cpl.
Stone, James L.*	Pine Bluff, Ark.	USArmy	1 Lt.
Story, Luther H.	Americus, Ga.	USArmy	Pfc.
Sudut, Jerome A.	Wausau, Wis.	USArmy	2 Lt.
Thompson, William	New York, N. Y.	USArmy	Pfc.
Turner, Charles W.	Boston, Mass.	USArmy	Sgt. 1/c
Van Winkle, Archie*	Everett, Wash.	USMC	S/Sgt.
Vittori, Joseph	Beverly, Mass.	USMC	Cpl.
Walmsley, John S., Jr.	Silver Spring, Md.	USAF	Capt.
Watkins, Lewis G.	Seneca, S. C.	USMC	S/Sgt.
Watkins, Travis E.	Gladewater, Tex.	USArmy	M/Sgt.
West, Ernest E.*	Wurtland, Ky.	USArmy	Pfc.

Wilson, Benjamin F.*	Vashon, Wash.	USArmy	1 Lt.
Wilson, Harold E.*	Birmingham, Ala.	USMC	T/Sgt.
Wilson, Richard G.	Cape Girardeau, Mo.	USArmy	Pfc.
Windrich, William G.	East Chicago, Ind.	USMC	S/Sgt.
Womack, Bryant H.	Rutherfordton, N. C.	USArmy	Pfc.
Young, Robert H.	Vallejo, Calif.	USArmy	Pfc.

* Living Awards.

Estimated Casualties of the Korean War

	DEAD	WOUNDED AND MISSING	TOTAL
Australia	265	1,387	1,652
Belgium	97	355	452
Canada	309	1,235	1,544
Colombia	140	517	657
Ethiopia	120	536	656
France	288	836	1,124
Greece	169	545	714
Netherlands	111	593	704
New Zealand	31	78	109
Philippines	92	356	448
Republic of Korea	415,004	428,568	843,572
South Africa (military and civilian)	20	16	36
Thailand	114	799	913
Turkey	717	2,413	3,130
United States	29,550	106,978	136,528
United Kingdom	670	2,692	3,362
TOTALS	447,697	547,904	995,601

COMMUNIST FORCES

China	900,000
North Korea	520,000
TOTAL	1,420,000

Bibliography

Appleman, Roy E., *South to the Naktong, North to the Yalu (June–November 1950)*, *U. S. Army in the Korean War*, Washington: Office of the Chief of Military History, published by Government Printing Office, 1960.

Attlee, C. R., *As it Happened*, New York: The Viking Press, 1954.

Berger, Carl, *The Korea Knot, A Military-Political History*, Philadelphia: University of Pennsylvania Press, 1957.

Boorstin, Daniel J., *The Americans*, New York: Random House, 1958.

Bowles, Chester, *Ambassador's Report*, New York: Harper and Brothers, 1954.

Cagle, Malcolm W., and Frank A. Manson, *The Sea War in Korea*, Annapolis: United States Naval Institute, 1957.

Chung, Henry, *The Russians Came to Korea*, Seoul: The Korean Pacific Press, 1947.

Clark, Gen. Mark W., *Calculated Risk*, New York: Harper and Brothers, 1950.

——, *From the Danube to the Yalu*, New York: Harper and Brothers, 1954.

Dean, Maj. Gen. William F., *General Dean's Story*, New York: The Viking Press, 1954.

Deane, Philip, *I Was a Captive in Korea*, New York: W. W. Norton and Company, 1953.

Donovan, Robert J., *Eisenhower, The Inside Story*, New York: Harper and Brothers, 1956.

Duncan, David Douglas, *This Is War, A Photo Narrative of the Korean War*, New York: Harper and Brothers, 1951.

Esposito, Col. Vincent J., Chief Editor, *The West Point Atlas of American Wars*, Vol. II, *1900–1953*, New York: Frederick A. Praeger, 1952.

Futrell, Robert F., *The United States Air Force in Korea 1950–1953*, New York: Duell, Sloan and Pearce, 1961.

Geer, Andrew, *The New Breed, The Story of the U. S. Marines in Korea*, New York: Harper and Brothers, 1952.

Goldberg, Alfred, editor, *A History of the United States Air Force, 1907–1957*, Princeton: D. Van Nostrand Co., 1957.

Grajdanzev, Andrew J., *Modern Korea,* New Yoık: Institute of Pacific Relations, 1944.

Green, A. Wigfall, *The Epic of Korea,* Washington: Public Affairs Press, 1950.

Gugeler, Capt. Russell A., *Combat Actions in Korea,* Washington: Combat Forces Press, 1954.

Higgins, Marguerite, *War in Korea, The Report of a Woman Combat Correspondent,* Garden City: Doubleday and Company, 1951.

Higgins, Trumbull, *Korea and the Fall of MacArthur, A Précis in Limited War,* New York: Oxford University Press, 1960.

Joy, Adm. C. Turner, *How Communists Negotiate,* New York: The Macmillan Company, 1955.

Kahn, E. J., Jr., *The Peculiar War, Impressions of a Reporter in Korea,* New York: Random House, 1952.

Karig, Capt. Walter, Cmdr. Malcolm W. Cagle, and Lt. Cmdr. Frank A. Manson, *Battle Report,* Vol. VI, *The War in Korea,* New York: Rinehart and Company, 1952.

Kinkead, Eugene, *In Every War But One,* New York: W. W. Norton & Co., 1959.

Korea Flaming High, Excerpts from Statements by President Syngman Rhee in Crucial 1953, Seoul: Office of Public Information, Republic of Korea, 1954.

Korea–1950, Washington: Office of the Chief of Military History, Department of the Army, 1952.

Leckie, Robert, *The March to Glory, The Marine Breakout from Chosin,* New York: World Publishing Company, 1960.

Lie, Trygve, *In the Cause of Peace,* New York: The Macmillan Company, 1954.

Linklater, Eric, *Our Men in Korea,* London: Her Majesty's Stationer's Office, 1952.

McCune, George M., *Korea Today,* Cambridge: Harvard University Press, 1950.

Marshall, S. L. A., *The River and the Gauntlet, Defeat of the Eighth Army by the Chinese Communist Forces, November, 1950, in the Battle of the Chongchon River, Korea,* New York: William Morrow & Co., 1953.

——, *Infantry Operations and Weapons Usage in Korea (Winter of 1950–51),* Chevy Chase: Operations Research Office, the Johns Hopkins University, 1953.

——, *Pork Chop Hill,* New York: William Morrow & Co., 1956.

Metcalf, Clyde H., *The History of the United States Marine Corps,* New York: G. P. Putnam's Sons, 1939.

Miller, John, Jr., Maj. Owen J. Carroll, and Margaret E. Tackley, *Korea, 1951–1953:* Washington: Office of the Chief of Military History, Department of the Army, 1956.

Miller, Lt. Cmdr. Max, *I'm Sure We've Met Before, The Navy in Korea,* New York: E. P. Dutton and Co., 1951.

Montross, Lynn, *Cavalry of the Sky,* New York: Harper and Brothers, 1954.

——, and Capt. Nicholas A. Canzona, *U. S. Marine Operations in Korea, 1950–1953,* Vol. I, *The Pusan Perimeter,* Vol. II, *The Inchon-Seoul Operation,* Vol. III, *The Chosin Reservoir Campaign,* Washington: Historical Branch, G-3, Headquarters, U. S. Marine Corps, 1954–1957.

Mulvey, Timothy J., O.M.I., *These Are Your Sons, Sketches of Men Who Fought in Korea,* New York: The McGraw-Hill Book Company, 1952.

Oliver, Robert T., *Why War Came in Korea,* New York: Fordham University Press, 1950.

Pate, Sgt. Lloyd W., *Reactionary!, Life in a Communist Prison Camp,* New York: Harper and Brothers, 1956.

Pierce, Lt. Col. Philip N., and Lt. Col. Frank O. Hough, *The Compact History of the United States Marine Corps,* New York: Hawthorn Books, Inc., 1960.

Poats, Rutherford M., *Decision in Korea,* New York: The McBride Company, 1954.

Ridgway, Gen. Matthew B., *Soldier: The Memoirs of Matthew B. Ridgway,* New York: Harper and Brothers, 1956.

Riley, John W., Jr., and Wilbur Schramm, *The Reds Take a City, The Communist Occupation of Seoul with Eye-Witness Accounts,* New Brunswick: Rutgers University Press, 1951.

Rovere, Richard H., and Arthur M. Schlesinger, Jr., *The General and the President, and the Future of American Foreign Policy,* New York: Farrar, Straus and Young, 1951.

Russ, Martin, *The Last Parallel,* New York: Rinehart, 1957.

Stewart, Col. James T., *Airpower: The Decisive Force in Korea,* Princeton: D. Van Nostrand Co., 1957.

Stone, I. F., *The Hidden History of the Korean War,* New York: The Monthly Review Press, 1952.

Thomas, Maj. R. C. W., O.B.E., *The War in Korea, A Military Study up to the Time of the Signing of the Cease-Fire,* Aldershot: Gale & Polden, 1954.

Thompson, Reginald, *Cry Korea, A British Correspondent's Report,* London: Macdonald & Col, 1951.

Truman, Harry S., *Memoirs by Harry S. Truman,* Vol. I, *Year of Decisions,* and Vol. II, *Years of Trial and Hope,* Garden City: Doubleday and Company, 1955–56.

Vatcher, William H., Jr., *Panmunjom, The Story of the Korean Military Armistice Negotiations,* New York: Frederick A. Praeger, 1958.

Voorhees, Lt. Col. Melvin B., *Korean Tales,* New York: Simon and Schuster, 1952.

Warner, Denis, *Hurricane from China, Mao Tse-tung's Plan for World Conquest,* New York: The Macmillan Company, 1961.

Westover, Capt. John G., *Combat Support in Korea,* Washington: Combat Forces Press, 1955.

White, Theodore H., and Annalee Jacoby, *Thunder out of China, Account of Civil War Between the Communists and Nationalists,* New York: William Sloane Associates, 1946.

White, W. L., *The Captives of Korea, Their Treatment of Our Prisoners and Our Treatment of Theirs,* New York: Scribner's, 1957.

————, *Back Down the Ridge, The Story of What Happens to the Men Who Get Clobbered in Korea,* New York: Harcourt, Brace and Company, 1953.

Whiting, Allen S., *China Crosses the Yalu, The Decision to Enter the Korean War,* New York: The Macmillan Co., 1960.

Whitney, Maj. Gen. Courtney, *MacArthur: His Rendezvous with History,* New York: Alfred A. Knopf, 1956.

Willoughby, Charles A., and John Chamberlain, *MacArthur 1941–1951,* New York: The McGraw-Hill Book Company, 1954.

Magazines:

Air University Quarterly Review

Army

Combat Forces Journal (predecessor of *Army*)

Leatherneck

Marine Corps Gazette

U. S. Institute of Naval Proceedings

Notes

PART I

Chapter Three
1. *Memoirs* by Harry S. Truman, Vol. II, *Years of Trial and Hope* (New York, 1955), p. 329.
2. Truman, *op. cit.*, Vol. II, p. 328.

Chapter Four
1. Truman, *op. cit.*, Vol. II, p. 332.
2. Truman, *op. cit.*, Vol. II, p. 333.

Chapter Five
1. Truman, *op. cit.*, Vol. II, p. 337.

Chapter Six
1. *U. S. Army in the Korean War, South to the Naktong, North to the Yalu,* by Roy E. Appleman (Washington, 1960), p. 60.
2. Appleman, *op. cit.*, p. 61.

Chapter Seven
1. *General Dean's Story*, by Maj. Gen. William F. Dean as told to William Worden (New York, 1954), p. 23.
2. Dean, *op. cit.*, p. 26.
3. Dean, *op. cit.*, p. 28.
4. Dean, *op. cit.*, p. 39.

Chapter Eight
1. Dean, *op. cit.*, p. 29.
2. *I Was a Captive in Korea*, by Philip Deane (New York, 1954), p. 18.
3. Deane, *op. cit.*, p. 26.
4. Appleman, *op. cit.*, p. 180.
5. Appleman, *op. cit.*, p. 181.
6. *The Americans*, by Daniel J. Boorstin (New York, 1958), p. 363.
7. *Korea–1950*, Office of the Chief of Military History, Department of the Army (Washington, 1952), pp. 15–16.

Chapter Nine
1. Appleman, *op. cit.*, pp. 207–8.
2. *The Compact History of the United States Marine Corps*, by Lt. Col. Philip N. Pierce and Lt. Col. Frank O. Hough (New York, 1960), p. 284.

Chapter Ten
1. Truman, *op. cit.*, p. 354.

Chapter Eleven
1. *The New Breed, The Story of the U. S. Marines in Korea,* by Andrew Geer (New York, 1952), p. 56.
2. Appleman, *op. cit.*, pp. 347–48.

Chapter Twelve
1. Appleman, *op. cit.*, pp. 387–88.

PART II

Chapter Two
1. *Battle Report, The War in Korea,* by Capt. Walter Karig, *et al.* (New York, 1952), pp. 254–55.
2. *Decision in Korea,* by Rutherford M. Poats (New York, 1954), pp. 67–69.

Chapter Three
1. *China Crosses the Yalu, The Decision to Enter the Korean War,* by Allen S. Whiting (New York, 1960), pp. 96–97.
2. Truman, *op. cit.*, Vol. II, p. 362.
3. *The River and the Gauntlet,* by. S. L. A. Marshall (New York, 1953), p. 7.
4. Whiting, *op. cit.*, pp. 169–70.

Chapter Five
1. Truman, *op. cit.*, Vol. II, pp. 379–80.

Chapter Six
1. Appleman, *op. cit.*, p. 770.
2. Marshall, *op. cit.*, pp. 170–71.
3. Marshall, *op. cit.*, pp. 318–20.

Chapter Seven
1. Truman, *op. cit.*, Vol. II, pp. 385–86.
2. *The March to Glory,* by Robert Leckie (New York, 1960), p. 192.
3. Leckie, *op. cit.*, p. 215.

PART III

Chapter One
1. Truman, *op. cit.*, Vol. II, pp. 406–7.
2. *Soldier: The Memoirs of Matthew B. Ridgway,* by General Matthew B. Ridgway as told to Harold H. Martin (New York, 1956), p. 204.
3. Ridgway, *op. cit.*, p. 210.
4. Ridgway, *op. cit.*, p. 213.

Chapter Three
1. Ridgway, *op. cit.*, p. 216.

Chapter Four
1. Truman, *op. cit.*, Vol. II, pp. 447–48.

2. *MacArthur: His Rendezvous with History,* Maj. Gen. Courtney Whitney (New York, 1956), p. 471.

Chapter Five
1. *The United States Air Force in Korea, 1950–1953,* by Robert F. Futrell (New York, 1961), p. 267.
2. *The Sea War in Korea,* by Cmdr. Malcolm W. Cagle and Cmdr. Frank A. Manson, (Annapolis, 1957), pp. 308–9.
3. Ridgway, *op. cit.,* pp. 219–20.

PART IV

Chapter One
1. *How Communists Negotiate,* by Admiral C. Turner Joy (New York, 1955), p. 11.
2. Joy, *op. cit.,* pp. 12–13.
3. Joy, *op. cit.,* pp. 4–5.

Chapter Two
1. Joy, *op. cit.,* p. 131.

Chapter Four
1. *Hurricane from China,* by Denis Warner (New York, 1954), p. 27.
2. *From the Danube to the Yalu,* Gen. Mark Clark (New York, 1954), p. 214.

Chapter Five
1. Clark, *op. cit.,* p. 108.
2. *Airpower: The Decisive Force in Korea,* edited by Col. James T. Stewart (Princeton, 1957), pp. 35–36.

Chapter Six
1. *The Last Parallel,* by Martin Russ (New York, 1957), pp. 238–39.

Chapter Seven
1. Clark, *op. cit.,* p. 264.
2. Clark, *op. cit.,* pp. 269–70.
3. Clark, *op. cit.,* pp. 279–80.

Chapter Eight
1. *The Captives of Korea,* by W. L. White (New York, 1957), pp. 301–2.

Acknowledgments

Acknowledgment is hereby made, and gratitude expressed, to D. Van Nostrand Co., Inc., for permission to quote portions of *Airpower: The Decisive Force in Korea,* edited by Colonel James T. Stewart, copyright 1957 by D. Van Nostrand Co.; to Holt, Rinehart and Winston, Inc., for permission to quote from *The Last Parallel,* by Martin Russ, copyright 1957 by Martin Russ; to The McBride Co. for permission to quote from *Decision in Korea* by Rutherford M. Poats, copyright 1954 by The McBride Co., Inc.; to The Macmillan Co. for permission to quote from *How Communists Negotiate,* by C. Turner Joy, copyright 1955 by C. Turner Joy, from *China Crosses the Yalu,* by Allen S. Whiting, copyright 1960 by the Rand Corp., and from *Hurricane from China,* by Denis Warner, copyright 1961 by Denis Warner; to William Morrow & Co., Inc., for permission to quote from *The River and the Gauntlet,* by S. L. A. Marshall, copyright 1953 by S. L. A. Marshall; to Harper & Brothers for permission to quote from *From the Danube to the Yalu,* by Mark Clark, copyright 1954 by Mark W. Clark, from *Soldier: The Memoirs of Matthew B. Ridgway,* by General Matthew B. Ridgway as told to Harold H. Martin, copyright 1956 by Matthew B. Ridgway and Harold H. Martin, and from *The New Breed,* by Andrew Geer, copyright 1952 by Andrew Clare Geer; to Random House for permission to quote from *The Americans,* by Daniel J. Boorstin, copyright 1958 by Daniel J. Boorstin; to Hawthorn Books, Inc., for permission to reprint a portion of *The Compact History of the United States Marine Corps,* by Lieutenant Colonel Philip N. Pierce and Lieutenant Colonel Frank O. Hough, copyright 1960 by Hawthorn Books, Inc.; to the Harold Matson Company for permission to quote from *I Was a Captive in Korea,* by Philip Deane, copyright 1953 by Gerassimos Svoronos-Gigantes; to the Office of the Chief of Military History for permission to quote from *South to the Naktong, North to the Yalu,* by Roy E. Appleman, copyright 1960 by James A. Norell, a volume in the series *U. S. Army in the Korean War,* published by that office; to The Viking Press, Inc., for permission to quote from *General Dean's Story,* as told to William L. Worden by Major General William F. Dean, copyright 1954 by William F. Dean and the Curtis Publishing Company; to *Life* Magazine for permission to quote from Volume II of the Truman Memoirs, *Years of Trial and Hope,* by Harry S. Truman, copyright 1956 by Time, Inc.; to Alfred A. Knopf, Inc., for permission to quote from *MacArthur: His Rendezvous with History,* by Major General Courtney Whitney, copyright 1955 by Time, Inc.; to Charles Scribner's Sons for permission to quote from

The Captives of Korea, by W. L. White, copyright 1957 by William Lindsay White; to the USAF Historical Division for a quotation from *The United States Air Force in Korea, 1950–1953*, by Robert F. Futrell, published and copyrighted by Duell, Sloan and Pearce, Inc., in 1961; and to the United States Naval Institute for permission to quote from *The Sea War in Korea*, by Commander Malcolm W. Cagle and Commander Frank A. Manson, copyright 1957 by United States Naval Institute.

The photographs in this book are taken from the following sources (numbers and letters reflect position of photographs in picture section):

U. S. ARMY PHOTOGRAPHS: 1a, 1b, 2–3a, 2–3b, 2–3c, 2–3d, 4a, 4c, 5, 7b, 8a, 8b, 10a, 10b, 14–15a, 14–15b, 14–15c, 14–15d, 16–17a, 16–17b, 18–19c, 20a, 20b, 21, 22–23a, 24, 25a, 25b, 26a, 26b, 28–29a, 28–29e, 30a, 30b, 31

U. S. NAVY PHOTOGRAPHS: 6b, 9a, 18–19a

U. S. AIR FORCE PHOTOGRAPHS: 9b, 12–13c, 16–17c, 18–19b

DEFENSE DEPARTMENT PHOTOGRAPHS (MARINE CORPS): 4b, 6a, 7a, 11a, 11b, 12–13a, 12–13b, 22–23b, 22–23c, 22–23d, 22–23e, 27a, 27b, 28–29b, 28–29d

LEATHERNECK MAGAZINE: 22–23f, 28–29c

All maps in this book have been created by Mrs. G. Kelley Fitch.

In a more personal way I am anxious to express my gratitude to Brigadier General S. L. A. Marshall, U.S.A. (Ret.), who, with customary grace and generosity, set me on the path which led to this book, as well as to Lieutenant Colonel William Schmitt of the U. S. Army, Dr. Stetson Conn and Dr. John Miller, Jr., historian and deputy historian, respectively, of the Army's Office of the Chief of Military History, and to Mr. Israel Wice and Mrs. Norma Sherris of that office; to Major James Sunderman of the U. S. Air Force; to Lieutenant Colonel Philip N. Pierce of the U. S. Marine Corps and Mr. Daniel M. O'Quinlivan of the Marine Historical Branch; to Mrs. Martha Holler of the Defense Department's Accreditation and Travel Division; to the staff of the Morristown (N. J.) Public Library and the Mountain Lakes (N. J.) Public Library, as well as to those helpful though unsung heroes of the research trail who staff the New York Public Library; to Mrs. Lois R. Williams of the Chicago booksellers, C. F. Petelle; to the many men of all ranks who fought in Korea and have been good enough to talk or write to me about their experiences there; to my wife, Vera, who typed the manuscript of this book; and, finally, to my editor, Mr. Peter Israel, for his criticism, advice, and patience. It should almost go without saying that any mistakes in this book are mine.

R. L.

Mountain Lakes, N. J.
April 25, 1962

Index

Fifth Air Force, U. S., 61, 75, 98, 100, 105, 242, 284, 285, 318
First Naktong Battle, 108-15
Florian, Dr. Istvann, 350
Flying Fish Channel, 136, 137, 138
Formosa, 30, 101, 102, 103, 154, 158, 281, 371, 394
Fort Marion, USS, 138
Fox Hill, 220
France, 55
Funchilin Pass, 221, 224

Gardner, Rear Admiral Matthias, 31
Gay, Maj. General Hobart, 177
Geneva Conventions, 332, 389, 394
George Washington University, 27
German Democratic Republic, *see* East Germany
Germany, 29
Germ warfare hoax, 348-56, 389, 398
Gordon, Corporal Charles, 368
Gordon-Ingram, Major A. I., 149
Greenwood, Lieut. Colonel Walter, 51
Gromyko, Andrei, 294, 303
Gross, Ernest, 46
Guderian, General Heinz, 38
Guerrilla warfare, 37, 98, 116, 143, 147, 175, 187, 257, 260, 263, 283
Gurke, USS, 136, 137

Hadong, 99
Hagaru-ri, 209, 211, 219, 220, 222
Hainan, 101
Halsey, Admiral William ("Bull"), 142
Hamyang, 147
Han River, 49, 50-51, 56, 58, 241, 242, 259, 261, 262
Harriman, Averill, 102, 270, 271
Harris, Maj. General Field, 198
Harris, Captain Theodore, 353
Harrison, Maj. General William, 347, 357, 358, 363, 377-78, 386
Harvard University, 27
Hate-America campaign, 158, 160, 163, 351
Heartbreak Ridge, 313
Helena, USS, 109, 143, 144, 173
Henderson, USS, 136, 137
Hermit Kingdom, 23
Hickey, Maj. General Doyle, 145, 194
Hideyoshi, Japanese warlord, 23
Higbee, USS, 95
Higgins, Rear Admiral John, 136, 137
Higgins, Trumbull, 167

Hill 282, 148
Hinton, Lieut. Colonel Bruce, 238
Hitler, Adolf, 49
Ho Chi Minh, 396
Hodes, Maj. General Henry, 300, 315
Hodge, Lieut. General John, 33, 34, 61
Hoengsong, 260, 261
Ho Loung, 183
Hong Kong, 249
Hope, Bob, 174
Hsieh Fang, Maj. General, 300, 301-02
Huff, Colonel Sidney, 273
Hughes, Emmett John, 364
Hungnam, 174, 209, 218, 226-27
Hwachon Reservoir, 176, 290, 313
Hwanggan, 94
Hyesanjin, 175, 196-97

Imjin River, 263, 288
Inchon, 126, 129-35, 136-37, 141-43, 218, 243, 259
Independence, 26
India, 155, 160, 165, 254, 369-70, 376, 397
Indo-China, 53, 55, 192, 386, 397
Inje, 45
International Red Cross, 330, 346, 350, 351-52
International Scientific Commission, 355
Iron Curtain, 30
Iron Triangle, 170, 176, 290, 291, 313, 361
Itazuke Airfield, 62
Ivan the Terrible, 23
Iwamura, Yoshimatsu, 131
Iwon, 175, 176, 197, 218

Jamaica, HMS, 64, 136, 137
Jamestown Line, 313
Japan, 23, 24, 25, 27, 28, 29, 37, 49
Jarrell, Captain Albert E., 217
Jebb, Sir Gladwyn, 154, 155
Johnson, Louis, 157, 188
Joint Chiefs of Staff, 74, 78, 126, 128, 132, 134, 153, 171, 188, 189, 194, 216, 237, 240, 245, 248, 249, 264, 269, 271, 357, 358, 365, 372
Joint Commission on Korea, 34-35
Joint Task Force Seven, 126, 136, 138, 142, 173
Joy, Admiral C. Turner, 55, 60, 132, 172, 299, 300, 301, 302, 303, 304-05,

443

446

Other titles of interest

THE BITTER WOODS
The Battle of the Bulge
John S. D. Eisenhower
New introd. by
Stephen E. Ambrose
550 pp., 46 photos & 27 maps
80652-5 $17.95

THE CONDUCT OF
WAR 1789-1961
J.F.C. Fuller
352 pp.
80467-0 $14.95

THE EVOLUTION OF
WEAPONS AND WARFARE
Colonel Trevor N. Dupuy
358 pp.
80384-4 $13.95

THE GI's WAR
American Soldiers in Europe
During World War II
Edwin P. Hoyt
638 pp., 29 illus.
80448-4 $16.95

THE GUINNESS BOOK
OF ESPIONAGE
Mark Lloyd
256 pp., 100 photos
80584-7 $16.95

THE KOREAN WAR
Matthew B. Ridgway
360 pp., 55 photos
80267-8 $13.95

MASTERS OF THE ART
OF COMMAND
Martin Blumenson and
James L. Stokebury
410 pp., 11 maps
80403-4 $14.95

MEMOIRS OF
HARRY S. TRUMAN
Volume II. 1946-1952:
Years of Trial and Hope
608 pp.
80297-X $14.95

NOW IT CAN BE TOLD
The Story of the Manhattan Project
Gen. Leslie R. Groves
New introduction by Edward Teller
482 pp.
80189-2 $14.95

REMINISCENCES
General Douglas MacArthur
440 pp., 30 photos
80254-6 $10.95

SURVIVORS
Vietnam P.O.W.s Tell Their Story
Zalin Grant
New introduction by the author
355 pp., 1 map
80561-8 $14.95

SWORDS AND PLOWSHARES
General Maxwell D. Taylor
434 pp., 59 photos
80407-7 $14.95

Available at your bookstore

OR ORDER DIRECTLY FROM

DA CAPO PRESS, INC.

1-800-321-0050